A

COMPLETE SYSTEM

OF

CHRISTIAN THEOLOGY;

OR,

A CONCISE, COMPREHENSIVE, AND SYSTEMATIC VIEW

OF THE

EVIDENCES, DOCTRINES, MORALS, AND INSTITUTIONS OF CHRISTIANITY.

By SAMUEL WAKEFIELD, D.D.

"Go ye into all the world, and preach the Gospel to every creature."

ISBN 0-88019-177-5

Printed by
Old Paths Tract Society Inc.
Shoals, Indiana 47581

PREFACE.

In presenting this volume of Christian Theology to the public, it may be necessary that the author should make some prefatory remarks, both in regard to the history of its origin, and to the distinctive character of the work itself.

There is perhaps no system of divinity extant which possesses more real merit than "Watson's Theological Institutes." As a body of purely evangelical theology, both theoretic and practical, it is nowhere surpassed; and in regard to its polemic character, for the clearness of its statements, the candor with which conflicting sentiments are considered, the fairness of its arguments, and the force of its logical conclusions, it has no equal. Its worth has been acknowledged by divines of various denominations both in Europe and America; and wherever it is known it cannot fail to reflect credit upon its able author, and to be regarded as the workings of a *master-mind*.

But notwithstanding its numerous excellencies, and its perfect adaptation to the *mature theologian*, it is not well suited to the wants of those who are *merely commencing* their theological course. The very style in which the work is written is quite too labored for that of a text-book on any subject. Many of its sentences are so long and complicated, that in order to gather their meaning the most rigid attention is required. This not only diminishes the pleasure of study, but prevents, in a great measure, that deep and lasting impression on the memory which the subject would otherwise produce. A considerable portion of the work consists in quotations from various authors. By this means the uniformity of its style is frequently interrupted; and as many of these quotations are from books of comparatively ancient date, the style is occasionally somewhat antiquated. Moreover, as the opinions of different authors are frequently brought to bear upon the same point of doctrine, there is often an uncalled for and wearisome repetition of the same ideas; and sometimes the introduction of matter which has no direct connection with the subject under discussion.

For many years the author entertained the opinion, that by a judicious abridgment of the "Institutes" these defects might be remedied; and that by this means a concise and simple theological text-book might be furnished, which would possess all the intrinsic value of the original, and at the same time conduct students to their desired acquisition by a shorter and easier path. Finding, however, after waiting long, and conversing with many upon the subject, that no one was willing to undertake the task, he finally commenced it himself; and, as his time and ability would allow, prosecuted it to its conclusion.

But at this point a new question arose. It is known by all that there are many topics of vast importance to the students of theology which are not at all discussed in the "Institutes." It became evident, therefore, that a mere abridgment of Watson, however well executed, would not *fully* meet the present wants of the Church. It was this fact, together with corresponding suggestions from an official source, which led to the preparation of the following work in its present form.

And now, in regard to the character of the work itself, it is only necessary to say that it has for its basis an abridgment of "Watson's Theological Institutes," which the author has given in his own style; that to this is added a considerable amount of original matter, for the purpose of completing the system; that the whole is presented in a new and strictly systematic form; and that it assumes to a very great extent, as every candid reader will allow, the character of originality.

As to the design of the author, it was to furnish a clear and comprehensive outline of scriptural theology, which, though especially intended for the benefit of those who are preparing for the Christian ministry, should at the same time be adapted to the wants of all classes of readers, from the aged theologian to the Sabbath-school scholar. How far he has succeeded in the accomplishment of his purpose others must judge. He knows that his work is imperfect, and will need the indulgence of a generous public. But he has done what he could; and now his earnest prayer is, that God may accept the humble offering, and render it subservient to the enlargement and edification of his Church: "To whom be glory for ever and ever. Amen!"

CONTENTS.

INTRODUCTION.

PART I.

	PAGE
OF THEOLOGY IN GENERAL	9
§ 1. The Nature of Theology	9
§ 2. The Objects of Theology	12
§ 3. Divisions of Theology	13

PART II.

OF THE SOURCES OF THEOLOGY	18
§ 1. Of Reason, as a Source of Theology	18
§ 2. Of Revelation, as a Source of Theology	22

BOOK I.

EVIDENCES OF A DIVINE REVELATION 39

CHAPTER I.

EVIDENCES NECESSARY TO AUTHENTICATE A DIVINE REVELATION 40
§ 1. External Evidence 40
§ 2. Internal Evidence 48
§ 3. Collateral Evidence 50

CHAPTER II.

GENUINENESS OF THE HOLY SCRIPTURES 51

CHAPTER III.

THE INTEGRITY OF THE SACRED SCRIPTURES 58

CHAPTER IV.

AUTHENTICITY OF THE SACRED SCRIPTURES 64

CHAPTER V.

DIVINE AUTHORITY OF THE SACRED SCRIPTURES: Inspiration 71

CHAPTER VI.

DIVINE AUTHORITY OF THE SACRED SCRIPTURES: Proof from Miracles 83

CHAPTER VII.

DIVINE AUTHORITY OF THE SACRED SCRIPTURES: Proof from Prophecy 90

CHAPTER VIII.

DIVINE AUTHORITY OF THE SACRED SCRIPTURES: Internal Evidence 98

CHAPTER IX.

DIVINE AUTHORITY OF THE SACRED SCRIPTURES: Collateral Evidence........... 109

CHAPTER X.

DIVINE AUTHORITY OF THE SACRED SCRIPTURES: Miscellaneous Objections answered. 114

BOOK II.

DOCTRINES RESPECTING GOD... 124

CHAPTER I.

THE EXISTENCE OF GOD... 124

CHAPTER II.

THE ATTRIBUTES OF GOD.. 139
    § 1. Unity of God.. 140
    § 2. Spirituality of God.................................... 142
    § 3. Eternity of God....................................... 145
    § 4. Omnipotence of God.................................... 146
    § 5. Omnipresence of God................................... 149
    § 6. Omniscience of God.................................... 151
    § 7. Immutability of God................................... 156
    § 8. Wisdom of God.. 159
    § 9. Truth of God... 162
    § 10. Justice of God...................................... 165
    § 11. Holiness of God..................................... 167
    § 12. Goodness of God.................................... 170

CHAPTER III.

THE TRINITY IN UNITY... 178
    § 1. The Importance of the Doctrine........................ 180
    § 2. Scripture Proofs of the Doctrine...................... 182

CHAPTER IV.

DIVINITY OF CHRIST... 187
    § 1. The Pre-existence of Christ........................... 187
    § 2. Christ the Jehovah of the Old Testament............... 190
    § 3. Divine Titles ascribed to Christ...................... 195
    § 4. Divine Attributes are ascribed to Christ.............. 199
    § 5. Divine Works are ascribed to Christ................... 201
    § 6. Divine Worship paid to Christ......................... 205

CHAPTER V.

THE SONSHIP OF CHRIST.. 210

CHAPTER VI.

THE PERSON OF CHRIST... 221

CHAPTER VII.

PERSONALITY AND DEITY OF THE HOLY GHOST.......................... 227

CHAPTER VIII.

THE DECREES OF GOD... 234

CHAPTER IX.

OF CREATION.. 242
    § 1. Of Creation in General............................... 242
    § 2. Of Creation in Particular............................ 249

CHAPTER X.

OF DIVINE PROVIDENCE... 261

BOOK III.

PAGE

DOCTRINES RESPECTING MAN 275

CHAPTER I.
MAN'S PRIMITIVE STATE 275

CHAPTER II.
THE FALL OF MAN 281

CHAPTER III.
THE EFFECTS OF THE FALL 290
    § 1. The Nature of that Death which was made the Penalty of Sin 291
    § 2. The Legal Relation which Adam sustained to his Posterity 292
    § 3. The Moral Condition in which Men are actually Born into the World 296

CHAPTER IV.
MAN'S MORAL AGENCY 308

CHAPTER V.
MAN'S MORAL AGENCY: Objections 322

INTRODUCTION.

Before we enter upon the discussion of the various topics which more strictly belong to the Christian system, we will offer a few introductory remarks in regard to theology in general, and the sources from which it is derived.

PART I.

OF THEOLOGY IN GENERAL.

In our remarks upon theology in general, we will notice its *Nature,* its *Objects,* and its *Divisions.*

§ 1. *The Nature of Theology.*

The term theology is derived from θεός, (*theos,*) God, and λόγος, (*logos,*) a *discourse ;* and literally signifies a *discourse concerning* God.

The ancient Greeks used the term according to its most literal signification, and hence, those who wrote the history of the gods, their works and exploits, were called θεολόγοι, or *theologians.* Pherecydes, of Scyros, was the first who was so denominated, and his work was entitled θεολογία, or *Theology.* Homer and Hesiod were theologians in this sense of the word.

In the writings of the Fathers the term is sometimes employed in a restricted sense to denote some particular doctrine concerning God. Accordingly, they speak of the theology of the sacred Trinity, and of the theology of the Son of God; that is, the doctrine of the Trinity, and of the Divinity of Jesus Christ.

But in the twelfth century Peter Abelard employed the term to denote particularly learned or scientific instruction in religion ; and this use of the word was preserved by most of the succeeding theologians. In the seventeenth century, however, many of the Protestant divines gave the name of *theology* to any knowledge respecting God and divine things, thus using the word in its etymological sense.

Theology, in its modern acceptation, is that science which treats of the existence, the character, and the attributes of God; his laws and government; the doctrines which we are to believe, the moral change which we must experience, and the duties which we are required to perform. In this sense *theology* and *divinity* are synonymous, both embracing the whole system of revealed religion, and both signifying learned or scientific instruction respecting God. Hence, a *theologian*, or *divine*, is one who is able thoroughly to explain, prove, and defend the doctrines of religion, and to teach them to others.

When we say that theology embraces the whole system of revealed religion, we do not intend to convey the idea that *theology* and *religion* are terms of precisely the same import; for though they should not be employed in opposition to each other, as some modern writers have done, yet they differ materially in regard to their signification. *Religion*, understood *subjectively* and in its most comprehensive sense, includes, 1. A knowledge of God in regard to his nature, his attributes, his relations to men, and his will respecting them; and, 2. Affections and conduct corresponding with this knowledge. The former, which may be denominated the *theory* of religion, is addressed to the human understanding; while the latter, which is the *practical* part, belongs to the will and affections.

These two essential parts of religion are always united in the teachings of Christ and his apostles. "If ye know these things, happy are ye if ye do them." John xiii, 17. "Be ye doers of the word, and not hearers only, deceiving your own selves." James i, 22. Religion, in this sense of the term, comprehends theology, as a system of doctrines, and also practical piety.

Thus far we have considered religion *subjectively*, or in its relation to those who possess it; but it may also be taken *objectively* to designate the whole sum of doctrines respecting God and his will. In this sense religion is nearly equivalent to theology, but with this difference, that the latter is commonly restricted to the knowledge of the true God, while the former is applied to any system of doctrines respecting either the true God, or false gods and their worship. We therefore speak of the religion of the Romans, of the Turks, of the Hindoos, or of the Indians, as well as of the Christian religion. We speak of *false* religions, as well as of that which is *true;* and also of embracing, professing, changing, or renouncing religion, using the term in the same sense.

It follows, therefore, that religion, as distinguished from theology, consists in practical piety, or the performance of all known duties to God and our fellow-men, in obedience to the divine law; and that theology, as distinguished from religion, is a systematic arrangement of *doctrines* respecting God, his will, and his worship.

As theology consists in a systematic arrangement of the general principles and leading doctrines of revealed religion, it is therefore called a *science;* and it is doubtless as worthy of that distinction as any other department of human knowledge. Indeed, it may be properly called the *science of sciences*, because it comprehends in its wide range every other science. It leads us back to the beginning of the world and the origin of man; and it directs our attention to the arts, manners, customs, religion, and history of ancient nations. It calls into its service language, astronomy, geography, and poetry; it explores the fields of natural, intellectual, and moral philosophy; it leads us to investigate the wonderful construction of our own bodies in the science of anatomy and of physiology; and, in a word, it takes in the entire circle of human knowledge, whether it be addressed to the memory, the understanding, or the imagination.

Many of the topics embraced in theology are abstruse, and nearly all of them have been perplexed by controversies which commenced as soon as our religion was promulgated, and have been continued from age to age with all the arguments that ingenuity and learning could supply.

The private Christian, ignorant of the subtle disputes which have arisen concerning almost every article of faith, humbly takes up the Bible as the word of God, and by a short and easy process acquires that measure of religious knowledge which makes him wise unto salvation. But the minister of religion proceeds more slowly, encounters obstacles at every step, and is often compelled to assume the character of a polemic. He must therefore study theology as a science, that he may be able not only to instruct the simple and illiterate, but also to contend with the wise and learned, whether as infidels they oppose revelation in general, or as heretics they impugn any of its doctrines.

From what has been said of theology in general, we must perceive the transcendent dignity and excellence of this science, and consequently the importance of theological study. Whether we turn our attention to the doctrines which theology embraces, or to the moral influence which it is intended to exert upon mankind, we can hardly fail to see that it claims the preference to every other study. To know God as far as he has revealed himself to us is the noblest aim of our understanding; to love him, the purest and holiest exercise of our affections; and to obey his commandments, the most rational, honorable, and delightful employment to which our time and talents can be devoted.

A man may be comparatively ignorant of human science and of the liberal arts, and yet by the sanctifying light of pure religion he may find his way to life eternal; but he who lives without a knowledge of God, though his mind may be stored with every other kind of knowledge, is living like a fool, and shall die without hope.

§ 2. *The Objects of Theology.*

There are three different objects that men may propose to themselves in the study of theology. They may pursue it, first, merely as a branch of liberal education, in order to gratify a laudable curiosity; or, secondly, to qualify themselves for the practical duties of the Christian life; or, thirdly, to fit themselves for the office of the Christian ministry. The first of these objects requires much more than the second; but more is necessary for the accomplishment of the third than for both the others.

So far as it relates to the first of these objects, it may be remarked that theological science, even apart from its utility, is both ornamental and entertaining; and no good reason can be assigned why theology should not be studied like any other science, purely for its own sake as a branch of liberal education. With regard to the second object, a qualification for the practical duties of the Christian life, every Gospel minister is thus far a professor of theology, and every attentive hearer of the Gospel is thus far a theological student. But it is chiefly for the accomplishment of the third and most comprehensive object—a qualification for the sacred office of the Christian ministry—that men pursue a regular course of theological training.

The least of what is required in the Christian pastor is that he be qualified to discharge the various duties of the Christian life, for in this respect he ought to be an example to his flock. Farther, he should labor to acquire a knowledge of whatever is necessary for the edification, the comfort, and the protection from all spiritual danger, of the people that may be committed to his care, or whatever may be of use in defending the cause of God. Again, whatever may enable him to make a proper application of all his acquisitions in knowledge, so as to turn them to the best account for the benefit of his people, is no less requisite.

To little purpose will it be for the minister to possess even the best materials, if he has not acquired the necessary skill to use them to advantage. The former we may call the *theory* of the profession; the latter the *practice*. The first without the second, however considerable, may be compared to wealth without economy. It will not be near so beneficial to the owner, and to those who depend upon him for support, as a more scanty portion would be where economy is understood and practiced. Nor will the second do entirely without the first, for the best economy can be of no real value where there is no subject on which to exercise it.

It follows therefore, that in the proper qualifications of a Christian minister there are two leading departments: the first regards the *science* of theology alone; the second, the *application* of that science to the purposes of the Christian pastor.

§ 3. *Divisions of Theology.*

Theology is divided, according to the sources from which it is derived, into *Natural* and *Revealed;* and it may be arranged under three general epithets, depending upon the distinctive manner in which it is treated, as *Didactic, Polemic,* and *Practical.*

1. *Natural Theology* is that knowledge of God and of divine things which is supposed to be derived from the light of nature, or from the exercise of reason and the suggestions of conscience. It is taught by the advocates of Natural Theology, that man, by a contemplation of the objects around him in the natural world, will be led to infer the existence of a Great First Cause, by whom these objects were created; and to ascribe to this Invisible Being certain attributes and perfections, the signatures of which are seen upon the works of his hands.

From this great first principle of natural religion other doctrines are deduced, such as that God governs the world; that man, in order to possess the favor of God, must practice piety, justice, and benevolence; that the human soul is immortal; and that there is a future state of retribution, in which the righteous shall be rewarded and the wicked punished. These are generally supposed to be the fundamental articles of Natural Theology; and much reason and eloquence have been employed in illustrating them, and in demonstrating their truth, in opposition to the objections of atheists.

By some theologians the division of Theology into *Natural* and *Revealed* is entirely rejected. They maintain that we owe all our knowledge of God, originally, to Divine Revelation; and that therefore, as to its origin, it cannot be *natural.* But though we allow that God revealed himself to men even in the earliest ages of the world, and that much of that revelation has been transmitted, from age to age, until the present time, yet this division is not to be rejected. The light of nature may not be the *primary source* of religious knowledge; but it is obviously an important means by which this knowledge is confirmed, enlarged, and perpetuated. Men are left to examine, in the diligent use of their natural powers, the grounds of revealed truth, to deduce from it its proper consequences, and to build higher upon this solid foundation. They thus obtain additional knowledge by the study and contemplation of nature; and why may not this religious knowledge, thus obtained, be called *Natural Theology?*

2. *Revealed Theology* is that system of divine truth which is contained in the Holy Scriptures. It is called Revealed, or supernatural, because it is derived exclusively from the word of God, and not from the deductions of human reason. It includes all the articles of natural religion; but it comprehends many other important doctrines, which never could have been known, had not God revealed them to the

world. What, for instance, could the light of nature teach with regard to the existence and character of angels, the origin of moral evil, and the redemption of man by Jesus Christ?

3. *Didactic Theology* consists in a plain exposition of the several doctrines of religion, and the adduction of the proofs by which they are sustained. The theologian who pursues his subject *didactically*, must proceed in the same manner as a teacher of any other science. It is his business to give a clear statement of the constituent doctrines of theology, and the conclusions which may be legitimately drawn from them, together with the train of reasoning upon which these conclusions are founded. He should not only state, explain, and prove the several doctrines of religion, but exhibit them also in their proper order and connection. Didactic Theology should therefore be *systematic*. Such a methodically arranged form of the great truths of religion will enable the student to contemplate them in their natural connection, and to perceive both the mutual dependence of the parts, and the symmetry of the whole.

It is granted that the doctrines of religion, as taught in the Bible, are not arranged in this systematic form, but are disclosed gradually, as providence required, and as Divine Wisdom directed. This circumstance, however, forms no objection either to the perfection of the Sacred Scriptures, or to a systematic arrangement of the doctrines which they contain. It forms no objection to the perfection of the Sacred Scriptures; for if we consider attentively the economy of divine grace in relation to the restoration of man, we can hardly fail to see that, in order to the perfecting of the whole plan, it was necessary that the several parts should be revealed by successive degrees, as the scheme advanced toward its completion. If therefore God has revealed, with sufficient clearness, the doctrines to be believed and the duties to be practiced, we have no reason to complain, nor should we dare to prescribe rules to Infinite Wisdom.

On the other hand, it is no ojection to a systematic arrangement of the doctrines of theology, that they are not thus digested in the Bible. God has given us a revelation of his will, that it may be employed for our spiritual instruction, our moral improvement, and our eternal salvation; he has given us a capacity to make a proper use of this revelation; he requires us to employ this capacity so as to turn the spiritual benefits which he has so graciously bestowed upon us to the best account; and we are therefore at liberty, nay, it becomes our duty, in the proper exercise of our reason, to arrange the doctrines of revealed religion into that form which will best assist us in obtaining the benevolent end that God had in view in revealing his will to man.

But while we admit that the doctrines of the Bible are not arranged in a systematic or scientific form, we are not to suppose, on the other hand, that revealed religion is destitute of all order; or that the Bible is an assemblage of writings which have no relation to one another but that of juxtaposition or collocation in the same volume. There is certainly an approach to system in some parts of the Bible, particularly in the writings of St. Paul. It is a consecutive revelation of the counsels of God toward man; and there is order here, as well as in all his other works, though it may require patient investigation to discover it to its full extent. We should therefore study the Scriptures, not to load the memory with a multitude of unconnected ideas, but that we may be able to bring together and systematize the saving truths which they reveal, and thus "understand what the will of the Lord is."

No intelligent man can be a careful and constant reader of the Bible without forming in his own mind a system of doctrines. And he will observe, moreover, that in proportion as this system advances toward completeness, its parts will reflect increasing light upon one another. Are we then to believe that the utility of such a system is either destroyed or diminished by its being communicated to others? Surely not.

Arrangement in any science is a great help both to the judgment and the memory; and the more simple and natural the arrangement is, the greater is the assistance which it affords. Theology, like any other science, may be digested according to different methods, each of which may have advantages peculiar to itself; but that arrangement is best, upon the whole, in which the order of nature is most strictly followed, and in which nothing is previously taught that presupposes a knowledge of what is afterward to be explained.

4. *Polemic Theology* consists in a vindication of the doctrines, precepts, and institutions of religion, against the opinions and attacks of errorists. The term *polemic* is derived from the Greek πολεμικός, (*polemikos*,) and signifies *warlike*. A polemic divine is therefore a warrior, in opposing error and defending truth.

It is acknowledged that this epithet sounds rather harshly when applied to a minister of the Gospel, who ought to be emphatically a messenger of peace; and it may be partly on this account that Polemic Theology has been often held in disrepute. It is loudly demanded by many that the voice of controversy be no more heard in the Church of God—that Christians bury all their religious disputes and differences of opinion in perpetual oblivion, and that they dwell together in brotherly union. This demand is no doubt often made in sincerity; but it always exhibits a great want of discernment. It proceeds upon the supposition that peace is of more value than truth, and that solid and lasting peace may exist without having truth for its foundation, neither of which can be admitted.

We believe, however, that this demand for peace is sometimes intended to conceal a sinister design under the plausible appearance of great liberality—a design to prevent one party from defending its doctrines, that another may propagate its opinions without opposition. Such cries for peace are like the conduct of Joab, when he took Amasa by the beard, saying, "Art thou in health, my brother?" and smote him in the fifth rib. 2 Sam. xx, 9.

There is nothing more evident than that when truth is assailed it ought to be defended. Thus we see that many of our Lord's discourses were intended to correct prevailing errors. St. Paul declares of himself, that he was "set for the *defense* of the Gospel;" and Jude exhorted those to whom he wrote to "*contend* for the faith which was once delivered to the saints." As it would therefore be base pusillanimity to yield, without a struggle, to the enemies of truth, so it would be disgraceful, as well as criminal, in the professed guardians of truth, not to be qualified to sustain the dignity of their office, and to uphold the sacred interests of Christianity. They should be "able, by sound doctrine, both to exhort and to convince the gainsayers." Titus i. 9.

It is not necessary for the theologian to acquire a knowledge of all the controversies that have ever arisen in the Christian Church. Such a task would be both tedious and unprofitable. But it is a matter of the utmost consequence that he be able to maintain the claims of revealed religion against the attacks of infidels, and to defend its fundamental doctrines against all errorists. He should therefore gain a particular acquaintance with the theological disputes and questions of the age and country in which he lives, and with the distinguishing tenets of the different sects with which he is surrounded.

5. *Practical Theology* is that which states and explains our moral and religious duties. In the two preceding departments of theological science the doctrines of religion are illustrated and defended. These doctrines are the foundation of Practical Theology, and supply the only motives that can lead us to the proper performance of the duties which God requires. In Didactic and Polemic Theology, therefore, the way is prepared for this; for Practical Theology is only the improvement which should be made of the doctrines of the Holy Scriptures.

No truth is more clearly sustained by the word of God than that the doctrines of Theology should be turned to a practical purpose. Christ declares: "Not every one that saith unto me, Lord, Lord, shall enter into the kingdom of heaven; but he that doeth the will of my Father which is in heaven." Matt. vii, 21. With this agree the teachings of the inspired apostles. "For the grace of God that bringeth salvation hath appeared to all men, teaching us that, denying ungodliness and worldly lusts, we should live soberly, righteously, and godly in this present world." Titus ii, 11, 12. "And hereby we know that we know him if we keep his commandments." 1 John ii, 3.

The practical intention of Theology appears, moreover, from the nature of revealed religion. If we take a view of the several parts of Christian doctrine, it will appear that they have a direct reference to piety and practice; and that if this point were given up, religion would be of no utility, and the whole subject might at once and forever be dismissed. But the several articles of Theology are such as tend to produce practical piety. This is particularly true in regard to what it teaches concerning God, his Attributes and his Works; as likewise concerning the Person and Offices of our Lord Jesus Christ.

The precepts of religion are given for practice, and would not be precepts if they were given only in order that they might be known, but not obeyed. The promises of Scripture always presuppose pious obedience, as they are made to those only who are truly pious; and they would cease to be promises if there were no established connection between obedience and reward.

It may be observed also that the threatenings of God would have no force, if the necessity of obedience were excluded. It becomes the duty, therefore, of every minister of the Gospel to represent religion as a practical system, to show the tendency of its doctrines to promote holiness of heart and life, and to explain as far as possible the nature of that "holiness without which no man shall see the Lord."

Theology is not a subject which belongs exclusively to the curious to investigate, and in which speculative men may spend their leisure hours; it is one which claims universal attention. Its instructions are addressed to all classes of men; to the learned and the illiterate; to the free and the bond; to them who abound in wealth, and to the children of poverty and want; to the retired student, and to the man of business engaged in the stirring scenes of life. To all it speaks with equal authority, and it should be equally interesting to all, as pointing out the only way that leads to life eternal.

But while this subject claims a share of every man's attention, because it has a direct bearing upon every man's welfare, there is an additional reason why those who have devoted themselves to the Christian ministry should make it the subject of their most careful and thorough investigation. Theology is their *profession*, as really as medicine is the profession of the physician, or law that of the barrister. In this profession they should labor to excel; not, indeed, from the same motives that actuate men of other professions—a desire of fame, and the prospect of worldly emolument; but with a view to the faithful and honorable discharge of the sacred duties of their holy calling.

The nature and responsibilities of this sacred office are concisely and forcibly presented, in the charge which God gave to the prophet Ezekiel. "So thou, O son of man, I have set thee a watchman unto the house of Israel; therefore thou shalt hear the word *at my mouth*, and warn them from me. When I say unto the wicked, O wicked man, thou shalt surely die; if thou dost not speak to warn the wicked from his way, that wicked man shall die in his iniquity, but his blood will I require at thine hand. Nevertheless, if thou warn the wicked of his way to turn from it, if he do not turn from his way, he shall die in his iniquity; but thou hast delivered thy soul." Ezekiel xxxiii, 7–9.

PART II.

OF THE SOURCES OF THEOLOGY.

WE now proceed to inquire into the sources from which theological knowledge is derived. These are *Reason* and *Divine Revelation*.

§ 1. *Of* REASON, *as a Source of Theology*.

By *Reason* we understand, in general, that faculty of the mind by which we distinguish truth from falsehood, and good from evil; or by which we are enabled to deduce inferences from facts and propositions. But when Reason is spoken of as a source of Theology, it means the rational and moral faculties of man, exercised, without any supernatural assistance, in the investigation of religion.

There are two aspects in which human reason may be regarded; and what is true of it in one, may not be true of it in the other. *First*, it may be taken for that high intellectual ability with which man was originally endowed, and which was as sufficient to direct him in all the various concerns of life, as instinct is to direct the lower animals. We do not say that even then Reason was man's only guide. The sacred history clearly shows that he lived in familiar intercourse with his Maker, and was favored with occasional communications of the Divine will.

But, *secondly*, Reason may signify the rational and moral powers of man in his fallen, sinful, and enfeebled state. It is to Reason, in this sense alone, that our inquiries are now to be directed; and we will try to ascertain, as nearly as we can, its true relation to the acquisition of theological or religious knowledge. Let us notice the *extent* of its discoveries, its real *use*, and its *limitation*.

1. *The* EXTENT *of its discoveries as a Source of Theology*.

Whether man, by the mere light of nature, can attain all the religious knowledge which is necessary to conduct him to virtue and happiness, is the great question of controversy between infidels and Christians. Of this question the advocates of natural religion take the affirmative, and contend that their theory is supported by what we know of the Divine Perfections. They assert that it would be inconsistent with the justice and the goodness of God to suppose that he would hold men responsible for their moral and religious conduct, if they had not in themselves sufficient means to acquire a knowledge of the Divine will;

that for this very purpose he endowed men with *Reason,* which must therefore be perfectly sufficient to direct them in every part of their duty; and that the notion of any supplementary means is a reflection upon the wisdom of God, as if he had not originally adapted man to his situation, and was therefore compelled to devise a new expedient for correcting the error.

Without examining these assertions one by one, and showing, as might easily be done, that they are mere gratuitous assumptions, it may be enough to observe, that there is not a single fact in the history of mankind by which they can be confirmed. They are fictions of the imagination, and not sober relations of things as they really exist. They are deductions from false premises, and not conclusions drawn from observation and experience.

It is not our business to inquire what *should be,* according to our own ideas of justice and fitness, but what *actually is;* not what Reason was designed to accomplish, but what it has actually accomplished. It is preposterous to give an arbitrary definition of Reason, and then to conclude that it is capable of exerting all the power which has thus been ascribed to it. It would be more consonant to sound philosophy to judge of the power of Reason by its effects. In a word, we must not waste our time and impose upon ourselves by endeavoring to show beforehand what Reason can do; we ought to proceed according to a different and a safer plan, and inquire what it has actually done.

Viewing the subject in this light, we are forced to the conclusion that it is, to say the least, extremely doubtful whether the doctrines embraced in what is called *Natural Religion* are within the reach of unassisted Reason as original discoveries.* That these doctrines, when clearly proposed to the mind, are approved by Reason, no one will deny. But whether men, by mere rational investigation, could arrive at the conclusion that there is a God, the Creator and Governor of the universe, and if they could, whether they would connect with this primary tenet the other articles of the system, are questions yet to be determined. Nor would it be any more an impeachment of the Attributes of God to affirm the incompetency of Reason in matters of religion, than it is to say that an eye which in consequence of disease does not see at all, or sees very imperfectly, is unfit for the purpose which it was originally intended to serve.

We admit that what is popularly called the *light of nature* may be so understood as to justify the opinion that it is sufficient, independent of a direct revelation, to lead men to a knowledge of God and of divine

* The phrase *Natural Religion* is often used equivocally. Some understand by it every thing in Religion, by whatever means it may be discovered, which has a real foundation in the nature and relations of things, and which unprejudiced Reason will approve. Others confine it to that system of Religion which they suppose to be discoverable by men, in the sole exercise of their natural faculties, without higher assistance.

things. But in this view of the light of nature three things are to be taken into the account. *First*, mankind generally possess, to a greater or less extent, a traditional knowledge of the existence, the attributes, and the will of God. *Secondly*, there is, to the eye of Reason, an adaptation in *surrounding nature* to confirm and illustrate these traditional discoveries, and to lead men of reflection to a knowledge of its Author. "The heavens declare the glory of God; and the firmament showeth his handy work." Psalm xix, 1. "For the invisible things of him from the creation of the world are clearly seen, being understood by the things that are made, even his eternal power and Godhead; so that they are without excuse." Romans i, 20. *Thirdly*, man possesses an additional source of the knowledge of God in *himself*, in his own *conscience;* which distinctly acquaints him with a Supreme and Invisible Judge of his thoughts and actions. Thus St. Paul represents the Gentiles, who were without the written law, as having "the law written in their hearts, their conscience also bearing witness, and their thoughts the mean while accusing or else excusing one another." Romans ii, 15.

The light of nature, therefore, as thus understood, includes a degree of supernatural instruction traditionally preserved; the deductions of right Reason from creation and providence, and the dictates of our *moral* nature. It is only in this connection that Reason is sufficient to conduct men to a knowledge of God; but even then it leaves them in perplexing doubts in regard to many very important points. It cannot, therefore, afford them *all* the assistance which they need for their religious instruction and moral improvement. But if Reason, even when thus assisted, is insufficient to discover many religious truths of the highest interest to man, *unassisted* Reason, as a source of theological knowledge, must be wholly inadequate.

We are not to conclude, however, from what has been said respecting the insufficiency of Reason, that it is to be entirely discarded from religion. It has important offices to perform in regard to this subject as well as to every other. If we were not rational creatures we would be as incapable of religion as the beasts that perish; and if we did not employ our Reason in the study of religion it would be addressed to us in vain. But as God has endowed us with rational powers, he requires us to exert them in search of truth; and they are never so worthily employed as in endeavoring to acquire just notions of his character, our relations to him, the duties which he has enjoined upon us, and the hopes which he has authorized us to entertain. Let us then consider,

2. *The* USE *of Reason, as an Instrument of Religious Knowledge.*

The *Use* of Reason in matters of religion is to investigate the evidences on which its claims to truthfulness are founded, and fairly and impartially to interpret its teachings. It belongs to Reason, then,

(1.) *To judge of the evidences of religion.* While reason is thus employed it not only collects proofs from observation and experience, in favor of the doctrines of natural theology, but it examines the grounds upon which any new doctrine claims to be a revelation from God. As various systems of religion claim this high origin, it is necessary that their pretensions should be carefully and critically investigated, and to do this is the legitimate work of human reason. There are two ways in which this investigation may be conducted. We may compare the system which demands our assent with our previous conceptions of the Divine character and will, in order to ascertain whether it harmonizes with them, because it is certain that sound Reason and a genuine Revelation cannot contradict each other. Or, we may consider certain circumstances extrinsic to the system itself, by which its claims to a supernatural origin may be determined.

The external circumstances to which we allude are such as these: The character of the publishers of the system, the nature of their testimony, and the works to which they appeal in attestation of their mission; and of all these Reason is competent to judge. The *doctrines* of the system may be so far beyond the range of Reason that it shall be incapable, by an abstract contemplation of them, to determine whether they are true or false; and yet the marks of truth which accompany the system may be so easy of apprehension as to carry conviction even to an ordinary understanding. For, though a man may be unable to comprehend a revealed truth, he may find no difficulty in estimating the force of the evidence by which its truth is established. We do not then retract what we have said respecting the insufficiency of Reason in matters of religion when we make it the judge of its evidences, for in this office it has nothing more difficult to perform than in the common affairs of life. But it is the office of Reason,

(2.) *To interpret a religious system,* or to ascertain what its real doctrines are. Here the same rules are to be applied as in the interpretation of any other record. The terms employed are to be taken in their plain and commonly received sense; figures of speech are to be interpreted with a reference to the local peculiarities of the country in which the writers resided; idioms are to be understood according to the genius of the language that is used; the key to allegorical or mystical discourses must be sought in the book itself, and not in our own fancies; what is obscure must be interpreted by what is plain; and the scope and tenor of a discourse must be regarded, and no conclusion formed on passages detached from their context, unless they are complete in sense, or evidently intended as axioms or apothegms. Notice is also to be taken of the *time* and *place* in which the record was written, the circumstances of the writer, and also of those to whom he wrote.

Reason may be farther employed in the *exhibition* and *statement* of the doctrines of religion. If these are brought together in a disconnected manner, as they evidently are in the Bible, we may use our Reason in collecting, arranging, and uniting them into such a system as shall suit our own convenience or the advantage of others. We may also illustrate the truth, the excellence, and the fitness of the various parts of the system, by analogies drawn from things around us, by the observation of human nature, by historical facts, and in many other ways which call Reason into exercise.

3. *The* LIMITATION *of Reason.* This is found in the *authority of God.* Reason may canvass the evidence, and proceed to settle by the laws of criticism and common sense the genuine import of Revelation; but here it should stop. The wisdom of God must not be tried by human reason. In the former case it acts as a servant, but in the latter it would assume the authority of a master. When, therefore, God has explicitly revealed any doctrine, that doctrine is to be humbly received, whatever degree of rational evidence may be afforded in its support; and no torturing or perverting criticism can be *innocently* employed to bring a doctrine into accordance with our favorite views, any more than to make a precept bend to our vicious inclinations.

§ 2. *Of* DIVINE REVELATION, *as a Source of Theology.*

A *Divine Revelation* is "a discovery of some proposition to the mind which came not in by the usual exercise of its faculties, but by some miraculous divine interposition, either mediate or immediate."*

In our remarks upon Divine Revelation as a source of theology, we will briefly point out its *Possibility*, its *Necessity*, and its *Probable Character*.

I. A REVELATION IS POSSIBLE.

No one who believes that there is a God, and that he is a Being of infinite knowledge, wisdom, and power, can reasonably deny that he can, if he thinks fit, make a revelation of himself and of his will to men in an extraordinary way, different from the discoveries made by men themselves in the ordinary use of their rational faculties; for if God is almighty his power must extend to whatever does not imply a contradiction, which cannot be pretended in this case.

We cannot distinctly explain the origin of our ideas, or the way in which they are excited or impressed upon the mind, but we know that this is done in various ways. And can it be supposed that the Author of our being has it not in his power to communicate ideas to our mind, in order to instruct us in those things which we are deeply concerned to know? Our inability to explain the manner in which this is done is no just objection against it. This has been acknowledged by Lord Bolingbroke, a distinguished antagonist of Revelation. He observes,

---

* DODDRIDGE'S Lectures, Part 5, Definition 68.

that " an extraordinary action of God upon the human mind, which the word *inspiration* is now used to denote, is not more inconceivable than the ordinary action of mind on body, or body on mind;" and that " it is impertinent to deny the existence of any phenomenon, merely because we cannot account for it."

As God can, if he sees fit, communicate his will to men in the way of extraordinary revelation, so he can do it in such a manner as to assure those to whom it is made that it is, indeed, a Divine Revelation. This is a natural consequence, for to suppose that God can communicate his will to men, and yet that he is not able to give them this assurance, is evidently absurd and contradictory. It is, in effect, to say, that he can reveal his will, but has no way of making men know that he does so, which is most unreasonable. If men can communicate their thoughts by language, so that we may certainly know who it is that addresses us, it would be a strange thing to affirm that God has no way of causing his rational creatures to know when he reveals to them his will that it is He, and no other, who makes the revelation. To deny that a God of infinite perfection has such a power is a glaring contradiction.

II. A Revelation is necessary.

This is a sentiment in which all will concur, except those who regard religious truth as a matter of absolute indifference, and those who believe that Reason is sufficient for all the discoveries which are necessary to guide men to virtue and happiness. Infidels profess to adopt the latter principle, but act according to the former; for, in no part of their conduct is there any indication of reverence for religious truth, or of a sincere desire to discover it. They continually betray symptoms of levity and impiety, a contempt for seriousness, a disposition to cavil, to raise objections, to perplex evidence, to involve everything in doubt, and to turn into ridicule the most solemn of all subjects.

But whatever may be the thoughts of men devoted to pleasure, and living without God in the world, every one who feels that he is an accountable being must desire to know by what means he may fulfill the design of his existence, and obtain the happiness of which he is capable. That a Revelation is necessary is evident,

1. *From the weakness and insufficiency of human Reason in the discovery of religious and moral truth.*

It is not from mere theory but from experiment, not from conjecture but from matters of fact, that we can ascertain what Reason can do in the discovery of religious truth. Let us, therefore, turn our attention to some of the doctrines of Natural Religion, which are supposed to be fairly within its province, that we may discover the results of its researches respecting them. We will notice,

(1.) *The existence of God.* This is the fundamental principle of all true religion. That it is demonstrable by Reason, when once the idea is suggested to the mind, we readily allow, for it has been evinced by arguments so strong and conclusive that it is hard to conceive how any one can resist them and continue to be an Atheist. The metaphysician should be overpowered by the profound reasonings of Clarke; and the man of plainer understanding by the more obvious arguments of Ray, Derham, and Paley. It should not be overlooked, however, that this triumphant demonstration of the Divine Existence is found only in the writings of Christians. For, though a similar train of argument was pursued by some of the heathen philosophers, as Cicero and Socrates, yet the illustration was not so ample as it is now made by the discoveries of modern philosophy, nor was the conclusion to which it naturally led drawn with equal clearness and confidence.

The cause of this difference is obvious. To the Gentile the existence of God was a question involved in doubt, an inference to be deduced from premises; and though he could see clearly some steps in the process, he was not always able, with equal distinctness, to perceive the result. But when Christians attempt to discuss this subject they are fully convinced of the fact; and we must perceive, upon the slightest reflection, that it is much more difficult to discover an unknown truth, by a slow process of induction, than to adduce proofs in support of what is already known. The former is like the voyage of Columbus, when he was in search of the new world. He did not know that there was such a country as America, and consequently he had nothing but *probability* to support him amid the difficulties and perils of the enterprise. But the latter is like a voyage to a well-known port, whither the skillful mariner can shape his course by his chart and his compass.

That nature, in all her works, declares the existence of a God, is readily admitted; but the sages of antiquity either disregarded her voice, or failed to interpret her language. Hence, their notions respecting him are so exceedingly imperfect and erroneous, as to afford indubitable proof that the God of NATURAL THEOLOGY will never be any thing more than the *dumb idol* of philosophy, neglected by the philosopher himself, and unknown to the multitude; acknowledged in the closet, but forgotten in the world.

To heathen philosophers, the idea of the distinct subsistence or *personality* of the Deity was in a great measure unknown. They regarded him, not so much an Intelligent Being, as an Animating Power diffused throughout the world. This notion was introduced into their speculative system, to account for the motion of passive matter, which they supposed to be coeval and co-existent with God himself.

In practice they adopted the polytheism of their country, and paid religious honors to an endless train of gods that were acknowledged by the vulgar. There was not a nation upon the earth, except the Jews, in which the living and true God was adored. Every natural object was mistaken for him, every part of the universe was deified, and fancy exerted its creative power in superadding a multitude of *imaginary* beings as objects of worship.   Even in Greece, that seat of refinement and philosophy, there were not less than thirty thousand gods.   In modern India, where science has long been cultivated, the number is still greater, for her gods are estimated by millions.

From these facts we have a right to conclude that the existence of *One God*, which is the first principle of what is called Natural Religion, is not discoverable by reason, or, at least, that reason cannot discover it with sufficient clearness to produce a permanent and practical conviction of it on the mind.   Philosophers sometimes spoke of the Deity as *One*, but there was no certainty or consistency in their opinions. Though the idea occurred to them, obscurity hung upon it, and to the wisest of them he remained " the unknown God."

(2.) *The creation of the world.*   We believe that all things were created by the almighty power of God; and though the production of the universe out of nothing is an event of which we can form no conception, yet we consider the Cause as adequate, Omnipotence being able to do whatever does not imply a contradiction.   But among those who had only the light of nature to guide them, very different sentiments were entertained.   Unassisted reason never arrived at the conclusion that the universe had a beginning.   Nor did it assent to this doctrine, even when it was suggested.   *Ex nihilo nihil fit*—nothing is made out of nothing—was an undisputed maxim among all the sages of antiquity.   In the details of their systems they differed, in many respects, from one another; but they all concurred in rejecting, as absurd, the idea of a proper creation.

Some believed that the universe was eternal, both in matter and form, that the heavens and the earth had always existed, and that the human race had no beginning, and would have no end.   Others maintained that the present order of things had a beginning, but they ascribed it to accident, to a fortuitous concourse of atoms, which, dancing up and down in infinite space, united themselves at last in the present regular system of nature.

Among those philosophers who acknowledged a Deity, some, instead of regarding him as the Creator of all things, confounded him with his works.   They supposed him to be the soul of the universe, giving life and motion to its various parts, as the soul of man animates his body. Others, though they distinguished him from the universe, did not believe that he created it, but held the opinion that he only reduced it to order from its previous chaotic state.   But according to all of them matter was co-eternal with the Diety, and depended upon him only in this, that his power was exerted in moving and arranging it.   Their notions, therefore, of the relation of the universe to God must have been very different from those which we entertain.   We hold that he created the earth on which we dwell, and the heavens which shed their influences upon us, and that "in him *we* live, and move, and have our being."

(3.) *Divine Providence.* We could hardly expect those who were so much mistaken, or so imperfectly informed, with respect to the character of God as *Creator* of the world, to entertain just ideas of his *government* of it.

It was natural for such philosophers as attributed the present system of the universe to accident, to deny a Providence altogether. Accordingly, the Epicureans represented the gods as indolently reposing in their own region of undisturbed felicity, and beholding with indifference the affairs of mortals. Aristotle taught that God "observes nothing, and cares for nothing beyond himself." The Stoics contended for a Providence, and occasionally said some fine things respecting it. "Of religion toward the gods," says Epictetus, "this is the principal thing: to form right conceptions of them as existing, and administering all things well and justly; to obey them, and acquiesce in all things that happen, and to follow willingly as being under the conduct of the most excellent mind."

But this elevated language loses much of its value when we remember that the Stoics held the doctrine of *fate*, by which all things were controlled, and to which both gods and men were subject. According to them, therefore, the world was not, properly, governed by the gods, for they, as well as their nominal subjects, were bound by the eternal and inviolable chain of causes and effects. Plato, and the followers of Pythagoras, professed to believe that all things happened according to Divine Providence; but this they overthrew by uniting God with *fortune*. "God, fortune, and opportunity," says Plato, "govern all the affairs of men."

In all the ancient heathen nations there were "gods many, and lords many." But wherever polytheism is admitted it is as destructive of the doctrine of Providence as fate, though by a different process. The fatalist supposes all things to be fixed and certain, and thus excludes the true idea of government; the polytheist gives up the government of the world to the will of contrary deities, and thus makes everything uncertain. If he gains the favor of one deity, the wrath of another equally powerful, or even more so, may be provoked; or the gods may quarrel among themselves. Such is the only Providence which can be discovered in the Iliad of Homer and the Æneid of Virgil.

We see, then, that though the idea of a Providence floated in the minds of heathen sages, they were not able to give it a distinct and consistent shape. All that reason could do was to point out the general truth. It failed to illustrate it, and to erect upon this foundation the superstructure of a rational piety.

(4.) *The immortality of the soul, and a future state of retribution.* Though in some form these doctrines were recognized in most pagan systems of religion, yet their evidence was either very defective, or they were mixed up with notions entirely subversive of that moral effect which they were originally intended to produce.

The doctrine of judicial astrology,* which perhaps originated in Chaldea, but was extensively received by the Egyptians, the Greeks, and the Romans, is so nearly allied to fatalism as to subvert the idea of a probationary state *here*, and of a retribution *hereafter*. But the doctrine which has done more than any other to destroy the moral effect of a belief in man's immortality is, that " God is the soul of the world," from which all human spirits come, and to which they will all return ; some immediately at death, and others through a course of transmigration. The Scriptures teach that the human soul is from God by creation. The refinement of pagan philosophy is, that it is from him by a separation of essence, and that it still remains a separate portion of God, seeking its return to him. Revelation shows that at death the souls of the just return to God, not to lose their individuality, but to be united to him in holy and delightful communion. The philosophic perversion is, that the parts so separated from God, and for a time connected with matter, will be reunited to the great Source by *refusion*, as a drop of water to the ocean.

When, therefore, the ancients attributed a proper eternity to the human soul, we must not suppose that they understood it to be eternal in its distinct and peculiar existence, but that it was discerpted from the substance of God in *time*, and would in *time* be rejoined to it again. They only differed about the time of this reunion or resolution, the greater number holding it to be at death; but the Pythagoreans not till after many transmigrations. Those of the Platonic school went between these two opinions, supposing that *pure* souls are joined to the Universal Spirit at death, while those which have contracted much defilement pass through a succession of bodies before they return to their parent substance. This theory is not only incompatible with the doctrine of future rewards and punishments, but it turns the immortality of man, so far as his distinct consciousness and personality are concerned, into absolute annihilation.

Another notion equally at war with the soul's immortality, and with a state of future retribution, was that of a periodical destruction and renovation of all things. This sprung up in the Egyptian schools, and was thence transmitted into Greece and India, and throughout all Asia. This theory is, according to Diodorus Siculus, "that the universe under-

* *Judicial astrology* is a science which is based upon the supposition that the heavenly bodies have a ruling influence over the physical and moral world, and which teaches men to judge of the influences of the stars, and to foretell future events by their situation and different aspects.

goes a periodical conflagration, after which all things are to be restored to their primitive form, to pass again through a similar succession of changes."

As the Stoics held that all inferior divinities, and all human souls, were portions separated from the soul of the world, and would return into the first celestial fire, so they supposed that at the same time the whole visible world would be consumed in one general conflagration. "Then," says Seneca, "after an interval the world will be entirely renewed, every animal will be reproduced, and a race of men, free from guilt, will repeople the earth. Degeneracy and corruption are, however, to creep in again, and the same process is to go on forever." This is evidently a corruption of the primitive doctrine of the destruction of the world, and the consequent termination of man's probationary state, preparatory to the general judgment; but it is one which effectually destroys the *moral influence* of that awful and most salutary revelation.

The doctrine of Aristotle and the Peripatetics gives no countenance to the opinion of the soul's immortality, or even of its existence after death. Democritus and his followers taught that the soul is material and mortal; Heraclitus, that when the soul is purified from soft vapors it returns into the soul of the universe, if not it perishes; and Epicurus and his followers, that "*when death is we are not.*" Pliny declares that "the soul and body have no more sense after death than before we were born; and Seneca, "that the day which he fears as his last is the birthday of eternity." The poets, it is true, spoke of the joys of Elysium, and the tortures of Tartarus; but both philosophers and poets regarded them as vulgar fables, as Virgil clearly shows. Thus the light of nature was too feeble to dispel the darkness that rested on all beyond the grave.

(5.) *The systems of heathen morality.* Here, it must be acknowledged, reason has had a degree of success. There are admirable treatises upon morality, which were composed by heathen philosophers, and which we may read both with pleasure and profit; but he who expects to find in any of them a perfect system of morality will be greatly disappointed.

It has indeed been affirmed by Lactantius that everything delivered in the Scriptures on the subject of morals is contained in the writings of one or another of the philosophers; but Lactantius, though a fine reasoner and an elegant writer, is not entitled to much deference in matters of theology, of which he has shown himself to be an incompetent judge. What he has affirmed is not true, for in the moral systems of the philosophers some duties of great importance are omitted, and some things which they call virtues, when brought to the Christian standard, are found to be vices.

Cicero declares that "virtue proposes *glory* as its end, and looks for no other reward;" and Zeno, that "all crimes are equal, and that a person who has offended or injured us should never be forgiven." The

Cynics held "that there was nothing shameful in committing acts of lewdness in public." Aristippus affirmed "that as pleasure was the *summmum bonum*, a man might practice theft, sacrilege, or adultery, as he had opportunity." With regard to veracity, the rule of Menander was that "a lie is better than a hurtful truth." Plato said, "He may lie, who knows how to do it *in a fit season ;*" and Maximus Tyrius, that "there is nothing decorous in truth, but when it is profitable." Humility, which is a Christian virtue of the first order, was despised by heathen philosophers as an indication of a mean and dastardly spirit; and the direct tendency of their moral lessons was to inspire men with notions of personal dignity, a feeling of self-approbation, a consciousness of worth, which, of all tempers, is most offensive to God.

We see, then, that the systems of heathen morality were exceedingly defective; but, in addition to this, they were entirely destitute of *any authority* that could give them force. Their authors claimed no commission from God ; they performed no miracles for the confirmation of what they taught; their doctrines were incapable of a mathematical demonstration, and consequently they could only be regarded as mere human opinions, which every one might receive or reject, as his judgment, his interest, or his passions might dictate. Such systems of morality had therefore no power over the conscience; and the motives to virtue which they contained were insufficient to counteract men's innate propensity to evil, or to overcome the strong temptations to which they were continually exposed. Hence, a general depravity of manners prevailed among the ancient Gentile nations, a depravity which was not confined to the lower and uneducated classes of society, but which extended to the higher and better informed, and even to the very men who professed to be teachers of wisdom.

It would be a great mistake to suppose that the heathen philosophers spent their days in the study and practice of virtue. There is abundant proof that they were, in general, a class of unprincipled declaimers, whose infamous conduct daily contradicted their eloquent harangues. It was in view of this fact that Cicero inquired: "Who is there of all the philosophers whose mind, life, and manners were conformable to right reason ? Who ever made his philosophy the law and rule of his life, and not a mere show of his wit and parts ? Who observed his own instructions, and lived in obedience to his own precepts ?"

This induction of facts must prove to every one that the principles of natural theology are beyond the reach of unassisted reason. It is therefore in vain for any man to contend for its sufficiency till he can point out an instance in which it has discovered and established, by satisfactory arguments, the great truths of natural religion.

But here we may observe, that little as reason has done in the discovery of religious truth, we have no evidence that it could have done even so much had it been left to work out its own discoveries alone.

Indeed, its solitary strength has never been fairly tried, for man has never been entirely destitute of a Revelation. Though this was in a great measure lost among the nations of the world, yet some fragments of it remained, from which the philosophers of antiquity made up their various systems of religion. From this source they derived the idea of a God, and their notions of Providence, of morality, and of a future state. Thus tradition was supplementary to reason; and though its light was faint, yet it led to the knowledge of some truths which the eye of reason, amid the surrounding darkness, could not have discovered.

Another remark to which this investigation leads us is, that those who contend for the sufficiency of reason in matters of morals and religion, owe all their best views to that fountain of inspiration from which they criminally turn away. How otherwise can it be accounted for, that the very principles which modern philosophers regard as demonstrable by unassisted reason were held doubtfully, or connected with some manifest absurdity, or utterly denied by the wisest moral teachers among the ancient Gentiles? They had the same works of God, and the same course of Providence to direct them; and to neither were they inattentive. They had intellectual endowments which have been admired in all subsequent ages; and their reason was rendered acute and discriminative by the discipline of mathematical and dialectic science. They had everything which the moderns have, *except the* BIBLE; and yet, on points which have been generally settled among modern philosophers as fundamental to natural religion, they had no just views, and no settled conviction.

The strongest advocates of natural religion must admit that of the ancient philosophers, some argued themselves into a belief of Atheism; some, by ascribing all things to chance, and others to absolute fatality, subverted all true notions of religion. Some patronized particular vices, while others professed open immorality. Even the better sort of them, who reasoned most correctly concerning the Providence of God, the immortality of the soul, and a future state of retribution, discoursed on all these subjects with much uncertainty and doubtfulness.

Were we even to allow that those just views of God and religion which sometimes appear in the writings of heathen philosophers are to be ascribed to the power of human reason, the argument for its sufficiency would not be greatly strengthened. It would only show that the reason which occasionally reached the truth had not power to hold it fast; that the pinion which sometimes bore the mind into fields of light could not maintain it in its elevation. But facts will not allow us to admit that the truth which they occasionally advanced was the discovery of their own powers. They were evidently indebted to a traditional knowledge much earlier than their own day, and they obtained additional light from the descendants of Abraham, whose sacred books contain noble and just views of God, and a correct morality.

We have now seen how defective Reason is in its application to natural theology; but if we apply it to the peculiar doctrines of Revelation, we shall soon find that here it cannot make a single discovery. It is like the eye, which, though it perceives objects within a given limit, cannot discern, unless aided by art, those parts of creation which lie in the profound abyss of space. To Reason, the line which is drawn between natural and revealed theology is impassable. On the one side of it are some gleams of light; but on the other all is impenetrable darkness.

Revealed theology is founded on that mysterious distinction in the Divine Essence which we call the *Trinity;* a distinction which Reason could never have discovered, and which only God himself could disclose. It also unfolds the wise and benevolent counsels of God respecting our *fallen race,* of which no trace can be looked for in creation, as they relate to a state of things posterior to creation, and differing from that state in which man was originally placed.

It is true some Christian writers have asserted that in the *works* of God there is an obscure revelation of *grace;* and the celebrated infidel, Lord Herbert, has laid it down as one of his five articles of natural religion, that "if men repent of their sins God will forgive them." But nature teaches no such doctrine, for there is nothing in Creation, or even in the dispensations of Divine Providence, which indicates an intention on the part of God to pardon his disobedient creatures. And farther, the principle which is assumed by Lord Herbert, as the dictate of nature, is false, for God does not pardon sinners on mere repentance. He requires an *atonement,* but of this nature gives no indication.

We conclude, then, from all which we have seen, that a Revelation was necessary, if even it had gone no farther than to shed light upon the doctrines of natural religion, and to dissipate the doubts which reason could not solve. These doctrines, which were more or less interesting to all, were especially so to men of reflection; but the success of their inquiries was by no means commensurate with the earnestness of their wishes. To men in these circumstances a Revelation must be as acceptable as is the rising of the sun to the bewildered traveler, who is anxiously seeking the place of his destination, but cannot find it amid the darkness of the night.

This necessity of a Revelation would exist to a very considerable extent, even if reason in some cases were capable of discovering all the religious knowledge that is necessary. The strongest believers in the sufficiency of reason will admit that we cannot gain a knowledge of the principles of natural theology from the investigation of nature itself without close and persevering study; but every one must see that this would place the acquisition beyond the reach of a majority of mankind. There are many whose intellectual faculties are naturally weak, whose minds have not been improved by education, and whose daily occupations afford them but little leisure for inquiry and reflection. Such persons are apt to be misled by false opinions, and distracted by worldly cares, and to neglect those objects which require abstraction of mind and patient investigation. The infidel himself is compelled to acknowledge that Reason has generally failed to lead men to a rational system of religion.

It is manifest, therefore, that a Revelation which should point out at once, and to all, the doctrines which reason could discover only by a tedious process, would be a most invaluable gift to the world. On this subject no doubt can be entertained. Such a Revelation has been granted, and what is the consequence? The doctrines of natural religion are better understood than they could otherwise be: they are known not only to men of contemplative minds, but to the illiterate, and we become acquainted with them in the morning of life. There are thousands of young persons in every Christian country whose religious knowledge far exceeds that of the wisest heathen philosopher. They have learned more by a few lessons of revealed truth than he could acquire by the painful researches of a long life.

The necessity of a Divine Revelation may be farther argued,

2. *From the concessions of heathen philosophers.*

There are many passages in the writings of the heathens which show, that while they were conscious of their ignorance on religious subjects, they were persuaded that there was no remedy for it, except in some Divine interposition. "The various apprehensions of wise men," says Cicero, "will justify the doubtings and demurs of skeptics, and it will then be sufficient to blame them when others agree, or any one has found out the truth. We say not that nothing is true, but that some false things are annexed to all that is true, and that with so much likeness, that there is no certain note of judging what is true, or assenting to it. We deny not that something may be true; but we deny that it can be perceived so to be, for what have we certain concerning good and evil? Nor for this are we to blame, but NATURE, which has hidden the truth in the deep."*

"The truth is," says Plato, speaking of future rewards and punishments, "to determine or establish anything certain about these matters, in the midst of so many doubts and disputations, is the work of God only." Again, one of the speakers in his Phædo says to Socrates concerning the immortality of the soul: "I am of the same opinion with you, that in this life it is either absolutely impossible, or extremely difficult, to arrive at a clear knowledge in this matter." In his apology for Socrates, he puts these words into his mouth: "You may pass the remainder of your days in sleep, or despair of finding out a sufficient expedient for this purpose, if God, in his providence, do not send you some other instruction."

But there is a most remarkable passage in Plato's dialogue between

* See *De Nat. Deorum*, l. 1, n. 10, 11. *Acad. Qu.*, l. 2, n. 66, 120.

Socrates and Alcibiades, on the duties of religious worship. The design of the dialogue is to convince Alcibiades that men, on account of their great ignorance, should be exceedingly cautious in their addresses to the gods, and should content themselves with very general prayers, or, what is better, not pray at all. "To me," says he, "it seems best to be quiet; it is necessary to wait till you learn how you ought to behave toward the gods and toward men." "When," exclaims Alcibiades, "when, O Socrates! shall that time be, and who will instruct me? for most willingly would I see this man, who he is." "He is one," replies Socrates, "who cares for you; but, as Homer represents Minerva as taking away darkness from the eyes of Diomedes, that he might distinguish a god from a man, so it is necessary that he should first take away the darkness from your mind, and then bring near those things by which you shall know good and evil." "Let him take away, if he will," rejoins Alcibiades, "the darkness or any other thing, for I am prepared to decline none of those things which are commanded by him, whoever this man is, if I shall be made better."*

This passage is truly curious, and deserves our particular attention as a proof of the longings of the ancient sages for such a Revelation as God has given to the world. The wisest philosopher of antiquity acknowledged its necessity, and ventured to anticipate it, without, however, knowing what he said. His disciple was transported at the thought, and declared his readiness to submit to the lessons of his desired teacher. It is only among unbelievers of modern times—the "men of reason," as they would be accounted—that the idea of a Divine Revelation is held up to ridicule, and the sufficiency of Reason maintained.

But we have a most conclusive proof of the necessity of a Revelation from God,

3. *In the debasing and demoralizing tendency of all pagan religions.*

It cannot be denied that the very systems of religion and established forms of worship among heathens, instead of being calculated to preserve men in the practice of morality and virtue, only served to plunge them into vice and degrading superstition. They paid divine worship to oxen, to crocodiles, to birds, and to reptiles. They metamorphosed beasts into gods, and conversely transformed their gods into beasts, ascribing to them drunkenness, unnatural lusts, and the most loathsome vices. They worshiped *drunkenness*, under the name of Bacchus; and *lasciviousness*, under that of Venus. Momus was to them the god of *calumny*, and Mercury the god of *thieves*. Even Jupiter, the greatest of their gods, they considered to be an *adulterer*. At length the worship of avowedly evil beings became prevalent among them; and hence, many of their rites were cruel and contrary to humanity, and the licentiousness and impurity of their whole religious system became notorious.

* Platonis Alcibiad., II.

Thus, to select a few instances out of many, the rites of the goddess Cybele were no less infamous for lewdness than for cruelty; and the practice of these rites spread far and wide, and formed part of the public worship at Rome. The *aphrodisia*, or festivals in honor of Venus, were observed with lascivious ceremonies in many parts of Greece; and Strabo tells us that there was a temple at Corinth so rich that it maintained more than a thousand harlots, sacred to her service. The feasts of Bacchus were equally impure and licentious; and according to Herodotus, many of the Egyptian rites were cruel and shockingly obscene. The *floralia* among the Romans, or their festivals in honor of Flora, the goddess of flowers, were celebrated for four days together by the most shameful actions, and with the most unbounded licentiousness.

The horrible practice of offering human sacrifices was for many ages very general in the heathen world. It obtained among the Phœnicians, Syrians, Arabians, Carthaginians, and other people of Africa; and among the Egyptians, till the time of Amasis. The same is asserted concerning the Thracians, the ancient Scythians, the Gauls, the Germans, and the Britons. And though this rite was not so common among the Greeks and Romans, as among some other nations, yet they practiced it for a long time on extraordinary occasions, as being the most meritorious sacrifice that could be offered to the gods.*

Indeed, when we examine the history of the ancient pagan world, we are struck with the accuracy of the description which is given of them by St. Paul in the first chapter of his Epistle to the Romans. He asserts that they "changed the glory of the uncorruptible God into an image made like to corruptible man, and to birds, and four-footed beasts, and creeping things." And as they were not willing to retain the knowledge of God, they were judicially given up to uncleanness and a reprobate mind. Hence the apostle tells us that they were "filled with all unrighteousness, fornication, wickedness, covetousness, maliciousness;" that they were "full of envy, murder, debate, deceit, malignity;" and that they were "whisperers, backbiters, haters of God, despiteful, proud, boasters, inventors of evil things, disobedient to parents, without understanding, covenant breakers, without natural affection, implacable, unmerciful."

If we direct our attention to heathen nations of the present age, such as Tartary, the Philippine Islands, and many parts of Africa, China, and Hindoostan, we learn, from the unanimous testimony of navigators and travelers, that they are enveloped in the grossest ignorance and idolatry, and that their religious worship, doctrines, and practices are equally corrupt with those of the pagan nations of antiquity.

With regard to Hindoostan in particular, though her inhabitants are

---

* See Leland's Necess. and Advan. of Revelation; Clarke's Evid. of Nat. and Rev. Religion; Gregory's Letters on Christian Religion; Horne's Introduction, vol. i; and Hartley on Man, vol. ii.

celebrated for their progress in the useful arts, and for intellectual acuteness, yet her polytheism is of the grossest and most debasing kind. There are not fewer than *three hundred and thirty millions of deities* claiming the adoration of their votaries! Her religion enjoins rites the most impure, penances the most toilsome, and modes of self-torture almost innumerable, and as exquisite in degree as human nature can sustain. The burying alive or burning of widows, infanticide, the immersion of the sick and dying in the Ganges, and self-devotement to destruction by the idol Juggernaut, are among the horrid practices which flow from her established system of idolatry, and which have never been exceeded in folly and ferocity by any to which Paganism has given birth.*

Let our argument then, be summed up.

We have seen that the light of human reason was too weak to conduct heathen philosophers to just conclusions, either with respect to the fundamental doctrines of *natural religion*, or to the principles of *a pure morality;* that the heathen sages themselves felt and acknowledged the insufficiency of reason in matters of religion, and strongly desired some direct communication from the gods; and that the religions of all Pagan nations, both ancient and modern, instead of elevating men and purifying their moral nature, have exerted upon them a most corrupting and demoralizing influence.

These are the facts, and they affect not only a small portion of mankind, but all who have not had the benefits of the Holy Scriptures. Where the Bible is unknown there is not, and never has been, since the corruption of the primitive religion, a religious system containing just views of God and of religious truth, or which has enjoined a correct morality, or even opposed any effectual barrier against the deterioration of public manners.

These facts cannot be denied, and the conclusion is therefore irresistible, that an express Revelation of the will of God, accompanied by efficient corrective institutions, had become necessary, and is still demanded by the religious and moral condition of every part of the earth into which Christianity has not been introduced.

Having then shown the possibility and the necessity of a Divine Revelation, we will proceed to consider,

III. Its probable character.

If there is ground to presume that God, in his compassion for his creatures, would not leave them without a direct and clear communication of his will, there is equal ground to presume that this communication, whenever made, should be of such a nature, and accompanied by such circumstances, as would most effectually meet the wants of the world.

Presumptions as to the nature and manner of such a Revelation, we

* Asiatic Researches, vol. viii.

will allow, ought to be guarded; but, without violating this rule, it may, from the obviousness of the case, be presumed, 1. That it should contain explicit information on those subjects which are of most importance to mankind, and in regard to which they have most fatally erred. 2. That it should accord with the principles of former revelations, should any have been given. 3. That it should have a satisfactory external authentication. And, 4. That it should contain provisions for its effectual promulgation among all classes of men. All this, allowing the necessity and the probability of a Divine Revelation, must certainly be expected; but this expectation is fully met in the Christian System.

1. It gives explicit information in regard to *the nature and perfections of* GOD; *his* WILL, *as the rule of moral actions; the means of obtaining* PARDON *and of conquering vice; the true* MEDIATOR *between God and man; Divine* PROVIDENCE; *the* CHIEF GOOD *of man*, respecting which alone more than three hundred different opinions among the ancient sages have been reckoned up; *the accountability and* IMMORTALITY *of man; and a* FUTURE STATE *of retribution.*

2. It accords with the principles of former Revelations. The veracity of God requires, that so far as one Revelation renews, explains, or adds to another, it must agree with the previous communication.

Now whatever direct proof may be adduced in favor of the Divine authority of the Jewish and the Christian Revelations, there is this in their favor: that they have a substantial agreement and harmony among themselves, and with that traditional system which existed in the earliest ages of the world. As to the patriarchal religion, to which reference has several times been made, we have ample information in the book of Job, from which venerable relic a copious body of doctrinal and practical theology might be collected.*

It recognizes in the clearest manner the Being and Attributes of God; the corrupt and helpless condition of man; the offering of propitiatory sacrifices, as of Divine appointment; the expectation of a Divine Redeemer; the immortality of the soul; the resurrection of the body; and a future judgment. It condemns immoral actions and vicious passions, as violations of the laws of God; and speaks of purity of heart, kindness, compassion to the poor, and cheerful submission to the will of God, as virtues of the highest obligation.

Such was the comprehensive system of patriarchal theology; and it would be easy to show that these great principles are all recognized and taken up in the successive Revelations by Moses, and by Christ. Here then are three religious systems, introduced at widely distant periods, and by agents greatly differing in their condition and circumstances,

---

* There is sufficient evidence that Job lived between the flood of Noah and the calling of Abraham; and that the book which bears his name was written not later than the time of Moses.

but they exactly harmonize in every leading doctrine, and agree in their great moral *end*—PERFECT PURITY OF HEART AND CONDUCT.

3. It was accompanied by an *external authentication*, of such a nature as to leave no reasonable doubt of its Divine authority.

The reason of this is obvious. A mere impression of truth on the understanding could not be distinguished from a discovery made by the human intellect, and could therefore have no authority as a Revelation from God, either with the person receiving it, or with others to whom he might promulge it. Hence an authentication of revealed truth, *external* to the Revelation itself, is necessary to give it authority, and to create the obligation of obedience.

The authority of the ancient patriarchal religion rested on external evidence. The received opinion was, that the Almighty Lawgiver, under celestial appearances, conversed with our first parents, and with the patriarchs; and that his laws thus delivered were authenticated by his kindness to the obedient and his judgments upon the rebellious. It was in consequence of the deep impress of Divinity which this system received in the earliest ages, from the attestation of singular judgments, and especially the flood, that it was universally transmitted, and waged so long a war against religious corruptions.

But the primitive system, being traditional, was liable to alteration and abuse. Hence, notwithstanding its original authentication as a matter of Divine Revelation, and the effects which it produced in the world for many ages, it was at length so much corrupted by transmission, and its external evidence so greatly weakened by the lapse of time, that some merciful interposition on the part of God was rendered necessary by the general ignorance of mankind. Indeed, the primitive Revelations supposed subsequent ones, and were not, in themselves, regarded as complete.

But if only a republication of the primitive truth had been necessary, it would have required a new authentication, in a form adapted to the circumstances of the world, and the same would be true of every enlarged or additional Revelation. If we presume, therefore, that a new Revelation was necessary, we must presume that, when given, it would have an external authentication as coming from God, from which there could be no reasonable appeal; and we therefore conclude, that as the Mosaic and the Christian Revelations profess both to republish and to enlarge former Revelations, the circumstance of their resting their claims on the external evidence of miracles and prophecy is a presumption in their favor.

4. It contains provisions for its effectual promulgation among all classes of men.

As the Revelation in question was designed to restore and enlarge the communications of truth, and as tradition had become an imperfect medium of conveying it, the fair presumption is, that the persons th ough whom the communication was made should record it in WRITING, as being the most natural and effectual means of preserving it. Any corruption of the record would be rendered impracticable, by its being publicly taught in the first instance; by a standard copy being preserved with care; or by such a number of copies being dispersed as to defy material alteration. This presumption is realized both in the Jewish and the Christian Revelations, as will be seen when the authority of the Holy Scriptures comes to be discussed. They were first publicly taught, then committed to writing, and copies were multiplied.

Another method of preserving and diffusing the knowledge of a Revelation once made would be the institution of public commemorative rites. These also we find in the Revelations of Moses and of Christ, at once preserving the memory both of great events themselves, and of the doctrines connected with them.

If it was reasonable to expect a Revelation, it was equally reasonable to presume that it should contain some injunctions favorable to its propagation among men of *all ranks*. For, as the compassion of God to the moral necessities of his creatures, generally, is the ground on which so great a favor rests, it is not to be restricted to any one class of men, but to be extended to all.

This reasonable expectation is also realized in the Mosaic and the Christian Revelations. Both provide for their general publication; both instituted an order of men, not to conceal, but to *read* and *teach*, the truth committed to them; both recognized a right in the people to search the record, and by it to judge of the ministrations of the priests; both made it obligatory on the people to be taught; and both separated one day in seven to afford leisure for that purpose.

Nothing but such a Revelation, and with such accompanying circumstances, appears capable of reaching the actual case of mankind, and of effectually instructing and bringing them under moral control; and, whether the Bible can be proved to be of Divine authority or not, this at least must be granted: that it presents itself to us under these circumstances, and claims, for this very reason, our most serious and candid attention.

CHRISTIAN THEOLOGY.

BOOK I.

EVIDENCES OF A DIVINE REVELATION.

WE now proceed to inquire whether we have sufficient reason to conclude that the Scriptures of the Old and the New Testament are a Revelation from God. This is a question of the greatest importance; for it is universally acknowledged among us that the Bible is the only book in the world whose claims to Divine authority are worthy of serious examination. If, therefore, the advantage of supernatural and infallible instruction has been afforded to man, it must be found in that alone.

Every humble and sincere man who is conscious of his own infirmity, and who knows the perplexities in which the wisest of men have been involved on religious and moral subjects, will desire to find at length an infallible guide, and will therefore examine the evidences of the Bible with an anxious wish that he may find sufficient reason to acknowledge its Divine authority. And should he be disappointed he will feel that he has met with a painful misfortune, and not a matter of triumph. This temper of mind is perfectly consistent with a full and even severe examination of the claims of Scripture, and he who is destitute of it is neither a *sincere* nor an *earnest* inquirer after truth.

That the Bible is in favor of the highest virtues, cannot be denied. It both prescribes them, and affords the strongest possible motives to their cultivation. It might be confidently put to every candid person, however skeptical, whether the universal observance of the morality of the Scriptures, by all ranks and classes of men, would not produce the most beneficial changes in society, and secure general peace, friendship, and happiness. If, therefore, he who investigates the Divine authority cf the Holy Scriptures has had the means of even a superficial acquaintance with their contents, he ought, if a lover of *virtue* as well as of *truth*, to be predisposed in their favor.

In the investigation of the truth of revealed religion we will direct our attention, 1. To the *evidences* which are necessary to authenticate a Divine Revelation; 2. To the *genuineness* of the Holy Scriptures; 3. To their *authenticity;* 4. To their *integrity;* and, 5. To their *Divine authority.*

CHAPTER I.

EVIDENCES NECESSARY TO AUTHENTICATE A DIVINE REVELATION.

THE Evidences in proof of the Divine authority of the Sacred Scriptures may be divided into EXTERNAL, INTERNAL, and COLLATERAL. The *External Evidence* consists of miracles and prophecy; the *Internal Evidence* is drawn from the nature and moral tendency of the doctrines taught; and the *Collateral Evidence* arises from a variety of circumstances, which indirectly prove the Revelation to be divinely inspired.

§ 1. *Of External Evidence.*

The principal and most appropriate evidence of a Revelation from God must be *external* to the Revelation itself. If, therefore, any person should profess to have received a Revelation from God to teach to mankind, and that he was directed to command their obedience to it on pain of the Divine displeasure, he would be asked for some *external* authentication of his mission. He might believe that a Divine communication had been made to himself; but *his* belief would have no authority to command *ours.* Nor could we have any means, without *external proof*, of knowing that he had received such communication. *Internal evidence alone* could not be a sufficient proof; for we could not tell whether his doctrines, however excellent, might not be the fruits of his own mental labor. To us, therefore, they could only have the authority of mere human opinions; and though their reasonableness and excellence might entitle him to attention and respect, without some *external* authentication he could not *command.*

Agreeable to this, the authors both of the Jewish and Christian Scriptures profess to have authenticated their mission by the two great external proofs, MIRACLES and PROPHECY; and it remains to be considered whether a mission to teach the will of God to man is sufficiently authenticated when *miracles* are really performed, and *prophecies* unequivocally accomplished.

I. MIRACLES.—In looking at these, as an external and authenticating proof of Divine Revelation, we may consider,

1. *Their Nature.*—In a *philosophic* sense, a miracle is an event which is inconsistent with some known law of nature, or contrary to the settled constitution and course of things. Accordingly, miracles presuppose an established system of nature, within the limits of which they operate, and with the order of which they disagree.

In a *theological* sense, a miracle is an event contrary to the established constitution and course of things, effected by the interposition of God for the proof of some particular doctrine, or in attestation of the authority of some particular person.*

The miracles recorded in the Holy Scriptures agree with the theological meaning of the term. They were wrought immediately by God himself, to attest the Divine mission of particular persons, and to authenticate their doctrines; or by some superior creatures, commissioned by him for the same purpose; or by men, in order to prove that they were invested with Divine authority.

In order to distinguish a real miracle, it is necessary that we should understand the common course of nature, for, without some knowledge of the operations of physical causes, we might deem an event miraculous merely because it is strange and inexplicable. Should an earthquake happen in a country where men had never heard of such a calamity, by the ignorant it might be considered miraculous; whereas, it is a regular effect of the established laws of nature.

But as we have at best only a partial knowledge of these laws, it seems necessary that such miracles as are intended to authenticate a Divine Revelation should be effected upon objects whose properties are well understood, and that they should be evidently contrary to some known laws by which such objects have been uniformly governed; or, that their apparent cause should be known to have no adequate power or adaptation to produce them. When these circumstances concur in any event, there is sufficient ground to conclude that it is miraculous.

Assuming, then, for the present, that the works ascribed to Moses and to Christ were actually performed by them, they are of such a nature as to leave no reasonable doubt of their miraculous character. The rod cast from the hand of Moses became a serpent. Here the subject was well known; it was a *rod;* and it was obviously contrary to the established course of nature that it should undergo so signal a transformation.

* Farmer, in his " Dissertation on Miracles," denies to created beings, however high, the power of working miracles when acting from themselves alone. If they perform miracles at all they must do it by a Divine commission, and by the interposition of Divine power. Dr. Taylor, of New Haven, takes the same ground.

The sea is parted at the stretching out of the rod of Moses, and the waters stand upon each side, leaving a passage for the host of Israel. But there is here no adaptation in the apparent cause to produce the effect, which was obviously in direct opposition to the known qualities of water.

It is in the nature of clouds to be carried about by the wind ; but the cloud which attended the Israelites in the wilderness rested on their tabernacle, moved when they were commanded to march, and directed their course. It rested when they were to pitch their tents ; and by night, when it is the nature of clouds to become dark, it shone with the brightness of fire. In all these cases, therefore, if the facts can be established, there can be no doubt as to their miraculous character.

" Were a physician instantly to give sight to a blind man, by anointing his eyes with a chemical preparation, to the nature and qualities of which we were absolute strangers, the cure would be to us wonderful ; but we could not pronounce it miraculous, because it might be the physical effect of the unguent upon the eyes. But were he to give sight to his patient merely by commanding him to receive it, or by anointing his eyes with spittle, we should, with the utmost confidence, pronounce the cure to be a miracle, because we know that neither the human voice nor human spittle has any such power over the diseases of the eye."

" Persons apparently dead are often restored to their families and friends by being treated, during suspended animation, in the manner recommended by the *Humane Society*. To the vulgar, and even sometimes to men of science, these resuscitations appear very *wonderful ;* but as they are known to be effected by physical agency, they cannot be miraculous. On the other hand, no one could doubt of his having witnessed a real miracle, who had seen a person that had been four days dead come alive out of the grave at the call of another."*

2. *Their Possibility.*—Those who believe in a Supreme Creator, and in the dependence of all things upon his power and will, cannot deny the *possibility* of miracles ; nor is there anything in them inconsistent with the wisdom and the immutability of God, or with the perfection of his works. They are departures from the ordinary course of God's operations ; but not to remedy unforeseen evils, or to repair imperfections in the system of nature. The reasons for them are *moral* and not natural reasons ; and they are wrought to accomplish *moral ends.* They remind us, when they occur, that the power of God is superior to nature, and that on him all nature depends.

3. *The Circumstances under which Miracles are an authenticating Evidence.*—Granting their possibility, the argument which is drawn from them is this : that as the established and known course of nature has been fixed by the Creator and Preserver of all things, it can never be

* Gleig's edition of Stackhouse's History of the Bible, vol. iii, p. 241.

counteracted but by himself, or by other beings at his command, and by his assistance. To deny this, is to deny the omnipotence and natural government of God.

But miracles, in order to be an authentication of a Divine mission, must be effected by the power of God for this very purpose. The following circumstances are sufficient to establish this fact : 1. When the miracles occur only in connection with an actual profession of certain persons that they have a mission from God, and while they are engaged in the proper functions of their office. In this there would be a strong presumption that the works were wrought by God in order to authenticate this pretension. 2. When they are performed by the persons themselves, at their own will, and for the express purpose of establishing their mission. If the works are real miracles, it is then clear that God is with them, and that his co-operation is an authenticating and visible seal upon their commission.

But though it should be allowed, that when real miracles occur under the circumstances which we have mentioned they are satisfactory evidences of a Divine mission, and that eye-witnesses of such miracles would be bound to admit the proof; it has been made a question, whether their testimony affords to others sufficient evidence that such events actually took place, and whether we are bound to acknowledge the authority of that mission in attestation of which the miracles are said to have been wrought.

If we assume the negative, either the benefits of a Revelation must be confined to those who witnessed its attestation by miracles, or similar attestations must be afforded to every man. But as no religious system can plead the authentication of *perpetual* miracles, either this principle is unsound, or we must abandon all hope of discovering a religion of Divine authority.

These remarks will lead us to notice,

4. *The Competency of human Testimony to establish the Credibility of Miracles.*—As miracles are facts, they, like other facts, may be reported ; and, from the nature of the miracles in question, the competency of any man of ordinary understanding to determine whether they were actually wrought, cannot be doubted. If, therefore, the witnesses are credible ; and if, in matters of the greatest moment in common life, we should not hesitate to act upon their testimony, it would be mere perverseness to reject it in the case of miracles.

Mr. Hume denies the credibility of miracles on the ground of human testimony. The substance of his objection is this : *Experience* is the ground of the credit which we give to human testimony ; but this experience is by no means constant, for men often prevaricate and deceive. It is *experience*, in like manner, which assures us of those laws of nature, in the violation of which the notion of a miracle consists ; but this experience is constant and uniform. Hence, it is contrary to experience that miracles should be true, but not contrary to experience that human testimony should be false; and, therefore, no human testimony can, in any case, render them credible.

To this objection, which has been met at large by many authors,* we oppose the following remarks:

There is an ambiguity in the term " experience," and in the phrase " contrary to experience," which ought to be removed. Strictly speaking, the narrative of a fact is contrary to experience when the fact is related to have existed at a time and place, at which time and place we, being present, did not perceive it to exist; as if it should be asserted that in a particular room, and at a particular hour of a certain day, a man was raised from the dead, in which room, and at the time specified, we, being present and looking on, perceived no such event. Here the assertion is contrary to experience in the proper sense of the phrase; and this is a contrariety which no evidence can surmount, whether the fact be miraculous or otherwise.

But is this the experience and contrariety which Mr. Hume intended in the objection? It certainly is not. When, therefore, he asserts that miracles are contrary to experience, he must be understood to mean, either that we ourselves have not experienced them, (which is properly a want of experience, and not a contradiction of it,) or, that they have not been generally experienced by others. We say, "not *generally;*" for to assert that no miracle was *ever* experienced is to assume the subject in controversy.

To argue against miracles from the supposed unalterable course of nature, is a mere begging of the question. It is to argue upon a supposition which is wholly incapable of proof: that the course of nature is indeed so *unalterably* fixed, that even God himself, by whom its laws were ordained, *cannot*, when he sees fit, suspend their operation. On the other hand, to expect that miracles should become a matter of common experience, is to expect what is contrary to their nature, what would make them cease to be miracles, and what would totally destroy the purpose for which they were wrought.

Mr. Hume attempts to adjust, in a sort of metaphysical balance, the degrees of probability resulting from what he is pleased to call " *opposite experiences;*" that is, the experience of men's veracity on the one hand, and of the unalterable laws of nature on the other. But it will at once appear, that he only weighs the experience of those who never had the opportunity of witnessing a miracle, against the experience of those who declare that they were eye-witnesses of the fact. Instead, therefore, of weighing *opposite experiences*, properly so called, he is only balancing total *inexperience* on the one hand, against positive *experience* on the other.

* See Campbell's Dissertations on Miracles; Paley's Evidences; Adam's Essay on Miracles; Bishop Douglas's Criterion; Dwight's Theology, vol. 2; and Chalmers.

There is a palpable fallacy in representing the experience of mankind as being *opposite* to the testimony on which our belief of miracles is founded. For the *opposite* experiences, as they are called, are not contradictory to each other, since there is no inconsistency in believing them both. A miracle necessarily supposes an established and *generally unaltered* course of nature, for in the interception of such a course lies the very essence of a miracle. Our experience, therefore, of the course of nature leads us to expect its continuance, and to act accordingly; but it does not prove that it is absolutely unalterable, nor does it set aside valid testimony of a deviation from it. How can our being personally unacquainted with a matter of fact which took place a thousand years ago, or in a distant part of the world, warrant us in rejecting the testimony of personal witnesses of the event? Common sense revolts at the absurdity of considering one man's ignorance or inexperience as a counterpoise to another man's knowledge and experience of a matter of fact. Yet on no better foundation does this favorite argument of infidelity rest.

But we may also remark, that " the evidence arising from human testimony is *not solely derived* from experience. On the contrary, testimony has a natural influence on belief, antecedent to experience. The early and unlimited assent given to testimony by children, gradually contracts as they advance in life; and it is therefore more consonant to truth to say, that our diffidence in testimony is the result of experience, than that our faith in it has this foundation."

" Besides, the uniformity of experience in favor of any fact is not a proof against its being reversed in a particular instance. The evidence arising from the single testimony of a man of known veracity, will go farther to establish a belief of its being actually reversed. And if his testimony be confirmed by a few others of the same character, we cannot withhold our assent to the truth of it."

" Now, though the operations of nature are governed by uniform laws, and though we have not the testimony of our senses in favor of any violation of them; still, if in particular instances we have the testimony of thousands of our fellow-creatures, and those, too, men of strict integrity, swayed by no motives of ambition or interest, but governed by the principles of common sense, that they were actually witnesses of these violations, the constitution of our nature obliges us to believe them."*

We have now shown the nature and possibility of real miracles; that under certain circumstances they are to be regarded as a sufficient authentication, both of the Divine mission of those who performed them, and of the doctrines which they taught; that as facts they are proper subjects of human testimony, and that credible testimony respecting them lays a competent foundation for our belief in them, and in those

* Reasonableness of Christianity.

Revelations which they were clearly designed to attest. Thus, the way is prepared for the consideration of the miracles recorded in Scripture.

II. PROPHECY. This is the other great branch of the external evidence of a Revelation from God, and its nature and force may be pointed out before we examine either the miracles or the prophecies of the Bible. For, by ascertaining the general principles on which this kind of evidence rests, the consideration of particular cases will be rendered more easy and satisfactory. We will notice,

1. *The Nature of Prophecy.*—It may be defined to be "*a miracle of knowledge.*" It is a declaration, description, or representation of something future, which is beyond the power of human sagacity to discover or calculate.

Prophecy is a *miracle*, because, to foresee and foretell future events, to which no existing cause necessarily and evidently leads, no train of probabilities points, is as much beyond the ability of man as to cure diseases with a word, or even to raise the dead. It is a miracle, too, the proof of which remains within itself. That such actions as may be properly termed *miracles of power* were ever performed, can be proved, at a distant period, only by human testimony, against which cavils may be raised, or causes for doubt advanced. But the man who reads a prophecy, and perceives the corresponding event, is *himself* the witness of the miracle. He sees that thus it was predicted, and that thus it has come to pass.

Prophecies yet unfulfilled are miracles which at present are incomplete. These may be regarded as the seeds of future conviction, ready to grow up and bear their fruit whenever the corresponding facts shall be exhibited on the theater of the world. This kind of evidence has been so admirably contrived by the wisdom of God, that, in proportion as the lapse of ages might *seem* to weaken the argument derived from miracles long since performed, that very lapse serves only to strengthen the argument derived from the fulfillment of prophecy.

2. *The Force of its Evidence.*—The force of the evidence arising from the prediction of such events as human sagacity could not anticipate is at once apparent. Such predictions, whether in the form of declarations, descriptions, or representations of things future, are evidently supernatural, and must be divinely inspired. When, for instance, the events are distant many years or ages from the time of the prediction; when they depend on causes not so much as existing when the prophecy was uttered and recorded, and likewise upon various circumstances and a long arbitrary series of things, and the fluctuating uncertainties of human volitions; and especially when they depend not at all upon any external circumstances, nor upon any created being, but arise merely from the counsels and appointment of God, such events can be foreknown only by an

omniscient Being, and can be foretold by him only to whom the "Father of lights" shall reveal them.

It follows, therefore, that whoever is manifestly endowed with this predictive power must, in that instance, speak and act by Divine inspiration, and what he declares must be received as the *word of God*.

The infidel author of "The Moral Philosopher" rather insinuates than attempts fully to establish a dilemma, with which to perplex those who regard prophecy as one of the proofs of a Divine Revelation. He thinks that either prophecy must respect "necessary events, as depending upon necessary causes, which might be certainly foreknown and predicted" without any Divine interposition; or that, if human actions are free, the possibility of prophecy must be given up, as it implies foreknowledge, which, if granted, would render them necessary.

To the first part of this objection we answer, that there are indeed many necessary events, dependent upon necessary causes, the existence and operation of which are within the compass of human knowledge. But to foretell such events would not be to prophesy, any more than to say that on a certain day and hour next year there will be an eclipse of the sun or moon, when that event has been previously ascertained by astronomical calculation.

Were we to allow that *all* events were necessary, yet, in a variety of instances, the argument from prophecy would not be at all affected; for the foretelling of necessary events in certain circumstances is beyond human intelligence, because they can be known to Him only by whose power those necessary causes on which they depend have been arranged, and who has prescribed the times of their operation.

Let us allow, for the sake of illustration, that the prophecy of Isaiah respecting the taking of Babylon by Cyrus was uttered, as it purports to have been, more than a century before Cyrus was born, and that all the actions of Cyrus and of his army, and those of the Babylonian monarch and his people, were necessitated. Is it to be maintained that the chain of necessitating causes, running through more than a century, could be traced by a *human* mind so as to describe the precise manner in which that fatality would unfold itself, even to the turning of the river, the drunken carousal of the inhabitants, and the neglect to shut the gates of the city? This being known to be above all human apprehension, would prove that the prediction was really a communication from God. Were events therefore subject to invincible fate, there might nevertheless be prophecy.

The other branch of the dilemma is founded on the notion that, if we allow the freedom of human actions, prophecy is impossible, because certain foreknowledge is contrary to that freedom, and renders events necessary.

Our reply is, that the objection is founded on a false assumption, the Divine foreknowledge having no more influence in making any future event necessary than human knowledge, in the degree in which it may exist. There is no moral causality in knowledge. This lies in the *will*, which is the determining and acting principle in every moral agent. The infallible judgment of God respecting contingent events no more causes them to be necessary, than our knowledge of a present truth is any cause of its being either *true* or *present*.

Things which depend upon a chain of *necessary* causes must be necessary, and as such God foreknows them; but it by no means follows that, from the foreknowledge of God concerning events which depend upon *free* causes, things otherwise supposed to be *free* will thereby unavoidably become *necessary*. The whole question lies in this: is the simple *knowledge* of an action a necessitating cause of the action? The answer must be in the negative, as every man's consciousness and common sense will assure him.

§ 2. *Of Internal Evidence.*

The second kind of evidence in attestation of a Divine Revelation is called *Internal ;* to the nature of which, as also to its rank in the scale of evidence, we will briefly turn our attention.

1. Its Nature.—*Internal evidence* is that kind of evidence which arises from a consideration of the doctrines taught in the Holy Scriptures, as being consistent with the character of God, and promotive of the happiness of man. It is derived from the wonderful sublimity of the sacred volume, the perfect purity of its moral precepts, the profundity and importance of its discoveries, the exact agreement of all its parts, and its obvious tendency to promote the wellbeing of mankind.

2. Its Rank *in the scale of Evidence.*—On this subject very different opinions have been entertained. Some have advanced the notion that internal evidence ought not to be ranked, as a *leading* proof, with miracles and prophecy, because the proof from them is decisive and absolute. But for the same reason prophecy might be excluded from the rank of *leading* evidence, inasmuch as miracles *alone* are decisive and absolute. If there is any force at all in the argument from miracles, it goes the full length of rational proof of a Divine attestation, both to him who witnesses the miracles, and to him to whom they are credibly reported; and nothing more is absolutely necessary to enforce a rational conviction.

But should it please the Author of a revelation to superadd the farther evidence of prophecy, and also that of the obvious truthfulness and beneficial tendency of this revelation, it ought not to be disregarded, or thought to be of trifling import in its favor. For, though this additional evidence may not be necessary to establish a rational proof, it may have a tendency to rouse attention, and to leave objectors more obviously without excuse.

By others, the internal evidence has been placed *first* in order and importance, and upon it the force of the evidence from miracles and prophecy has been made to depend. Nothing, say they, is to be received as a revelation from God which does not contain doctrines worthy of his character and promotive of the good of mankind.

This, we reply, is readily admitted. But are we to try a professed Revelation by our own notions of what is worthy of God and beneficial to mankind? This would be to assume, that, independent of a Revelation, we know what God is, and that we are so perfectly acquainted with the character, relations, and wants of man as to determine what is most for his benefit. This, however, cannot be granted.

But again, to make internal evidence the *primary* test of a Divine Revelation, is to render the *external* testimony comparatively unimportant. For, if a Revelation is to contain an evidence of its truth, which shall be independent of all external testimony, the utility of the evidence of miracles is rendered very questionable. It is either unnecessary, or it is subordinate and dependent. But this notion is contradicted by the whole tenor of the Scriptures; for miracles are everywhere represented as a complete and absolute demonstration of the mission and doctrines of those by whom they were performed.

It is easy to discover the causes which have led to this error in regard to the true *office* and *rank* of the internal evidence of Revelation.

First, a hypothetical case has been assumed, and it has been asked, "If a doctrine absurd and wicked should be attested by miracles, is it to be admitted as Divine upon their authority?" The answer is, that this is a case which in the nature of things can never occur, and which cannot, therefore, be made the basis of an argument. We have seen already that a *real* miracle can be wrought by none but God, or by his commission. Therefore, whenever a real miracle takes place, in *attestation* of any doctrine, that doctrine cannot be either unreasonable or impious.

The *second* cause of the error has been, that the *rational* evidence of a Revelation has been confounded with the *authenticating* evidence. When the character, plans, and laws of God are made known, they carry to the reason of man, so far as they are comprehended, the demonstration which accompanies truth of any other kind. For, as the eye is formed to received light, so the rational powers of man are formed to receive conviction when the congruity of propositions is made evident. This is *rational* evidence, but it is not *authenticating* evidence.

Let us suppose that there is no *external* evidence to attest the Divine mission of those teachers from whom we have received the doctrines which appear to us to be so sublime, so important, so true. It will then follow that they had no means of knowing these doctrines to be from God, or of distinguishing them from the discoveries of their own mind.   And if even they had, we can have no means of knowing that they are anything more than mere human opinions.   They may be true, but of this we can have no infallible proof; for neither our own rational faculties, nor those of any other human being, are infallible. But even granting them to be true, they cannot be attested to be Divine.   Add, then, the *external* testimony, and we have the attestation required.   The *rational* evidence of the doctrines, in both cases, is the same; but this evidence is no proof that God revealed them.   It is in *external* evidence alone that this proof is found.

From this distinction the relative importance of the External and Internal evidence may be further illustrated.

Rational evidence of the doctrines proposed to us, when it can be had, goes to establish their *truth*, so far as we can depend upon our judgment; but external testimony, if satisfactory, establishes their *Divine authority*, and consequently their absolute truth, leaving no appeal.   It is of the most simple and decisive kind, and gives to unbelief the character of obvious perverseness and inconsistency : *perverseness*, because there is a clear opposition of the will rather than of the judgment in the case; *inconsistency*, because men act upon a much lower degree of evidence in the most important concerns of life.

In difficult doctrines, of a kind to give rise to a variety of opinions, rational evidence is accompanied with doubt; but the attestation of miracles rests on principles supported by the universal and constant experience of mankind : 1. That a real miracle is above human power; 2. That men unquestionably virtuous in every other respect are not likely to propagate a deliberate falsehood; and, 3. That they should do· so not only without advantage, but at the hazard of reproach, persecution, and death, contradicts all the known motives to action in human nature.

In strict propriety, therefore, miracles may be considered as the *primary* evidence of the truth of a Revelation, and every other species of proof as *confirmatory*.   Prophecy and the internal evidence are *leading proofs*, but neither of them stands in the foremost place.

§ 3. *Of Collateral Evidence.*

The third kind of evidence by which a Revelation from God may be confirmed is the *collateral*.   But here we will only adduce a few instances, merely to illustrate this kind of testimony.

The collateral evidence of a Revelation from God may be its agreement with former Revelations, should any have been given; its adaptation to the condition of the world at the time of its communication, and to effect the great moral ends which it proposes; the agreement of its record of facts with the credible traditions and histories of the same times; the monuments, either natural or instituted, which may remain to attest the truth of its history; the concessions of adversaries in its favor; and, finally, the continuance of its adaptation to the case of the human family to the present day.

We have now briefly considered the several classes of evidence by which a Divine Revelation may be authenticated; but before we proceed to a practical application of these evidences it will be necessary to establish the *Genuineness*, the *Authenticity*, and the *Integrity* of the Holy Scriptures.

CHAPTER II.

GENUINENESS OF THE HOLY SCRIPTURES.

THE genuineness of a book consists in its having been written by the author whose name it bears, and should be distinguished from its authenticity, with which it is often confounded. The former refers exclusively to the authorship of the book in question; the latter, to the correctness of the facts which are detailed in it. A book may therefore be genuine which is not authentic, and one may be authentic which is not genuine.

The history of Sir Charles Grandison is genuine, being indeed written by Richardson, the author whose name it bears; but it is not authentic, being a mere production of fictions. Again, the Account of Lord Anson's Voyages is an authentic book, being a relation of facts; but it is not genuine, for its real author was not Walters, whose name is appended to it, but Benjamin Robins. Hayley's Memoirs of the Life of Cowper are both genuine and authentic. They were written by Mr. Hayley, and the information which they contain is perfectly reliable.

In establishing the genuineness of the sacred Scriptures it will be proper,

I. *To ascertain* THE EXISTENCE, AGE, *and* ACTIONS *of the leading persons mentioned in them*, as the instruments by whom the Revelations were made.

It is not necessary that our attention should be directed to more than two of these persons, MOSES and CHRIST; because the evidence which establishes their existence and actions, and the period of both, will also establish all that is stated in the same records as to the subordinate and succeeding agents.

The existence and the respective antiquity of Moses and of Christ may be satisfactorily proved,

1. *From the Existence of the Jewish Polity and of the Christian Religion.*—The writings which are ascribed to Moses claim that he was the

leader and legislator of the Jews, near sixteen hundred years before the Christian era, according to the common chronology. That the Jews existed very anciently as a nation cannot be doubted. And that it has been an uninterrupted tradition among them, that Moses led them out of Egypt, and first gave them their system of laws and religion, is equally certain. The history of that event they have in writing, and also the laws attributed to him. This history is uncontradicted by the authentic records of other nations; and as their institutions bear the marks of a systematic arrangement, established at once, they must have been enforced by some political authority, and are to be attributed to one superior and commanding mind. The Jews refer them to Moses, and if this be denied, it cannot be shown that any other person is entitled to that honor. The history therefore can only be denied on some principle of skepticism which would equally shake the foundation of all history.

The same observations may be made in regard to the existence of the Founder of the Christian religion. In the records of the New Testament he is called JESUS CHRIST, and his birth is fixed upward of eighteen centuries ago. This also is at least uncontradicted testimony.

The Christian religion exists, and must have had an author. Like the institutions of Moses, it bears the evidence of being the work of one mind; and, as a theological system, it presents no indications of a gradual and successive elaboration. There was a time when there was no such religion as Christianity, and it follows that there once flourished a teacher to whom it owed its origin. All tradition and history unite in their testimony, that this teacher was JESUS CHRIST.

2. *By the Testimony of Ancient Writers.*—MANETHO, CHEREMON, APOLLONIUS, and LYSIMACHUS are quoted by Josephus as agreeing that Moses was the leader of the Jews when they departed from Egypt, and the founder of their laws. STRABO, JUSTIN, PLINY, TACITUS, JUVENAL, LONGINUS, and DIODORUS SICULUS all speak of Moses; and Justin Martyr expressly says, that most of the historians, poets, lawgivers, and philosophers of the Greeks mention him as the leader and prince of the Jewish nation. From all these testimonies it is clear that it was commonly received among ancient nations generally, as well as among the Jews themselves, that Moses was the founder and lawgiver of the Jewish state.

AS TO CHRIST, it is only necessary to give the testimony of two historians, whose antiquity no one ever thought of disputing. SUETONIUS mentions him by name, and says that Claudius expelled from Rome those who adhered to his cause.* TACITUS records the progress which the Christian religion had made; the violent death its founder had

* Judæos impulsore Christo assidue tumultuantes Româ expulit.—SUET., Edit. Var., p. 544.

suffered; that he flourished under the reign of Tiberius; that Pilate was then procurator of Judea, and that the original author of this profession was *Christ*.* Thus both the real existence of Christ, and the period in which he lived, are exactly ascertained.

Another important fact in proof of the genuineness of the sacred Scriptures is,

II. THEIR ANTIQUITY.

In establishing the antiquity of the books which contain the Jewish and the Christian Scriptures we will direct our attention,

1. *To those of the Old Testament.* The question before us is, whether the books of the Old Testament were written at the respective times assigned to them. It is not necessary to go into a critical examination of the date of each book separately, for if we can ascertain the period in which the five books of Moses were written it will not be a difficult matter to settle the date of all the rest. To prove, therefore, that the *Pentateuch* was written synchronically with the exodus of the Jews from Egypt, we will present a chain of historical facts which, if duly considered, must prove satisfactory to every candid mind. We will begin with the apostolic age, and travel backward step by step, as the evidence of facts may lead the way.

(1.) Josephus, who was himself a Jewish priest, and also cotemporary with the apostles, gives us a catalogue of the sacred books of the Jews, in which he expressly mentions the five books of Moses, thirteen of the prophets, four of Hymns and Moral Precepts; and if, as many critics maintain, Ruth was added to Judges, and the Lamentations of Jeremiah to his Prophecies, the number agrees with the books of the Old Testament as it is received at the present day.

This threefold division of the Jewish Scriptures into the *Law*, the *Prophets*, and the *Psalms*, mentioned by Josephus, was expressly recognized before his time by Jesus Christ,† as well as by the subsequent writers of the New Testament. We have therefore sufficient evidence that the Old Testament existed at that time; and if we only allow that Jesus Christ was a person of a virtuous character, we are bound to conclude that these Scriptures were not corrupted in his day. For, when he accused the Pharisees of making the law of no effect by their traditions, and when he exhorted his hearers to "search the Scriptures," he could not have failed to mention the corruptions or forgeries of Scripture had any in that age existed.

(2.) The books of the Old Testament were translated into Greek, for the use of the Alexandrian Jews, about two hundred and eighty-seven years before the Christian era. This Greek translation, of which almost every one has some knowledge, is proof positive that the Hebrew Pen-

---

* Auctor nominis ejus Christus, qui Tiberio imperitante, per procuratorem Pontium Pilatum supplicio affectus erat.—Annal., 1, 5.

† See Matt. xi, 13; Luke xvi, 16; Acts xxvi, 22; Rom. x, 5.

tateuch existed at that period. But if it existed two hundred and eighty-seven years before Christ it must have existed in the days of Ezra, five hundred and thirty-six years before Christ; for this simple reason, that the circumstances of the Jews rendered its composition impossible at any point between these two periods. This will appear evident if we weigh the next fact to be adduced.

(3.) The Hebrew language, in which the Old Testament was written, ceased to be the living language of the Jews soon after the Babylonish captivity; and the learned agree that there was no grammar for the language till many ages after that event. It follows, therefore, that every book which is written in *pure* Hebrew must have been composed either before or about the time of the captivity. It is also an important fact, that after that period the writings of the Jews were generally either in Chaldee or Greek. Hence it is utterly impossible that the Hebrew Pentateuch could have been written at any period subsequent to the return of the Jews from Babylon.

(4.) As this cannot be rationally denied, some have thence contended that it was written by Ezra. But to this opinion, however plausible some may think it to be, there are insuperable objections. In the book of Ezra, "*the Law of Moses, the man of God,*" is particularly referred to as a well known *written* document then actually existing.* And in the book of Nehemiah we have an account of the manner in which that same *written* document was openly read to the people, under the precise name of "*the book of the Law of Moses, which the Lord had commanded to Israel.*"† Nor is this all. It was not that Ezra produced a new volume, and then called upon the people to receive it as the authentic Law of Moses; but the *people themselves* called upon Ezra to bring forth and read that book, as a work with which they had long been acquainted.

The Law of Moses, therefore, must have been known to exist as a *written document* previous to the return from Babylon; and as Ezra could not have produced under that name a mere compilation of oral traditions, so neither could he have suppressed the ancient volume of the Law, nor have set forth, in its stead, that volume which the Jews have ever since received as the genuine Pentateuch. Add to this, that when the foundation of the second temple was laid, many persons were there who well remembered the first temple. These, consequently, must have known whether there had or had not been a written Law of Moses anterior to the captivity; nor could they have been deceived by the introduction of a new composition, either by Ezra or by any one else.

(5.) We have now extant two Hebrew copies of the Law of Moses. One is received by the Jews, and the other by the Samaritans; each maintaining that their own is the genuine record. The coincidence of

* Ezra iii, 2; vi, 18.   † Neh. viii, 1.

these two copies is such as to demonstrate that they were taken from the same original. But if so, that original must have existed long before the Captivity, as circumstances will show. For, since the Pentateuch was received as the book of the Law both by the ten tribes, and also by the two tribes it follows as a necessary consequence, that they each received it *before* they became divided into two kingdoms, which event took place about nine hundred and seventy years before Christ. Had it been forged in a later age among the Jews, the perpetual enmity that existed between them and the Israelites would utterly have prevented it from being adopted by the Samaritans; and had it been a spurious production of the Samaritans, it would never have been received by the Jews.

(6.) The universal admission of the Pentateuch, as the inspired Law of Moses, throughout the whole commonwealth of Israel, prior to its disruption into two hostile kingdoms—the magnificent temple of Solomon, and the whole ritual attached to it, are plain proofs of the *previous existence* of this sacred document. And as the Law strictly prohibits more than one practice of Solomon, it is incredible either that he should have been its author, or that it should have been written under his sanction and authority.

(7.) And with as little probability can we ascribe it to David. His life was occupied with almost incessant troubles and warfare ; and it is difficult to conceive how a book written by that prince could, in the space of a few years, be universally received as the inspired composition of Moses.

(8.) The Pentateuch might be more plausibly ascribed to Samuel than to either of those two princes ; but this supposition will not stand the test of rational inquiry. For, besides the impossibility that he should persuade all Israel to adopt, as the inspired Law of Moses, a mere modern composition of his own, there is this additional fact, that in a speech which he made to the assembled Israelites he expressly referred to the well known commandment of Jehovah, and to the Divine legation of Moses and Aaron.

(9.) We have now ascended to within four centuries of the exodus from Egypt, and the alleged promulgation of the Law from Mount Sinai ; and, from Ezra to Samuel, we have found no person to whom the composition of the Pentateuch can reasonably be ascribed. The only remaining question is, whether it could have been written during the three hundred and fifty-six years that intervened between the entrance of the Israelites into Palestine, and the appointment of Saul to be their king.

Now, the whole history of that period utterly forbids such a supposition. The Israelites are uniformly described as acknowledging the authority of a written Law of Moses. It is declared that Joshua wrote the book which bears his name, as a supplement to a *prior* book, which is denominated the "*book of the* Law." It is likewise asserted that this book of the Law is "*the book of the Law of Moses ;*" a copy of which, Joshua declares, he had written in the presence of the children of Israel.

Thus, finally, we come to the *original*, whence the copy of Joshua was taken; for we are told that Moses, with his own hand, wrote the words of THIS LAW in a BOOK, and commanded the Levites to put THIS BOOK into the ark of the covenant, that it might be preserved throughout their generations.

These arguments fully establish the genuineness of the books of Moses. As to those of the Prophets, it can be proved, from Jewish tradition, the list of Josephus, the Greek translation, and from their being quoted by ancient writers, that they existed many ages before some of those events occurred, to which we shall refer in the proper place, as unequivocal instances of prophetic accomplishment.

In pursuing the argument respecting the antiquity and genuineness of the sacred books, we will consider,

2. *Those of the New Testament.*—Of the ancient date of these books we have sufficient proof,

(1.) *In the Quotations which are made from them by early Christian Authors.*—Quotations from the books of the New Testament are found in the writings of *Clement*, of the first century; and also in those of *Ignatius*, of *Polycarp*, of *Justin Martyr*, of *Irenæus*, Bishop of Lyons, of *Athenagoras*, of *Theophilus* of Antioch, and many others. Thus we have the testimony of a series of Christian writers, beginning with those who were cotemporary with the apostles, or who immediately followed them, and proceeding in close and regular succession from their time to the present.

This medium of proof is most unquestionable, and is not to be diminished by the lapse of ages. Bishop Burnet, in the History of his Own Times, inserts various extracts from Lord Clarendon's History. *One* such insertion is a proof that Lord Clarendon's History was extant when Bishop Burnet wrote, that it had been read and received by him as a work of Lord Clarendon's, and that he regarded it as an authentic account of the transactions which it relates, and it will be a proof of these facts a thousand years hence.

The application of this argument to the Gospel History is obvious. If the books in which it is contained have been quoted as genuine, by a series of writers, up to the age in which their authors lived, it is then clear that they must have existed prior to the earliest of those writings in which they are quoted, and that they were then regarded as genuine.

(2.) *In the early Catalogues of the Christian Scriptures.*—Catalogues of the books of the New Testament were drawn up by different persons at an early period, from which we learn that the books which are now acknowledged existed then, and were received as genuine.

The first catalogue is that of Origen in the year 210, who omits the

Epistle of James, and the Epistle of Jude; but he acknowledges both of them in other parts of his writings.

The second is the catalogue of Eusebius in the year 315, which is the same with ours. He says, however, that a few of the books were disputed by some. Of the same date is the catalogue of Athanasius, which exactly accords with ours.

The catalogue of Cyril of Jerusalem, drawn up in 340, that of the Council of Laodicea in 364, and that of Gregory Nazianzen in 375, omit the Revelation, but contain all the other books.

Philostrius, Bishop of Brescia, in 380, leaves out Revelation and the Epistle to the Hebrews; but Jerome in 382, Ruffinus in 390, and Augustine in 394, have all the books of the New Testament, as they are now acknowledged.

Nothing farther is necessary to prove that these books were written at the time assigned for their publication, and by the persons to whom they are ascribed. There seems, indeed, to have been no doubt relative to this matter in the early ages of Christianity. It is true, that by some the genuineness of a few of these books was called in question; but this circumstance supplies additional evidence of the genuineness of the New Testament Scriptures, by showing that the clearest proof was required before any of the books could be acknowledged. When we find that men are far from being credulous, and that while they give assent in some instances they withhold it in others, we rest with the greater confidence in their decisions.

(3.) *In the Testimony of the Enemies of Christianity.*—No public contradiction of the Gospel history was ever put forth by the Jewish rulers, and this silence on their part is important evidence in its favor. But the *direct* testimonies of its adversaries to the facts of the Gospel are both numerous and clear.

Celsus in the second century, Porphyry and Hierocles in the third, and Julian in the fourth, all wrote against Christianity. They have given evidence that they were well acquainted with the New Testament Scriptures, and that they believed them to have been written by Christ's own disciples. Indeed, they never pretended to call this in question, or to produce any contrary account, as they surely would have done had it been in their power. They quoted passages from the writings of the apostles, touching nearly all the leading facts of the Gospel history; nor did they deny even the *miracles* of our Saviour. True, they mentioned these things only with a design to ridicule and expose them; but they afford incontestible proof, that in their times these Scriptures were in existence.

Among the evidences in support of the genuineness and truth of the Christian Scriptures, perhaps none are of more value than the testimonies of those learned philosophers who wrote against Christianity in its first ages. They express no doubt concerning the authenticity of these

Scriptures, nor do they ever insinuate that Christians were mistaken in regard to the authors to whom they ascribe them. They confirm the prevailing sentiments of the Church respecting those books of the New Testament which are called *canonical;* for their writings show that those very books, and not any others, are the books which Christians then acknowledged as the rule of their faith, as they now are of ours.

These writers proposed to overthrow the arguments for the Christian religion, and to arrest its progress. But in these designs they had very little success in their own times; and their works, composed and published in the early days of Christianity, are now a testimony in its favor, and will be of use in its defense to the latest ages.

We have thus established the genuineness of the books of the New Testament by the testimony of those who had the best opportunities of ascertaining whether they were indeed written by the persons whose names they bear; because they lived in the age when these books were published, or soon after, and were led by their circumstances to make a critical investigation of the whole matter. We receive them, therefore, as the genuine works of their respective authors, for the very same reason that we receive as genuine the writings of Xenophon, of Polybius, of Cesar, or of Tacitus; namely, because we have the uninterrupted testimony of ages to their genuineness, and have no reason to suspect imposition.

CHAPTER III.

THE INTEGRITY OF THE SACRED SCRIPTURES.

Having established the genuineness of the Sacred Scriptures, we will proceed, in the next place, to consider their *Integrity.*

By the *Integrity* of the Scriptures is meant, *their entire and uncorrupted preservation.* This implies, *first,* that we have now all the books which formerly belonged to the *Canon;* and, *secondly,* that these books have come down to us without any material alteration. We assert,

I. The Integrity of the Canon.*

We are now in possession of all the books which were ever received as canonical, either by the Jews or by the primitive Christians. This is sufficiently evident,

1. *With respect to the Books of the Old Testament.*—The list of Josephus, the Septuagint translation, and the Samaritan Pentateuch clearly prove that the books which we now receive as sacred are the very same that were received by the Jews and the Samaritans, long before the Christian era. But it is equally evident,

---

* See the note at the end of this chapter.

2. *In regard to the Books of the New Testament.*—We have already shown, that in the writings of the earliest Christian authors there are numerous quotations from nearly all the books now included in the New Testament, and references to them by name; and also, that catalogues of the books which the ancient Christians received as Divine were drawn up by Origen, Eusebius, and others. These catalogues, which were published at early periods, and in countries distant from one another, differ in no material point, and all contain the four Gospels. It is therefore certain that we have at present the very books which were received by the ancient Christian Church, and that not one of them has been lost.

To this it has been objected, that the Scriptures themselves make mention of books which are not now extant: as "the book of the wars of the Lord," Num. xxi, 14; "the book of Jasher," Josh x, 13; "the book of Nathan " and "the book of Gad," 1 Chron. xxix, 29; and the Epistle from Laodicea," Col. iv, 16.

Our answer is this: It cannot be made appear that these are different books from what are extant under different titles. But if even this could be done, it is not at all requisite to the integrity of the canon of Scripture that we should have all the writings of holy and inspired men, or all the histories quoted in the Bible. This is proved from the consideration that the ancient Jews and Christians had not these books in the canon, and yet they never entertained the least doubt of their having the entire canon of Sacred Scripture.

But we maintain the integrity of the Scriptures,

II. With respect to the particular Books.

These have come down to us without corruption, or any material alteration. This we hold to be true,

1. *With regard to the Old Testament.*—The integrity of these Scriptures will appear both from the impossibility of corrupting them, and from the agreement of numerous ancient manuscripts. We will call attention,

(1.) *To the Impossibility of corrupting the Jewish Scriptures.*—This is put beyond all dispute by the consideration of a few historical facts.

Before the time of Christ, the profound regard which the Jews had for their sacred books rendered any material change in their contents impossible.

The Law being the deed by which the land of Canaan was divided among the Israelites, it is improbable that they would suffer it to be altered or falsified. The distinction of the twelve tribes, and their separate interests, made it more difficult to alter their Law than that of any other nation.

The Samaritans had the Pentateuch as well as the Jews; and the jealousy and hatred which existed between the two nations made it impracticable for either to corrupt or alter the text, in anything of consequence, without certain discovery.

The general agreement between the Hebrew and the Samaritan Pentateuch plainly demonstrates that they were originally the same. Nor can there be any better evidence that the Jewish Scriptures have not been corrupted or interpolated than this very book of the Samaritans, which, after more than two thousand years of discord between the two nations, varies as little from the Jewish Pentateuch as any classic author has varied from itself in less time by the unavoidable mistakes of transcribers.

After the Jews returned from Babylon, the Law and the Prophets were publicly read in their synagogues every Sabbath day, which was an excellent method of securing their purity; and a law was also enacted by them which denounced him to be guilty of inexpiable sin who should presume to make the slightest possible alteration in their sacred books.

Since the birth of Christ the Old Testament has been held in high esteem both by Jews and Christians. They have been a mutual guard upon each other, which must have rendered any material corruption impossible if it had been attempted. For if such attempt had been made by the *Jews*, it would have been detected by the Christians; and if any such attempt had been made by the *Christians*, it would certainly have been detected by the Jews. Nor could such a purpose have been effected by any other body of men without its being exposed by both Jews and Christians.

But as the Jews were dispersed among all the nations of the then known world, and as it was therefore impossible that they should collect all the copies of the Law, with the intention of corrupting them, the accomplishment of such a design was on their part utterly impracticable. But we will notice,

(2.) *The Agreement of Ancient Manuscripts.*—The agreement of all the manuscripts of the Old Testament which are known to be extant, amounting to more than eleven hundred, is a clear proof of its uncorrupted preservation. These manuscripts are not all entire, some containing one part and some another. But it is absolutely impossible that *every* manuscript, whether in the original Hebrew or in any ancient version, should or could be *designedly* altered or falsified in the *same* passages without detection either from Jews or Christians.

These manuscripts are, confessedly, liable to errors and mistakes from the negligence and inaccuracy of copyists; but they are not *all* uniformly incorrect in the same words or passages, for what is incorrect in one is correct in another. And although the various readings which learned men have discovered in the Hebrew Scriptures amount to many thousands, yet these differences are of very little real moment.

Equally satisfactory is the evidence for the integrity of the Scriptures,

2. *With regard to the Books of the New Testament.*—This is manifest,

(1.) *From their Contents.*—For, as early as the first two centuries of the Christian era, we find the very same *facts* and the very same *doctrines* universally received by Christians which we of the present day believe on the authority of the New Testament.

(2.) *From the impossibility of their being universally corrupted.*—They could not be corrupted during the life of their authors; and before their death copies were dispersed among the different communities of Christians, who were scattered throughout the world.

Within twenty years after the ascension, Churches were planted in all the principal cities of the Roman Empire; and in all these Churches the books of the New Testament, especially the four Gospels, were read as a part of their public worship, just as the writings of Moses were read in the Jewish synagogues.

Copies of these books were multiplied and disseminated as rapidly as the boundaries of the Church increased, and translations were made into as many languages as were spoken by its members. This rendered it impossible to corrupt these books in any one important word or phrase; for it is morally impossible that *all* Christians should agree in such a design.

But as these books could not be corrupted during the life of their respective authors, so neither could any material alteration take place after their death while the original manuscripts were preserved in the Churches.

The Christians who were instructed by the apostles, or by their immediate successors, traveled into all parts of the world, carrying with them copies of the apostolic writings, from which other copies were multiplied and preserved. We have therefore an unbroken series of testimonies for the uncorrupted preservation of the New Testament, which can be traced back from the fourth century of the Christian era to the very time of the apostles.

It is known that a division commenced in the fourth century, between the Eastern and the Western Church, which exists to the present day. Now, if it had been possible to alter all the copies in one of these divisions, those of the other would have detected the alteration. But the fact is, that both the eastern and the western copies agree; and this proves that on neither side were they altered or falsified.

The Church was early rent with fierce contentions on doctrinal points; but in all such disputes the New Testament was appealed to by every sect, as being conclusive in all matters of controversy. It was therefore morally impossible that any man or body of men could corrupt this book in any fundamental article.

3. *From the Agreement of Manuscripts.*—Of these upward of three

hundred and fifty were collected by Griesbach for his celebrated critical edition. True, they were not all entire. Most of them contained only the four Gospels; others the Gospels, Acts of the Apostles, and the Epistles; and a few contained the Apocalypse. They were all written in different and distant parts of the world, and some of them are upward of twelve hundred years old; but in all essential points they perfectly agree, as any one may ascertain by examining the critical editions published by Mill, Bengel, Wetstein, and Griesbach.

The thirty thousand various readings by Dr. Mill, and the one hundred and fifty thousand of Griesbach's edition, in no degree whatever affect the general credit or integrity of the sacred text. They consist almost wholly of palpable errors in transcription, grammatical and verbal differences, such as the insertion or omission of an article, the substitution of a word for its equivalent, or the transposition of a word or two in a sentence.

Even the few various readings that do change the sense, affect it almost exclusively in passages relating to unimportant, historical, and geographical circumstances, or other collateral matters; and the still smaller number that make any alteration in things of consequence do not place us in any absolute uncertainty. For, either the true reading may be found by a reference to different manuscripts and versions, or, should these fail, we may explain the point in question by other *undisputed* passages of Scripture.

4. *From the Agreement of the Ancient Versions of the New Testament with Quotations made from it by Christian Writers of the first three centuries, and by the succeeding Fathers of the Church.*—These quotations are so numerous that almost the whole body of the Gospels and Epistles might be compiled from the various passages which appear in the writings of those authors. And though the citations were, in many cases, made from memory, yet they correspond with the original records from which they were extracted. Thus we have an irrefragable argument for the purity and integrity of the New Testament Scriptures.

Note.—The word *canon*, in its general sense, means anything which is determined according to a fixed measure, rule, or law. It was employed by the early ecclesiastical writers to designate a catalogue of things that belonged to the Church. Hence they applied the term to a collection of hymns which were to be sung on festival occasions; to a list, in which were introduced the names of Church members; and particularly to a publicly approved catalogue of all the books that might be read in Christian assemblies for instruction and edification. But by modern theologians the word *canon* is usually employed to designate our authorized collection of Inspired Writings.

The establishment of the Jewish canon is by some ascribed to Ezra, and by others to Nehemiah; but it can hardly be doubted that in a work so important the priests, the lawyers, and all the leading men of the nation must have been unitedly engaged, as the grammarians of Alexandria were in determining the canon of the Greek classics. It is probable, however, that in this undertaking both Ezra and Nehemiah had a principal share.

The canon of the Old Testament Scriptures appears to have originated somewhat in the following manner. When the Jews returned from Babylon and re-established Divine worship, they collected the inspired books which they still possessed, and commenced with them a sacred library, as they had done before with the books of the Law. To this collection they afterward added the writings of Zechariah, Malachi, and other distinguished prophets and priests, who wrote during the Captivity, or shortly after; and also the books of Kings, Chronicles, and other historical writings, which had been compiled from the ancient records of the nation. The collection thus made was ever after considered complete, and the books composing it were called THE HOLY SCRIPTURES; or, THE LAW AND THE PROPHETS.

It is evident from the historical information which we possess, that the canon of the New Testament was not finished at once, but was commenced a considerable time before it was made complete. The Gospels were collected as early as the second century, and in the third century were regarded as of undoubted authority throughout the Christian Church. They were prefixed to the other books of the New Testament, because the history of Jesus was considered, at that early period, as the basis of Christian truth; just as the historical writings of Moses were prefixed to the Old Testament as the basis of the Mosaic economy.

As to the *Epistles*, a collection of them was commenced at a very early period, and was gradually enlarged and completed. It appears, indeed, to be of somewhat later origin than the collection of the Gospels; but both of them must have existed before the beginning of the third century. As early as the third century most of the copies of the apostolic Epistles contained all the books which now belong to this collection, as appears from the catalogues of Origen and Eusebius.

CHAPTER IV.

AUTHENTICITY OF THE SACRED SCRIPTURES.

WE have produced, in a former chapter, a variety of proofs in support of the genuineness of the sacred books. Should any one still deny that they were written by the persons to whom they are ascribed, we have a right to ask, By whom then were they composed? We do not, however, expect an answer to this question; for, as they never were attributed to any other authors by those who had the best opportunities of knowing their history, it would be ridiculous, at this late day, to attempt to trace them to a different origin. It remains, then, for us to inquire whether they are a faithful record of the facts and transactions of which they give us information.

The authenticity of the Scriptures may be proved,

I. FROM THEIR INTERNAL MARKS OF CREDIBILITY.

Mr. Leslie has laid down four rules for determining the truth of historical facts in general. These rules are, 1. That the fact be such as that men can judge of it by their outward senses; 2. That it be public; 3. That it be kept in memory both by public monuments and by the performance of some outward actions; 4. That such monuments exist, and such actions be observed, from the time that the matter of fact came to pass.

With these rules in view, let us direct our attention,

1. *To the Books of Moses.*—In these we have a history of the Jewish people from the call of Abraham to the death of Moses, embracing a period of nearly five hundred years, and detailing a succession of the most wonderful events that ever took place in the history of nations. But, in addition to their historical character, they were the standing and municipal law of the Jewish nation, binding both the king and the people. They required the king to prepare himself a copy, and to "read therein all the days of his life;" and the people were commanded to lay up the words of this law in their hearts, and faithfully and diligently to teach them to their children.*

These books teach us moreover that God appointed and consecrated the tribe of Levi as his priests, by whom alone the sacrifices of the people were to be offered and their solemn institutions celebrated; that their high priest wore a glorious miter, and magnificent robes of God's own contriving;† and that at his word the king and the people were to go out and to come in. They teach us that the Levites were the chief judges in all matters, and that it was death to resist their sentence.

* Deut. xi, 18, 19; xviii, 18.　　　　　　　† Num. xxvii, 21.

But the books of Moses, while they contain the history of the Jews, together with the laws by which their civil and religious affairs were regulated, give us an account of the institution of various commemorative rites, and of the commemoration of particular actions and events. For examples we may take the *Passover*, in memory of God's passing over the children of the Israelites when he slew all the first-born of Egypt;* the *Rod of Aaron*, which was kept in the ark, in memory of the destruction of Korah, Dathan, and Abiram, and of the confirmation of the priesthood in the tribe of Levi;† the *Pot of Manna*, in memory of their having been fed on manna in the wilderness;‡ the *Brazen Serpent*, which was kept to the days of Hezekiah, as a memorial of their wonderful deliverance from the biting of the fiery flying serpents;§ and the *Feast of Pentecost*, in memory of the dreadful appearance of God upon Mount Horeb.‖

There were other solemn institutions among the Jews in memory of their deliverance out of Egypt; as the Sabbath, their daily sacrifices and yearly expiation, and their new moons, and other feasts and fasts. Of these things, therefore, there were yearly, monthly, weekly, and daily recognitions.

Now, if the books of Moses had not been a faithful record of all these facts, they never could have been received by the Jews as authentic, unless they could have been made to believe that they had received them from their fathers, had been instructed in them when they were children, and had taught them to their children; that they had all been circumcised, and had circumcised their children, in pursuance of what was commanded in these books; that they had observed the yearly passover, the weekly Sabbath, the new moons, and all the several feasts, fasts, and religious ceremonies commanded in these books; and that they had a magnificent tabernacle, with a visible priesthood to administer in it, which was confined to the tribe of Levi, over whom was placed a glorious high priest, clothed with great and mighty prerogatives. Was it possible to have persuaded a whole nation of men that they had known and practiced all these things if they had not done it? or to have received a book for truth, which said that they had practiced them when they knew they had not?

But now let us suppose that these things were practiced before the books of Moses were written, and that the only imposition was in making the people believe that they had kept these observances in memory of certain events recorded in those books; will not the same impossibility appear upon this supposition, as in the former case? It must then be supposed that the Jews kept all these observances in memory of nothing, or without knowing anything of their origin or why they kept them; whereas these very observances express the reason of their

* Num. viii, 17, 18.   † Num. xvi; xvii.   ‡ Deut. xvi, 32, 33.
§ Num. xxi, 8, 9; 2 Kings xviii, 4.   ‖ Exod. xix; xx.

being kept; as the Passover, in memory of God's passing over the children of the Jews when he slew all the first-born of Egypt.

But if the Israelites knew no reason at all why they kept these observances, was it possible to make them believe that they had kept them in memory of events of which they had never heard before the time when it is supposed these books were written? Take, for illustration, the Stonehenge in Salisbury Plain. Every body knows it; and yet no one knows by whom, or for what reason, these great stones were placed there. Now, suppose we should write a book, and tell the world that these stones were set up by Hercules, in memory of his catching the stag with golden horns. And suppose we should say in this book that it was written by Hercules himself, or by eye-witnesses, at the time of that event; that it had been received as truth, and quoted by the most reputable authors in all ages since; that it was enjoined by legislative authority to be taught to our children, and that when we were children it was taught to us. We would ask the deist whether he thinks it possible that such a cheat could be palmed upon an enlightened community? or whether, if we should insist upon it, we should not, instead of being believed, be regarded as insane?

Let us now compare this with the twelve stones set up at Gilgal, the history of which is given in the fourth chapter of Joshua. There we learn that these stones were designed for a memorial unto the children of Israel of their miraculous passage over Jordan. The miracle in memory of which they were set up was such as could not possibly be imposed upon that nation when it is said to have been done. It was as wonderful as their passage through the Red Sea. Notice was given to the Israelites the day before this great miracle was performed.* It was done at noonday, before the whole nation. When the waters of Jordan were divided it was not at low ebb, but when that river overflowed all its banks.† And it was done not gradually, as by the action of winds, but suddenly, as soon as "the feet of the priests that bare the ark were dipped in the brim of the water."‡

Now, to form our argument, let us suppose that there never was any such thing as that passage over Jordan—that these stones at Gilgal were set up on some other occasion—and then, that some designing man invented this book of Joshua, saying that it was written by Joshua at that time, and giving these stones for a testimony of its truth. Would not everybody say to him, I know these stones at Gilgal, but I never before heard of this reason for them, nor of this book of Joshua? Where has it been all this time? Besides, this book tells us that our children were to be instructed, from age to age, in regard to this passage over Jordan and this memorial at Gilgal. But we never heard of that event when we were children, nor did we ever teach our children any such thing; and it could hardly have been forgotten while so

---

* Josh. iii, 5.   † Josh. iii, 15   ‡ Josh. iv, from verse 18.

remarkable a memorial continued. If, therefore, we could not be imposed upon as to the Stonehenge in Salisbury Plain, much less could we be in regard to the twelve stones at Gilgal.

If the books of the Law were written by Moses, as has been shown, it is easy to prove that he could not have deceived the people by a mere pretense of miraculous attestations. The very instances of miracles which he gives renders this impossible. Suppose a man should pretend that yesterday he divided the Thames, in sight of all the people of London, and carried the whole city, men, women, and children, over to Southwark on dry land, the waters standing like walls on both sides; is it not morally impossible that he could persuade the people of London to believe this to be true, when every man, woman, and child would know it to be a notorious falsehood? Equally impossible was it for Moses to persuade six hundred thousand men that he had brought them out of Egypt through the Red Sea, or that he had fed them forty years with manna if it had not been true, because the senses of every man that was then alive must have contradicted it. And, for the same reason, it was impossible for him to make them receive his five books as truth, which declared that these things had been done before their eyes, if they had not been so done.

But Mr. Leslie's four rules for determining the truth of historical facts will apply with equal force,

2. To THE GOSPEL HISTORY.—The works and miracles of our Lord were done publicly in the face of the world. He said to his accusers, "I spake openly to the world, and in secret have I said nothing." John xviii, 20. But his works were as public as was his teaching. Some of his most notable miracles were performed in the presence of many witnesses. Take, for instance, his first miracle in Cana of Galilee,* the healing of the paralytic,† the raising of the widow's son from the dead at the city of Nain,‡ and the feeding of five thousand men, besides women and children.§ Equally public were the miracles wrought by the apostles; and as it is impossible that men could have been deceived in regard to what was done thus publicly before their eyes, these facts accord with the first two rules before mentioned.

Then, for the other two, we have Baptism and the Lord's Supper. These were instituted by the Author of the Christian religion, to be observed in his Church to the end of time: the former, as a *sign* and *seal* of God's gracious covenant with his people; and the latter, as a *memorial* of the sacrificial death of Christ. Accordingly, they have been observed, without interruption, down to this time.

Moreover, Christ ordained men to preach his Gospel, administer the sacraments, and govern his Church; and these ministers of religion have continued, in regular succession, until the present day. The exist-

---

* John ii, 1–10.   † Matt. ix, 2–8.   ‡ Luke vii, 11–15.   § Matt. xiv, 15–21.

ence of the Christian clergy is therefore as notorious a matter of fact as was that of the tribe of Levi among the Jews; and that such an order of men was appointed by Christ the Gospel positively declares.*

But if the Gospel is a fiction, and was invented in some age after Christ, then, at the time when it was invented, there could have been no public sacraments of Christ's institution, and no order of clergy to administer them. For it is impossible that these things could have existed before they were invented; and it is equally impossible that they could have been received, when invented, as matters of fact that had existed long before.

And now, to apply what has been said, we may safely affirm that the Sacred Scriptures never could have been received had not their historical records been true. The institution of the Priesthood of Levi, of the Sabbath, of the Passover, and of circumcision; as also that of the Gospel ministry, of Baptism, and of the Lord's Supper, are there related as having been handed down, without interruption, from the time in which they were severally appointed. But it was impossible to persuade men that they had been circumcised or baptized, that they had circumcised or baptized their children, that they had celebrated passovers, Sabbaths, and sacraments, under the administration of a certain order of priests, if they had done none of these things. And without believing such facts, it would have been impossible for men to receive either the Law or the Gospel.

These public institutions, then, are an appeal to the senses of mankind for the truth of the matters of fact recorded in the Jewish and the Christian Scriptures. For, as it is impossible that the senses of men could have been imposed upon at the time when such public matters of fact took place; so it is equally impossible that any one should have invented such stories in after ages without being detected at the time.

The authenticity of the Sacred Scriptures may be farther argued,

II. From the Credibility of the Sacred Writers.

There are four facts which cannot fail to give credibility to any witness: 1. That he is virtuous and sober; 2. That he has had an opportunity to know the truth of what he relates; 3. That he has no interest in making good his story; and, 4. That his account is circumstantial. These guarantees of faithful testimony meet, in the highest degree, in the authors of the New Testament, and to them our remarks shall be principally confined.

1. *They were Men of strict and exemplary Virtue.*—Indeed, this has not been denied even by the most malicious enemies of Christianity. Of their sincerity they gave the utmost proof in the openness of their testimony, never affecting reserve or shunning inquiry. They were so fully convinced of the truth of the Gospel, that they were willing for

---

* Matt. x, 1–7; xviii, 18–20; xxviii, 19, 20.

its sake to endure all manner of shame, reproach, and persecution. They constantly exhibited, in the bright and faithful mirror of their own behavior, the amiableness and excellence of the religion which they taught; and, in every scene and circumstance of life, were distinguished for their devotion to God, their love for mankind, their sacred regard for truth, their self-government and moderation, and for every social and moral virtue that can adorn and exalt the character of man. They were never dejected or intimidated by their severest sufferings; but when persecuted in one city they fled to another, and there proclaimed their message with intrepid boldness and heaven-inspired zeal. They were patient in tribulation, joyful under reproach and persecution, and, when in dungeons, they cheered the silent hours of the night with hymns of praise to God. They met death itself in some of its most dreadful forms, but with a serenity and exultation that *Stoic philosophy* never knew.

2. *They were in Circumstances certainly to know the Truth of what they relate.*—They were the select companions and familiar friends of the hero of their story. They had free access to him at all times, heard both his public and private discourses, and were spectators of his amazing works. Some of them were his inseparable attendants, from the commencement to the close of his public ministry. No writers ever enjoyed a more favorable opportunity for publishing just accounts of persons and things than did the Evangelists for giving a true history of Jesus Christ.

Most of the *Greek* and *Roman* historians lived long after the persons whom they immortalize and the events which they record; but the sacred writers commemorate actions which they saw and discourses which they heard. They describe characters with which they were familiar and scenes in which they were deeply interested.

And as it was contrary to their character to deceive others, so neither could they be deceived themselves. They could not be deceived in the case of Christ's feeding the five thousand, of his suddenly healing those who were leprous, lame, and blind. They could not but know whether he who professed to be the risen Saviour, and with whom they conversed forty days, was the same Jesus with whom they had daily and familiar intercourse before his crucifixion. They could not be mistaken as to Christ's ascension to heaven; as to their being suddenly endowed with the gift of tongues; and as to their being able to work miracles, and to impart the same power to others.

3. *The Apostles were not influenced by Worldly Interests.*—Not only were they *disinterested* in their testimony, but their interests were on the side of concealment. One of the Evangelists, Matthew, occupied a lucrative situation when called by Jesus, and was evidently an opulent man. The fishermen of Galilee were at least in circumstances of comfort, and never had any worldly inducement held out to them by their

Master. St. Paul, from his education, connections, and talents, had encouraging prospects in life. But they voluntarily abandoned every temporal expectation, and embarked in a cause which the world regarded as wretched and hopeless to the last degree.

The *earthly* rewards which the apostles of our Lord obtained for their devotedness to his cause are thus graphically presented by St. Paul: "Even unto this present hour we both hunger and thirst, and are naked, and are buffeted, and have no certain dwelling-place; we are made as the filth of the world, and are the offscouring of all things unto this day." 1 Cor. iv, 11, 13. Finally, they sealed their testimony with their own blood; a circumstance of which they had been fore-warned by their Master, and in the daily expectation of which they lived. From such facts the conclusion is irresistible, that these men *could not be deceivers.*

4. *Their Testimony was in the highest degree circumstantial.*—The writings of the Evangelists are full of references to persons then living, many of whom were persons of consequence, and to places in which miracles and other transactions had publicly taken place. If these things had not been true they would have been contradicted; and if contradicted on good evidence, the authors must have been over-whelmed with confusion.

This argument is strengthened by the consideration that "these things were not done in a corner;" nor was the age dark and illiterate, or prone to admit fables. The *Augustan Age* was the most learned that the world had ever seen. The love of arts, sciences, and literature was the universal passion in almost every part of the Roman Empire, where Christianity was first taught in its doctrines and proclaimed in its facts. In this inquisitive and discerning age it rose, flourished, and established itself, with much resistance to its doctrines, *but without being once questioned as to the truth of its historical facts.* And yet how easily might they have been disproved had they been false.

But we may add, finally, that the history of the Evangelists is impressed with every feature of credibility. An artless simplicity characterizes all their writings. They use no studied arts to adorn their story; but record the most astonishing events in as plain a man-ner, and with as much dispassionate coolness, as if they had been the most common transactions. They are distinguished above all other writers for their sincerity and integrity. Impostors never proclaim to the world the defects of their own character. But the Evangelists inform us of the lowliness and poverty of their condition, their dullness of apprehension, and of their ambitious views and warm contentions among themselves. They even tell us that they basely deserted their Master when he was seized by his enemies; and that, after his cruci-fixion, they returned to their former secular employments, abandoning the cause in which they had been so long engaged, notwithstanding the conviction which they had before entertained that Jesus was the *Messiah.*

Such men could neither suffer themselves to be deceived, nor be capable of imposing a falsehood upon others. We have therefore as much reason to believe that they have given us a true history of the life and transactions of JESUS, as that Xenophon and Plato have given a faithful narrative of the character and doctrines of SOCRATES. Their sacred regard for truth appears in everything which they have written; and to reject such a history is to insult the common understanding of mankind, and to renounce all faith in history. As well might we reject everything that is related in *Herodotus, Thucydides, Diodorus Siculus, Livy,* and *Tacitus,* and confound all history with fable, truth with falsehood, and veracity with imposture.

We have now considered the Genuineness, the Integrity, and the Authenticity of the Sacred Scriptures, and it only remains for us to show that these Scriptures are of DIVINE AUTHORITY. This question, therefore, will now be examined.

CHAPTER V.

DIVINE AUTHORITY OF THE SACRED SCRIPTURES: INSPIRATION.

WHEN we say that the Sacred Scriptures are of Divine authority, our meaning is that they are *an inspired Revelation from God to man.* But before we attempt to adduce the evidences by which this proposition is infallibly established, we will inquire into the nature and extent of that Divine inspiration which is claimed for the sacred writers, and to this subject the present chapter will be devoted.

It has been shown that the sacred writers were men of the utmost integrity, and entitled to the most implicit confidence of mankind. But since it is possible that honest men may be mistaken, if we had nothing more to urge in behalf of these writers than the excellence of their character their writings would only be of human authority. Something more was therefore required than a pious life, and a mind purified from prejudice and passion, to qualify them for being infallible teachers of the will of God, namely, *Divine inspiration.*

This may be defined to be that extraordinary influence of the Holy Spirit upon the human mind by which men are qualified to communicate to others religious knowledge without error or mistake.

In the discussion of this subject it will be necessary, 1. To offer a few preliminary observations; 2. To show that the sacred writers claimed to be divinely inspired; and, 3. To ascertain, as nearly as we can, in what sense and to what extent they were supernaturally assisted in writing the Holy Scriptures.

I. WE WILL OFFER A FEW PRELIMINARY OBSERVATIONS.—It will be proper to observe,

1. *That Inspiration is possible.*—The Father of spirits may act upon the mind of his creatures, and this action may be extended to any degree which the purposes of God may require. He may superintend those who write, so as to prevent the possibility of error in their writings, which is the lowest degree of inspiration. He may enlarge their understanding, and elevate their conceptions beyond the measure of ordinary men, and this is the second degree. Or, he may suggest to them the thoughts which they should express, and the very words which they shall employ, so as to make them merely the vehicles of conveying his will to others. This is the highest degree of inspiration, and no sound Theist will deny that all these degrees are possible.

2. *It is reasonable*, that the sentiments and doctrines developed in the Holy Scriptures should be suggested to the mind of the writers by the Supreme Being himself. They are every way worthy of his character, and promotive of the highest interests of man; and the more important the communication is, the more it is calculated to preserve men from error, to stimulate them to holiness, and to guide them to happiness, the more reasonable it is to expect that God should make the communication free from every admixture of error. Indeed, the notion of inspiration enters essentially into our ideas of a revelation from God, so that to deny it is the same as to affirm that there is no revelation.

3. *Inspiration is necessary.*—This is evident from the nature of the *subjects* which the Scriptures unfold. Some past facts are recorded in the Bible which could not possibly have been known if God had not revealed them in a supernatural way. How, for instance, could Moses have given a correct history of the creation of the world, and of antediluvian times, if he had not been divinely inspired? The Scriptures contain predictions of future events which God alone could foreknow and foretell; and many of the doctrines which they unfold are so far above the capacity of the human mind to discover, that they must have been delivered by Divine inspiration.

The authoritative language of the Scriptures, too, if we admit the veracity of the writers, argues the necessity of inspiration. They propose things, not as matters for consideration, but for adoption. They do not grant us the alternative of receiving or rejecting their instructions. They do not present to us their own thoughts, but preface their communications by *"Thus saith the Lord,"* and on this ground demand our assent. It follows, therefore, either that the sacred writers spoke and wrote " as they were moved by the Holy Ghost," or that they were impostors. But as the latter is too absurd to be admitted, we must adopt the former.

If the Scriptures were not divinely inspired they could not claim our entire confidence as an infallible standard of religious truth. For, however fully we might be convinced of the honesty of the sacred writers, and of the general truthfulness of our religion, when we should proceed to examine its nature, and to investigate its doctrines, its precepts, its promises, and its institutions, we could not have perfect confidence in the detailed account, unless we had reason to believe that its authors had been so assisted by supernatural influence as to be infallibly preserved from all error.

4. *Divine Inspiration has always been ascribed to the sacred penmen,* both by the Jewish and the Christian Church. By the Jews the Law of Moses was accounted the Law of God himself, and their other canonical books were held in like veneration. Accordingly Josephus tells us that they were accustomed, from their infancy, to call these Scriptures *the doctrines of God;* and that they were ready, at any time, to lay down their life in vindication of them.

The primitive Christians entertained the same respect for the writings of Moses and the Prophets that the Jews did; but they received also, by universal consent, the Scriptures of the New Testament as being composed by the direction and Inspiration of the Holy Spirit. They regarded, therefore, both the Jewish and Christian Scriptures as *Oracles,* to decide all differences in matters of religion; and every sentence in them was looked upon as a Divine *axiom,* from which there was no appeal. And thus the case was viewed for nearly seventeen centuries, for it is only in modern days that the plenary inspiration of the Scriptures has been called in question.

The opinion of the Church in the first centuries, respecting the inspiration of the sacred writers, is explicitly set forth in the testimony of the Christian Fathers.

Clemens, Bishop of Rome, a cotemporary with the apostles, tells us that "the apostles preached the Gospel, being **filled** with the Holy Ghost;" that "the Scriptures are the true words of the Spirit;" that "Paul wrote to the Corinthians things true by the aid of the Spirit;" and that "he, being divinely inspired, admonished them by an epistle concerning himself, Cephas, and Apollos."

Justin Martyr says that "the Gospels were written by men full of the Holy Ghost."

Irenæus declares that "all the apostles received the Gospel by Divine revelation; that the Scriptures were dictated by the Spirit of God; and that, therefore, it is wickedness to contradict them, and sacrilege to make any alteration in them."

Theophilus, citing the authors of the Old and the New Testament, says that "both the one and the other spake, being inspired by one and the same Spirit." And again he says, "These things the Holy Scriptures teach us, and all who were moved by the Holy Spirit."

Clemens Alexandrinus says that "the whole Scriptures are the law of God—that they are all Divine; and that the evangelists and apostles wrote by the same Spirit that inspired the prophets."

Origen tells us that "the Scriptures proceeded from the Holy Spirit; that there is not one tittle in them but what expresses a Divine wisdom; that there is nothing in the Law, or the Prophets, or the Gospels, or the Epistles which did not proceed from the fullness of the Spirit; that we ought, with all the faithful, to say that the Scriptures are divinely inspired; that the Gospels are admitted as Divine in all the Churches of God; and that the Scriptures are no other than the organs of God."

II. The Sacred Writers themselves claimed to be divinely inspired. This is true,

1. *With regard to the Writers of the Old Testament Scriptures.*—The Jewish lawgiver often reminded those whom he addressed of the Divine authority of his communications by the well known declaration, "the Lord spake unto Moses;" and the language of David is, "the Spirit of the Lord spake by me, and his word was in my tongue." 2 Sam. xxiii, 2. Thus, too, the Jewish prophets delivered their predictions, not only in the name of Jehovah, but also as being received directly from him. Isaiah introduces many of his prophetic messages by the declaration, "Thus saith the Lord;" and Jeremiah, Ezekiel, and others by asserting, "The Lord said unto me," or, "The word of the Lord came unto me."

But the plenary inspiration of the Old Testament Scriptures is most distinctly asserted by Christ and his apostles. They recognize the whole Jewish Canon in their threefold division of the Law, the Prophets, and the Psalms. It is upon the evidence of these Scriptures that our Lord proves himself to be the Messiah; and to them he constantly appeals, both in proving his own doctrines and in refuting the errors of the Jews. But farther, what Moses wrote in the Pentateuch is expressly declared by Christ to have been spoken by God himself. "Have ye not read that which was *spoken unto you by God,* saying, I am the God of Abraham, and the God of Isaac, and the God of Jacob?" Matt. xxii, 31, 32.

What David wrote in the Psalms is declared by St. Peter to have been spoken by the Holy Ghost. "This Scripture must needs have been fulfilled, which the Holy Ghost by the mouth of David spake before concerning Judas." Acts i, 16. He tells us, moreover, that what the prophets delivered was by the Spirit of Christ speaking in them; and that they spoke "as they were moved by the Holy Ghost."*

St. Paul also bears the most unequivocal testimony to the inspiration of the Jewish prophets. "Well spake the Holy Ghost by Esaias the prophet unto our fathers." Acts xxviii, 25. And again, enlarging the terms which he employs to their utmost latitude, but undoubtedly hav-

* 1 Peter i, 11; 2 Peter i, 21.

ing a special reference to the Jewish Canon, he declares, " All Scripture is given by inspiration of God." 2 Tim. iii, 16. Thus we see that the writers of the New Testament Scriptures bear witness to the inspiration of those of the Old. But,

2. *They claim the same kind of Inspiration for themselves.*—The proof of this is seen,

(1.) *In the general tone of Confidence and Authority with which they delivered their Discourses.*—To feel the force of this argument, we must take a view of the apostles, first in themselves, and then in their changed condition, when the gifts of the Spirit had qualified them for the duties of their office.

Behold these weak, dismayed, and timid fishermen of Galilee, who had fled at the apprehension of their Master, and had with difficulty been persuaded of his resurrection. The day of Pentecost arrives, and they are all together in one place, waiting for the promised Comforter. The house is shaken where they are assembled, and the Divine Spirit descends and rests upon each of them under the external appearance of " cloven tongues like as of fire." They are suddenly endowed with new and surprising powers, assume a new character, and speak with new tongues. Unlearned as they were, and discouraged and cowardly as they had proved themselves to be, they discourse with the greatest readiness and propriety, and with a boldness which nothing could daunt, in every tongue and dialect of the assembled crowds. New courage, discernment, skill in argument, and fortitude in bearing testimony to the truth, appear in all their discourses. " With *great power* gave the apostles witness of the resurrection of the Lord Jesus, and great grace was upon them all." Acts iv, 33. But the apostles give us additional proof of their claim to Divine inspiration,

(2.) *In classing their own Teachings with the Scriptures of the Old Testament, as being of equal Authority with them.*—Hence St. Paul, in speaking of believers as " the household of God," declares that they " are built upon the foundation of the apostles and prophets." Eph. ii, 20. St. Peter occupies the same ground when he says, " I stir up your pure minds by way of remembrance; that ye may be mindful of the words which were spoken before by the holy prophets, and of the commandment of us the apostles of the Lord and Saviour." 2 Peter iii, 1, 2.

Again, they apply to the writings of the New Testament, as well as to those of the Old, the peculiar and solemn title of *Scripture*. " For the *Scripture* saith, Thou shalt not muzzle the ox that treadeth out the corn ; and, the laborer is worthy of his reward." 1 Tim. v, 18. Here it is seen that the first part of the authoritative citation is taken from the Law of Moses; the second, from the Gospel of St. Luke.* Peter speaks of the Epistles of St. Paul as being indited by more than human

* Deut. xxv, 4; Luke x, 7.

wisdom, and evidently claims for them Divine authority. They are revelations of Divine truth, "which they that are unlearned and unstable wrest, as they do also the other Scriptures, unto their own destruction." 2 Peter iii, 16. To these considerations it may be added that the claim of the apostles to Divine inspiration is evinced,

(3.) *By their own positive and express Declarations.*—If the prophets began their discourses with the solemn formula, "Thus saith the Lord," the apostles begin with the same claim of a Divine command: "Paul, an apostle of Jesus Christ, by the commandment of God our Saviour." 1 Tim. i, 1. "If any man think himself to be a prophet, or spiritual, let him acknowledge that the things that I write unto you are the commandments of the Lord." 1 Cor. xiv, 37.

In the fifteenth chapter of the Acts of the Apostles we have the account of an epistle which was addressed by the College of Apostles to the brethren of the Gentiles. In this short letter we have this remarkable passage: "For it seemed good *to the Holy Ghost and to us* to lay upon you no greater burden than these necessary things." Hence it follows that the Apostolical Epistles claim to be inspired by the Holy Ghost.

St. Paul, in his First Epistle to the Corinthians, uses this language: "My speech and my preaching was not with enticing words of man's wisdom, but in demonstration of the Spirit and of power, that your faith should not stand in the wisdom of men, but in the power of God." He then declares that his doctrine was "the wisdom of God in a mystery;" that it was what "none of the princes of this world knew;" but that God had revealed it to him "*by his Spirit.*" Here the apostle evidently claims Divine inspiration; but to put this beyond all possibility of doubt, he expresses himself in terms which cannot be misunderstood: "Which things also we speak, not in the words which man's wisdom teacheth, but which the *Holy Ghost teacheth,* comparing spiritual things with spiritual," or, as some render it, adapting spiritual expressions to spiritual things.

Again, the apostle's solemn injunction to the Galatians to adhere strictly to his doctrines demands our attention. On a particular point of prudential discipline, such as the marriage of Christians under certain circumstances, he had received no inspired communication, and he mentions the exception. But on all the truths of the Christian revelation he had received the most positive command. What then is his language when he approaches the doctrines of Christianity? "I marvel that ye are so soon removed from him that called you into the grace of Christ, unto another Gospel. But though we, or an angel from heaven, preach any other Gospel unto you than that which we have preached unto you, let him be accursed. I certify you, brethren, that the Gospel which was preached of me is not after man; for I neither received it of man, neither was I taught it, but by the revelation of Jesus Christ. It pleased God to reveal his Son in me, that I might preach him among the heathen." Gal. i, 6–16.

Correspondent to these declarations is the language of the apostle, when, in his Epistle to the Ephesians, he is speaking of the revelation of Gospel privileges to the Gentile world. "If ye have heard of the dispensation of the grace of God which is given me to you-ward: how that by *revelation he made known unto me the mystery,* as I wrote afore in few words; whereby, when ye read, ye may understand my knowledge in the mystery of Christ, which in other ages was not made known unto the sons of men, as *it is now revealed unto the holy apostles and prophets by the Spirit.*" Eph. iii, 2–5.

We have now seen that Divine inspiration is possible, reasonable, and necessary; that the Church, in all ages, has ascribed it to the sacred writers; and that they have claimed it in terms which cannot be mistaken. Let us then proceed to inquire,

III. *In what sense and to what extent they were supernaturally assisted in writing the Holy Scriptures?*

This question has given rise to a diversity of opinions. Some have had the boldness to deny inspiration altogether, while others have circumscribed it within very narrow limits. "I think," says Dr. Priestley, "that the Scriptures were written, without any particular inspiration, by men who wrote according to the best of their knowledge, and who, from their circumstances, could not be mistaken with respect to the greater facts, of which they were proper witnesses." He assumes, however, that they were liable, like other men, "to adopt a hasty and ill-grounded opinion concerning things which did not fall within the compass of their own knowledge." But it is a sufficient refutation of this theory that it directly contradicts what the sacred writers declare of themselves, and is an impeachment of their veracity.

Some who advocate the doctrine of Divine inspiration limit it to the prophetical parts of Scripture; while others extend it to the *doctrinal* parts also, but not to the historical. There are many who maintain that the inspiration of the sacred writers was only occasional; that they were not always under that immediate and plenary influence of the Holy Spirit which renders their writings the unerring word of God; and that consequently, as they were sometimes left to themselves, they then thought and reasoned like ordinary men. According to this notion, an intermixture of human infirmity and error is by no means excluded from the Sacred Scriptures. But if it is once granted that they are in the least degree alloyed with error, an opening is made for every imaginable corruption. And to admit that the sacred writers were only occasionally inspired, would involve us in the greatest perplexity; because, not knowing when they were or were not inspired, we could not determine what parts of their writings should be regarded as the infallible word of God. To tell us, therefore, that they were inspired only on certain occasions, while we have no means of ascertaining what those occasions were, is the same as to say that they were not inspired at all.

Many learned men have held the *plenary* inspiration of the Scriptures; the import of which is that every part of them is inspired. This doctrine has been violently opposed, and even treated with ridicule; but the objections against it have arisen, in some cases at least, from misconception. It has been supposed to imply that every part of the sacred books was immediately communicated to the mind of the writers. Hence it has been argued that as some parts of them relate to things which might have been known from other sources, it is absurd to suppose a revelation where the bodily senses and natural reason were adequate to the purpose. But this is not the true idea of plenary inspiration. It extends, indeed, to every part of the Scriptures; but it admits of degrees suited to the nature of the various subjects which the writers were employed to record, and did not supersede the use of their natural faculties, so far as these could contribute to the general design.

We do not then apply the term inspiration in the same sense to every portion of Scripture, because the same degree of Divine assistance was not necessary in the composition of every part. When the prophets predicted future events, or when the apostles made known the mysteries of redemption, it was God alone who spoke, and they were employed merely as instruments for the communication of his will. When Moses related the miracles of Egypt and the journeyings of the Israelites in the wilderness, and when the Evangelists related the history of Christ, they only declared what they had previously known; but without the assistance of the Holy Spirit they could not have performed their work so well.

The true doctrine of plenary inspiration may be drawn from the special promises which our Lord made to his apostles respecting the gift of the Holy Spirit. "But the Comforter, which is the Holy Ghost, whom the Father will send in my name, he shall teach you all things, and bring all things to your remembrance, whatsoever I have said unto you." John xiv, 26. And again, "When he, the Spirit of truth, is come, he will guide you into all truth; for he shall not speak of himself; but whatsoever he shall hear, that shall he speak; and he will show you things to come." John xvi, 13.

If we examine these promises we can hardly fail to see that they must have related to those supernatural endowments which were necessary to render the apostles infallible teachers of the doctrines of Christianity. The Holy Ghost is here promised, not as a *Spirit of Miracles* but as a SPIRIT OF TRUTH; an expression which, if taken in connection with other terms of the passages, manifestly includes an unerring direction in the communication of religious instruction. The Spirit was also promised to abide with them *"for ever;"* and this promise secured to them his constant operations, without change or intermission, whenever and wherever they were engaged in the execution of their office.

Again, the Holy Ghost is called "*another* Comforter," from which phraseology the apostles must have drawn the conclusion that he would fully supply the place of their Master's personal presence; and with the distinct promises before them that the Comforter would teach them all things, bring all things to their remembrance, guide them into all truth, and show them things to come, they could not, from the most obvious meaning of these declarations, expect anything less than the constant help of the Holy Spirit to secure them from all error in the communication of religious instruction.

But we have a more particular account of the nature and extent of that supernatural influence which these promises imply in the language of our Saviour on another occasion. "When they bring you unto the synagogues, and unto magistrates and powers, take ye no thought how or what thing ye shall answer, or what ye shall say; for the Holy Ghost shall teach you in the same hour what ye ought to say." Luke xii, 11, 12. To this it is added by Matthew: "For it is not ye that speak, but the Spirit of your Father which speaketh in you." Matt. x, 20. Such, then, is the nature of Divine inspiration; it is the Spirit of God speaking in or by men, and teaching them what they ought to say. But if the apostles were thus divinely assisted in defending themselves before their persecutors, we surely have a right to conclude that they were at least equally assisted in composing their sacred books, as these were to be the rule of faith and practice to the Church in all succeeding ages.

The different degrees of Inspiration which theologians have usually mentioned are *superintendence, elevation,* and *suggestion.* Let us briefly inquire into the nature of each.

1. *Superintendence* signifies that controlling influence of the Holy Spirit by which the sacred writers, in relating what they knew by ordinary means, were preserved from error, and directed to what they should record.

There are many things in the Scriptures which the writers must have known without any direct communication from God. They did not need a revelation to inform them of what passed before their eyes, or to point out those inferences and moral maxims which were obvious to every attentive observer. Moses could record, without a Divine afflatus, the deliverance of the Israelites from bondage, and the history of their journeyings toward the Promised Land. So Solomon could remark that "a soft answer turneth away wrath, but grievous words stir up anger;" or, that "better is a dinner of herbs where love is, than a stalled ox and hatred therewith." In such cases as these no supernatural influence was required to enlighten the mind of the writers. It was necessary, however, that they should be infallibly preserved from error.

But the true notion of superintendence implies also that the sacred penmen were moved or excited by the Holy Ghost to record particular events, and to set down particular observations. They were not like common historians, who introduce facts and reflections into their narratives according to their own judgment and sense of propriety; but they were rather like amanuenses, who commit to writing such things only as are selected by their employers. Passages which are thus recorded under the direction and superintendence of the Spirit are, in a proper sense, divinely inspired. But if the writers had recorded them at the suggestions of their own minds they would be mere human compositions, and, though free from error, would be exactly on a level with profane history, so far as it is agreeable to truth.

2. *Elevation* denotes that Divine influence by which the mental faculties of the sacred writers, though acting in a natural way, were raised and invigorated to an extraordinary degree; so that their compositions were more truly sublime, noble, and pathetic than what they could have produced merely by the force of their natural genius.

By some this kind of inspiration is restricted to such parts of Scripture as are lofty and sublime; but it is easy to perceive that there must have been, in some cases at least, an elevation of the mind above its ordinary state, even when the province of the writer was simple narrative. This may be seen in the case of the Evangelists. It is not to be supposed that illiterate men, unskilled in the art of composition, such as we may conceive Jewish fishermen and publicans to have been, could, if they had not been supernaturally assisted, have expressed themselves with that perspicuity and dignity of language by which their writings are so eminently characterized. It must be granted, therefore, that a Divine influence was exerted upon the mind of the Evangelists by which they were enabled to relate the discourses and miracles of our Lord, and to record the facts of his history, not only with fidelity, but in that manner also which was most appropriate and impressive.

Further, in many passages of Scripture there is such a grandeur, such a sublimity of ideas and expressions, as must inevitably lead us to conclude that the faculties of the writers were elevated far above their ordinary capacity. " Should a person of moderate talents give as elevated a description of the majesty and attributes of God, or reason as profoundly on the mysterious doctrines of religion, as a man of the most exalted genius and extensive learning, we could not fail to be convinced that he was supernaturally assisted; and the conviction would be still stronger if his composition should transcend the highest efforts of the human mind. In either of these cases it would be impossible to account for the effect by the operation of any ordinary cause; and yet sentiments so dignified, and representations of Divine things so grand and majestic occur in their writings, that the noblest flights of human genius, when compared with them, appear cold and insipid."*

3. *Suggestion* is the highest degree of inspiration, and includes all those direct revelations which were made to the sacred writers, of such things as they could not have discovered by ordinary means.

It is manifest, with respect to many passages of Scripture, that the subjects of which they treat must have been matters of direct revelation. They could not have been known by natural means, nor was the knowledge of them attainable by a simple elevation of the mental faculties. They were founded on the free determinations of God and his prescience of human affairs, and with the abilities of an angel we could not explore the thoughts and purposes of the Divine mind. Such subjects, therefore, could not have been known but by a direct communication from the "Father of lights." This degree of inspiration is properly ascribed to those who were employed to predict future events, to those who were sent with particular messages from God to his people, and to those who were empowered to make known the mysteries of the Gospel.†

From the preceding account of inspiration, it is easy to perceive in what sense the Scriptures, taken as a whole, may be called the *Word of God*. We give them this denomination because they were written by persons who were moved, directed, and assisted by the Holy Spirit, and who were, therefore, infallibly preserved from error. Hence we are authorized to consider all the doctrines, precepts, promises, and threatenings which they contain, as true, righteous, and faithful; and to believe also that the events which are said to have happened did so happen, and that the words which are said to have been spoken were so spoken.

We are not to conclude, however, that all the sentiments contained in the Scriptures are just, and that all the examples are worthy of imitation. Some, from the want of reflection, fall into a mistake in this matter. They quote a sentiment as authoritative because they read it in the Scriptures, without waiting to consider by whom it was uttered. They draw arguments for the regulation of their own conduct and that of others from some recorded action, without inquiring into its moral quality. Yet it is certain that the sacred writers recorded not only the imperfections and misdoings of those who were confessedly pious, but also the words and actions of wicked men and devils. No moral action, therefore, is proved to be right merely from its being recorded in the Scriptures. This only proves that the action did really take place, and that it was the will of God that we should know it; but its conformity or disconformity to the standard of truth and rectitude must be determined by the judgment pronounced in the Scriptures themselves on par-

* Dick's Theology, vol. i, Lecture xi.
† See Gal. i, 12; Eph. iii, 3, 5; 1 Cor. ii, 9, 10.

ticular cases, or by applying those principles and general rules which are laid down in them to regulate our decisions.

Whether inspiration extended to the *language* of the Scriptures, as well as to the subjects recorded, is a question which has engaged a considerable share of attention. In answering this question it may be of some importance to distinguish one part of Scripture from another. We cannot rationally suppose that in those commands, messages, and communications which were delivered in the name of God the writers were left to choose their own language; but the very words, as well as the thoughts, must have been dictated by the Holy Spirit. This was evidently the case when they announced new and mysterious doctrines, of which they could have had no conception if the words had not been suggested to them; and when they delivered predictions which they did not understand, the inspiration consisted solely in presenting the words to their mind. That the prophets did not always understand their own predictions is obvious from the language of Peter, who represents them as trying to search out their meaning: "Searching what, or what manner of time the Spirit of Christ which was in them did signify when it testified beforehand the sufferings of Christ, and the glory that should follow." 1 Peter i, 11. Thus far, therefore, it must be allowed that inspiration extended to the words.

With regard to other parts of Scripture, consisting of histories, moral reflections, and devotional pieces, we would not contend for the inspiration of the language in the same sense. It is reasonable to believe that the writers were permitted to exercise their own faculties to a certain extent, and to express themselves in their natural manner; but, at the same time, we have no right to suppose that even when they were most at liberty, they were in no degree directed by a secret influence in the selection of words and phrases.

It was of the utmost importance that the facts and observations which God intended for the instruction of mankind in all ages should be properly expressed. But if we had nothing to depend upon for the accuracy of Scripture language but the skill and attention of the writers themselves, most of whom were illiterate and ignorant of the art of composition, we could have no certainty that it is always correct; and our faith would be frequently disturbed by the suspicion, that what is only a difficulty might be a mistake. It must be granted, therefore, that the sacred writers, even in relating what they knew, what they had seen, and what they had learned from the testimony of others, were divinely assisted in the words which they employed; and consequently, their very language bears the seal of God's approbation.

To this it is objected, that each of the sacred penmen has written in his own peculiar *style*, and therefore the *language* of Scripture cannot be a matter of inspiration. We admit the statement, but deny the inference, because the diversity of style observable in the sacred writers is by no means inconsistent with the inspiration of their language. It is possible, and in the highest degree probable, that God, in communicating his will to mankind, accommodated himself to the character and genius of those whom he employed as his instruments; and surely no man in his senses will affirm that there was only one style in which he could communicate his will.

"God employs second causes in all his operations so far as we can trace them. In employing these second causes he conforms to the laws to which he himself has subjected them. God waters the earth, but how? Here, by gentle and oft-repeated showers; there, by the silent and refreshing dews; and yonder, by the overflowing river. God destroys the wicked nation: in this instance, by turning the waters of the river and sending an invading army through the channel; in that, by the crow and the battering-ram; in another, by the bomb-shell and the bayonet. God, in condescension to human infirmities, uses human *language*. Is it any more wonderful that he should avail himself of human *peculiarities?* that, in conveying truth to the prophet's lips, he should take the route of the prophet's imagination, emotions, and mental habits? Truly, there is nothing incredible in this to him who knows that the hearts and minds of men are in the hands of God, as well as all the modifications of external nature."*

------------•◆•------------

CHAPTER VI.

DIVINE AUTHORITY OF THE SACRED SCRIPTURES: PROOF FROM MIRACLES.

It has already been proved that Miracles are possible; that they are appropriate, necessary, and satisfactory evidences of a revelation from God; and that, like other facts, they are capable of being authenticated by credible testimony. These points having been established, the main questions before us are, whether the facts alleged as miraculous in the Old and the New Testament have sufficient claim to that character, and whether they were wrought in confirmation of the doctrines and mission of the founders of the Jewish and the Christian religion.

As miracles are manifestly above human power, and as no created being can effect them, unless empowered by the Author of nature, when they are wrought in proof of some particular doctrine, or in attestation of the authority of some particular person, they are authentications of a Divine mission by a special and sensible interposition of God himself.

* Dr. Thomson's Essays.

Let us, then, in examining the miracles of Scripture, turn our attention, 1. To those of Moses; and, 2. To those of Christ.

I. THE MIRACLES OF MOSES.

From the numerous miracles wrought by the agency of Moses we will select only a few. We notice,

1. *The Plague of* DARKNESS.*—Two circumstances are to be noted in this event. It continued three days, and it afflicted none but the Egyptians; for "all the children of Israel had light in their dwellings." The phenomenon was not produced by an eclipse of the sun, for no eclipse of that luminary can continue so long. Some of the Roman writers mention a darkness by day so great that persons were unable to know each other; but we have no account of any other darkness so long-continued as this, which was so intense that the Egyptians "rose not up from their places for three days."

But if any such circumstance had again occurred, and a natural cause could have been assigned for it, yet even then the miraculous character of this event would remain unshaken; for the distinction made between the Israelites and the Egyptians, while they inhabited the same district of country, must be attributed to a supernatural cause. "Moses stretched out his hand," and the darkness prevailed everywhere except in the dwellings of his people. The fact being allowed, the *miracle* of necessity follows. We will consider,

2. *The destruction of the* FIRST-BORN *of Egypt.*†—This judgment was threatened in the presence of Pharaoh, *before* any of the other plagues were brought upon him and his people. The Israelites also were forewarned of it, and were directed to slay a lamb, to sprinkle the blood upon their door-posts, and to prepare for their departure that same night. The stroke was inflicted only upon the first-born of the Egyptians, and not upon any other part of the family—it occurred in the same hour; but the first-born of the Israelites escaped, without a single exception.

The history, therefore, being established, the *miracle* must be admitted; for if a pestilence were to be assumed as the agent of this calamity, every one knows that an epidemic disease comes not upon the threat of a mortal, and makes no such selection as the first-born of every family.

3. *The dividing of the* RED SEA.‡—This miracle has already been mentioned, but merits a more particular consideration. The miraculous character of this event is strongly marked. An expanse of water from nine to twelve miles broad, known to be exceedingly subject to agitations, is divided, and a wall of water is formed on each side, affording a passage on dry land for the Israelites. The instrument is a strong east wind, which begins its operation upon the waters at the stretching out of the hand of Moses and ceases at the same signal. The phenomenon

* See Exod. x, 21–23.   † See Exod. xii, 29, 30.   ‡ Exod. xiv, 21–23.

occurs just as the Egyptians are on the point of overtaking the Israelites, and ceases when the latter reach the opposite shore in safety; and when the former are in the midst of the passage, and in the only position in which the closing of the waters could insure the entire destruction of so large a host.

It has been asked whether there were not some ledges of rocks where the water was shallow, so that an army, at particular times, might pass over; and whether the *Etesian* winds might not blow so violently against the sea as to keep it back " on a heap." But if there were any force in these questions, such suppositions would not account for the destruction of the Egyptians.

At the place where the passage of the Red Sea was effected its depth, according to Bruce, is about fourteen fathoms, and its breadth between three and four leagues. But there is no "ledge of rocks;" and as to the *Etesian* winds, if they could keep the sea as a wall on one side, still the difficulty would remain of building the wall on the other. It is also worthy of remark, that the *monsoon* of the Red Sea blows the summer half of the year from the north and the winter half from the south, neither of which could have produced the miracle in question. For the wind which actually did blow, according to the history, was an "*east wind*," and, as Dr. Hales observes, "seems to be introduced, by way of anticipation, to exclude the *natural* agency which might be afterward resorted to for solving the miracle."

4. *The Miracle of the* MANNA.—The falling of the manna in the wilderness for forty years is another unquestionable miracle. That this event was not produced by the ordinary course of nature is rendered certain by the fact that the same wilderness has been traveled by individuals and by large bodies of men from the earliest ages to the present, but no such supply of food was ever found, except on this occasion. Its miraculous character is marked by the following circumstances: 1. It fell but six days in the week; ·2. It was so abundant as to sustain three millions of people; 3. A double quantity fell on every Friday, so as to serve the Israelites for the next day, which was their Sabbath; 4. What was gathered on the first five days of the week bred worms and became offensive if kept over one day, but that which was gathered on Friday kept sweet for two days; and, 5. It continued to fall while the Israelites remained in the wilderness, but ceased as soon as they obtained corn to eat in the land of Canaan. Let these very extraordinary particulars be considered and they will unequivocally establish the miracle.

II. THE MIRACLES OF CHRIST.

When we proceed to the examination of these we find that their miraculous character becomes, if possible, still more indubitable. Even a slight investigation of the feeding of the multitudes in the desert, the healing of the paralytic, the raising from the dead of the daughter of Jairus, of the widow's son, and of .Lazarus, and many other such instances of miraculous power, will be sufficient to convince any ingenuous mind that all the characters of real and adequately attested miracles meet in them.   But to complete this branch of external evidence it is only necessary to adduce that greatest of all miracles, the resurrection of our Lord from the dead.

That it is a miracle, in its highest sense, for a person actually dead to raise himself again to life cannot be doubted; and when wrought, as the raising of Christ was, in attestation of a Divine commission, it is evidence of the most irrefragable kind.   So this miracle has been regarded by unbelievers, who have bent all their force against it; and so God himself regarded it, rendering its proofs ample and indubitable in proportion to its importance.   That we may perceive it in its true light, let us attend to the following remarks:

1. *There can be no dispute in regard to the Reality of Christ's Death.* —His execution was public, where all could witness the tragedy. When the soldiers who broke the legs of the two malefactors came to Jesus they saw that he was already dead.   Pilate refused to deliver the body for burial until he had learned, from the officer on duty, that he was really dead.   But if no such circumstantial evidence could be adduced, it is not to be supposed that they who had sought his death with so much eagerness would be inattentive to the full execution of the sentence for which they had clamored.   The reality of Christ's death is therefore established.

2. *He was not taken away to some unknown or distant place of interment.*—Joseph, of Arimathea, made no secret of the place where he had buried him.   It was in his own family tomb, " which was nigh at hand;" and the Pharisees knew where to direct the watch which was appointed to guard the sepulcher.

3. *It is agreed on all hands that the Body of Christ was removed from the Tomb,* and that in a state of death it was never more seen. How then is this fact accounted for?   The disciples affirm that in the midst of a great earthquake, and while the affrighted keepers became as dead men, an angel descended from heaven and rolled back the stone from the door of the sepulcher, proclaiming that Jesus Christ had risen from the dead; that they examined the tomb for themselves, and saw his grave-clothes, but found not his body; that at different times he appeared to them, both separately and when assembled; that he continued to make his appearance among them for about forty days, allowing them to converse with him and to handle his body; and that he finally led them out to Bethany and, in the presence of them all, ascended to heaven.

The manner in which the Jewish Sanhedrim accounted for the absence of our Lord's body from the sepulcher is, that "his disciples came by night and stole him away," while the Roman soldiers were sleeping. As we have no other account, we are warranted in the conclusion that the Pharisees had nothing but this to oppose to the positive testimony of the disciples. But it must be seen that in this attempt they fell far below their usual subtilty, for the story which they circulated carries with it its own refutation. This, however, may be accounted for from the hurry and agitation of the moment, and from the necessity under which they were laid to invent *something* to amuse the populace, who were rather inclined to charge them with the death of Jesus.

This absurd rumor was not only hastily gotten up, but it was almost as hastily abandoned; for it is remarkable that it was never adverted to by the Pharisees in any of those legal proceedings which were instituted against the first preachers of Christ as the risen Messiah. Peter and John were first brought before the great council, then the whole body of the apostles twice. On all these occasions they affirmed the resurrection of Christ before the very men who had originated the tale of the stealing away of his body; but in none of these instances did the chief priests oppose their story to the explicit testimony of the disciples, or bring forward even *one* of the sixty soldiers to disprove what they asserted.

That a Roman guard should be found off their watch, or asleep, a fault which the military law of that people punished with death, is most incredible. Or that the timid disciples of Christ should dare to steal away his body, even if the guard were asleep, is very improbable. The soldiers were either awake or asleep: if awake, why did they suffer a few unarmed men and women to take away the body? and if asleep, how came they to know that the disciples had done it?

There is really, therefore, no testimony whatever against the resurrection of Christ. The very inability of the Jewish rulers to account for the absence of his body, which had been entirely in their own power, affords strong presumptive evidence in favor of the statement of the disciples. The tomb was carefully closed and sealed by officers appointed for that purpose, a guard was set, and yet the body was removed. The story of the Pharisees does not at all account for the fact, being too absurd to be for a moment credited; and unless the history of the Evangelists be admitted, that singular fact remains still to be accounted for.

But, in addition to this presumption, let the circumstances of credibility in the testimony of the disciples be collected, and the evidence will become indubitable.

(1.) *Their own account sufficiently proves that they were incredulous as to the fact of the Resurrection of Christ when it was first announced,* and therefore they were not likely to be imposed upon by a mere conceit. Indeed this, under all the circumstances, was *impossible;* for the appearances of Christ were too numerous, and continued for too long a time, forty days. And it was equally impossible that they should persuade upward of five hundred persons that they had seen and conversed with Christ, or to agree, not only without reward, but in renunciation of all interests, and in hazard of all dangers and of death itself, to continue to assert a falsehood.

(2.) *The account given by the disciples is highly probable;* for if we allow the miracles wrought by Christ during his life, his resurrection follows as a *natural* conclusion. Before that event can be maintained to be in the lowest sense improbable, the whole history of his public life, in opposition not to the Evangelists merely, but to the testimony of Jews and heathens also, must be proved to be a fable.

(3.) *The manner in which their testimony is given is in its favor.* They give an account of the transaction so variant as to make it clear that they wrote independent of one another; and yet so agreeing in the leading facts, and so easily capable of reconcilement in those minute circumstances in which some discrepancy at first sight appears, that their evidence in every part carries with it the air of honesty and truth.

(4.) *A long period did not elapse before the fact of the Resurrection was proclaimed;* nor was a distant place chosen in which to make the first report of it. These would have been suspicious circumstances. But, on the contrary, the disciples testified the fact *from the very day of the resurrection.* One of them, in a public speech at the feast of Pentecost, addressed to a mixed multitude, affirmed it; and the same testimony was given by the whole college of apostles, before the great council, twice. This, too, was done *at Jerusalem,* the scene of the whole transaction, and in the presence of those most interested in detecting the falsehood had it indeed been false. Their evidence was given before magistrates and tribunals; before philosophers, rabbies, and lawyers; before people expert in examining and cross-examining witnesses; and yet they were never convicted of prevarication, nor were they ever confronted with others who could contradict them, as to this or any other matter of fact.

(5.) *To this testimony of the Apostles was added the seal of Miracles.* The gift of tongues was in proof of the resurrection and ascension of Jesus Christ; and the miracles of healing, which were wrought by the apostles in their Master's *name,* were proofs both of his resurrection and of their Divine commission.*

We may close this chapter by observing that the miracles which the Scriptures record, while they prove the Divine authority of the sacred books, are connected, in a most remarkable manner, with that system of human recovery which has been carried on in the world from the fall of Adam to the present time.

The mark set upon Cain served as a memorial of the first apostacy from the true religion under a dispensation of grace. The general

* See West on the Resurrection; Sherlock's Trial of the Witnesses; and Dr. Cook's Illustration of the Evidence of Christ's Resurrection.

deluge was an awful instance of Divine vengeance against an ungodly world. The confusion of tongues was intended to preserve the worship of the true God from the influence of atheism and idolatry. The wonders wrought in Egypt, by the hand of Moses, were manifestly designed to expose the senseless and abominable idolatries of that devoted country; and the subsequent miracles in the desert had an evident tendency to wean the Israelites from an attachment to the false deities of the surrounding nations. The wonders connected with the settlement of the Israelites in Canaan, and with their subsequent history, all conspired to the separation of that people from a wicked and apostate world, and to the preservation of a chosen seed, through whom all the nations of the earth should be blessed. Every miracle wrought under the Jewish theocracy appears to have been intended, either to correct the superstitions and impieties of the neighboring nations, or to reclaim the Jews whenever they betrayed a disposition to relapse into heathenish abominations and to forsake the true religion.

In the miracles of our Lord he not only evinced his Divine power, but fulfilled many important predictions relating to himself as the Messiah, and thus afforded a twofold evidence of his authority. And in those of the apostles there is nothing done for mere ostentation, but all have a direct reference to the great purpose of the Gospel, that of turning men "from darkness to light, and from the power of Satan unto God."

Whoever will take this view of the peculiar design and use of Scripture miracles must perceive in them the unerring counsels of Infinite *Wisdom*, as well as the undoubted exertions of Infinite Power. He will be compelled to acknowledge that they exhibit proofs of *Divine agency*, carried on in one continued series, such as no other system can claim; and that such agency is not only beyond the power of created beings, but demonstrates the impossibility of imposture in any part of the proceeding.

On miracles, therefore, like those which attest the mission of Moses and of Christ, we may safely rest the proof of the authority of both, and say to each of them, though with a due sense of the superiority of the "Son" to the "servant," "*Rabbi, we know that thou art a teacher come from God, for no man can do these miracles that thou doest, except God be with him.*" John iii, 2.

CHAPTER VII.

DIVINE AUTHORITY OF THE SACRED SCRIPTURES: PROOF FROM PROPHECY.

THE nature and force of the argument from Prophecy have already been stated,* and it has been proved that *real predictions* can be uttered only by inspired men, and that the author of such communications can be no other than the infinite and omniscient God, showing to his servants things to come in order to authenticate their mission, and to fix upon their doctrines the stamp of his own infallible authority.

The only subject of inquiry proper to this chapter is, therefore, the *prophetic character* of the predictions contained in the Old and the New Testament. In order to place this subject in as clear a light as possible, it will be necessary, 1. To make a few general observations; and, 2. To adduce some examples of Scripture prophecy which prove themselves to be real predictions.

I. GENERAL OBSERVATIONS IN REGARD TO THE PROPHECIES OF THE HOLY SCRIPTURES.

1. *The instances to be considered by those who would fully satisfy themselves on this point are numerous.* There are prophecies relative to individuals, to cities and states, to the person and offices of Christ, and to the Christian Church. Some of these have been unequivocally fulfilled; and there are others which are now taking place, or which are to be fulfilled hereafter.

2. *Men may differ in regard to the fulfillment of some particular prophecies;* but there are many others the accomplishment of which has been so evident as to defy rational doubt. Nor can it be shown that any clear prediction of the Holy Scriptures has ever been falsified by the event.

3. *The Predictions of Scripture chiefly relate to a grand scheme for the moral recovery of the human race from ignorance, vice, and wretchedness.* They speak of the agents to be employed in it, and especially of the REDEEMER himself; and of those mighty and awful proceedings of Providence, as to the nations of the earth, by which judgment and mercy are exercised with reference both to the ordinary principles of moral government, and especially to this restoring economy.

Prophecy is of very great extent. It commenced at the fall of man, and reaches to the consummation of all things. For many ages it was delivered darkly to but few persons, and with long intervals from the date of one prophecy to that of another; but at length it became more

* See chapter i of this book, § 1.

clear and more frequent. It was uniformly carried on in the line of one people, who were separated from the rest of the world that they might be the repository of the Divine Oracles; and, with some intermission, the spirit of prophecy subsisted among them to the coming of the Messiah. But Christ and his apostles exercised this power in the most conspicuous manner, leaving behind them many predictions, recorded in the New Testament, which profess to respect very distant events, and even to run out to the end of time.

Farther, besides the extent of this prophetic scheme, the dignity of the *Person* whom it mainly concerns deserves our consideration. He is described in terms which excite the most august and magnificent ideas. He is indeed spoken of as "*the seed of the woman,*" and as "*the Son of man;*" yet so as being at the same time of more than mortal extraction. He is represented as the Word and the Wisdom of God; as the eternal Son of the Father; and the "brightness of his glory, and the express image of his person." Such is the transcendent excellence of that Jesus to whom all the prophets bear witness.

But we may add, that the declared purpose for which the Messiah came into the world corresponds to all the rest of the representation. It was not to deliver an oppressed nation from civil tyranny, or to erect a great civil empire. It was another and far sublimer purpose—a purpose, in comparison of which all our policies are poor and little, and all the performances of man as nothing. It was to deliver a world from ruin; to abolish sin and death; to purify and immortalize human nature; and thus, in the most exalted sense, to be the Saviour of men and a blessing to all nations. Such is the scriptural delineation of that economy which we call prophetic.

4. *Prophecy in this peculiar sense, and on this ample scale, is found nowhere but in the Holy Scriptures,* and to them therefore the advantage of this species of evidence exclusively belongs. It is a *growing* evidence, gathering strength by length of time, and affording from age to age fresh proofs of its Divine origin. Heathenism never made any clear and well-founded pretensions to it; and Mohammedanism, though it stands as a proof of the truth of Scripture prophecy, is unsupported by a single prediction of its own.

5. *The Objection raised to Scripture Prophecy from its supposed obscurity has no solid foundation.* There is, it is true, a prophetic language of symbol, or emblem; but it is a language which is definite in its meaning, and as easily understood as that of poetry. This, however, is not always used. The style of prophecy often differs in nothing from that of the Hebrew poets, or sinks into the plainness of historical narrative.

The two great ends of prophecy are, to excite expectation before the event, and to confirm the truth by an unequivocal fulfillment; and it is a sufficient answer to the allegation of the obscurity of prophecy, that it has abundantly accomplished both these objects. It cannot be denied, for instance, that by means of predictions an expectation of the advent of a *Divine Restorer* was kept up among the Jews; that as these predictions multiplied their expectation became more intense; and that at the time of our Lord's coming this expectation prevailed, not only among the Israelites, but also among other nations. This purpose then was sufficiently answered, and the objection is met. It is in this way that prophecy serves as a basis for our hope in regard to things yet to come, such as the final triumph of truth and righteousness, the universal establishment of the kingdom of our Lord, and the ultimate rewards of the righteous.

The second end of prophecy is, to confirm the truth by the subsequent event. Here the question of the actual fulfillment of Scripture prophecy is involved, to which we shall immediately advert.

6. *From what theologians call the "double sense" of prophecy* an objection of another kind has been raised, as though no definite meaning could be assigned to the prophecies of Scripture but that they resembled the ambiguity of the pagan oracles. Nothing, however, can be more unfounded. The equivocations of the heathen oracles arose from their ignorance of future events, and from their endeavors to conceal that ignorance by such indefinite expressions as might be equally applicable to two or more events of a *contrary* description. But the double sense of Scripture prophecy springs from a foreknowledge of its accomplishment in *both* senses; whence the prediction is purposely so framed as to include both events, the one being *typical* of the other.

So far, then, are these seeming ambiguities of meaning from forming any valid objection to the credibility of Scripture prophecies, that we may urge them as additional proofs that these predictions came from God. For, who but the Being who is infinite in knowledge and in counsel could so construct predictions as to give them a twofold application to events not only distant from one another, but to *human* foresight, unconnected with each other?

II. Examples of Prophecy which prove themselves to be real Predictions.

We now proceed to enumerate a few predictions contained in the Scriptures which most unequivocally show a perfect knowledge of future events, and which, therefore, as certainly prove that they were uttered by men who spoke "as they were moved by the Holy Ghost." Let us notice,

1. *The Prophecy respecting the Seed of the Woman.*—"I will put enmity between thee and the woman, and between thy seed and her seed; it shall bruise thy head, and thou shalt bruise his heel." Gen. iii, 15. In vain is it attempted to resolve the whole of the transaction with which this prediction stands connected into *allegory*, or to show that the language expresses a mere fact of natural history, the enmity

between the human race and serpents. In no intelligible sense can the passage be understood but in that fixed upon it by other portions of the sacred volume.

The serpent and the seed of the woman are representatives of two invisible and mighty powers, the one good, the other evil; the one Divine, though incarnate, the other diabolic. Between them enmity is placed, which is to express itself in a long and fearful struggle, in the course of which the seed of the woman shall sustain a temporary wound; but the conflict shall issue in the infliction of a fatal blow upon the power of the serpent.

The scene of this contest is our globe, and *generally* the visible agents in it are men under their respective leaders. The serpent is endeavoring to render dominant error, vice, and rebellion against the Divine government; while the seed of the woman is advocating truth, virtue, and obedience to God.

Now, that such a contest of principles and powers has existed in the world no one can deny. It commenced with Cain and Abel, and was continued in the wickedness and punishment of the antediluvians, and in the prevalence of idolatry and the judgments of God upon idolatrous nations; and we trace it in the history of the Jews down to the coming of our Lord. We witness the sufferings and death of the incarnate Redeemer, the bruising of his *heel;* but he died only to revive again, more visibly and powerfully to establish his kingdom and to commence his spiritual conquests. The history of the Christian Church is but the history of this mighty struggle between light and darkness. The contest still continues, but with increasing zeal on the part of Christianity, and with a success which warrants the hope that the time is not far distant when the *head of the serpent shall be bruised* throughout the entire world, and the idols of modern heathenism be displaced to introduce the worship of the universal Saviour.

Infidels may scoff at a redeemer, and deride the notion of a tempter; but they cannot deny that such a contest as is here foretold has actually taken place and still continues. This contest, so extended, so continued, and so to be terminated, no human foresight could have foretold; and the fact is therefore established that no one could have uttered this first promise made to fallen man but He whose eye looks through the depths of future ages.

2. *The Prediction of Jacob in regard to the coming of* "Shiloh."— "The scepter shall not depart from Judah, nor a lawgiver from between his feet, until Shiloh come." Gen. xlix, 10.

The word " *Shiloh*" signifies *the Peacemaker,* or *he who is to be sent.* In either sense it is applicable to the Messiah. Nor is this application an invention of Christians, for it was so understood by the ancient Jews, and the modern ones are unable to resist the evidence drawn from the passage in favor of the claims of our Lord. That the prophecy has received a singular accomplishment in the person of Christ is certain, and it is equally certain that in no other person has it been accomplished in any sense whatever.* Judah, *as a tribe*, remained till after the advent of Christ, which cannot be said of the long-dispersed ten tribes, and scarcely of Benjamin, which was merged into the tribe of Judah.

It has been asked, Where was the supremacy of Judah when Nebuchadnezzar carried the whole nation captive to Babylon, when Alexander subdued Palestine, and when it was a tributary province of the Roman empire? We reply that the prediction does not convey the idea of either independent or supreme power, but that the tribe of Judah should retain its *ensigns*, its *chiefs*, and its *tribeship* until the coming of Shiloh. During the captivity in Babylon this tribe was kept distinct, and had its own internal government and chief. Under the dominion of the Asmonean kings the Jews had their rulers, their elders, and their council; and so under the Romans.

It is, therefore, matter of unquestionable historic fact, that until our Lord came and had accomplished his work on earth the tribe of Judah continued; and that in a short time afterward it was dispersed, and mingled with the common mass of the Jews of all tribes and countries. We see, then, that this prediction implies a prescience of countless contingencies, occurring in the lapse of successive ages, which can only belong to God.

3. *Predictions respecting the Jewish Nation.*—These predictions, beginning with those of Moses and running through all the Jewish prophets, are too numerous to be adduced; but there are three prominent topics contained in them which demand consideration. These are, the frequent and gross departures of the Jews from the Divine Law, their signal punishments, and their final restoration to their own land. All these have taken place. Even the last was accomplished by the return of the Jews from Babylon, though, in its highest sense, it is still future.

(1.) *Their Apostasies.*—These were foretold by Moses. "I know," said he, "that after my death ye will utterly corrupt yourselves, and turn aside from the way which I have commanded you." Deut. xxxi, 29. This prediction proves very clearly that Moses was an inspired prophet. The rebellious race whom he had led into the wilderness had died there, the new generation were much more disposed to obey their leader, and when these words were written appearances were all in favor of the future obedience of that people.

But even if this had not been the case, it would have been the last thought with Moses, as a merely political man, that his favorite institutions should fall into disuse and contempt. Nor is it to be supposed that he would have closed his public life by declaring that he foresaw

* See Newton on the Prophecies.

such an event if even he had feared it. Nothing, therefore, but the spirit of prophecy could have influenced him to make such an announcement.

(2.) *Their threatened Punishments.*—The Jews were threatened with signal punishments in famines, pestilences, invasions, dispersions, captivities, and subjugations to foreign enemies; and these are represented as being solely the consequences of their vicious departures from God and from his laws.

It may be said that Moses uttered his predictive menaces to deter the people from departing from institutions which he was anxious, for the sake of his own fame, that they should observe. To this we answer, that he could not expect the Israelites to attach any weight to his threats, unless their former rebellions had been punished by such visitations. For forty years his laws had been often disobeyed, and if no infliction of Divine displeasure had followed, what reason had they to credit the menaces of Moses as to the future? But if such inflictions had resulted from their disobedience, everything in regard to these threatenings is rational and consistent.

The infidel may choose which of these positions he pleases. If he thinks that Moses aimed to deter the people from departing from his institutions by empty threats, he ascribes an incredible absurdity to a man of unquestionable wisdom and policy; but if his predictive threatenings were enforced by former marked and acknowledged interpositions of Divine Providence, he was God's inspired prophet. Who but an inspired man could foresee that no famine, no blight, no invasion would befall the Jews, except in obvious punishment for their offenses? What was there in the common course of things to prevent them, though observant of their laws, from falling under the dominion of more powerful nations but the special protection of God? And what but this could guard them from the plagues and famines to which their neighbors were liable?

If we turn to matters of fact as recorded in the sacred history, we will find that every instance of singular calamity is consequent on a previous departure from the laws of Moses; the one following the other with almost as much regularity and certainty as natural effects follow their causes. In this the predictions of Moses and the Prophets are strikingly fulfilled, and a more than human foresight is proved.

Let us look farther into the detail of these threatened punishments of the Jews. Besides the ordinary inflictions of failing harvests and severe diseases in their own country, they were, according to the predictions of Moses, (Deut. xxviii,) to be scattered "among all people, from the one end of the earth even unto the other." And where is the trading nation in Asia, Africa, Europe, or America in which they are not? Who could foresee this but God; especially when their singular preservation as a distinct people, a solitary instance in the history of nations, is implied?

This remarkable chapter, written more than three thousand years ago, contains other predictions equally striking, and as evidently accomplished. The siege of Jerusalem by the Romans is pointed out with that particularity which demonstrates, in the most unequivocal manner, the prescience of Him to whom all events are known with absolute certainty. That the Romans are intended in verse 49, by the nation brought from "*the end of the earth*," distinguished by their well-known ensign, "*the eagle*," and by their fierce and cruel disposition, is exceedingly probable. And it is remarkable, that the account of Moses in regard to the horrors of the siege of which he speaks is exactly paralleled by those well-known passages in Josephus, in which he describes the siege of Jerusalem by the Roman army.

(3.) *Their final Restoration.*—Moses and other prophets agree, that after all the captivities and dispersions of the Jews they shall again be restored to their own land. This was in one instance accomplished, as we have seen, in their restoration by Cyrus and his successors, after which they became a considerable state. Jeremiah had fixed the captivity so unequivocally to seventy years, that the Jews in Babylon, when the time drew near, began to prepare for their return. But there was nothing in the circumstances of the Babylonian empire, when the prediction was uttered, to warrant the hope of such a deliverance. No one therefore but He who determines the affairs of the world by his power and wisdom could foretell that event.

A future restoration, however, awaits this people, and will be to the world a glorious demonstration of the truth of prophecy. This being future, we cannot argue upon; but three things are certain: the Jews themselves expect it; they are preserved by the providence of God as a distinct people *for their country;* and their country, which in fact is possessed by no one, is preserved *for them.*

4. *Prophecies respecting the Messiah*—the great end and object of the prophetic dispensation. Divines have selected more than *one hundred* predictions, generally of very clear and explicit meaning, and each referring to some different circumstance connected with the appearing, the person, or the history of Jesus Christ. How are all these to be disposed of, if the inspiration of the Scriptures which contain them be denied?

These predictions are in books written many ages before the birth of our Saviour; and that no interpolations have taken place to accommodate them to him is evident, for the same predictions are found in copies which are in the hands of the Jews, and which have descended to them from before the Christian era. On the other hand, the history of Jesus answers to these predictions, and exhibits their exact accomplishment.

The Messiah was to be of the seed of David; born in Bethlehem; born of a virgin; an incarnation of deity, *God* with us; and an eminent but unsuccessful teacher. He was to open the eyes of the blind, heal the diseased, and raise the dead. He was to be despised and rejected of his own countrymen, arraigned on false charges, denied justice, and condemned to a violent death. He was to rise from the dead, ascend to the right hand of God, and being there invested with power and authority, he was to punish his enemies, and to establish his own spiritual kingdom, which shall never end.

We need not enter into more minute predictions, for the argument is irresistible when founded on these alone. If we deny that the prophets were divinely inspired, how shall we account for the fact that these circumstances, strange as they are, have all met in one person, and in one only of all the millions of men, and that person Jesus of Nazareth? We may assert that no man, or number of men, could have made such conjectures. It is therefore impossible to evade the evidence in favor of the prophetic character of these predictions, which their fulfillment affords, unless it could be shown that Jesus and his disciples, by some kind of concert, made the events of his life and death to correspond with the prophecies in order to substantiate his claim to the Messiahship.

No infidel has ever been so absurd as to hazard this opinion except Lord Bolingbroke. He asserts that Jesus Christ brought on his own death, by a series of willful and preconcerted measures, merely to give his disciples the triumph of an appeal to ancient prophecies! But this hypothesis does not reach the case. He ought to have shown that our Lord preconcerted his descent from David, his being born of a virgin, and in the town of Bethlehem; and that he contrived not only his death, but his resurrection and ascension also, and the spread of his religion in opposition to human opinion and human power, in order to give his disciples the triumph of an appeal to the Prophecies! Thus men do violence to their own understanding by denying the truth.

That wonderful series of particular prophecies respecting our Lord, contained in the fifty-third chapter of Isaiah, will illustrate the foregoing observations, and may properly close this chapter.

The style of this portion of Scripture is that of *narrative;* it is also entire in itself, and unmixed with any other subject; and it evidently refers to one single person. So the ancient Jews understood it, and applied it to the Messiah; and though modern Jews, in order to evade its force in the argument with Christians, allege that it describes the sufferings of their nation, and not of an individual, the objection is refuted by the terms of the passage.

The Jewish people could not be the *sufferer*, because he was to bear *their* griefs, to carry *their* sorrows, and to be wounded for *their* transgressions; so that the person of the sufferer is clearly distinguished from the Jewish nation. Moreover, his death and burial are spoken of, which in no sense can be applied to the Jews. To some *individual* it must be applied; to no one but our Lord can it be applied; and applied to him, the prophecy assumes the appearance of real history.

Let the infidel meditate thoroughly and soberly upon these predictions. Their priority to the events admits of no question, and their fulfillment is obvious to every competent inquirer. Here, then, are facts, and we must account for these facts on rational and adequate principles. Is human foresight equal to the task? Is conjecture? Is chance? Is political contrivance? If none of these can account for the facts, neither can any other principle that may be devised by the sagacity of man. As, therefore, every effect must have a cause, true philosophy, as well as true religion, will ascribe them to the inspiration of the Almighty.

CHAPTER VIII.

DIVINE AUTHORITY OF THE SACRED SCRIPTURES: INTERNAL EVIDENCE.

THE Internal Evidence of a revelation from God has been stated to be that which is drawn from the nature and moral tendency of the doctrines taught.* This is at least its chief characteristic, though other particulars may also be included in this species of proof.

There are some truths, made known to us through the medium of a revelation from God, which, though not discoverable by the unassisted reason of man, yet, when once revealed, are attended by strong *rational* evidence, so far as we can understand them. Of other truths revealed to us in the Bible, and those in many instances fundamental to the Christian system, we have no proof of this kind; but they stand alone on the firm basis of Divine attestation as their *authenticating* evidence. Such are the doctrines of the Trinity, of the hypostatic union of the two natures in Christ, and of his Divine and eternal Sonship.

The Internal Evidence of the Holy Scriptures, so far as *doctrines* are concerned, is restrained to truths of the former class; but there are facts and circumstances connected with all Scripture from which this kind of evidence may be drawn. Our remarks, however, will be confined to the *excellence of the doctrines*, their *moral tendency*, the wonderful *agreement of the sacred* writers, and their *style and manner*.

I. THE EXCELLENCE OF THE DOCTRINES OF SCRIPTURE.

In presenting this feature of the subject we will not attempt to do

* See chap. i, § 2.

anything more than to consider a few of the more prominent doctrines of the Bible. We will notice,

1. *The Scripture Doctrine respecting the Nature and Attributes of God.* —That this doctrine presents itself to the mind of man with strong rational evidence is clearly shown by that astonishing change of opinion on this great subject which took place in pagan nations on the promulgation of Christianity, and which continues to this day. The discoveries of revelation have satisfied the human mind on this great and primary doctrine, and have given it a resting-place which it never before found. A class of ideas the most elevated and sublime, and which the most profound philosophers in former times sought without success, have thus become familiar to the most illiterate in Christian nations.

2. *The Moral Condition of Man.*—Of this, as it is represented in the Scriptures, the evidence from fact and from our own consciousness is very copious. What man is in his relations to God we never could have discovered without revelation; but now, as this is made known, confirmatory facts crowd in on every side, affording evidence of the truth of the doctrine. The Scriptures represent the human race,

(1.) *As absolutely vicious, and capable, without moral check and control, of the greatest enormities.*—To this the history of all ages bears witness, and present experience gives its testimony. All the states of antiquity crumbled down or were suddenly destroyed by their own vices; and the general character and conduct of the people who composed them may be read in the works of their historians, poets, and satirists, which have been transmitted to our times.

These testimonies fully bear out the dark coloring of man's moral condition as it is found in the first chapter of St. Paul's Epistle to the Romans, and in other passages of the Scriptures; and to this day the same representation depicts the condition of almost all pagan countries. Even where the redeeming influence of revealed religion has been most powerfully exerted, the same appetites and passions may be seen in perpetual contest with the laws of the state, the example of the virtuous, and the commands of God. The Scriptures therefore characterize man as he has been found to be in all ages and in all places. But they assume,

(2.) *That Man is vicious in consequence of a Moral Taint in his Nature.*—This assumption is the basis of the whole scheme of moral restoration through Jesus Christ. Accordingly the Scriptures constantly remind him that he is " *conceived in sin and shapen in iniquity,*" and that being " *born of the flesh,*" he " *cannot please God.*" That man is strongly inclined to do evil cannot be denied, for the doctrine appeals to our reason through the evidence of unquestionable facts. It is supported by every penal law in civil legislation; by every legal deed, with its seals and witnesses; and by the history of nations, which is chiefly a record of human crime.

This tendency to evil, the Scriptures tell us, arises from "*the heart;*" nor is it otherwise to be accounted for. It cannot be the result of association and example, as some have supposed; for if men were naturally inclined to good and averse to evil, how is it that the whole race have become evil by association? This not only involves the absurdity of supposing the weaker cause to be more efficient than the stronger, but it is also contrary to the reason of the case; for with persons *naturally* well disposed, example and association can produce no other effect than that of maturing and confirming their good dispositions.

Nor is there any plausibility in the opinion that this general corruption is the result of bad education. If man in all ages had been rightly affected in his moral inclinations, how could a course of deleterious education have commenced? and if it could have commenced, why was it not arrested and a better system introduced? The Scriptures, therefore, assign the only rational cause for this phenomenon: that man is by NATURE *prone to evil.* But as it is unreasonable to suppose that this disposition was implanted in him by his Maker, we are bound to admit the Scripture doctrine of the FALL of the human race from a higher and better state.

The Scriptures also teach,

(3.) *That the Divine Administration in regard to Man is of a mixed Character, exhibiting both Severity and Kindness.*—As he is corrupt in his nature and tendencies, he is placed under a rigidly *restraining* discipline; and as he is an actual offender, he is under correction and a penal dispensation. But, on the other hand, as he is a being for whose pardon and recovery Divine Mercy has made provision, moral ends are connected with these severities, and the administration of God is crowned with instances of benevolence to the sinning race.

The proof of these different relations of man to God surrounds us in that admixture of good and evil, of indulgence and restraint, of felicity and misery, to which he is so manifestly subject. Life, in all ordinary circumstances, is felt to be a blessing; but it is short and uncertain, and subject to numerous evils. Many enjoyments fall to the lot of men, yet with the majority they are attained by means of great and exhausting labors; or they are accompanied with so many disappointments, fears, and cares, that their number and quality are greatly lessened.

The globe itself, the residence of man, bears evident marks of the mixed character of the Divine government. It is subject to destructive earthquakes, volcanoes, and inundations; to blights and dearths, the harbingers of famine; and to those atmospheric changes which induce wide-wasting epidemic disorders. These and many other instances show a course of discipline very incongruous with the most enlightened views of the Divine character, if man be considered as an innocent being.

On the contrary, he cannot be under an unmixed *penal* administration; for the earth yet ordinarily yields her increase to industry; the destructive convulsions of nature are but occasional; and, generally, the health of men predominates over sickness, and their animal enjoyments exceed their positive misery.

To those *diverse* relations of man to God, as stated in the Bible, the *contrarieties* of nature and providence bear an exact adaptation. Assume man to be anything else than what the Scriptures represent him to be, and they would be discordant and inexplicable; but in this view they harmonize. Man is neither *innocent* nor *finally condemned*—he is fallen and guilty, but not excluded from the compassion and benignity of his God.

3. *The Doctrine of Atonement.*—The great article of Christianity is, the restoration of man to the Divine favor, through the merits of the VICARIOUS AND SACRIFICIAL DEATH OF CHRIST, the incarnate Son of God. The rational evidence of this doctrine, we grant, is partial and limited; but this does not affect its *authority.* It is indeed not unreasonable to suppose that the internal evidence of such a doctrine should be somewhat obscure, for we must not expect as clear information in regard to the Divine conduct as concerning our own duty. There is nevertheless a reasonableness in this doctrine, when fairly understood, and a wonderful adaptation to the moral condition of man, which strongly commend it to every sober and thoughtful mind.

The doctrine of the atonement is grounded upon man's liability to be eternally punished in a future life for sins committed in this. That men are capable of committing sin, and that sin is productive of misery and disorder, cannot be denied; for the great sum of human misery is the effect of actual offense. And as it is a principle in human legislation to estimate the guilt of individual acts by their general tendency, and to proportion their punishment by that consideration, the same reason of the case is in favor of that future and eternal punishment which the Scriptures declare to be the penalty of the Divine law.

That atonement for sin which was made by the death of Christ is represented in the Christian system as the means by which mankind may be delivered from this awful catastrophe. This end it proposes to accomplish by means which preserve the character of the Supreme Governor from mistake, and maintain the authority of his government; and which give to man the strongest possible reason for hope, and render most favorable the circumstances of his earthly probation.

How sin may be forgiven without leading to such misconceptions of the Divine character as would encourage disobedience, and thereby weaken the influence of the Divine government, is a problem of very difficult solution. A government which never punishes offense is a contradiction—it cannot exist; but one which admits no forgiveness sinks the guilty to inevitable destruction, and where all are guilty, makes the destruction universal.

The Ruler of the world is not careless in regard to the conduct of his creatures ; for that penal consequences are attached to offense is manifest from daily observation. It is a principle already laid down, that the authority of God must be maintained ; and it ought to be observed, that in the kind of administration which restrains evil by penalty, and encourages obedience by favor and hope, we and all moral creatures are the interested party, and not the Divine Governor. The reasons therefore which move him to maintain his authority do not terminate in himself. If he becomes a party against offenders it is for our sake, and for the sake of the moral order of the universe. And if the granting of pardon be strongly and even severely guarded, we are to refer it to the moral necessity of the case in order to secure the general welfare ; and not to any reluctance on the part of God to forgive, or to anything vindictive in his nature.

If, then, the interests of the moral universe require that man's restoration to the Divine favor ought to be so granted that no license shall be given to offense, that the holiness and justice of God shall be as clearly manifested as his compassion, and that the awful authority of his government shall be fully maintained, we ask, on what scheme, save that which is developed in the New Testament, are these necessary conditions provided for ?

But may not sin be pardoned in the exercise of the Divine prerogative? The reply is, that if this prerogative were exercised toward a part of mankind only, the passing by of others could not be reconciled to the character of God ; but if the benefit were extended to all, government would be at an end. Nor is this scheme improved by confining the act of grace to *repentant* criminals. What offender, in the immediate view of danger, feeling the vanity of guilty pleasures now past forever, and beholding the approach of delayed but threatened punishment, would not repent ? Were this principle to regulate human governments every criminal would escape, and judicial forms would become a subject for ridicule.

Nor is this the principle on which the Divine Being governs men in the present state. Repentance does not restore health injured by intemperance, property wasted by profusion, or character once stained by dishonorable practices. If repentance alone can secure pardon, then all must be pardoned and government dissolved, as in the case of forgiveness by mere prerogative ; but if a selection be made, then different and discordant principles of government are introduced into the Divine administration.

To avoid the force of these obvious difficulties some have added *reformation* to repentance, and would restrain forgiveness to those only who to their penitence add a course of future obedience to the Divine law. But a change of conduct does not, any more than repentance, repair the mischiefs of former misconduct. The sobriety of the reformed man does not always restore health; and the industry and economy of the formerly negligent and wasteful do not repair the losses of extravagance. This theory is in direct opposition to the principles and practice of human governments, which in flagrant cases never suspend punishment in anticipation of a change of conduct; but in the infliction of the penalty look steadily to the crime actually committed, and to the necessity of vindicating the majesty of violated law.

But we may go farther and show that the reformation anticipated is *impracticable*. To make this clear, it must be recollected that they who advocate this theory leave out of it, not only the vicarious sacrifice of Christ, but also that agency of the Holy Spirit which awakens the thoughtless to consideration, and prompts and assists their efforts to attain a higher character. Man is therefore left, unassisted and uninfluenced, to his own endeavors, and in the unalleviated circumstances of his morally depraved state. How then is this supposed reformation to commence? If man is totally corrupt, the only principles from which reformation can proceed do not exist in his nature; and if only his propensity to evil is stronger than it is to good, it would be absurd to suppose that the weaker propensity should resist the stronger, that the rivulet should force its way against the tides of the ocean. The *reformation*, therefore, which is to atone for his vices is impracticable.

How then can mercy be extended to our guilty race consistent with the character and government of God and with the highest interests of his moral creatures? The only answer is found in the Holy Scriptures. They alone show, and indeed they alone *profess* to show, how God may be *just*, and yet the *justifier* of the ungodly. Other schemes show how he may be *merciful;* but the difficulty lies not there. This meets it by declaring " the righteousness of God," at the same time that it proclaims his mercy. The voluntary sufferings of an incarnate Divine person " for us," in our room and stead, magnify the justice of God, display his hatred to sin, proclaim the " exceeding sinfulness " of transgression by the deep and painful agonies of the Substitute, warn the persevering offender of the terribleness and certainty of his punishment, and open the gates of salvation to every true penitent.

The same Divine plan secures the influence of the Holy Spirit to awaken the wanderer to repentance and lead him back to God; to renew his fallen nature in righteousness at the moment he is justified through faith, and to qualify him to " walk not after the flesh, but after the Spirit." *All the ends of government are here answered.* No license is given to sin, the moral law is unrepealed, the day of judgment is still appointed, future and eternal punishments still display their awful sanctions, a new and singular manifestation of the Divine purity is afforded, pardon is offered to all who seek it, and the whole world may be saved!

With such evidence of suitableness to the case of mankind, and under such lofty views of connection with the principles and ends of moral government, does the doctrine of THE ATONEMENT present itself. But other important considerations are not wanting to mark the united wisdom and goodness of this method of extending mercy to the guilty. All that can most powerfully illustrate the united tenderness and awful majesty of God, and the odiousness and destructive tendency of sin; all that can win back the heart of man to his Maker and Lord, and render future obedience a matter of affection and delight as well as duty; all that can extinguish the angry and malignant passions of man toward man; all that can inspire a mutual benevolence, and dispose to a self-denying charity for the benefit of others; and all that can arouse by hope, or tranquilize by faith, may be found in the vicarious death of Christ, and in the principles and purposes for which it was endured.

4. *The Doctrine of the Influence of the Holy Spirit.*—The Scriptures represent man as being influenced, in his moral course, by spiritual agencies, as being solicited to persevering rebellion by the seductions of *evil spirits*, and to obedience by the influences of the Holy Spirit.

It would be easy to show, if it were at all necessary, that no valid objection, either *physical* or *moral*, can be urged against the Scripture doctrine of Divine influence. But assuming for the present what we know to be true, that the doctrine itself is not *unreasonable*, we will inquire at once into some of its excellencies.

(1.) *It is suited to Man's Moral Condition.*—The moral helplessness of man has been universally felt and universally acknowledged. To see the good, and to follow the evil, has been the complaint of all; and precisely to such a state is the doctrine of Divine influence adapted. As the atonement of Christ stoops to the *judicial* destitution of man, the promise of the Holy Spirit meets the case of his *moral* destitution. One finds him without any means of satisfying the claims of justice, the other without either inclination or strength to avail himself of offered pardon. The one relieves him from the penalty, the other from the disease of sin. The former restores him to the favor of God, the latter renews him in the Divine image.

(2.) *It gives an affecting view of the Divine Character.*—That tenderness and compassion of God to his offending creatures; that reluctance that they should perish; that sympathizing anxiety to accomplish their salvation, which were displayed by the "cross of Christ," are here in continued and active manifestation. It is the office and work of the Spirit to convince the mistaken, to arouse the conscience of the guilty, to comfort the penitent and humble, and to plant, foster, and bring to maturity in the hearts of the obedient every grace and virtue. These are views of God which we could not have but for this doctrine; and their obvious tendency is, to fill the heart with gratitude for a condescension so wonderful and a solicitude so tender.

(3.) *It elevates our Aspirations, and encourages our Virtuous Efforts.*— Were we left wholly to our own resources we should despair; and perhaps it is exactly in proportion to the degree in which this promise of the Holy Spirit is apprehended by those who truly receive Christianity that they advance the standard of possible moral attainment. If God works in us "both to will and to do of his own good pleasure," it is a reason why we should "work out our own salvation with fear and trembling;" for, as our freedom is not destroyed by the operations of the Spirit, and as even the Spirit may be *grieved* and *quenched*, our fall would be unspeakably aggravated by our advantages. Surely no one who cordially embraces this doctrine can despair of conquering any evil habit, of being fully renewed in the image of God, or of being sustained in the performance of any duty to which he may be called, even the most difficult and painful. Such are the practical effects of this doctrine. It prompts to attainments in inward sanctity and outward virtue which it would have been chimerical to consider possible but for the aid of a Divine influence, and it leads to exertion for the benefit of others the success of which would otherwise be too doubtful to encourage the undertaking.

It would be easy to adduce many other doctrines of our religion which, from their obvious excellence and correspondence with the experience and circumstances of mankind, furnish much interesting internal evidence in favor of its divinity. But as this would greatly exceed the limits of a chapter, and as those doctrines have been considered against which the most strenuous objections from pretended rational principles have been urged—the moral state and condition of man, the atonement made by the death of Christ for the sins of the world and the influences of the Holy Spirit—it is sufficient for the argument to have shown that even such doctrines are accompanied with important and interesting reasons, and that they powerfully commend Christianity to universal acceptance. What has been offered is only a mere specimen of the rational proof which accompanies many of the doctrines of revelation; but a considerate mind may extend the argument at pleasure.

II. THE MORAL TENDENCY OF THE SACRED SCRIPTURES.

If these Scriptures declare to us the before "*unknown God*," unknown even to the wisest of the heathen philosophers; if they reveal man's true moral condition, and the only means by which he can be restored to the favor of God and renewed in his image; if they contain every moral direction which can safely guide us, every promise which is suitable to our condition, and every hope which can animate us to run our course of probation and aspire to the high rewards of another life, then must their moral influence be as powerful as their doctrines are lofty and important. That the Bible, in this respect, is superior to every other system of religion, will appear evident from a few observations.

1. *A perfect System of Morals is nowhere to be found but in the Holy Scriptures; and the deficiencies of Pagan morality only exalt the purity, comprehensiveness, and practicability of ours.*—The character of the Being acknowledged as supreme must always impress itself upon that morality which rests upon his will for its obligation. We have seen the views entertained by pagans on this all-important point, and their demoralizing effects. But the God of the Bible is " *holy,*" without spot; "*just,*" without intermission or partiality; "*good,*" boundlessly benevolent and beneficent; and his law is the image of himself, " *holy, just,* and *good.*"

2. *With Pagans the great Principles of Morality, so far as they comprehend them, were mere Abstractions, and therefore comparatively feeble in their influence.* But in the person of Christ, our God incarnate, they are exemplified in *action,* displaying themselves amid human relations, and the actual circumstances of human life. With them the authority of moral rules was either the opinion of the wise or the tradition of the ancient, confirmed, it is true, in some degree by observation and experience; but to us they are given as commands immediately from the Supreme Governor, and ratified as HIS by the most solemn and explicit attestations. With them many great moral principles, being indistinctly apprehended, were matters of doubt and debate; but with us the clear and authoritative manner in which they are revealed excludes both.

3. *Those who never had the benefit of Revelation have no just conception of that moral state of the heart from which alone pure morality can flow.* When, therefore, they speak of the same virtues as those enjoined in the Scriptures they attach to them a lower idea, and in this we see the great superiority of Christianity. It forbids not only the overt acts of vice, but even the very thoughts and desires of the heart from which they spring. It enjoins humanity, meekness, placability, and charity as clearly and solemnly as the grosser vices are prohibited. Nor are the injunctions feeble; they are strictly LAW, and not mere *advice* and *recommendations.*

4. *The Superiority of Christian Morality is also seen in the number and strength of its motives.*—A sense of duty to God and the fear of his displeasure are the highest motives of heathen morality. But to these Christianity adds the motive of tender and supreme love to God, excited by his infinite compassion to us in the gift of his Son; and another, which heathen moralists never knew, the testimony that we please God, manifested in the acceptance of our prayers and in spiritual and felicitous communion with him. A pagan could draw, though with imperfect lines, a *beau ideal* of virtue which he never thought to be attainable; but to all who seek the renovation of their moral nature the religion of Christ gives the "*full assurance of hope* " that they shall obtain the desired object.

What, then, is the moral tendency of Christianity ?　It is this : to free man from every passion which wastes, and burns, and frets, and enfeebles his spirit; and to lead him to the possession of that new nature, that peace of mind, and that joy unspeakable which will render his obedience voluntary, cheerful, and entire.　On vast numbers of men it has superinduced these moral changes; its way is still onward, and he who would arrest its progress, were he able, would quench the only hope which remains to our world and prove himself to be an enemy to mankind.

We conclude, therefore, that the Scriptures are worthy of God, and that they propose the very ends which rendered a revelation necessary. To this whole system of practical religion we may apply the language of Mr. Wesley, in relation to our Lord's Sermon on the Mount : " Behold Christianity in its native form, as delivered by its great Author.　See a picture of God, as far as he is imitable by man, drawn by God's own hand.　What beauty appears in the whole!　How just a symmetry! What exact proportions in every part!　How desirable is the happiness here described!　How venerable, how lovely is the holiness !"*

III. The Wonderful Agreement of the Sacred Writers.

The Bible contains the compositions of a vast variety of writers, men of every rank and condition, of every diversity of character and turn of mind.　Among them are the monarch and the plebeian, the learned and the illiterate, the talented and the moderately gifted, the historian and the legislator, the orator and the poet.　Some of them lived in ages distant from one another, under different modes of civil government and in different dispensations of the Divine economy, filling a period of time which reached from the first dawn of heavenly light to its meridian glory.　Each had his peculiar province; "some *apostles*, and some *prophets*, and some *evangelists* and *teachers*."　Here we have the writers of the Old Testament and of the New, the prophets predicting future events and the Evangelists recording them; the doctrinal yet didactic epistolary writers, and him who closed the sacred canon in the Apocalyptic vision.　These writers furnished their respective portions of the sacred volume under circumstances as varied as we can possibly imagine; and yet in all its bearings, parts, and designs we find a most striking harmony, fitness, and adaptation of its component parts to one beautiful, stupendous, and united whole.

"This instance of uniformity without design, of agreement without contrivance; this consistency maintained through a long series of ages, without a possibility of the ordinary methods for conducting such a plan; these unparalleled congruities, these unexampled coincidences, form altogether a species of evidence of which there is no other instance in the history of all the other books in the world."　The inevitable conclusion from all this is, that these sacred writings, of which the Bible is

* Wesley's Sermons.

composed, were dictated by one and the same *omniscient and eternal* Spirit.

IV. The Style and Manner of the Sacred Writers.

The *style* of the sacred writers is *various*, and thus accords with the profession that the Bible is a collection of books by different authors. Each has his own peculiarity so strongly marked and so equally sustained throughout the book ascribed to him as to be a forcible proof of genuineness. The writers of the New Testament employ Hebrew idioms, words, and phrases. The Greek in which they wrote is not classic Greek, but is such a dialect as would be used by persons acquiring the language, by frequent intercourse with strangers, where Chaldee or Syriac was spoken as the vernacular tongue. This affords an argument, from internal evidence, that the books were written by the persons whose names they bear. And as this particular style was changed after the destruction of Jerusalem, they must have been written in the first century.

The *manner* of the sacred writers is in proof that they were conscious of the truth of what they related. The whole narrative is simple and natural. Even in the accounts given of the creation, the flood, the exodus from Egypt, and the events of the life and death of Christ, where designing men would have been most inclined to heighten the impression by glowing and elaborate description, the same chastened simplicity is preserved. "These sober recorders of events the most astonishing are never carried away, by the circumstances they relate, into any pomp of diction or use of superlatives. Absorbed in their holy task, no alien idea presents itself to their mind. The object before them fills it. They never digress; are never called away by the solicitations of vanity or the suggestions of curiosity. They never fill up the intervals between the events which they record. They leave circumstances to make their own impression, instead of helping out the reader by reflections of their own. They preserve the gravity of history and the severity of truth without enlarging the outline or swelling the expression."*

* See Mrs. More's Character of St. Paul.

CHAPTER IX.

DIVINE AUTHORITY OF THE SACRED SCRIPTURES: COLLATERAL EVIDENCE.

MUCH of the *Collateral Evidence* of the Divine authority of the Scriptures has been anticipated in the course of this discussion, and need not again be resumed.

The *agreement* of the final revelation of the will of God, by the ministry of Christ and his apostles, with former authenticated revelations, has been pointed out; so that the whole constitutes one body of harmonious doctrines, gradually introduced, and at length fully unfolded and confirmed.

The *suitableness* of the Christian revelation to the state of the world, at the time of its communication, follows from the view we have given of the necessity, not only of a revelation generally, but of such a revelation as God has granted to the world through his Son.

It has also been shown that its historical facts accord with the credible histories and traditions of the same time, that monuments remain to attest its truth in the institutions of the Christian Church, and that adversaries have made concessions in its favor.

These sources of Collateral Evidence having been sufficiently considered, we must confine our further remarks upon this subject to two particulars, but each of very convincing character. The first is, the marvelous diffusion of Christianity in the first three centuries; the second is, its ameliorating influence upon the condition of mankind.

I. ITS MARVELOUS DIFFUSION IN THE FIRST THREE CENTURIES.

How are we to account for the fact, that the first preachers of the Gospel, though unaided by human power or philosophic wisdom, and even in opposition to both, effected a revolution in the opinions and manners of a great portion of the civilized world to which in the history of nations there is no parallel.* In the face of all opposition, and in a short period of time, they induced multitudes in various nations, distinguished both by the peculiarity of their manners and the diversity of

---

* The success of Mohammed, though sometimes presented as a parallel, is, in fact, both as to the means employed and the effect produced, a perfect contrast. The *means* were conquest and compulsion; the *effect* was to legalize and sanctify the natural passions of man for plunder and sensual gratification; and it is indeed strange that a contrast so marked should ever have been regarded as a correspondence. Men were persuaded, when they were not *forced*, to join the ranks of the Arabian impostor by the hope of plunder, and a present and future life of brutal gratification; but they were persuaded to join the apostles by the evidence of truth and by the hope of future spiritual blessedness, but with the certainty of present disgrace and suffering.

their language, to forsake the religious institutions of their ancestors, though sanctified by age, defended by vigorous authority, and associated with the most alluring gratification of the passions, and to embrace the religion of the despised Nazarene. Let us look both at the historical proof of the fact, and the evidence which it affords of the Divine authority of our holy religion.

1. *The Historical Proof of the Fact.*—We have the testimony of Tacitus, about thirty years after the crucifixion, to the extensive propagation of Christianity even in the apostolic age. Speaking of the Christian religion, he says: "This pernicious superstition, though checked for a while, broke out again, and spread not only over Judea, but reached the city of Rome also. At first they only were apprehended who confessed themselves to belong to that sect; afterward a *vast multitude* were discovered and cruelly punished."* This testimony is of great value, because it shows in how short a period of time Christianity had passed from the distant province of Judea to Rome, and with what success it was attended in the capital of the world.

We learn from the younger Pliny, who presided over Pontus and Bithynia in the beginning of the second century, that in his province the Gospel could boast of numerous disciples. "The contagion of this superstition," says he, in his well-known letter to Trajan, "has not only invaded cities, but the smaller towns also, and the whole country." He tells us, moreover, that until he began to use severities against the Christians the temples of the heathen gods were almost deserted, and that those who sold victims for sacrifice could hardly find purchasers.†

These are testimonies of heathens, who could have no interest in magnifying the number of the Christians; but they agree substantially with the testimony of the Christian fathers, as a few quotations will show. About the middle of the second century Justin Martyr writes: "There is not a nation, Greek or Barbarian, or of any other name, even of those who wander in tribes and live in tents, among whom prayers and thanksgivings are not offered to the Father and Creator of the universe in the name of the crucified Jesus." Near the close of this century Tertullian, in his Apology, appeals thus to the Roman governors: "We were but of yesterday, and we have filled your cities and towns; the camp, the senate, and the forum." Origen, in the early part of the third century, says: "By the good providence of God the Christian religion has so flourished and increased that it is now preached freely, and without molestation."

But the great fact in connection with this subject is, that in the year A. D. 300 *Christianity became the established religion of the Roman empire*, and Paganism was abolished. It follows from this event that the religion which thus became triumphant must have been embraced

* Annal., lib. xv, cap. 44.   † Plin., Ep. x, 97, 98.

by a large majority of *the one hundred and twenty millions* supposed to be contained in that empire; for otherwise no emperor would have attempted to change the religion of so vast a state, nor could such a change have been effected had the attempt been made. Let us then look at this wonderful success of the Christian cause,

2. *As a Proof of the Divine Authority of the Holy Scriptures.*—To present the argument in its true light a few remarks will be necessary.

(1.) *We do not affirm that mere success is a decisive proof of the truth and divinity of a religion;* for this success may not be owing to the justice of its claims, but to other causes. A religion may spread, not indeed as rapidly as did Christianity, but gradually, through its adaptation to the opinions, prejudices, inclinations, and worldly interests of men. Great effects may be produced in the course of time, by the united influence of artifice and authority, when there is a disposition to yield to them. We can account in this manner for the progress of idolatry in the heathen world, and in the Christian Church during the dark ages. A religion may be rapidly and extensively propagated by *force.* Of this we have an example in that of Mohammed, which diffused itself in a short time over several countries in the East.

(2.) *But to none of these causes can we attribute the success of the Christian Religion during the first three centuries.*—We know of one religion which was propagated by the sword; but our Lord, unlike Mohammed in this, as in every other part of his character, made no use of carnal weapons to disseminate his religion, and positively disclaimed them. "My kingdom," said he, "is not of this world. If my kingdom were of this world then would my servants fight, that I should not be delivered to the Jews: but now is my kingdom not from hence." John xviii, 36. Hence said the apostle, "The weapons of our warfare are not carnal;" but still these weapons were "mighty through God." 2 Cor. x, 4.

(3.) *Nor did its success depend upon any support or protection which it received from the civil authority.*—It is a well-authenticated fact, not only that Christianity was unaided by the secular arm, but that it made its way in the face of strong and persevering opposition. Those who professed this despised religion were exposed to the loss of property, of country, of liberty, and of life. They were tortured with every species of cruelty, and accounted the enemies of the human race. The emperors armed the magistrates with authority, and the fury of the populace supplied additional means of destruction. Neither age nor sex was spared; and for centuries a succession of sanguinary persecutions, with only short intervals of repose, marked the progress of the Christian Church. The struggle was prolonged nearly three hundred years, during which the blood of Christian martyrs flowed in torrents in almost every part of the Roman empire. But truth ultimately prevailed, and the religion of the man whom his countrymen rejected was established in every Roman province.

(4.) *It was not because Christianity was suited to the opinions, the prejudices, the carnal inclinations, and the worldly interests of men that it so wonderfully prevailed.*—The Gospel was "to the Jews a stumbling-block, and to the Greeks foolishness." Each of these classes found something in it which was irreconcilable with their preconceived opinions. It was a stumbling-block to the Jews, because it proclaimed a suffering Messiah, a spiritual kingdom, and salvation to the Gentiles, as well as to the sons of Abraham. It was foolishness to the Greeks, because, setting aside their learned speculations and splendid superstitions, it called upon them to acknowledge a God unknown to their ancestors, and a Mediator of whom they had never before heard, and to yield an unhesitating assent to doctrines which were new, strange, and inexplicable by the principles of philosophy. It demanded of its votaries the renunciation of all sinful habits and pursuits, the sacrifice of worldly honors and pleasures, and, conditionally, of life itself. It prescribed humility, the mortification of appetite, and a course of circumspect and persevering obedience; and the promised recompense lay in another world, of which they could have no knowledge but by implicitly depending upon the word of its Author.

(5.) *But who were the immediate instruments in this marvelous diffusion of Gospel truth?*—Were they the wise, the learned, and the eloquent? These, according to human policy, would have been regarded as the fittest persons to accomplish the work; but with such our Lord had no connection. He used no means to secure their assistance, nor did he seem to desire it. He selected, for the execution of this great enterprise, those whom every other person would have rejected as being destitute of the necessary qualifications. They were fishermen and tax-gatherers, without learning, reputation, or friends. They were men whose appearance was ungainly, whose manners were unpolished, and who, instead of drawing attention to their doctrines by the arts of oratory, would render it still more revolting by the rudeness of their speech. Yet these are the persons who were chosen to propagate a religion which was unacceptable to all classes of men; but which nevertheless aimed at universal dominion, requiring the priest, the philosopher, and the statesman to bow to its authority and become its lowly disciples.

(6.) *Now, as the human means employed in the propagation of the Gospel were manifestly inadequate, we must attribute its success to supernatural agency.*—It is a species of miracle which does not strike the eye, but the mind. Something has been done, not indeed without means, but above them; and it is as truly wonderful as was the flowing of water from the rock when Moses smote it with his rod. A power was exerted beyond that which resided in the means employed: it was the power of God. And if means and instruments were selected apparently incompetent in themselves, it was for the express purpose of making that power manifest, and of furnishing a decisive evidence that Christianity is Divine. This thought is forcibly presented by St. Paul. "God hath chosen the foolish things of the world to confound the wise; and God hath chosen the weak things of the world to confound the things which are mighty; and base things of the world, and things which are despised, hath God chosen, yea, and things which are not, to bring to naught things that are: that no flesh should glory in his presence." 1 Cor. i, 27–29. The same writer, in speaking directly of the Gospel, says: "We have this treasure in earthen vessels, that the excellency of the power may be of God, and not of us." 2 Cor. iv, 7.

We come now to consider,

II. The Ameliorating Influence of Christianity upon the Condition of Mankind.

The actual effects which Christianity produced in the world, and which it is still producing, are strong arguments in support of its Divine authority.   In every pagan country where it has prevailed it has abolished *idolatry* with its sanguinary and polluted rites. It has raised the standard of *morality;* and by that means, even where its full effects have not been exerted, it has insensibly improved the manners of every Christian state. It abolished *infanticide* and *human sacrifices,* which were so prevalent among ancient and modern heathens.

Christianity has borne its testimony against *polygamy* and *divorce;* and, by the institution of marriage in an indissoluble bond, has given birth to a felicity and sanctity in the domestic circle which it never before knew. It has exalted the character and condition of *woman,* and by that means has humanized *man.* He no longer imposes upon her feeble shoulders the meanest and most servile occupations of life, thus treating her with injustice, cruelty, and ungenerous contempt; but, inspired by the refining and ennobling principles of the Gospel, he feels in his breast a *new and important affection,* which Christianity alone can create, the love of woman, founded on *esteem.*

Christianity abolished domestic slavery in ancient Europe, and from its principles the struggle which is now maintained against this great evil draws its energy and promises a triumph as complete. It has given a milder character to *war,* and taught modern nations to treat their prisoners with humanity, and to restore them by exchange to their respective countries. It has laid the basis of a *jurisprudence* more just and equal, given civil rites to subjects, and placed restraints on absolute power, and crowned its achievements by its *charity.* Hospitals, schools, and many other institutions for the benefit of the aged and the poor, are almost exclusively its own creations; and they abound most where its influence is most powerful.

The same effects are still resulting from its influence in every heathen country into which it has been carried. In some of them idolatry has been renounced; infants, and widows, and aged persons, who would have been immolated to their gods or abandoned by their cruelty, have been preserved, and are now "*living to praise its Divine Author, as they do at this day.*" In other instances the light is prevailing against the darkness, and those systems of dark and sanguinary superstition which have stood for ages only to pollute and oppress, without any symptom of decay, now betray the shocks which they have sustained by the preaching of the Gospel of Christ and nod to their final fall.

Such are the leading evidences of the truth of the Holy Scriptures, and of the religious system which they unfold, from the first promise made to the first fallen man to its perfected exhibition in the New Testament. The Christian will review these solid and immovable foundations of his faith with unutterable joy. They leave none of his moral interests unprovided for in time, and they set before him a certain and felicitous immortality.

The infidel may be entreated by every compassionate feeling to a more serious consideration of the evidences of this Divine system, and the difficulties and hopelessness of his own; and we would remind him that "if Christianity be true it is *tremendously* true." Let him turn to an insulted, but yet merciful Saviour, who even now prays for his enemies as once he prayed for his murderers: "FATHER, FORGIVE THEM; FOR THEY KNOW NOT WHAT THEY DO!"

CHAPTER X.

DIVINE AUTHORITY OF THE SACRED SCRIPTURES: MISCELLANEOUS OBJECTIONS ANSWERED.

IN meeting the objections which are urged against the Bible, it will be our purpose to expose them, in as few words as possible, to the sunlight of truth. The mere cavils of infidel writers may be hastily dismissed, but the most plausible objections shall be considered more at large.

1. It is objected that reason is a sufficient guide in religion, that revelation is therefore unnecessary, and that it reflects upon the wisdom of the Creator, as if he had not at first duly fitted man for the end of his being, and consequently found it expedient afterward to supply the defect.

This specious infidelity, called "*deism,*" or "*the religion of nature,*" made its appearance in France and Italy about the middle of the sixteenth century, and was first advocated in England early in the seventeenth century by Lord Herbert of Cherbury. He lays down five primary articles of religion which, he says, are all discoverable by our natural faculties, and contain everything that is necessary to be believed. They are, that there is a supreme God, that he is chiefly to be worshiped, that piety and virtue are the principal parts of his worship, that repentance expiates offense, and that there is a state of future rewards and punishments.

The history of infidelity from this time is, however, a striking comment upon the words of St. Paul, that "evil men and seducers shall wax worse and worse, deceiving and being deceived;" for in the progress of this deadly error every one of Lord Herbert's five articles has been called in question or given up. HOBBES regarded our duty to God as a chimera, the civil magistrate being supreme in all things. SHAFTESBURY denied the doctrine of future rewards and punishments. HUME attempted to overthrow the argument for the existence of God from the frame of the universe, by denying the relation between cause and effect. By some the worship of God has been rejected as unreasonable because he needs not *our praises*, and is not to be turned from his purposes by *our* prayers.

And as to future rewards and punishments, philosophy has discovered, since the days of Lord Herbert, that the human soul, being a mere result of organization, dies with the body. The great principle of the English proto-infidel, "the sufficiency of our own natural faculties to form a religion for ourselves," is, however, the foundation of all these theories; and this being conceded, the instances just given are a sufficient refutation of the objection. Nothing, therefore, can be more absurd than to wrangle about the sufficiency of reason when it has proved itself to be insufficient in every trial. The fact is a stubborn one, and no speculation can set it aside.

Nor does this fact imply a reflection upon the wisdom of the Creator. With us there is no difficulty in accounting for it. We believe that reason, when first conferred, was fully adequate to all the purposes which it was intended to serve; but that it has since been impaired and perverted by sin, which has both darkened the understanding and corrupted the heart. It is, therefore, subject to be led astray by the imagination and the passions, to adopt false principles, and to draw erroneous conclusions.

2. It is alleged, as an objection to the Divine authority of the prophetic Scriptures, that some of the prophecies have failed. The following are the principal instances referred to:

(1.) It has been said that a false promise was made to Abraham when he was told that his descendants should possess the territory which lies between the Euphrates and the river of Egypt. But this objection is evidently made in ignorance of the Scriptures; for the fact is that

David conquered that territory, and that the dominions of Solomon were thus actually extended.*

(2.) Voltaire objects that the prophets made promises to the Jews of the most unbounded riches, dominion, and influence; but they have lost their possessions instead of obtaining either property or power, and therefore the prophecies are false. But the case is here unfairly stated, for the prophets never made such exaggerated promises. They predicted many spiritual blessings, to be bestowed in the times of Messiah, under figures drawn from worldly opulence and power, which no attentive reader can mistake. They also promised many civil advantages, but conditionally, on the obedience of the nation; and they spoke in high terms of the state of the Jews upon their final restoration, for which objectors must wait before they can determine the predictions to be false.

Moreover, Voltaire should have known that the reverses of the Jews of which he speaks were clearly predicted, and that his very objection acknowledges the truth of prophecy. The promises of the prophets have not been falsified, while their threatenings have been signally fulfilled.

(3.) Paine asserts that the prophecy of Isaiah to Ahaz was not verified by the event. The history of this prophecy, as delivered in the seventh chapter of Isaiah, is this: Rezin king of Syria, and Pekah king of Israel, made war upon Ahaz king of Judah, with the declared purpose of making an entire revolution in the government of Judah, of destroying the royal house of David, and of placing another family on the throne. Their purpose is thus expressed: "Let us go up against Judah, and vex it, and let us make a breach therein for us, and set a king in the midst of it, even the son of Tabeal." Now what did Isaiah say to Ahaz? Did he say, The kings shall not vex thee? shall not conquer thee? shall not succeed against thee? No: but he said, "It (*the purpose of the two kings*) shall not stand, neither shall it come to pass." Did it stand? did it come to pass? Was there any revolution effected? Was the house of David dethroned and destroyed? Was Tabeal ever made king of Judah? No. The prophecy was therefore perfectly accomplished.

(4.) The same writer attempts to fix a charge of false vaticination upon Jeremiah. He refers to a prediction which the prophet delivered to King Zedekiah, and which is recorded in the thirty-fourth chapter of his prophecies, in these words: "Thine eyes shall behold the eyes of the king of Babylon, and he shall speak with thee mouth to mouth, and thou shalt go to Babylon. Thou shalt not die by the sword; but thou shalt die in peace. And with the burnings of thy fathers, the former kings which were before thee, so shall they burn odors for thee."

* See 2 Sam. viii; 1 Chron. xviii.

Mr. Paine alleges that this prediction was not fulfilled; but that the very reverse was the case, according to the eleventh verse of the fifty-second chapter. It is there stated that the king of Babylon "put out the eyes of Zedekiah, and bound him in chains, and carried him to Babylon, and put him in prison till the day of his death." He asks, therefore, "What can we say of these prophets but that they are impostors and liars?" This, however, can be said in truth, that the prophecy was fulfilled in all its parts. Zedekiah beheld the eyes of the king of Babylon when he was brought before him at Riblah. The king spoke with Zedekiah mouth to mouth when he gave judgment upon him, or, as the margin has it, "*spake judgments with him.*" He was carried to Babylon. He did not die by the sword, nor did he fall in battle. He died in peace, for he neither expired upon the rack nor on the scaffold; he was neither strangled nor poisoned; he died upon his bed, though that bed was in a prison. It cannot be shown from the history that the prediction in regard to the funeral burnings was fulfilled, nor can it be proved that it was not; but as every other part was accomplished, the fair conclusion is that this was also.*

(5.) Mr. Paine quotes also a passage from the twenty-ninth chapter of Ezekiel, where, speaking of Egypt, the prophet said: "No foot of man shall pass through it, nor foot of beast shall pass through it, neither shall it be inhabited forty years." This, he says, "never came to pass, and consequently is false."

Now, as the history of Egypt at that remote period is very imperfectly known, it is at least hasty to conclude, even if we had no evidence in support of the prophecy, that it never was accomplished. But that the predicted invasion of Egypt by Nebuchadnezzar did come to pass we have the testimony of Megasthenes and Berosus, two heathen historians, who lived about three hundred years before Christ. This invasion was as devastating in its character as was that of Judea; and we know that the greater part of the inhabitants of that country were destroyed or led captive, and that the land, though not absolutely left without inhabitants, generally remained uncultivated for seventy years. In such circumstances, from the total cessation of all former intercourse between the different parts of the kingdom, it might without exaggeration be said that the foot of man and of beast did not "PASS THROUGH IT," their going from one part to another on business or for worship at Jerusalem being wholly suspended. And as we have no reason to suppose that Nebuchadnezzar was more merciful to Egypt than to Judea, the same expressions might be used, in a popular sense, in regard to that country.

It is admitted that no period can be pointed out, from the time of Ezekiel to the present, in which there was *no* foot of man or of beast to be seen in all Egypt for forty years. The language is evidently hyper-

* See 2 Kings xxv, 5–7; Jer. lii, 10, 11.

bolical, and we are not to expect a literal accomplishment of a hyperbolical expression. We only claim for the prediction that it denotes a great desolation; importing that the trade of Egypt, which was carried on by caravans—by the foot of man and of beast—should be suspended for forty years. No one, however, can prove that the prophecy was not so fully accomplished that the expression might be used without violent hyperbole.

3. It is objected that the Bible has a demoralizing influence upon society, and therefore cannot be divinely inspired. In proof of this various facts and circumstances are urged, the strongest of which we will consider.

(1.) It records the failings and vices of some of its leading characters. The fact is not denied; but the objectors suppress what is equally true, that these vices are never mentioned with approbation; that the characters stained with them are not, in those respects, held up for our imitation; and that such things are recorded for our admonition. They dwell upon the crimes of David, and sneer at his being called "*a man after God's own heart.*" But they seem not to know that this character was ascribed to David long before he committed those crimes; that, even if this were not so, the language had respect to his qualifications as a king, and not to his moral character, and that those very crimes were tremendously visited by the displeasure of the Almighty. This objection to the Bible has therefore no force in the direction intended, but it furnishes a strong argument in favor of the honesty and sincerity of the sacred writers. Had they been cunning impostors no such acknowledgments of crimes and frailties would have been made.

But what has been the effect of infidelity upon the morals of its advocates? Blount committed suicide because he was prevented from an incestuous marriage; Tyndal was notoriously infamous; Hobbes changed his principles with his interests; Morgan continued to profess Christianity while he wrote against it; the moral character of Voltaire was mean and detestable; Bolingbroke was a rake and a flagitious politician; Collins and Shaftesbury qualified themselves for civil office by receiving the Lord's Supper, while they were endeavoring to prove the religion of Christ to be an imposture; Hume was revengeful, disgustingly vain, and an advocate of adultery and self-murder; Paine was the slave of low and degrading habits; and Rousseau was an abandoned sensualist, and guilty of the basest actions. Was it ever found that a truly virtuous and humble man was an infidel? Does infidelity abound among the devout, the pure, the modest, and the dispassionate inquirers after truth? Or, are not rather its advocates profane and dissipated, smatterers in knowledge, false pretenders to philosophy and self-conceited speculatists, who, from their imaginary eminence, look down with contempt upon the opinions and pursuits of the multitude.

(2.) The extermination of the Canaanites by the Jews, according to the Divine command, is urged as an act of the greatest cruelty and injustice.   But this objection cannot be urged upon the mere ground that it is contrary to Divine justice or mercy to cut off a people indiscriminately, for this has been done by earthquakes and pestilences.   What is here ascribed to the God of the Bible, does not therefore contradict the character of the God of nature.

But was it consistent with the character of God to employ *human agents* in this work of destruction?   Who can prove that it was not?   Surely no one; and yet here lies the whole stress of the objection. The Jews were not rendered more cruel by their being so commissioned, for we find them much more merciful in their institutions than other ancient nations.   Nor can this instance be pleaded in favor of exterminating wars; for there was in the case a special commission for a special purpose, and by that it was limited.

Moreover, the sins of the Canaanites were of so gross a nature that it was necessary to mark them with signal punishments for the benefit of surrounding nations.   And the employing of the Israelites as instruments, under a special and publicly proclaimed commission, connected the punishment more visibly with the offense than if it had been inflicted by the array of warring elements; while the Israelites themselves would be more deeply impressed with the guilt of idolatry, and its ever accompanying polluted and sanguinary rites.

(3.) That law in the twenty-first chapter of Deuteronomy, which authorizes parents to bring a rebellious and intemperate son before the elders of the city that, if guilty, he might be stoned to death, has been called inhuman and brutal.   In point of fact, however, it was a merciful regulation.   In almost all ancient nations parents had the power of taking away the life of their children.   This was a branch of the old patriarchal authority which did not all at once merge into the kingly governments which were afterward established.   There is reason, therefore, to believe that it was possessed by the heads of families among the Israelites, and that this was the first attempt to control it, by requiring the crimes alleged against their children to be proved before regular magistrates, that the effects of unbridled passions might be prevented.

(4.) The intentional offering of Isaac by Abraham has also had its share of censure.   The answer is: 1. That Abraham had no doubt of the Divine command in the case, and of the right of God to take away the life which he had given.   2. That he proceeded to execute the command of God in *faith*, as St. Paul has stated, that God would raise his Son from the dead.   Had this transaction been so stated as to encourage human sacrifices it might be fairly objected to, but here are sufficient guards: an indubitable Divine command was given, the sacrifice was prevented by the same authority, and the history stands in a book which prohibits human sacrifices.

(5.) *Indelicacy* and *immodesty* have been charged upon some parts of the Scriptures. We reply, that in no instance is any statement made *in order* to incite impurity; and nothing throughout the whole Scriptures is represented as being more offensive to God than the unlawful gratification of the senses. It is also to be noted, that many of the passages objected to are in the *laws* and *prohibitions* of both Testaments; and as well might the laws of the land be held up as tending to encourage vices of various kinds because they must, in order to prohibit them, describe them with more or less circumstantiality.

We must also take into the account the simplicity of manners and language in early times. We observe, even among the peasantry of modern states, a language on the subject referred to which is more direct, and what refined society would call gross; but greater real indelicacy does not follow.

These cases have been adduced as specimens of the objections which infidels urge against the Scriptures, and of the ease with which they may be met. For others of a similar kind, and for answers to objections founded upon supposed contradictions between different passages of Scripture, reference must be made to commentators.* A little skill, however, in the original languages of the Scriptures, and in the times, occasions, and scope of the sacred books, as also in the antiquities and customs of those countries in which the recorded transactions took place, will always clear the main difficulty.

4. It is objected to the Bible that it contains mysteries and doctrines contrary to reason. It has been a favorite practice with unbelievers to institute a contrast between natural philosophy and revelation, the book of nature and the book of God, and to set the plainness and simplicity of the one against the mysteriousness of the other. The ground of all this is an unwillingness to receive as authorized doctrine what is incomprehensible. They contend that if a revelation has been made there can be no mysteries in it; and that to hold things incomprehensible to be a part of it is a contradiction, and fatal to its claims as a *revelation.*

The sophism here is easily answered. There are many doctrines and duties in which no mystery at all is involved; and as to incomprehensible subjects, nothing is more certain than that a fact may be clearly revealed, as that God is eternal and omnipresent, and still remain mysterious and incomprehensible. The fact is not revealed in a difficult, obscure, or mysterious manner, the only sense in which the objection could be valid. As a fact, it is clearly revealed that these are attributes of the Divine nature; but notwithstanding this clear and indubitable revelation they are still incomprehensible. It is not revealed HOW God is eternal and omnipresent, nor is such a revelation pretended; but

---

* See a copious collection of these supposed contradictions, with judicious explanations, in the Appendix to volume i of Horne's Introduction.

that HE IS SO.   The same remarks will apply to the doctrine of the Trinity, and to many other doctrines of the sacred Scriptures.

But if men hesitate to admit incomprehensible subjects as matters of faith, they cannot be permitted to fly for relief from revelation to philosophy, much less to claim that the latter is superior to the former in the clearness of its manifestations.   Here too it will be seen that mystery and truth go inseparably together, and that he who embraces *facts* embraces at the same time the mystery of their *causes.*   For instance, attraction, gravitation, cohesion, electricity, and magnetism are all admitted facts; but though the experimental and inductive philosophy of modern times has led to many discoveries of the *relations*, and in some cases of the *proximate causes* of these phenomena, yet their *real causes* are all confessedly hidden.   And here it may be added, that if we turn our attention to the science of mechanics, or even to that of pure mathematics, we will still meet with much that is incomprehensible.

5. Analogical reasoning has made it probable that the planets of our system, and those of others, may be inhabited by moral beings like ourselves.   Hence, infidels have argued the improbability that a Divine Person should have been sent into this world for its instruction and salvation, when, in comparison with the solar system, it is but a point, and that system itself, in comparison with the universe, may be nothing more.

Plausible as this may appear, nothing can have less weight, even if only the philosophy and not the theology of the case be considered. The intention with which man is thus compared with the universe is, to prove his insignificance; and the comparison must be made either between man and the *vastness* of planetary and stellar matter, or between the *number* of mankind and the *number* of supposed planetary inhabitants.   If the former, we make corporeal magnitude the standard of real worth.   It will therefore follow that a mountain is of more value than a man, in proportion as its magnitude is greater than his; that the smaller the disproportion between the man and the mountain, the less would be the relative insignificance of the former; and that if the smaller object be increased in magnitude, its dignity must be proportionately increased in the *true nature of things.*   The *Irish giant*, therefore, whose altitude exceeded eight feet, would exceed in relative dignity, by the same proportion, BACON or NEWTON, whose height did not attain to six feet.   But if this is *nonsense*, then must that also be *nonsense* from which these conclusions are legitimately drawn.

If we consider the dignity of an intelligent being, and put that in the scale against mere matter, we may affirm, without overvaluing human nature, that the soul of one virtuous man is of greater worth and excellence than the sun and his planets, and all the stars in the universe. Let us not then make bulk the standard of value, nor judge of the importance of man from the weight of his body, or from the size or situation of the planet which is now the place of his abode. If, therefore, man possesses *another magnitude*, which can be brought to another and different scale of computation, a scale which determines him to be of more value than the material universe, then it would not be irrational to suppose that the highest mountains and the widest regions, and the entire system to which they pertain, may be made subservient to his interests.

Such a scale is that by which the *intelligent, moral,* and *immortal* nature of MAN is to be measured, and which the sacred historian calls a formation " *after the image and likeness of God ;*" a scale but little regarded in the science of *mere physics.* As soon, however, as the mind clearly apprehends this moral scale of magnitude, and perceives that though man's present existence is bounded by a very short period, yet his *moral nature* is unlimited in time, and will outlast all the mountains of the globe, it then perceives, at the same moment, the deceitful character of the objection which was urged with so much apparent humility.

If the comparison of man with mere material magnitude will not then support this effort to effect his degradation and to shame him out of his trust in the lovingkindness of his God, so neither will the argument which may be drawn from the supposed *number* of other intelligent beings. Their number cannot alter his character; for, though there may be myriads of immortal beings besides himself, yet he is still immortal, and still has his immense capacity for pleasure and for pain. Unless, therefore, it could be proved that the care of God for *each* of his creatures must be diminished as their number is increased, the argument can have no force. But such a supposition would be a base and unworthy reflection upon the supreme Creator himself, as though he could not bestow upon *all* the beings he has made a care and a love adequate to their circumstances.

That man is governed by the providence of God none but an atheist will deny; but any argument drawn from such premises as the preceding would conclude as forcibly against Providence as it can be made to conclude against redemption. And if, by a stupendous exuberance of animal, vegetable, and mineral productions, and the wonderful distribution of light and heat, God supplies the means of life and comfort to the short-lived inhabitants of this globe, can it be incredible, nay, does not this consideration render it in the highest degree probable that he has also prepared the means of eternal happiness for beings whom he has formed for endless duration ?

There is, however, another consideration, which gives a sublime and overwhelming grandeur to the Scripture view of redemption, but of which infidel philosophers appear never to have entertained the least conception. It is the moral connection of this world with the whole universe of intelligent creatures, and the intention of God to convey moral instruction to other beings by the history of his moral government in regard to man.   Intimations of this great and impressive view are found in various passages of the New Testament, and it opens a scene of inconceivable moral magnificence, " to the intent that now unto the principalities and powers in heavenly places might be known by the Church the manifold wisdom of God."*

* See Dr. Beattie's Evidences of the Christian Religion, and Dr. Chalmers's Discourses on Modern Astronomy.

BOOK II.

DOCTRINES RESPECTING GOD.

THE Divine Authority of the Sacred Scriptures having been established, our next step is to examine their contents, and to collect from them that religious and moral instruction which they contain.

CHAPTER I.

THE EXISTENCE OF GOD.

A BELIEF in the *existence* of God lies at the foundation of all religion, and is the only basis of true morality. This will appear evident if we inquire into the meaning of the terms *religion* and *morality*. By religion is meant either a system of doctrines of which God is the subject, or a system of affections and conduct of which he is the object. Morality sometimes denotes the practice of moral duties merely from motives of convenience or from a regard to our own reputation, and in this sense it may be distinguished from religion; but when it is understood in its true light it means the practice of moral duties from love to God and in obedience to his will, and consequently it is necessarily included in the idea of religion.

It follows, therefore, that if there were no God there could be no religion, no moral obligation, no hope of reward, no fear of punishment. There could in reality be neither virtue nor vice; for men would be under no law but that of stern necessity, and could propose to themselves no higher end than the securing of their temporal happiness by every possible means. But if there is a God of infinite power, wisdom, and goodness, he ought to be loved, worshiped, and obeyed by all his intelligent creatures.

The opinion has been entertained that it is irreverent to adduce proofs in favor of the Divine existence, because it seems to call in question a truth which it is impiety to doubt. There are considerations, however, that will show the propriety and the utility of an investigation of this kind.

Though it is true that mankind generally believe in the existence of God, yet it is equally true that a large proportion of them have embraced the tenet upon the ground of mere authority, without any careful examination of the evidence on which it rests. Such persons would be unable to give a rational account of their faith, or to defend themselves against the attacks of infidelity. Hence it is necessary for every man to examine the ground of his faith, that he may be able to give a reason of his hope.

Moreover, it is of the utmost importance that a truth on which the hopes and happiness of mankind are suspended should be deeply impressed upon the mind. But there is nothing so well suited to produce this result, in relation to the Divine existence, as a thorough and frequent review of the evidences of this fact by which men are everywhere surrounded.

It may also be added that no one knows to what severe trials his faith may be subjected through the temptation of the devil. Men of deep piety have sometimes experienced moments of darkness, in which they have entertained doubts, not only of the providence and goodness of God, but even of his very existence. This is a subject, therefore, which every man should examine for himself, and in regard to which he should obtain clear and enlightened views.

The word God is supposed to be derived from the Icelandic *godi*, which signifies Supreme Magistrate, or Governor of the Universe. It is also a pure Anglo-Saxon term, which among our ancestors literally signified *good*. When, therefore, they thought or spoke of the being whom we call God, they were taught by the primary meaning of the term employed to regard him as being emphatically *the Good Being*, the fountain of infinite benevolence.

The Hebrew word which is translated God is *Elohim*. This, the learned say, is derived from the Arabic *alaha*, which means *to worship, to adore*. Thus God is characterized as the only proper object of worship and adoration. In Greek the name of God is *Theos*, and in Latin, *Deus ;* both of which signify the *Supreme Divinity*, or Ruler of the Universe.

The question has been asked, Can God be defined? To this we reply, *first*, that if a definition must necessarily contain a complete description of the nature and attributes of the object defined a definition of God is impossible, because no definition can be given which will fully exhaust the idea in question. But, *secondly*, if it is only necessary that a definition should present so many characteristics of the object defined as will enable us to distinguished it from all others, then, in this sense, God can be defined.

A definition of this great First Cause may be given thus: God is an

Eternal, Independent, Immutable, Omnipotent, Omniscient, Omnipresent, Just, Holy, and Infinitely Benevolent Spirit; the Creator, Preserver, and Governor of all things.

Before we enter upon an examination of the arguments by which the Divine Existence is sustained, we may inquire,

I. By what means is the Idea of God originated? On this subject the three following opinions have been advanced: 1. That the idea is innate; 2. That it is the result of rational investigation; and, 3. That it depends alone upon Divine Revelation. Let us examine each of these briefly.

1. *That the Idea is innate.*—If the notion of a supreme First Cause were an innate idea, it would be as natural for man to believe that there is a God, as to believe in the existence of an external universe. Such an idea would have all the force of a self-evident proposition, and could be doubted by no one possessing rationality. But how does this theory correspond with matters of fact? Is it not evidently inconsistent with the existence of atheism? I am aware some suppose that no man can be an atheist, but this is assuming what cannot be proved. That there are those who profess atheism, and who manifest all possible zeal in its propagation, no one will deny; and, until we can claim the ability to discern the thoughts and purposes of the human heart, we have no right to call in question the truth of their profession or the sincerity of their zeal.

The theory in question is also at war with the true philosophy of mind. The doctrine of innate ideas is a mere hypothesis, which no man has ever been able to prove; but which is contradicted by all experience, and is, therefore, unworthy of our confidence. It is now generally admitted that we gain all our ideas by the use of our natural faculties, sensation and reflection; and if so, we have no reason to believe that our idea of God forms an exception to the general rule.

2. *There seems to be a degree of plausibility in the opinion that men may acquire an idea of God by rational induction, or from the light of nature;* but however plausible this theory may at first sight appear to be, we will find, on further examination, that it is wholly untenable. It is true, *nature* is a volume of theological instruction to those who are capable of reading it. But, as a book may be stored with wholesome and important matter, and yet be of no benefit to the man who understands not the language in which it is written; so the volume of nature may contain a thousand arguments in favor of the Divine existence, and yet men, for the want of a sufficient degree of moral instruction, may be unable in the slightest degree to feel their force or follow their tendency.

To the Jew it is evident that "the heavens declare the glory of God," and that "the firmament showeth his handiwork." To the Christian philosopher it is equally evident that "the invisible things of him from the creation of the world are clearly seen, being understood by the things that are made, even his eternal power and godhead." And to deists and heathen sages, who enjoy a light which they are either unable to trace to its proper source or unwilling to acknowledge, the voice of nature proclaims the existence of a supreme First Cause.

These facts, however, have no direct bearing upon the present subject. The question to be investigated is not, whether the light of nature sustains the proposition that there is a God, for of this there can hardly be a doubt; but it is simply this: Is the light of nature sufficient of itself to lead men to the knowledge of God? In other words, Can men who are entirely destitute of the idea of a God derive that idea from rational investigation? Of the question as understood in this sense we feel disposed to take the negative, and in support of our position we offer the following arguments.

(1.) *The Opinion is not supported by a single matter of fact.*—The history of ages does not afford a single instance in which any man, by a course of philosophic research, obtained the idea of God as an original discovery. On the other hand it is worthy of remark, that the wisest among heathen philosophers confessed themselves to be indebted to *tradition* for the ideas which they entertained upon this point; and no one, in any age or country, has ever pretended to have arrived at an original idea of God by rational investigation.

Had such a discovery ever been made by any man, there would most certainly have been preserved, in some way or other, a notice of so wonderful an event. This is true in regard to all the great discoveries of mankind in arts and science. Thus, the name of *Copernicus* is associated with the present system of astronomy. The name of *Hervey* is connected with the common theory of the circulation of the blood. *Fulton* stands at the head of steam power; and the memory of *Morse* runs with lightning speed along every telegraphic wire. So it is with almost every important discovery. But nothing of this kind marks the discovery of a great First Cause; and the only reason is, that such a discovery was never made by any human being. In every case, where a process of reasoning upon this subject has been instituted, it has been to corroborate the belief in the being of a God, and not to gain a knowledge of him as an original discovery. But,

(2.) *This Theory is incredible in itself, because it is absurd and contradictory.*

To suppose that a man can commence a rational investigation of this kind without an idea of God, and as the result of his researches to arrive at such an idea, is to suppose that he will put forth an effort without any object in view. Or, which is the same thing, to inquire after an object of which he has no conception—a subject of which he has not the least idea. It is, in a word, to have an idea of an object and no idea at the same time; and to suppose that of which he has no knowledge to be the subject of his thought and reasoning.

How, then, is a man to come by the first idea of God, with regard to whose existence he is to decide? Were we to suppose human beings to be without such an idea, is it probable that they would ever institute an inquiry respecting him? Or, if such an intention should somehow or other be formed by them, is it likely that they would be able to prosecute it? No one who understands the philosophy of the human mind will answer these questions in the affirmative. Every one knows that it requires more intellectual strength and effort to discover an unknown truth than to comprehend it when fairly stated, or to see the force of the evidence on which it rests. But,

(3.) *The opinion supposes a degree of mental culture that never has existed, and never can exist, where there is no idea of a God;* and, therefore, the discovery is not probable.

Man, without some degree of education, is wholly a creature of appetite. The gratification of his animal nature occupies all his thoughts, and he is therefore unqualified for rational investigation. If we suppose that God is at all discoverable by the light of nature, we must look to those whose civilization and intellectual culture have fitted the mind for the investigation of abstract and philosophic truth. For, to a people who have never heard of God, his existence must be a question of mere philosophy.

But where is such a state of mental cultivation found? Is it among those from whose mind the idea of God is entirely obliterated? To suppose this is to suppose that men can be raised from a state of barbarism to one of civil and scientific cultivation without the influence of religion; for no religious motives can exist where the foundation of all religion is unknown. It is to suppose that civil and scientific cultivation can exist independent of moral control, without a sense of the principle of justice, without hope or fear in regard to another life.

This is what never was. No civilized nation ever existed under such circumstances. It is utterly impossible to raise any body of men, by mere civil improvement, to that degree of mental cultivation which will fit them for philosophic research without the aid of religion in some form. Accordingly, wherever there has been a sufficient amount of mental improvement to prepare men for the investigation of moral and spiritual truth, there the idea of a great First Cause has been previously known and acknowledged.

Under the influence of religion in one form or other, all states or civil communities, both ancient and modern, have been formed and maintained. It has entered essentially into all their legislative and gubernative institutions. Even the atheists of Greece and Rome acknowledged the necessity of maintaining the public religion as the means of restraining the multitude. We conclude, therefore, that where no idea of a Supreme Ruler or Creator has been suggested to the mind, either by instruction or tradition, it is not to be supposed that men could gain a knowledge of such a truth even in an imperfect form.

absurdities. The phrase, the "angel of Jehovah," is not accounted for by a visible symbol, unless that symbol be considered as distinct from Jehovah. We have then the name Jehovah given to a cloud, a light, a fire. The fire is the *angel of the Lord*, and yet the angel of the Lord calls to Moses *out of the fire*. This visible symbol says to Abraham, "By MYSELF I have sworn," for these are said to be the words of the angel of Jehovah; and this angel, the visible symbol, spake to Moses on Mount Sinai. Such are the absurdities which flow from error! Most clearly, therefore, is it determined on the testimony of several Scriptures, and by necessary induction from the circumstances attending the numerous appearances of the angel of Jehovah in the Old Testament, that the person thus manifesting himself, and thus receiving supreme worship, was not a created angel, as the Arians would have it, nor an *atmospheric appearance*, the theory of modern Socinians, but that he was a DIVINE PERSON.

2. THIS DIVINE PERSON WAS NOT GOD THE FATHER.—We do not claim that the Father never manifested himself to men, as distinct from the Son; for this is contradicted by Scripture testimonies.* It is amply sufficient for the argument with which we are now concerned to prove that the angel of the Lord, whose appearances are so often recorded, is *not* the Father. This is clear from his appellation *angel*, with respect to which there can be but two interpretations. It is either a name descriptive of *nature* or of *office*. In the first view it is generally employed in the sacred Scriptures to designate one of an order of intelligences superior to man, but still *finite* and *created*. We have, however, already proved that the angel of the Lord is not a *creature;* and he cannot therefore be called an angel with reference to his *nature.*

The term must then be considered as a term of *office*. He is called the *angel* of the Lord because he was the *messenger* of the Lord—because he was *sent* to do his will and to be his visible image and representative. His office, therefore, under this appellation, was ministerial; but ministration is never attributed to the Father. He who was *sent* must be a distinct person from him *by whom* he was sent; the *messenger* from him whose *message* he brought, and whose will he performed. The angel of Jehovah is therefore a different person from the Jehovah whose messenger he was; and yet the angel himself is Jehovah, and, as we have proved, truly Divine. Thus does the Old Testament most clearly reveal to us, in the case of Jehovah and the angel of Jehovah, *two Divine persons*, while it still maintains its great fundamental principle, that there is but *one God.*

3. THE DIVINE PERSON SO OFTEN CALLED THE ANGEL OF THE LORD WAS THE PROMISED MESSIAH, *and is consequently* THE LORD AND SAVIOUR OF THE CHRISTIAN CHURCH.—We have seen that it was the angel of

* See Exod. xxiii, 20; Matt. iii, 17; xvii, 5.

the Lord who gave the law to the Israelites, and that in his *own name*, though still an *angel*, a *messenger* in the transaction ; being at once servant and Lord, angel and Jehovah—circumstances which can only be explained on the hypothesis of his divinity, and for which neither Arianism nor Socinianism can give any solution. He was therefore the person who made the Mosaic covenant with the children of Israel. But the prophet Jeremiah says that the *new* covenant with Israel was to be made by the same person who had made the old. " Behold, the days come, saith the Lord, that *I will make* a new covenant with the house of Israel, and with the house of Judah ; not according to the covenant that *I made* with their fathers, in the day that I took them by the hand, to bring them out of the land of Egypt." Jer. xxxi, 31, 32. The angel of Jehovah, who led the Israelites out of Egypt and gave them their law, is here plainly introduced as the author of the new covenant. But this new covenant, as we learn from the Epistle to the Hebrews,* is the Christian dispensation ; and if Christ is its author, the Jehovah of the Old Testament and Christ of the New are the same Divine person.

Equally striking is the celebrated prediction of Malachi, the last of the Jewish prophets : " Behold, I will send my messenger, and he shall prepare the way before me ; and the Lord, whom ye seek, shall suddenly come to his temple, even the messenger of the covenant whom ye delight in ; behold, he shall come, saith the Lord of hosts." Mal. iii. 1. Here the prophet describes the coming Messiah, not only as the messenger of the covenant, but also as the Lord and Owner of the Jewish temple ; and, consequently, as a Divine prince or governor—he shall " come to *his temple*." The Lord of any temple is the divinity to whose worship it is consecrated. The temple at Jerusalem, of which the prophet here speaks, was consecrated to the true and living God ; and we have therefore the express testimony of Malachi that the Christ, the Deliverer, whose coming he announced, was no other than the Jehovah of the Old Testament.

This prophecy is expressly applied to Christ by St. Mark. " As it is written in the prophets, Behold, I send my messenger before thy face, which shall prepare thy way before thee." Mark i, 2. It follows from this that Jesus Christ is the Lord, the Lord of the temple, the messenger of the covenant mentioned in the prophecy. The appearing Jehovah of the Old Testament was the *King* of the Jews ; their temple was HIS, because he resided in it ; and he was the *messenger* of *their covenant*. But as all these characters are ascribed to Jesus Christ, the identity of the persons cannot be mistaken. One coincidence is singularly striking. It has been proved that the Angel Jehovah had his residence in the Jewish tabernacle and temple, and that he took possession of both at their dedication, suddenly filling them with his glory. On one occasion Jesus himself, though in his state of humiliation, came

* Heb. viii, 8–13.

in public procession to the temple at Jerusalem, and called it *his own ;* thus at once declaring that he was the ancient and rightful Lord of the temple, and appropriating to himself this eminent prophecy.

It would be easy to multiply quotations in which the name Jehovah and other Divine titles are applied to the Messiah; and to show, moreover, that these very passages are applied, in the New Testament, to our Lord Jesus Christ. We will, however, notice only two others. The first is Isaiah xl, 3 : "The voice of him that crieth in the wilderness, Prepare ye the way of the LORD, (JEHOVAH,) make straight in the desert a highway for our GOD." This prediction is applied, in the Christian Scriptures, to John the Baptist, as the harbinger of Christ; and it is, therefore, evident that our Lord is the person whom the prophet calls JEHOVAH and "*our* GOD."

The other passage is 1 Cor. x, 9 : "Neither let us tempt Christ, as some of them (that is, the Jews in the wilderness) also tempted, and were destroyed of serpents." The pronoun *αυτὸν, him,* must be understood after "tempted," as referring to Christ just before mentioned. The Jews in the wilderness are here said to have tempted some person; and to understand by that person any other than Christ, who is just before mentioned, is against all grammar, which never allows, without absolute necessity, any other accusative to be understood with the verb than that of some person or thing previously mentioned in the same sentence. The conjunction *και, also,* establishes this interpretation beyond a doubt. Neither let us tempt CHRIST as some of them ALSO tempted—tempted whom? The obvious answer is, *Christ.* If, therefore, the Israelites tempted Christ in the wilderness he is the Jehovah of the Old Testament.

It has now been established that the Angel Jehovah and Jesus Christ our Lord are the same person; and this is the first great argument by which his divinity is proved. He not only existed before his incarnation, but is seen at the head of the religious institutions of his Church up to the earliest ages. In every manifestation of himself he has given evidence that he "thought it not robbery to be equal with God." No name is given to the Angel Jehovah which is not given to Jehovah Jesus. No attribute is ascribed to the one which is not ascribed to the other. The worship which was paid to the one by patriarchs and prophets was paid to the other by evangelists and apostles; and the Scriptures declare them to be the same august person, *the Redeeming Angel, the Redeeming Kinsman, and the Redeeming* GOD.

§ 3. *Divine Titles ascribed to Christ.*

The next argument in support of the divinity of Christ is drawn from the titles which are ascribed to him in the sacred volume. If they are such as can designate a Divine Being, and a Divine Being *only,* then is

Christ truly Divine. To deny this conclusion would be to charge the word of truth with direct deception, and that, too, in a fundamental article of religion. This is our argument, and we will proceed to the illustration. Our attention will be directed to only four of the Divine titles which are ascribed to our Lord. These are, *Jehovah, Lord, God,* and *King of Israel.*

1. JEHOVAH.—That this name is applied to the Messiah in many passages of the Old Testament is admitted even by our opponents. But Dr. Priestley attempts to destroy the force of the argument deduced from this fact, by alleging that "several things in the Scriptures are called by the name of Jehovah; as, Jerusalem is called Jehovah our righteousness."* It is, however, a miserable pretense to meet this argument by asserting that the name Jehovah is sometimes given to places. It is so, but only in composition with some other word; as Jehovah-Jire, Jehovah-Nissi, Jehovah-Shallum. Such names are used, not as descriptive of particular localities, but as *memorials* of events connected with them, which mark the interposition and character of Jehovah himself. Thus: "Jehovah-Jire," *the Lord will see* or *provide,* referred to HIS interposition to save Isaac, and probably to the *provision* of the sacrifice of Christ. Nor is it true that Jerusalem is called "Jehovah our righteousness." The parallel passage clearly shows that this is the name, not of Jerusalem, but of "THE BRANCH."† No instance can be given in which a created being is called Jehovah in the Scriptures, or was so called among the Jews. The peculiar sacredness attached to this name among them was a sufficient guard against such an application of it in their common language; and as for the Scriptures, they explicitly represent it as peculiar to divinity itself. "I am JEHOVAH, that is my name, and my glory will I *not* give to *another.*" Isa. xlii, 8. "Thou, whose NAME ALONE is JEHOVAH, art the Most High above all the earth." Psa. lxxxiii, 18.

We see, then, that this is the peculiar and appropriate name of God, that name by which he is distinguished from all other beings, and which imports perfections so exclusively belonging to the living and true God that it cannot, in truth, be applied to any other being. This name, however, is *solemnly* and *repeatedly* given to the *Messiah;* and, unless we can suppose Scripture to contradict itself, by making that a peculiar name of God which is not peculiar to him, and by establishing an inducement to that idolatry which it so sternly condemns, then this adorable name itself declares the absolute divinity of him who is invested with it.

2. LORD.—Our Lord's disciples not only applied to him those passages of the Old Testament in which the Messiah is called Jehovah, but they saluted and worshiped him by the title κυριος, LORD, which is of precisely the same original import. We admit that it is sometimes

* History of "Early Opinions."   † Jer. xxiii, 5, 6; xxxiii, 16.

used as the translation of other names of God, which import simply dominion, and that it is applied also to merely human masters and rulers; but, in its *highest sense*, it is universally allowed to belong to God. If in this *highest sense* it is applied to Christ, then are we to regard it as denoting true and absolute divinity.

The *first* proof of this is, that both in the Septuagint and by the writers of the New Testament, κύριος is the term by which the name Jehovah is translated. In all those passages, therefore, in which the Messiah is called by that peculiar title of divinity, we have the authority of the LXX for applying it in its full and highest signification to Jesus Christ, who is that Messiah. Accordingly, the New Testament writers apply this appellation to their Master when they quote these prophetic passages as fulfilled in him. They found it used in the Greek version of the Old Testament, in its *highest possible import*, as a rendering of Jehovah. Had they thought Jesus to be less than God, they could not have given him a title which would have misled their readers, unless they had intimated that they did not use it as a title of divinity, but in its lowest sense, as a term of merely human courtesy, or at most, of human dominion. But we have no such intimation; and, if they wrote under Divine inspiration, it follows that they used it as being fully equivalent to the title JEHOVAH itself, as their quotations will show.

St. Matthew quotes, and applies to Christ, Isaiah xl, 3 : "The voice of one crying in the wilderness, Prepare ye the way of the LORD, κυρίου." The other Evangelists make the same application of it, representing John as the herald of Jesus, the Jehovah of the prophet, and their κύριος, *Lord*. On this point St. Paul also adds his testimony, Romans x, 13 : "Whosoever shall call on the name of the LORD (κυρίου) shall be saved," which is quoted from Joel ii, 32 : "Whosoever shall call on the name of JEHOVAH shall be delivered."

But, *secondly*, even when the title κύριος, LORD, is not employed as the rendering of the name JEHOVAH, but is used as a common appellation of Christ, it is so connected with other terms, and with circumstances which clearly imply divinity, as to afford additional proof that the disciples themselves considered it as a Divine *title*, and intended that it should be so understood by others. It is put *absolutely*, and by way of *eminence*, "THE LORD." Christ is called by St. Luke "the LORD GOD;" and Thomas adoringly addresses him, "My LORD and my GOD." When κύριος is used to express dominion, that dominion is represented as *absolute* and *universal*, and therefore *Divine.* Hence Peter declares of Jesus Christ that "he is (κύριος) LORD of all." Acts x, 36.

3. GOD.—That this title is ascribed to Christ, even the adversaries of his divinity are obliged to confess. It is indeed said, that the term is sometimes used in an inferior sense; but this proves nothing against the Deity of Christ, for it must still be allowed that it is *generally* used in

Scripture to designate the Divine Being. The question is, therefore, limited to this: Is our Lord called *God* in the highest sense of that appellation?

Before we proceed to the examination of this question, it will be necessary to show that the term *God*, in its highest sense, involves the idea of absolute divinity. This has been denied by Sir Isaac Newton and Dr. Samuel Clarke, who considered it a *relative* term, importing nothing more than dominion. But if we trace the Scripture notion of what is *truly* and *properly* God, we shall find it made up of these several ideas: infinite wisdom, invincible power, immutability, all-sufficiency, and the like. These are the foundation of *dominion*, which is a secondary consideration; but it must be nothing less than dominion *supreme*, which will accord with the Scripture notion of *God*. It is not merely that of a *ruler*, a *governor*, a *lord*, or a *protector;* but a *Sovereign* Ruler, an *Omniscient* and *Omnipresent* Governor, an *Almighty* Lord, an eternal, immutable, and all-sufficient *Creator*, *Preserver*, and *Protector*. Whatever falls short of this is not *properly* God, in the Scripture import of that term, and cannot be so denominated, except by way of figure.

If *God* were merely a relative term, having reference to *subjects*, it would necessarily follow, either that some of those subjects had an eternal existence, or that there was a time when there was no God. We have, however, the express testimony of Divine truth, that it is not dominion *only*, but absolute divinity, that is designated by the term. Thus, "Before the mountains were brought forth, or ever thou hadst formed the earth or the world, even from everlasting to everlasting, thou art God." Psa. xc, 2. Here the term *God* is applied to that eternal Being who "formed the earth and the world." He is declared to be God "from everlasting," and consequently before any creature existed, and so before he had any *subjects*, or exercised any *dominion*.

The import of the term God, in its highest sense, being thus shown to include all the excellences and glories of the Divine nature, if in this sense it is ascribed to Christ, it will prove, not as Arians would have it, his *dominion* only, but his divinity. Nor will it set aside this conclusion to say, that men are sometimes called gods; for in the New Testament the term God is never applied in the singular to any man.

Let us then adduce a few passages of Scripture in which this appellation is applied to Jesus Christ. Matt. i, 23: "Behold, a virgin shall be with child, and shall bring forth a son, and they shall call his name Emmanuel, which being interpreted is, God with us."

John i, 1: "In the beginning was the Word, and the Word was with God, and the Word was God."

John xx, 28: "And Thomas answered and said unto him, My Lord and my God."

Romans ix, 5: "And of whom, as concerning the flesh, Christ came, who is over all, GOD blessed forever."

Titus ii, 13: "Looking for that blessed hope, and the glorious appearing of the great GOD and our Saviour Jesus Christ."

Hebrews i, 8: "But unto the Son he saith, Thy throne, O GOD, is for ever and ever."

1 John v, 20. "And we are in him that is true, even in his Son Jesus Christ. This is the true GOD, and eternal life."

4. KING OF ISRAEL.—This title has an allusion to Christ's pre-existence, and to his sovereignty over Israel under the law. It has been already established that the "*Jehovah*," "the *Holy One of Israel*," "the *Lord of hosts*," "the *King of the Jews*" of the Old Testament, is not the Father, but another Divine person, who, in the New Testament, is affirmed to be *Jesus Christ*. This being the view of the sacred writers of the evangelical dispensation, it is evident that they could not use the appellation "KING OF ISRAEL" in a lower sense than that in which it stands in the Old Testament, and it is equally evident that the Jews understood it to imply divinity.

Nathanael, upon a satisfactory proof of Christ's Messiahship, exclaimed, "Thou art the Son of God, thou art the KING OF ISRAEL." John i, 49. While our Saviour hung upon the cross, the chief priests, the scribes, and the elders said, "If he be the KING OF ISRAEL, let him now come down from the cross, and we will believe in him." Matt. xxvii, 42.

§ 4. *Divine Attributes are ascribed to Christ.*

Having considered the import of some of the titles applied to our Lord in the Scriptures, and having proved that they imply divinity, we may next consider the *attributes* which are ascribed to him. If, to names and lofty titles which imply divinity, we find added attributes never given to creatures, and from which all creatures are excluded, the Deity of Christ will be established beyond reasonable controversy. No argument can be more conclusive than this. Of the essence of Deity we know nothing, but that he is a Spirit. He is made known to us by his attributes, and it is from them we learn that there is an *essential* distinction between him and his creatures. He has attributes which they have not, and those which they have in common with him he possesses in an absolutely perfect degree. From this it follows, that HIS is a *peculiar* nature, a nature *sui generis*, to which no creature can possibly approximate. Should, then, these same attributes be found ascribed to Christ as explicitly and literally as to the Father, it will follow of necessity that, the attributes being the same, the essence must be the same, and that this essence is the exclusive nature of the θεοτης, or Godhead.

Of the peculiar attributes of Deity which are ascribed to Jesus Christ we may notice,

1. ETERNITY.—Isaiah calls him "The mighty God, the *Everlasting Father*, the Prince of Peace." Isa. ix, 6. The phrase "Everlasting Father" is variously rendered by the best orthodox critics; but every rendering is consistent with the application of a positive eternity to the Messiah, of whom this is evidently a prediction. Christ declares of himself, "I am THE FIRST and THE LAST;" and again, "I am Alpha and Omega, the beginning and the ending, saith the Lord, which is, and which was, and which is to come, the Almighty." Rev. i, 8, 17. Now, it is by these very terms that the eternity of God is declared. "Before me there was no God formed, neither shall there be after me." Isa. xliii, 10. "I am the first, and I am the last; and besides me there is no God." Isa. xliv, 6. These titles clearly indicate that the Being to whom they properly belong had no beginning, and will have no end; and as they are explicitly and absolutely claimed by Christ, they are proofs of his eternity.

2. OMNIPRESENCE.—Our Lord declares himself to be, at the same time, both in heaven and upon the earth; which is surely a property of divinity alone. "No man hath ascended up to heaven, but he that came down from heaven, even the Son of man which is in heaven." John iii, 13. Again, "Where two or three are gathered together in my name, *there am I in the midst of them.*" Matt. xviii, 20.

How futile is the Socinian comment on this text, that this promise is to be "limited to the apostolic age!" Were that even granted, what would the concession avail? In that age the disciples met in the name of their Lord many times in the week and in many parts of the world at the same time. He, therefore, who could be "in the midst of them," whenever and wherever they assembled, must be *omnipresent*. The text is as literal a declaration of Christ's presence everywhere with his true worshipers, as that similar promise of Jehovah to the Israelites: "In all places where I record my name, I will come unto thee, and I will bless thee." Exod. xx, 24. At the very moment, too, of Christ's ascension, and when, as to his bodily presence, he was about to leave his disciples, he promised still to be with them, calling their attention to this promise by an emphatic exclamation: "Lo, I AM WITH YOU ALWAY, even to the end of the world." Matt. xxviii, 20.

3. OMNISCIENCE.—This is an attribute which cannot be ascribed to a creature; for though it may be difficult to say how far the knowledge of the highest order of intelligent creatures may be extended, yet there are two kinds of knowledge which God solemnly and exclusively claims as peculiar to himself. The *first* is a perfect knowledge of the thoughts and purposes of the human heart. "I the Lord search the heart, I try the reins." Jer. xvii, 10. "Thou, even thou only, knowest the hearts of all the children of men." 1 Kings viii, 39. This knowledge is

attributed to our Lord, and claimed by him; not, however, as a supernatural *gift*, but as an original attribute.   Hence St. John declares that "HE KNEW ALL MEN, and needed not that any should testify of man; for HE KNEW WHAT WAS IN MAN." John ii, 24, 25.   After his exaltation he claimed this prerogative, in the full style and majesty of the Old Testament Jehovah.   "And all the Churches shall know that *I am he which* SEARCHETH THE REINS AND HEARTS." Rev. ii, 23.

The *second* kind of knowledge, to which reference has been made, is the knowledge of *futurity;* which is so peculiar to Deity that God distinguishes himself from all the false divinities of the heathen by this circumstance alone.   "I am God, and there is none else; I am God, and there is none like me; declaring the end from the beginning, and from ancient times the things that are not yet done." Isa. xlvi, 9, 10.   This kind of knowledge is also ascribed to Christ.   All the predictions which he uttered are in proof that he possessed this attribute; for they are nowhere referred to *inspiration*, the source to which all the prophets and apostles ascribed their prophetic gifts, but resulted from his own prescience.   He "*knew from the beginning* who they were that believed not, and who should betray him." John vi, 64.

4. OMNIPOTENCE.—This also is peculiar to the Godhead; for, though power may be communicated to a creature, yet a finite capacity must limit the communication; nor can it exist in an infinite degree any more than wisdom, except in an infinite nature.   Christ claims "all power in heaven and in earth;" and in Rev. i, 8, he is expressly styled "THE ALMIGHTY."   To the Jews he said, "What things soever he [the Father] doeth, THESE ALSO DOETH THE SON LIKEWISE." John v, 19.

Thus we have seen that the Scriptures ascribe to our Lord Jesus Christ *Eternity*, *Omnipresence*, *Omniscience*, and *Omnipotence*—attributes which prove him to be "The true God;" and we may now close the argument with his own remarkable declaration: "ALL THINGS which the Father hath ARE MINE." John xvi, 15.   If the Son possess all things that belong to the Father, then he possesses all the attributes and perfections of the Father, and must necessarily be of the same nature, substance, and Godhead.

§ 5. *Divine Works are ascribed to Christ.*

This argument is confirmatory of the foregoing; for if acts have been done by Christ which, in the nature of things, cannot be performed by any creature, however exalted, then must he be truly God.   That such works are ascribed to him in the Holy Scriptures, we will now proceed to show.

1. CREATION.—The Socinians themselves acknowledge that the production of things out of nothing is possible only to Divine power; and they, therefore, attempt to prove that the creation of which Christ is

said to be the author, is a *moral* creation. To correct this error it is only necessary to exhibit two or three passages of Scripture which evidently ascribe to him the whole physical creation. St. John affirms, in the introduction of his Gospel, that "all things [without limitation or restriction] were made by" the Divine Word; and that "without him was not *anything* made that was made." If he had reference to a *moral*, and not a *physical* creation, he could not have expressed himself in this manner without intending to mislead: a supposition which is equally contrary to his piety and to his inspiration. His meaning must, therefore, be, that there is no created object which had not Christ for its creator.

But the apostle shows most clearly that the physical creation was the work of Christ, by asserting that "THE WORLD WAS MADE BY HIM;" that world into which he came as "the light;" that world *in* which he was when he was made flesh; that *world* which "knew him not." It matters nothing to the argument whether "the world" be understood of men or of the material world. On either supposition "the world was made by him," and the creation was, therefore, *physical.* In neither case could the creation be a *moral* one, for the *material* world is incapable of a moral renewal; and the world which "knew not" Christ, if understood of *men*, was not renewed by a moral creation, but was unregenerate.

Another passage, equally explicit in ascribing to Christ the physical creation, is found in Heb. i, 2: "By whom also HE MADE THE WORLDS." "God," says the apostle, "hath in these last days spoken unto us by his SON, whom he hath appointed heir of all things;" and he then proceeds to give *farther* information in regard to the nature and dignity of the personage thus denominated the "SON" and "HEIR." In order to prove him greater than angels, who are the greatest of all created beings, the apostle declares that "by him also God made the worlds." That the term "worlds" is here to be understood of the material universe, is evident from Heb. xi, 3: "Through faith we understand that the WORLDS were framed by the word of God, so that things which are seen were not made of things which do appear:" words which can only be understood of the physical creation.

Another consideration which fixes the meaning of the clause, "by whom also he made the worlds," is, that in the same chapter the apostle reiterates the doctrine of the creation of the world by Jesus Christ. "But unto THE SON he saith," not only, "Thy throne, O God, is for ever and ever;" but also, "Thou, Lord, [Jehovah,] in the beginning hast laid the foundation of the earth; and·the heavens are the works of thine hands." This language is, beyond all controversy, addressed to Christ, and will forever attach to him, on the authority of inspiration, the title of "*Jehovah*," and array him in all the majesty of creative power and glory.

The only additional passage which it is necessary to adduce, in order to show that Christ is the creator of all things, and that the creation of which he is the author is not a *moral* but a *physical* creation; not the framing of the Christian dispensation, but the forming of the whole universe of creatures out of nothing, is Colossians i, 16, 17: "For by him were all things CREATED, that are in heaven, and that are in earth, visible and invisible, whether they be thrones, or dominions, or principalities, or powers; all things were created BY him and FOR him; and he is BEFORE all things." The terms here employed are an abundant refutation of the notion, that the creation mentioned is to be understood in a *moral* sense. The objects created are " all things in heaven and in earth;" and lest immaterial beings should be thought to be excluded, the apostle adds, "visible and invisible." And, lest things *invisible* should be understood of *inferior* angels only, to the exclusion of those of the higher orders, the apostle becomes still more particular, and adds, " whether they be thrones, or dominions, or principalities, or powers;" terms by which the Jews expressed the different orders of angels, and which are thus employed in the Scriptures.* The passage shows, moreover, that in the creation of all things Jesus Christ was both the *efficient* and the *final* cause, and not merely the *instrumental* cause, working by and for another. " All things were created BY him and FOR him."

2. PRESERVATION.—The sacred Scriptures declare that Jesus Christ is the preserver of all things as well as their creator, for " by him all things CONSIST," ($\sigma\upsilon\nu\varepsilon\sigma\tau\eta\kappa\varepsilon$, *sunesteke*,) are kept together, or preserved from falling into confusion or annihilation. This is surely a Divine work; nor could it be said, consistent with reason and piety, that the universe is sustained by a created being. The same doctrine is taught in Heb. i, 3, where Christ is spoken of as " *upholding all things* by the word of his power." Τὰ πάντα (*ta panta*) signifies the universe, which the Son of God bears up, or sustains, by his almighty word. If, then, to preserve the created universe is the work of JEHOVAH, as the Scriptures declare,† and if this work is ascribed to our Lord, there can remain no doubt whatever that he also is JEHOVAH.

3. THE FORGIVENESS OF SINS.—This is unquestionably one of the peculiar acts of God. In the manifest reason of the thing, no one can forgive but the party offended; and, as sin is the transgression of the law of God, he alone is the offended party, and, therefore, he only can forgive. *Mediately* others may *declare* his pardoning acts, or the conditions on which he proposes to forgive; but *authoritatively*, there can be no actual forgiveness of sins but by God himself.

But Christ forgives sins by his own authority, and therefore he is God. One single passage will prove this. " He said to the sick of the palsy, Son, be of good cheer, *thy sins be forgiven thee.*" Matt. ix, 2.

* See Eph. i, 21; Col. ii, 10. † Neh. ix, 6; Psa. xxxvi, 6.

The scribes understood that he did this *authoritatively*, and that he thereby assumed a Divine prerogative. They, therefore, said among themselves, "This man blasphemeth." What then was the conduct of our Lord on that occasion? Did he admit that he only ministerially *declared*, in consequence of some revelation, that God had forgiven the sins of the paralytic? On the contrary, he performed a miracle to prove that the very right which they disputed was vested in him. "That ye may KNOW that the Son of man hath power on earth to forgive sins, then saith he to the sick of the palsy, Arise, take up thy bed, and go unto thine house." Matt. ix, 6.

4. THE RAISING OF THE DEAD.—It will be acknowledged by all, that to raise the dead is a Divine work. He only who first framed the human body, and connected with it a living spirit, can restore that body again to life, and bring back the soul from the invisible world to its original abode. It is "God who quickeneth the dead." Rom. iv, 17. But this power is claimed by Jesus Christ: "As the Father raiseth up the dead, and quickeneth them; even so the Son quickeneth whom he will." John v, 21. Here Christ explicitly assumes equal power with the Father, and the same uncontrolled and sovereign exercise of it in the restoration of life. This power was exerted by our Lord, while he sojourned upon the earth, in raising to life the daughter of Jairus, the widow's son, Lazarus, and others; but it will be more gloriously displayed at the end of time, in restoring to life the millions of the human race who shall then be sleeping in the dust. "The hour is coming, in which all that are in the graves shall hear his voice, and shall come forth." John v, 28, 29.

It may be objected that this work is not a decisive proof of divinity, because the dead were raised by some of the prophets and by the apostles of our Lord. To this it is only necessary to reply, that the prophets raised the dead *in the name* of the God of Israel, and the apostles *in the name* of Jesus Christ; but he performed this miracle of power in his own name, and spoke of himself in terms which no prophet or apostle would have dared to employ: "I am the resurrection and the life; he that believeth in me, though he were dead, yet shall he live." John xi, 25.

5. THE FINAL JUDGMENT IS ASCRIBED TO CHRIST.—The Scriptures declare that "the *Lord* (JEHOVAH) is our Judge," and that "every one of us shall give account of himself to *God;*" but they declare also, that "we must all appear before the judgment-seat of *Christ;*" that "before him shall be gathered all nations;" and that "he shall separate one from another, as a shepherd divideth his sheep from the goats."* To him who will pronounce the final sentence omniscience is necessary as well as omnipotence to execute it; for it will proceed not merely upon the external actions of men, but upon their motives and their

---

* See Isa. xxxiii, 22; Rom. xiv, 12; 2 Cor. v, 10; Matt. xxv, 32.

thoughts, which are known to him alone who searches the heart. Christ will indeed act in concurrence with the Father, who is hence said to judge the world by him; but this high office necessarily supposes him to be truly God.

§ 6. *Divine Worship is paid to Christ.*

It will be our business in this section, *first*, to establish the fact that Jesus Christ is the object of worship; and *secondly*, to consider the bearing which this fact has upon the doctrine of his Supreme Divinity.

1. CHRIST IS THE OBJECT OF WORSHIP.—Of this fact there are numerous proofs in the sacred Scriptures, a few of which we will notice.

(1.) *He was worshiped by his disciples prior to his ascension to heaven.*—"When he was come down from the mountain, great multitudes followed him; and behold, there came a leper and WORSHIPED HIM, saying, Lord, if thou wilt, thou canst make me clean." Matt. viii, 1, 2. When Jesus said to the man whom he had previously cured of blindness, "Dost thou believe on the Son of God? he answered and said, Who is he, Lord, that I might believe on him? And Jesus said unto him, Thou hast both seen him, and it is he that talketh with thee. And he said, Lord, I believe; and he WORSHIPED HIM." John ix, 35–38. He worshiped Christ, be it observed, under the character, "Son of God," a title which the Jews regarded as implying actual divinity. The worship paid by this man must, therefore, in its intention, have been supreme, for it was offered to a person who was acknowledged to be Divine, "the Son of God." Again, when the disciples, fully yielding to the demonstration of our Lord's Messiahship, arising out of a series of splendid miracles, recognized him *also* under his personal character, "they WORSHIPED HIM, saying, Of a truth thou art the Son of God." Matt. xiv, 33.

It is admitted that the word προσκυνέω, (*proskuneo*,) *to worship*, is sometimes used to express that lowly reverence with which, in the East, it has been always customary to salute persons of rank, and especially rulers and sovereigns; but it is frequently used to express also the worship of the Supreme Jehovah. Whether, then, it denotes an act of civil respect or of Divine adoration, the circumstances of the case must determine.

Our Lord could not have received the worship which was paid to him in the character of a civil governor. He had cautiously avoided the least intimation that he had any civil pretensions, or that his object was to make himself a king; and, therefore, to have suffered himself to be saluted with the homage proper to civil governors would have been a marked inconsistency. Nor could he have received it in compliance with the custom of the Jewish Rabbins, who exacted great external reverence from their disciples, for he sharply reproved their haughtiness, and their love of adulation and honor. The circumstances, then, which accompany these instances make it evident that the worship which the disciples paid to Christ was of the highest order—they *worshiped him as* GOD.

(2.) *Christ was worshiped by his disciples subsequent to his resurrection and ascension.*—When "he was parted from them, and carried up into heaven, they WORSHIPED HIM." Luke xxiv, 51, 52. Here the act must necessarily have been one of Divine adoration, since it was performed *after* "he was parted from them," and, therefore, it cannot be resolved into the customary token of *personal* respect paid to superiors, which was always exhibited in their *presence.*

When the apostles were assembled to fill the place of Judas, the lots being prepared " they prayed, and said, Thou, Lord, which knowest the hearts of all men, show whether of these two thou hast chosen." Acts i, 24. That this prayer was addressed to Christ is clear, from its being his special prerogative to choose his own apostles. They are, therefore, styled "apostles," not of the Father, but "of Jesus Christ." Here, then, is a direct act of worship, because it is an act of prayer, and our Lord is addressed as one who knows " the hearts of all men."

When Stephen, the protomartyr, was stoned, he prayed, "LORD JESUS, RECEIVE MY SPIRIT;" and again, "LORD, LAY NOT THIS SIN TO THEIR CHARGE." Acts vii, 59, 60. In the former petition he acknowledges Christ to be the disposer of the eternal states of men; in the latter, he acknowledges him to be the governor and judge of men, having power to remit, pass by, or visit their sins. These are so manifestly Divine acts that Stephen must have prayed to Christ, believing him to be truly GOD.

St. Paul, in that affliction which he metaphorically describes by " a thorn in the flesh," " besought the Lord thrice, that it might depart from " him; and the answer shows that " *the Lord* " to whom he addressed his prayer was CHRIST; for he adds, " And he said unto me, My grace is sufficient for thee: for my strength is made perfect in weakness. Most gladly therefore will I rather glory in my infirmities, that the POWER OF CHRIST may rest upon me." 2 Cor. xii, 7–9. The invoking of Christ was not only practiced by the apostle himself, as several passages show ;* but is adduced by him as a distinctive characteristic of Christians, so that among all the primitive Churches this practice must have been universal. " Unto the Church of God which is at Corinth, with all that IN EVERY PLACE CALL UPON THE NAME OF JESUS CHRIST our Lord." 1 Cor. i, 2.

To these instances are to be added all the *doxologies* to Christ, in common with the Father and the Holy Spirit, and all the *benedictions* made in his *name* in common with theirs, for all these are forms of wor-

* See 2 Thes. ii, 16, 17 ; 2 Tim. iv, 22.

ship. The first consist of ascriptions of equal and Divine honors, with grateful recognitions of the Being addressed as the author of benefits received. The following may be given as a few out of many instances: " But grow in grace, and in the knowledge of our Lord and Saviour Jesus Christ. To him be GLORY, both now and for ever. Amen." 2 Pet. iii, 18. " Unto him that loved us, and washed us from our sins in his own blood, and hath made us kings and priests unto God and his Father, to him be GLORY and DOMINION for ever and ever. Amen." Rev. i, 5, 6. When we consider the serious and reverential manner in which these doxologies are introduced, and the superlative praise which they convey, so far surpassing what humanity can deserve, we must suppose that the Being to whom they refer is really Divine. The ascription of eternal glory and everlasting dominion, if addressed to any creature, however exalted, would be idolatrous and profane.

Benedictions are blessings solemnly pronounced upon persons in the name of God, and were derived from the practice of the Jewish priests, and the still older patriarchs, who blessed others in the name of Jehovah, as his representatives. These are so regular in their form as to make it clearly appear that the apostles constantly *blessed* the people *ministerially* in the name of Christ as one of the blessed Trinity. " Grace to you, and peace from God our Father, and the Lord Jesus Christ." Rom. i, 7. " The grace of the Lord Jesus Christ, and the love of God, and the communion of the Holy Ghost, be with you all." 2 Cor. xiii, 14.

In answer to the Socinian perversion, that these are mere " wishes," or " expressions of good-will," it may be observed that this objection overlooks, or notices very slightly, the main point on which the whole question turns, the *nature* of the blessings sought, and consequently, the *qualities* which they imply in the Person who is desired to bestow them. The blessings sought are *grace, mercy,* and *peace;* which are the highest gifts that Omnipotent Benevolence can bestow, or a dependent nature receive. To desire such blessings, either in the mode of direct address, or in that of precatory wish, from any being who is not possessed of omnipotent goodness, would be absurd, and sinful in the highest degree.

(3.) *The worship of Christ is practiced among heavenly beings.*— " When he bringeth in the first-begotten into the world, he saith, And let ALL THE ANGELS OF GOD WORSHIP HIM." Heb. i, 6. The Apocalypse, in its scenic representations, exhibits Christ as, equally with the Father, the object of the worship of angels and glorified saints ; placing every creature in the universe, except the inhabitants of hell, in prostrate adoration at his feet. "And every creature which is in heaven and on the earth, and under the earth, and such as are in the sea, and all that are in them, heard I saying, Blessing, and honor, and glory, and power, be unto him that sitteth upon the throne, AND UNTO THE LAMB forever and ever." Rev. v, 13. Having now established the fact, that Jesus Christ is the object of *worship*, we will proceed to consider,

2. The bearing which this fact has upon the doctrine of his Supreme Divinity.—To perceive this clearly, we should first inquire into the religious principles and practice of the early disciples of our Lord. As to their religious principles, they were Jews; and Jews, too, of an age in which their nation had shaken off its idolatrous propensities, and which was distinguished by its zeal against all worship or religious trust of which any creature was the object. The great principle of the law was, "Thou shalt have no other gods before (or *beside*) me."* It was, therefore, commanded by Moses, "Thou shalt fear the Lord thy God, and *him* shalt thou serve;"† which words are quoted by our Lord in his temptation, when solicited to worship Satan, so as to prove that to *fear* God and to *serve* him are expressions which signify *worship*, and that all other beings but God are excluded from it. "Thou shalt worship the Lord thy God, and him *only* shalt thou serve." Luke iv, 8. Accordingly, we find the apostles teaching and practicing this as a first principle of their religion.

St. Paul charges the heathen with not *glorifying* God when they *knew* him, and with worshiping and serving "the *creature* more than (or *besides*) the Creator." Rom. i, 25. Again, when he mentions it as one of the crimes of the Galatians, previous to their conversion to Christianity, that they "did service unto them which by *nature* are no gods," he plainly intimates that no one has a title to religious *service* but he who is by *nature* God; and if so, he himself could not have worshiped Christ had he not believed him to be truly Divine.

The *practice* of the apostles was in strict accordance with this principle. Thus, when worship was offered to Peter by Cornelius, who certainly did not take him to be God, he forbade it. So also Paul and Barnabas prevented the people at Lystra from offering to them religious honors with expressions of horror. An eminent instance is recorded, also, of the exclusion of all creatures, however exalted, from the honor of religious worship, in Rev. xix, 10, where the angel refused to receive so much as even the outward act of adoration. His language is, " See thou do it not: *worship God*," clearly intimating thereby that all acts of religious worship are to be appropriated to God alone.

From the known and avowed religious sentiments, then, of the apostles, both as Jews and as Christians, as well as from their practice, it follows that they could not have paid religious worship to Christ, a fact which has already been established, unless they had considered him as a Divine person, and themselves as bound on that account, according to his own words, to *honor the* Son, *even as they honored the* Father. It is the testimony of St. Paul that he, " being in the form of God, thought it not robbery to be equal with God,"—a passage which inci-

* Exod. xx, 4.   † Deut. x, 20.

dentally teaches the Godhead of Christ, and which cannot be reconciled to any hypothesis that excludes his essential Deity.

Arians devised the doctrine of *supreme* and *inferior* worship, and a similar distinction was maintained by Dr. Samuel Clarke, to reconcile the worship of Christ with his semi-Arianism. The same sophistical distinction is resorted to by Roman Catholics to vindicate the worship of angels, the Virgin Mary, and departed saints. But it is a sufficient refutation of this theory,

(1.) *That it has no countenance in the Sacred Scriptures.*—We often read of prayer; but there is not a word respecting absolute and relative, supreme and inferior prayer. We are commanded to pray fervently and incessantly, but never to pray sovereignly or absolutely. Nor have we any rules left us about raising or lowering our intentions, in proportion to the dignity of the object.

(2.) *That the Scriptures are directly opposed to it.*—Sacrifice was a mode of worship required under the law, and was doubtless not more solemn in its character than the exercise of prayer; but it is said, "He that sacrificeth unto any god, save unto the Lord only, he shall be utterly destroyed." Exod. xxii, 20. Now suppose any person, considering that this law referred only to absolute and sovereign sacrifice to God, had sacrificed to other gods, and had been convicted of it before the judges. His apology for the act must have run thus: "I did, indeed, sacrifice to other gods, but it was not absolute or supreme sacrifice, which is all that the law forbids. I considered the gods to whom I sacrificed as inferior beings, and I offered them, therefore, only a relative and inferior service; reserving all sovereign sacrifice to the Supreme God of Israel." But is it likely that such an apology would have saved him from the penalty of the law? If it would not, which we think is evident, then the law appropriated all sacrifice to God.

Such being the case with respect to sacrificial worship, we may ask, What is there so peculiar in invocation and adoration that they should not be governed by the same law? Why should not absolute and relative prayer and prostration appear as absurd as absolute and relative sacrifice? They are, like the other, acts of religious worship, and are appropriated to God in the same manner, by the same laws, and upon the same grounds and reasons. We are not at liberty to fix what signification we please to the acts of religious worship, making them high or low at discretion; for God himself has determined their signification to be supreme by claiming to be their only lawful object. It follows, therefore, that we can never use them in any other sense without being guilty of profaneness or idolatry.

14

CHAPTER V.

THE SONSHIP OF CHRIST.

THAT the title "SON OF GOD" is applied to Jesus Christ is not denied. His disciples, occasionally before and frequently after his resurrection, gave him this appellation, and he assumed it himself. The question, therefore, is, In what sense is this title to be understood? In answering this question we will, *first*, notice several false theories that have been adopted respecting the Sonship of Christ; *secondly*, adduce the testimony of Scripture in support of the doctrine that the title "Son of God" is a designation of his Divine nature; and, *thirdly*, make some remarks on the importance of maintaining the orthodox view upon this subject.

I. WE ARE TO NOTICE SEVERAL FALSE THEORIES THAT HAVE BEEN ADOPTED RESPECTING THE SONSHIP OF CHRIST.

1. Various attempts have been made to restrict the title "Son of God" to the mere humanity of our Saviour, and to rest its application upon his *miraculous conception*. It is true that this opinion is held by some who hesitate not to acknowledge that Jesus Christ is a Divine person; but, by denying his Deity as "THE SON OF GOD," they both depart from the faith of the early Christian Church, and give up to Socinians the whole argument for the divinity of Christ, which is founded upon that eminent appellation.

Those who think that it was assumed by Christ, and given to him by his disciples because of his miraculous conception, are obviously in error. Our Lord, when he adopted the appellation, never urged his miraculous birth as a proof of his Sonship; but when he called God his Father, he grounded the proof of his claim upon the *miracles* which he performed. The Jews clearly conceived that, in making this profession of Sonship with reference to God, he assumed a Divine character, and made himself "*equal with God*." They, therefore, took up stones to stone him.

Nor did the disciples themselves give him this title with reference to his conception by the Holy Ghost. Certain it is, that Nathanael did not know the circumstances of his birth, for he was announced to him by Philip as Jesus of *Nazareth*, "the *Son* of *Joseph;*" and he, therefore, asked, "Can any good thing come out of *Nazareth?*" He did not know but that Jesus was the son of Joseph; he knew nothing of his being born in Bethlehem; and yet he confessed him to be "THE SON OF GOD" and "the KING OF ISRAEL."

It may also be observed that in the celebrated confession of Peter,

"Thou art the Christ, the Son of the living God," there is no reference at all to our Lord's miraculous conception. Nor did this form any part of the ground on which he confessed "the *Son of Man*" to be the "Son of God;" for our Lord replied, "Flesh and blood hath not revealed this unto thee, but my Father which is in heaven." Peter had, therefore, been taught the doctrine of the Sonship of Christ by a special revelation from God the Father, an unnecessary thing, certainly, if the miraculous conception had been the only ground of that Sonship; for the evidence of that fact might have been collected from Christ and his virgin mother.

2. This ground, therefore, not being tenable, it has been urged that "Son of God" was simply an appellation of Messiah, and is, consequently, an *official*, and not a *personal* designation. Against this, however, the evangelic history affords decisive proof.

That the Messiah was the Jehovah of the Old Testament has been shown in a former chapter; and this is to be regarded as the faith of the ancient Jewish Church. But it is certain that at the period of our Lord's advent the great body of the Jews had given up the Divine character of the Messiah, and held the opinion that he was to be a *temporal monarch.* The true doctrine was retained only among the faithful few, as Simeon, who expressly ascribed divinity to the Messiah, and Nathanael, who connected "Son of God" and "King of Israel" together, one the designation of the Divine *nature*, the other of the *office* of the Messiah.

Three things are therefore clear, from the writings of the Evangelists : 1. That the Jews recognized the existence of such a being as the "Son of God." 2. That they regarded it blasphemy for any created being to claim this designation. 3. That for a person to profess to be the Messiah simply was not considered blasphemy, and did not exasperate the Jews. Our Lord certainly professed to be the Messiah; many of the Jews also, at different times, believed on him *as such;* and yet these same Jews were not only offended, but took up stones to stone him as a blasphemer when he declared himself to be the "Son of God." We cannot, therefore, account for the use of this title among the Jews of our Lord's time, whether by his disciples or his enemies, by considering it as synonymous with Messiah. The Jews regarded the former as *necessarily* involving a claim to divinity, but not the latter; and the disciples did not conceive that they fully confessed their Master by calling him the Messiah without adding to it his higher designation. "Thou art Christ," said Peter; but he immediately added, "The Son of the Living God." So Nathanael, under the influence of a recent proof of his omniscience, and, consequently, of his divinity, salutes him, first, as the "Son of God," and then as Messiah, "the King of Israel."

We conclude, therefore, that the title "Son of God," as it is applied to Jesus Christ, is a *personal* designation and not one of office; that it was *essential* in him to be a Son, and only *accidental* that he was the Messiah; that he was the first by *nature*, the second by *appointment;* and that, in constant association with the name *Son*, as given to him alone, and in a sense which shuts out all creatures, however exalted, are found ideas and circumstances of full and absolute divinity.

3. Another opinion is, that the title "*Son of God*" is applied to Christ because God raised him from the dead. Those who adopt this theory rest it mainly on a passage in the second Psalm: "The Lord hath said unto me, Thou art my Son; this day have I begotten thee." They suppose that the *day* spoken of in the text is the day of Christ's resurrection, and interpret his being "begotten" of the Father as denoting the act of raising him from the dead, thus making his resurrection the ground of his Sonship.

From apostolic authority we know that the "*Son*" here represented as speaking is Christ, for to him this passage is explicitly applied at least twice in the New Testament.* But he is so frequently called the Son, when there is no reference to his resurrection, that this cannot be the ground of that relation. This point, however, may be settled by the following considerations:

(1.) It is clearly indicated in the Scriptures that Christ raised himself from the dead by his own power. He explicitly declared, when speaking of his *life*, "I have power to lay it down, and I have power to take it again." John x, 18. Accordingly he said to the Jews, "Destroy this temple, and in three days *I will raise it up*." John ii, 19. Hence it would follow, if the preceding interpretation were true, that our Lord begat himself, and is therefore his own son, which is absurd.

(2.) He was declared from heaven to be the beloved Son of the Father at his very entrance upon his public ministry, and, consequently, before his resurrection. "And lo, a voice from heaven, saying, This is my beloved *Son*, in whom I am well pleased." Matt. iii, 17.

(3.) St. Paul tells us (Rom. i, 4) that the resurrection of Christ was the DECLARATION of his Sonship, and not the ground of it— "DECLARED to be the Son of God with power, by the resurrection from the dead." This was, therefore, the declaration of an *antecedent* Sonship.

(4.) The titles and honors ascribed in this Psalm to the extraordinary person who is the chief subject of it far transcend what the Scriptures ascribe to any mere creature. He is the Lord's *Anointed*, the *King of Zion*, and the rightful *Sovereign of the nations*. Accordingly, kings and judges of the earth are exhorted to "kiss the Son;" and all are pronounced blessed who "*put their trust in him*." This is surely an unequivocal declaration of divinity; for it is written, "Cursed be the man that trusteth in man and maketh flesh his arm." Jer. xvii, 5.

* See Acts xiii, 33; Heb. i, 5.

(5.) It is also to be noted that St. Paul employs the very passage under consideration to prove that Christ is superior to angels: "For unto which of the angels said he at any time, Thou art my Son, this day have I begotten thee?" Heb. i, 5. The force of this argument lies in the expression "begotten," importing that the person addressed is the Son of God, not by creation, but by generation. Christ's pre-eminence over the angels is here stated to consist in this, that whereas they were *created*, he was *begotten;* and the apostle's reasoning would be fallacious if the expression did not intimate a proper and peculiar filiation. The argument shows, therefore, that the title Son, which is given to the Messiah in this Psalm, implies real divinity.

Having noticed and refuted some of the false theories respecting the Sonship of Christ, we will now proceed,

II. To adduce the testimony of Scripture in support of the doctrine that the title "Son of God" is a designation of his Divine Nature.

We will direct our attention,

1. *To a few passages in the Old Testament in which a Divine Son is spoken of.*—We have seen that the term *Son*, in the second Psalm, is applied to Jesus Christ, and that it denotes real divinity. To this we may add Prov. viii, 22, in which Solomon introduces, not the personified, but the *personal* wisdom of God, under the same relation of a Son, and in that relation ascribes to him Divine attributes. "The Lord possessed me in the beginning of his way, before his works of old. I was set up (appointed) from everlasting, from the beginning, or ever the world was. When there were no depths I was brought forth," or *born*. Here, from a consideration of the excellence of wisdom in the abstract, there is an easy transition to that of its infinite Source; and hence the inspired writer proceeds to delineate a Divine Being, who is portrayed in colors of such splendor and majesty as can be attributed to no other than the eternal Son of God.

To say of wisdom, as an attribute, that God possessed it in the beginning of his way, is certainly too trifling an observation to be attributed to the wise monarch of Israel. In what way can it be predicated of a quality that it was set up or appointed from everlasting? But every attribute which is here ascribed to wisdom is strictly applicable to the divine *Logos*, who "was in the beginning with God," and in whom "dwelleth all the fullness of the Godhead bodily."

The eternal Sonship of Jesus Christ is most unequivocally expressed in the prophecy of Micah: "But thou, Bethlehem Ephratah, though thou be little among the thousands of Judah, yet out of thee shall he come forth unto me that is to be Ruler in Israel; whose goings forth have been from of old, from everlasting;" or, as it is in the margin, "from the days of eternity." Micah v, 2. There is here ascribed to the person spoken of a twofold birth or going forth. By a natural birth he was to come forth from Bethlehem of Judah; but by another and higher birth he had been "from the days of eternity."*

This passage is so signal a description of Christ, the eternal Son of God, who assumed our nature and was born in Bethlehem, that it evidently belongs to him, and to no other being; and it is so decidedly indicative of that peculiar notion of his divinity, which is marked by the term and the relation of Son, that Socinians have resorted to the utmost violence of criticism to escape its powerful evidence. Dr. Priestley says "that it may be understood concerning the promises of God, in which the coming of Christ was signified to mankind from the beginning of the world."

To this we reply that the word which is rendered "goings forth" never signifies the work of God in predicting future events, but is often used to express natural birth and origin. It is unquestionably so used in the preceding clause, and cannot be taken in a different sense in that which immediately follows, and especially when a clear antithesis is marked and intended. He was born in time, but was not, on that account, merely human; for though born in Bethlehem, his "goings forth," his production, his heavenly birth or generation, was from *everlasting.*

Others refer the phrase, "his goings forth," to the purpose of God that Christ should come into the world; but this is too absurd to need refutation. It would be mere trifling solemnly to affirm of the Messiah what is just as true of every other man born into the world. This passage is, therefore, an irrefutable proof of the faith of the ancient Jewish Church, both in the divinity and the Divine Sonship of the Messiah.

The same relation of Son, in the full view of Supreme Divinity, and where no reference appears to be had to the office and work of the Messiah, is found in Prov. xxx, 4: "Who hath ascended up into heaven, or descended? who hath gathered the wind in his fists? who hath bound the waters in a garment? who hath established all the ends of the earth? what is his name, and what is his son's name, if thou canst tell?" Here the Deity is contemplated, not in his redeeming acts, but in his works of creation and providence, managing at will and ruling the operations of nature; and yet, even in these peculiar offices of divinity alone, he is spoken of as having a Son, whose "name," that is, according to the Hebrew idiom, whose *nature* is as *deep, mysterious,* and *unutterable* as *his own.* "What is His name, and what is his Son's name; canst thou tell?"

It was thus that the Scriptures of the Old Testament furnished the Jews with the idea of a personal Son in the Divine nature. They were

---

* The word רָצָא, YATZA, *to come forth,* is frequently used in reference to *birth,* or *generation,* as in Gen. xvii, 6; 2 Kings xx, 18; and so the Jews understood it, when they replied to the inquiry of Herod in regard to the place where Christ should be born, by quoting this very passage. According to a common Hebraism in order to denote *eminency,* the word for birth, which is rendered "goings forth," is used in its plural form.

not only acquainted with the phrase "Son of God," but in a good degree they understood its true import. Nor is it any objection to this, that among their ancient writers it was sometimes applied to the Messiah. It is granted that the Messiah is the Son of God; but that the phrase *Son of God* ceases, on that account, to be a personal designation, or that it imports the same as *Messiah*, is what we deny. David was the son of Jesse and the king of Israel. He, therefore, who was king of Israel was the son of Jesse; but the latter is the *personal*, the former only the *official* description. The latter marks his origin and family; for before he was king of Israel he was the son of Jesse. In like manner "Son of God" marks the *natural* relation of the Messiah to God, and the term *Messiah* his *official* relation to men. This relation to God subsists not in the human, but in the *higher* nature of the Messiah; and this higher nature being proved to be Divine, it follows that the phrase "Son of God," as applied to Jesus Christ, is a title of absolute divinity, importing his participation in the very nature and essence of God.

2. *The same ideas of a* Divine Sonship *are suggested by almost every passage in which the phrase occurs in the New Testament.*—When Jesus was baptized "the heavens were opened unto him, and he saw the Spirit of God descending like a dove, and lighting upon him; and lo, a voice from heaven, saying, This is my beloved Son, in whom I am well pleased." Matt. iii, 16, 17. The circumstances of this testimony are of the most solemn and impressive kind, and there can be no rational doubt but that they were designed authoritatively to invest our Lord with the title "Son of God" in its fullest sense—rendered stronger and more emphatic by the epithet "*beloved*," and by the declaration that in him the Father was "*well pleased.*" It is evident that the title was applied to him on grounds independent of the circumstances of his *birth*, or of his *official relation* to men; and that he was in a higher *nature* than his human, and for a higher reason than an *official* one "the Son of God." Accordingly, as soon as John the Baptist had heard the testimony of the Father respecting our Lord, and had seen the descent of the Holy Spirit upon him, he declared him to be "the Son of God."

To the transaction at his baptism our Lord himself adverts in John v, 37: "And the Father himself, which hath sent me, hath borne witness of me." He had just adverted to the evidence of his divinity arising from his miraculous works, and, in addition to this, he introduces that distinct personal testimony of the Father which was given at his baptism. Now, the witness of the Father on that occasion is that Christ is his "*beloved* Son;" and it is remarkable that our Lord introduces this testimony of the Father at a time when his claim to be the Son of God was a matter of dispute with the Jews. They denied that God was his Father in the high sense in which he was obviously to be understood; and "they sought to kill him, because he had said that

God was his Father, *making himself equal with God*." What then, in this case, was the conduct of our Lord? He reaffirmed his Sonship even in this very objectionable sense, claiming the power to perform the works of God, to raise the dead, and to exercise all judgment, and the right to be honored of all men, "even as they honor the Father."[*]

The epithet "ONLY BEGOTTEN," which several times occurs in the New Testament, affords further proof of the Sonship of Christ in his Divine nature. One of these instances *only* need be selected: "The Word was made flesh, and dwelt among us, and we beheld his glory, the glory as of the ONLY BEGOTTEN of the Father, full of grace and truth." John i, 14. If the term "only begotten" referred to Christ's miraculous conception, then the glory "as of the only-begotten" must be a glory of the human nature of Christ only, for that alone was capable of being thus conceived. This, however, is clearly contrary to the scope of the passage, which does not speak of the glory of that nature which the Word assumed, but of the glory of the WORD HIMSELF, who is here said to be the "only-begotten of the Father." It is, therefore, the glory of his Divine nature that is here intended.

It is also clear that the miraculous conception of Christ could not constitute him a Son, except as it consisted in the immediate formation of his manhood by the power of God; but, in this respect, he was not the "*only-begotten*," not the *only Son*, because Adam was thus also immediately produced, and for this very reason is called by St. Luke "the son of God." The note in the Socinian version tells us, "that this expression," only-begotten, "does not refer to any particular mode of derivation or existence; but is used to express merely a higher degree of *affection*, and is applied to Isaac, though Abraham had other sons." Isaac, however, was so called because he was the only child which Abraham had by his wife Sarah; and this instance is therefore against the Socinian theory. It would be easy to show that μονογενης, *only-begotten*, does not anywhere import the affection of a parent, but the peculiar relation of an *only son*, and as this peculiarity does not apply to the production of the mere humanity of our Lord, the first man being in this sense, and for this very reason, a "son of God," the epithet must be applied to his Divine nature, in which alone he is at once *naturally* and *exclusively* "the SON OF THE LIVING GOD."

Those passages which declare that "all things were made by" the SON,[†] and that "God *sent* his Son into the world,"[‡] may be considered as declarations of a Divine Sonship. The former imply that the CREATOR was a SON at the very period of creation, and the latter, that he was the SON OF GOD before he was *sent* into the world; and thus both will prove that this relation is independent of his incarnation, or of his official appointment as Messiah.

---

[*] See John v, 18–29.　　　　　[†] See John i, 3; Col. i, 16; Heb. i, 2.
[‡] See John iii, 17; Gal. iv, 4: 1 John iv, 9, 10, 14.

The only plausible objection to this is, that a person may be said to perform actions under a title which he subsequently receives. Thus we ascribe the "*Principia*" to *Sir* Isaac Newton, though that work was written before he received the honor of knighthood. Accordingly, we are told by those who allow the divinity of Christ, while they deny his Divine Sonship, that the sacred writers ascribed creation and other Divine acts to the Son merely by an interchange of appellations between his human and his Divine nature; meaning thereby, that they were done by that same Divine Person who, in consequence of his incarnation and miraculous conception, became the Son of God. Thus it is said that "the Lord of glory" was crucified, and that God purchased the Church "with his *own blood*." So, also, in familiar style, we speak of the divinity of Jesus, and of the Godhead of the Son of Mary.

To this our reply is, that though an interchange of appellations is acknowledged, yet even this supposes that some of them are designations of our Lord's Divine nature, while others describe the nature which he assumed. But the simple circumstance of such an interchange will no more prove the title Son of God to be a human designation than it will prove Son of Mary to be a *Divine* one. If "Son of God" does not relate to the divinity of our Lord, then, as God, he has no distinctive name in all the Scriptures. The title "God" does not distinguish him from the other persons of the Trinity, and the term "word" stands in precisely the same predicament as "Son;" for the same kind of criticism may reduce it to merely an *official* appellative.

But the notion that the title "Son of God" is an appellation of the human nature of our Lord, and that it is applied to him in his Divine character merely by a customary interchange of designations, is an assumption which cannot be proved; while all those passages which connect the title "*Son,*" immediately and by way of eminence, with his divinity, remain wholly unaccounted for on this theory, and are therefore contrary to it. It is evident, that in direct relation to his Divine nature, and without reference to any other circumstance, he claimed God as his Father. When he said to the Jews, "My Father worketh hitherto and I work," they understood him to assert that in this high sense "God was his Father, [πατερα ιδιον, his own proper Father,] making himself equal with God." John v, 17, 18. And when our Lord said, "I and my Father are one," the "Jews took up stones to stone him," saying, "For a good work we stone thee not, but for blasphemy; and because thou, being a man, makest thyself God." John x, 31–33.

His unequivocal answer to the direct question of the Jewish council, when he was on his trial before them, is also in point here. "Then said they all, Art thou then the Son of God? And he said unto them, Ye say that I am." Luke xxii, 70. The obvious meaning of our Lord's reply is, *I am that,* or *what ye say ;* thus declaring that, in the very sense in which they put the question, he was the Son of God. But in confessing himself to be in that sense the SON, he did more than claim to be the Messiah, for the counsel judged him to be guilty of blasphemy, and therefore worthy of death; a charge which could not lie against any one, by the Jewish law, for professing to be the Messiah. His blasphemy was alleged to consist in his making himself "THE SON OF GOD," which was, in their view, an assumption of positive divinity; and the conduct of our Lord shows that they did not mistake his intention, for he suffered them to proceed against him without lowering his claims or correcting their opinion.

The whole argument of the apostle in the first chapter of Hebrews is designed to prove that our Lord is superior to angels, and he adduces, as conclusive evidence on this point, that to none of the angels did God ever say, "Thou art my SON, this day have I begotten thee." He argues, therefore, on this very ground of *Sonship* that Christ is superior to angels; that is, superior in *nature* and in *natural relation* to God; for in no other way is the argument conclusive. He has his title SON by way of INHERITANCE; that is, by *natural* and *hereditary* right. "He hath by *inheritance* obtained a more excellent name than they;" that is, by his being OF the Father, and therefore by virtue of his Divine filiation. Angels may be, in an inferior sense, the sons of God by *creation;* but they *cannot inherit* that title for this plain reason, that they are *created,* not *begotten;* while our Lord inherits "the more excellent name" because he is *begotten,* not *created.* "For, unto which of the angels said he at any time, Thou art my SON, this day have I BEGOTTEN thee?" The same ideas of absolute divinity connect themselves with this title throughout the chapter. "The SON," by whom "God hath in these last days spoken unto us," is "the brightness of his glory and the express image of his person;" but it is only to the Divine nature of our Lord that these expressions can refer.

As in none of these passages the title "Son of God" can possibly be considered as a designation of his human nature or office, so we find proof of equal force that it is used even by way of *opposition* and *contradistinction* to the inferior nature. Thus St. Paul says of the "Son Jesus Christ" that he "was made of the seed of David according to the flesh; and declared to be the Son of God with power, according to the Spirit of holiness, by the resurrection from the dead." Rom. i, 3, 4. A very few remarks will be sufficient to point out the force of this passage. The apostle is speaking not of what Christ is officially, but of what he is personally and essentially, for the truth of all his official claims depends upon the truth of his personal ones. If he is a Divine person he is everything else that he assumes to be. He is, therefore, considered by the apostle in his twofold nature. As a man he was "of the seed of David according to the flesh;" but in a superior nature he was "declared to be the Son of God." That an opposition is expressed between what Christ is "according to the flesh," and what he is according to a higher nature, must be allowed, or else there is no force in the apostle's observation; and it must be equally clear that the nature put in *opposition* to Christ's fleshly nature can be no other than his Divine nature, which the apostle calls "the SON OF GOD."

We also learn, from Romans viii, 3, that God sent "his own Son in the likeness of sinful flesh." The person who is here entitled the SON was sent "in the likeness of sinful flesh;" but in what other way could he have been sent if he were *Son* only as a *man?* It is, therefore, most clearly intimated that he was a SON before he was sent, and that FLESH was the nature which the Son *assumed*, but not the nature in which he was "the Son of God."

With the same idea of the absolute divinity of the SON, as distinguished from his humanity, the apostle applies that lofty passage from the forty-fifth psalm. "But unto the Son he saith, Thy throne, O God, is for ever and ever." Heb. i, 8. It is allowed by all who hold the Deity of Christ that he is here addressed as a being composed of two natures, Divine and human. As man, he is anointed " with the oil of gladness," and elevated above his "fellows;" while the stability of his throne, and the unsullied justice of his government, declare his GODHEAD. He is, however, called the SON; but this term could not characterize the being here introduced, unless it agreed with his higher and Divine nature. The SON is addressed—that Son is addressed as GOD, and as God whose throne is *for ever and ever*.

Thus we think it fully established, that the title "SON OF GOD" is not given to Christ on account of his miraculous conception; that it is not an appellative of his human nature, occasionally applied to him by metonymy, when Divine acts and relations are spoken of, as any other human title might be applied; that it is not ascribed to him simply because of his assuming our nature, as is supposed by some who admit the divinity of our Lord but deny his eternal filiation; and that the use of the title cannot be fully explained by any *office* with which he is invested, or any *event* in his mediatorial undertaking. It follows, therefore, that it is a title characteristic of his mode of existence in the Divine essence, and of the relation which exists between the first and the second person in the ever blessed Trinity.

It only remains for us now,

III. TO MAKE SOME REMARKS ON THE IMPORTANCE OF MAINTAINING THE ORTHODOX VIEW RESPECTING THE SONSHIP OF JESUS CHRIST.

It is granted that some divines, truly decided on the question of our Lord's divinity, have rejected the Divine Sonship; but in this they have gone contrary to the judgment of the Church of Christ in all ages, and would certainly have been ranked among heretics in her earliest and purest times. This consideration alone is worthy of attention, and ought to induce caution; but there are many considerations to show that points of great moment are involved in the denial or maintenance of the doctrine in question. A few of these we will present in the following remarks:

1. The loose and general manner in which many passages of Scripture, which speak of Christ as a Son, must be explained by those who deny the Divine filiation of Christ, seems to sanction principles of interpretation which would be highly dangerous, or rather absolutely fatal, if generally applied to the Scriptures.

2. The denial of the Divine Sonship destroys all *relation* among the persons of the Godhead. No other relation of the Divine persons is mentioned in Scripture except those which are expressed by *paternity*, *filiation*, and *procession*. If these *natural* relations are removed, we must then conceive of the *persons* in the Godhead as perfectly independent of each other, a view which is incompatible with the *unity* of the Divine *essence*.

3. It is the doctrine of the Divine paternity only which preserves the Scripture idea that the Father is the *fountain* of deity, and as such, the *first*, the *original*, the *principle*. He must have read the Scriptures to little purpose who does not perceive that this is their constant doctrine—that " OF him are all things ;" that though the Son is Creator, yet BY the Son the Father made the worlds, and that " as the Father hath life in himself, so hath he given to the Son to HAVE LIFE IN HIMSELF," which can only refer to his Divine nature, nothing being the source of life in itself but what is *Divine*. But where the essential paternity of the Father and the correlative filiation of the Son are denied, these Scriptural representations have no foundation in fact, and are incapable of interpretation.

4. The perfect EQUALITY of the Son with the Father, and, at the same time, the SUBORDINATION of the Son to the Father, are to be equally maintained only by the doctrine of the Divine Sonship. Deny this, and the Son might as well be the *first* as the *second* person in the Godhead, and the *second* as well as the first. The Father might have been *sent* by the Son without incongruity, or either of them by the Holy Spirit. These are most absurd and repulsive conclusions, which the doctrine of the Sonship avoids, and thus proves its accordance with the Holy Scriptures.

5. A denial of the Divine filiation of Christ is derogatory to the *love* of the Father in the gift of his Son. It insensibly runs into the Socinian heresy, and restricts the Father's love to the gift of a *mere man*, if the Sonship of Christ is only *human ;* and in that case, the permission of the sufferings of Christ was no greater manifestation of God's love to the world than if he had permitted any other good man to die for the benefit of his fellow-creatures.

CHAPTER VI.

THE PERSON OF CHRIST.

In the present day the controversy respecting the person of Christ is almost wholly confined to the question of his divinity; but in the early ages of the Church it was necessary to establish his proper humanity. The denial of this seems to have existed as early as the time of St. John, who, in his epistles, excludes from the pale of the Church all who denied that "Christ is come in THE FLESH." As his Gospel, therefore, proclaims his Godhead, so his epistles defend also the doctrine of his humanity.

As the Divine nature of Christ has been fully established, it is only necessary in this chapter to prove his true humanity, and to show that the two natures, the human and the Divine, are united in *one person*. But before we proceed to the discussion of these points it will be proper for us to notice, very briefly,

I. A FEW OF THE LEADING ERRORS WHICH HAVE BEEN MORE OR LESS DISSEMINATED IN THE CHURCH RESPECTING THE PERSON OF CHRIST.— These have related both to his human and his Divine nature.

1. *Errors in regard to the human nature of our Lord.*—The *Gnostics* denied the real existence of the *body* of Christ. The things which the Scriptures attribute to his human nature they did not deny, but affirmed that they took place in appearance only. The source of this error appears to have been a philosophical one. Both in the Oriental and Greek schools it was a favorite notion, that whatever was joined to *matter* was necessarily contaminated by it; and that the highest perfection of this life was abstraction from material things, and in another, a total and final separation from the body.

While the Gnostics denied the real existence of the *body* of Christ, the *Apollinarians* maintained that his body was endowed with a sensitive and not with a rational soul, and that the Divine nature supplied the place of the intellectual principle in man. Thus both these views denied to Christ a proper humanity, and both were, accordingly, condemned by the general Church.

Even among those who held the union of the Divine and the human nature in Christ, which in theological language is called the *hypostatical* or *personal* union, several distinctions were also made which led to a diversity of opinion. The *Nestorians* acknowledged two *persons* in our Lord, mystically and more closely united than any human analogy can explain. The Monophysites contended for one person and one nature, the two being supposed to be, in some mysterious manner, confounded. The Monothelites two natures and one will.

2. *Errors respecting the Divine Nature of Christ.*—Among the various errors of this class, which formerly sprung up in the Church, three only can be said to have much influence in the present day, Arianism, Sabellianism, and Socinianism. The two former are now almost entirely merged into the last, whose characteristic tenet is the simple humanity of Christ. Arius, who gave his name to the first, seems to have wrought some of the floating errors of previous times into a kind of system, which, however, underwent various modifications among his followers. The distinguishing tenet of this system was that Christ was the first and most exalted of creatures ; that he was produced in a peculiar manner, and endowed with great perfections ; that by him God made the worlds ; that he alone proceeded immediately from God, while other things were produced mediately by him ; and that all things were put under his administration.

The semi-Arians divided from the Arians, but still differed from the orthodox in refusing to admit that the Son was ὁμοούσιος, or of the *same substance* with the Father ; but they acknowledged him to be ὁμοιούσιος, or of a *like* substance with the Father. It was only in appearance, however, that they came nearer to the truth than the Arians themselves, for they contended that this *likeness* to the Father in essence was not by *nature*, but by peculiar privilege. In their system, therefore, Christ was but a creature.

A still further refinement on this doctrine was advocated by Dr. Samuel Clarke. His theory was that there is one Supreme Being who is the Father, and two subordinate, derived, and dependent beings. But he objected to call Christ a creature, thinking him something between a created and a self-existent nature. This hypothesis, however, still implies, unless an evident absurdity be admitted, that Christ is a created being.

The *Sabellian* doctrine stands equally opposed to Trinitarianism and to the Arian system. It asserts the divinity of the Son and the Holy Spirit against the latter, and denies the personality of both in opposition to the former. Sabellius taught that the Father, Son, and Holy Ghost are only denominations of one hypostasis ; in other words, that there is but one person in the Godhead, and that the Son and the Holy Spirit are virtues, emanations, or functions only ; that under the Old Testament God delivered the law as Father ; under the New dwelt among men, or was incarnate as the Son ; and descended on the apostles as the Holy Spirit. In the early ages they were often called *Patripassians*, because their scheme, by denying a real Sonship, obliged them to acknowledge that it was the Father who suffered for the sins of men.

On the refutation of these errors it is not now necessary to dwell, both because they have at present but little influence, and chiefly because both are involved in the Socinian question, and are decided by the establishment of the scriptural doctrine of a Trinity of Divine persons in the Unity of the Godhead. If Jesus Christ is the Divine Son of God; if he was "sent" from God and "returned" to God; if he distinguished himself from the Father both in his Divine and human nature, saying, as to the former, "I and my Father are ONE," and as to the latter, "My Father is GREATER than I;" if there is any meaning at all in his declaration, that "no man knoweth the Son but the Father, neither knoweth any man the Father save the Son," words which cannot, by any possibility, be spoken of *official* distinction, or of an *emanation* or *operation;* then all these passages prove a real personality, and are incapable of being explained by a *modal* one. This is the answer to the Sabellian opinion; and as to the Arian hypothesis, it falls, with Socinianism, before that series of proofs which has already been adduced from the Scriptures to establish the eternity of our Lord, his consubstantiality and coequality with the Father, and, consequently, his Supreme Divinity. But,

II. WE ARE TO PROVE THAT OUR LORD WAS TRULY MAN AS WELL AS GOD.

That he assumed *humanity*, in the full and proper sense of that term, is, we think, abundantly evident from the following considerations:

1. *The prophets who predicted the coming of the Messiah often spoke of him as a Man.* Hence he is represented as being the seed of the woman;* the seed of Abraham;† a prophet like unto Moses;‡ and "the son of David."§

2. *He is called a* MAN, *and the* SON OF MAN, *in a multitude of instances.*—He is designated by the latter appellation no less than seventy-one times in the sacred Scriptures. In sixty-seven of these instances the title is employed by our Lord *himself*, once by *Daniel*, once by *St. Stephen*, and twice by *St. John*. It must surely be acknowledged that in giving this appellation to himself he disclosed his true character, and that he was therefore, in reality, what he called himself, *the Son of Man*. When spoken of as a man he is ascribed with just such characteristics as belong to other men, those only excepted which involve error or sin. He is exhibited as meek, lowly, and dutiful to his parents; as hungering, thirsting, and being weary; as sustained and refreshed by food, drink, and sleep; as the subject of temptations, infirmities, and afflictions; as weeping with tenderness and sorrow; and, in general, as having all the innocent characteristics of our nature.

3. *The history of the birth, life, and death of our Lord is unanswerable proof that he was really Man.*—He was born, he lived, and he died essentially in the same manner as other men. He "increased in wisdom

* Gen. iii, 15. † Gen. xxii, 18. ‡ Deut. xviii, 15. § Matt. xxii, 42.

and stature;" wrought with his hands; ate, drank, slept; suffered on the cross; gave up the ghost, and was buried, as other men.

4. *The humanity of Christ is argued at large and proved by St. Paul in the second chapter of Hebrews.*—In the passage containing this argument are the following declarations: "Forasmuch then as the children are partakers of flesh and blood, he also himself likewise took part of the same;" and again, "in all things it behooved him to be made like unto his brethren." That Christ had a human body cannot be denied. It is equally undeniable that to increase in wisdom, to be sorrowful, to be tempted, to be obedient to parents, together with many other things of a similar nature, cannot be attributed either to *God* or to *a mere human body*, but are appropriate characteristics of *the human soul*. Christ, therefore, possessed a human *soul* as well as a human body, and was perfectly *man;* or, as it is very properly expressed in the Shorter Catechism, he "became man by taking to himself a true body and a reasonable soul."

While we maintain the integrity of Christ's human nature, we admit that he assumed it with all its *innocent infirmities*. He was not subject to any of the *sinful* infirmities of man, nor was there any stimulus or incentive to sin in the constitution or temperament of his body. The Scriptures declare that he was "without sin;" that "in him is no sin;" and that, though he came "in the likeness of sinful flesh," he was "holy, harmless, undefiled," and "separate from sinners." Nor does it appear that he was subject to any of those bodily diseases which are the portion of man. Infirmities of this kind would have discommoded him in the discharge of his duty, and he was exempted from them on account of his personal purity. But he was subject to hunger and thirst, to cold and heat, to pain of body arising from external injuries, and to distress of mind, from various causes. Against all such annoyances he might have been defended by the order of Omnipotence; but this would not have accorded with the design of his mission. He submitted to our infirmities that he might acquire an experimental knowledge of our sufferings, both corporeal and mental, and that we might be more fully assured of his sympathy. "We have not a high priest which cannot be touched with the feeling of our infirmities; but was in all points tempted like as we are." Heb. iv, 15.

III. WE ARE TO SHOW THAT THE HUMAN AND THE DIVINE NATURE OF OUR LORD ARE UNITED IN ONE PERSON.

The true sense of Scripture appears to have been very accurately expressed by the Council of Chalcedon, in the fifth century, that in Christ there is *one person*, in the unity of person *two natures*, the Divine and the human; and that there is no change, or mixture, or confusion of these two natures, but that each retains its own distinguishing properties. With this agrees the Athanasian Creed; and the Church of England professes, in her second article, that "The Son, which is beauty. A combination of earth, water, and the gases of the atmosphere forms the strength and majesty of the oak, and the grace, beauty, and odor of the rose; and from the principle of *evaporation* are formed clouds which drop fatness upon the earth, dews which refresh the languid fields, and springs and rivers which cause the valleys to rejoice through which they flow.

(3.) *That in the works of God there is an endless variety of equally perfect operations.*—" O Lord, how manifold are thy works!" All the three kingdoms of nature pour forth the riches of *variety*. It is seen in the varied forms of crystalization and composition in *minerals;* in the colors, forms, and qualities of *vegetables;* and in the kinds, properties, and habits of *animals*. No two things are exactly alike, even when of the same kind. Plants of the same species, and the leaves and flowers of the same plant, have all their varieties. Animals of the same kind have their individual character. The wisdom of this appears more strongly marked when we consider that important ends often depend upon it. The *resemblance* of various natural things in greater or less degree becomes the means of acquiring a knowledge of them with greater ease, because it is made the basis of their arrangement into kinds and sorts, without which the human memory would fail and the understanding be confused.

But a *difference* in things is as important as their resemblance. I domestic animals did not differ individually, no property could be claimed in them, nor when lost could they be recovered. The countenance, the voice, and the manner of every man differ from all the rest of his species. This is not only an illustration of the resources of creative power and wisdom, but of design and intention, to secure a practical end. Parents, children, and friends could not otherwise be distinguished, nor the criminal from the innocent. No felon could be identified by his accusers, and courts of judgment would not only be obstructed, but often rendered of no avail for the protection of life and property.

To variety of kind and form we may add that of *magnitude*. In the works of God we have the extremes of minuteness and magnificence, and those extremes filled up in perfect gradation from the one to the other. We adore the mighty sweep of that power which scooped the bed of the fathomless ocean, moulded the mountains, and filled space with innumerable worlds; but the same hand formed the animalcule which requires the strongest magnifying power of optical instruments to make it visible. The workmanship, however, is as complete in the smallest as in the most massive object. But we may add,

(4.) *That the connection and dependence of the works of God are as wonderful as their variety.*—Every created object fills its place, not by accident, but by design. The meanest weed that grows stands in intimate connection with the mighty universe. It depends upon the atmosphere for moisture, which atmosphere supposes an ocean, clouds, winds, and gravitation. It depends upon the sun for its color, and for its required degree of temperature; and this supposes the revolution of the earth, and the adjustment of the whole planetary system.

We have, however, the highest manifestation of the Divine Wisdom,

3. In the Plan of Human Redemption.

It is in this that God "hath abounded toward us in all *wisdom* and prudence." Herein does the perfection of his wisdom shine forth, in his reconciling the exercise of mercy with the claims of justice, and in his doing this by such an expedient as is perfectly consistent with the ends of his moral government. There is Divine wisdom reflected even from the cross of Christ. His ignominious death was no doubt intended by his enemies, to defeat the benevolent purpose for which he came into the world; but in the wisdom of God it was made the means by which he triumphed over men and devils, overturning the powers of darkness, and filling heaven and earth with wonder and joy.

§ 9. *The Truth of God.*

By the *Truth* of God we understand his perfect and undeviating *veracity* in all his communications to mankind. When we speak of him as the *True God*, we mean to distinguish him from the imaginary gods of the heathen, and to ascribe to him supreme divinity. But when we say that he is a *God of Truth*, our design is, not directly to assert his divinity, but to declare his veracity. We virtually say, that all his communications to us are in exact accordance with the real nature of things; and that there is the utmost sincerity in all his declarations, and faithfulness in all his promises and purposes. This attribute of God may be proved,

1. From the Sacred Scriptures.

To this it may be objected, that it is absurd to bring God's own declarations to evince his truth, since this is to take for granted the very doctrine to be proved and to reason in a circle. We acknowledge this objection to be a specious one, but contend that it is unsound. It must be granted, that the mere declaration on the part of any being that *he is sincere*, furnishes, by itself, no evidence of his sincerity; for we know that insincere persons will as readily claim sincerity as those who are sincere. But the uniform agreement of a man's declarations *with facts* is justly regarded by his fellow-men as a satisfactory proof of his sincerity and truthfulness. In the same manner God may evince his veracity by his own declarations, and this he has done in the Scriptures, as may easily be shown.

(1.) *God has declared himself to be a God of Truth.*—"For the word of the Lord is right, and all his works are done in *truth*." Psa. xxxiii, 4. "My covenant will I not break, nor alter the thing that is gone out of my lips." Psa. lxxxix, 34.　"The *truth* of the Lord endureth forever." Psa. cxvii, 2.　"God is not a man, that he should lie; neither the Son of man, that he should repent.　Hath he said, and shall he not do it? or hath he spoken, and shall he not make it good?" Num. xxiii, 19. "It was impossible for God to lie." Heb. vi, 18.　These passages are adduced, not to *prove* the veracity of God, but to show that he *claims* to be a God of truth.

(2.) *The declarations of God are all in strict agreement with the facts professedly declared.*—The history which the Scriptures contain is, even at this day, capable of being satisfactorily examined as to its accordance with facts.　Some parts of it are, indeed, beyond the reach of a direct examination; but, as almost all of it can be thus examined, and can at any time be proved to be true, the truth of the rest cannot reasonably be called in question.　In these declarations we have as convincing evidence of the truth of God, as we can have of the veracity of men from the agreement of their declarations with the real state of things.

(3.) *God has uttered numerous predictions which have been exactly fulfilled.*—In this manner he has not only proved his omniscience, but also his truth; especially in the exact accomplishment of such predictions as appeared, at the time when they were uttered, altogether unlikely to be fulfilled.　Such were those which related to the advent, the character, and the mediation of the Messiah.　Such, also, were those which respected his dispensations to the Jewish Church and nation, and the establishment and progress of Christianity.　Of the fulfillment of these and other similar predictions no explanation can be given which will not firmly establish the truth of God.

(4.) *God has verified both his promises and his threatenings in regard to men.*—So far as he has promised blessing to them in this life, or threatened them with punishments, he has not failed, in the course of his providence, to bestow those blessings and to inflict those punishments.　In this, therefore, we have another strong scriptural argument in support of the Divine veracity.　But the truth of God may be argued,

2. FROM HIS OTHER PERFECTIONS.

If he possesses in himself all power, wisdom, justice, holiness, and goodness, he must be at an infinite distance from all those influences which lead men to practice deceit and falsehood.　Men sometimes speak what is not agreeable to truth from ignorance, or misconception of the subject of discourse; but with God there can be no such defect. He knows perfectly the nature of all things, with all their various relations; and, therefore, he cannot be deceived or err in judgment. "God is light, and in him is no darkness at all." 1 John i, 5.

The declarations of men may be made rashly, without a foresight of consequences, or they may not be distinctly remembered; and, therefore, they are not always, nor with full confidence, to be received and depended on. But the perfect knowledge and wisdom of God, which must, under all circumstances, be the same, infallibly secure him from precipitancy, instability, and forgetfulness. Men may violate their engagements for the want of ability to fulfill them; but the omnipotence of God precludes every idea of difficulty where his word is concerned. Men may be disposed to deceive one another, or violate their promises through malevolence of nature, or from selfish motives; but "the Holy One of Israel," being self-existent, and perfectly independent, cannot be liable to such temptations. The veracity of God may be inferred,

3. FROM HIS HAVING IMPLANTED IN MAN A DISPOSITION TO ESTEEM TRUTH AND DESPISE FALSEHOOD.

This respect for truth and contempt for falsehood are irresistible, from two causes: *First*, they are the necessary dictates of the understanding, and are perfectly independent of any feeling or influence on the heart. Knaves, as truly and irresistibly as honest men, despise knavery and falsehood; and no other dictate of the understanding was ever found or can ever exist among men. But, *secondly*, truth is known to be absolutely necessary to the *happiness* of mankind, and invariably productive of it; and falsehood utterly inconsistent with our happiness, and invariably productive of misery. We see, then, in this great practical lesson that men are compelled to respect truth, without a possibility of its being otherwise, and to despise deceit and falsehood.

It is unreasonable to suppose that God, as a perfectly independent being, would impress on the mind of his creatures any character which is not in strict accordance with his own. But if the necessary dictates of the human understanding, in regard to truth and falsehood, are in accordance with the character of God, he must be a God of truth. Moreover, as God has so constituted us that we are compelled to esteem truth and to despise falsehood; and as he has commanded us to "love him with all the heart, and with all the understanding, and with all the soul," it follows, as a necessary consequence, that he is a God of absolute veracity; for if he were not we could not love him at all, much less as he requires. But the veracity of God is proved,

4. FROM THE CONSEQUENCES WHICH WOULD FOLLOW A DENIAL OF IT.

If no confidence could be placed in God, none could be placed in any other being. Every thought, purpose, interest, and hope would be afloat on the waves of a boundless and perpetually disturbed ocean, where rest and safety could never be found. Suspicion and jealousy would make all men strangers and enemies to one another. Suspense would fill every mind, and hang, as a dark cloud, over every enjoyment. Truth would be known, if known at all, only as a thing unattainable;

and, wandering in endless doubt and perplexity, we should close our comfortless existence without being able to tell whence we had come, or whither we were going. A Divine revelation would afford no satisfaction; because, amid the subversion of all evidence, it would be impossible to ascertain that it had proceeded from the Author of our being. But if even this point could be settled, that would not prove its statements to be worthy of credit.

It is by the *truth of God* that this restless and stormy ocean is hushed to peace. All men know, or may know, that the purposes, the declarations, and the promises of God are immutable; and that he can neither deceive their confidence nor disappoint their reasonable hopes. However fluctuating and uncertain the state of things may be with respect to creatures, the soul rests on God with perfect reliance and final safety.

It only remains to be observed that the truth of God, when we consider it in its relation to the accomplishment of his predictions, his promises, or his threatenings, is denominated FAITHFULNESS. In this God manifests his veracity by declaring beforehand what his subsequent conduct will be; and afterward, by acting according to his previous declarations. The *truth* and the *faithfulness* of God are, then, in reality the same moral perfection, only viewed under different circumstances; nor can we conceive of his possessing the one and not the other. There is, therefore, no reason for making them separate subjects of examination.

§ 10. *The Justice of God.*

The *Justice* of God is defined by Dr. Ryland to be, " the ardent inclination of his will to prescribe equal laws as the Supreme Governor, and to dispense equal rewards and punishments as the Supreme Judge." It is that attribute by which God actively manifests his approbation of what is good, and disapprobation of what is evil. It is, therefore, the same in essence with his *holiness.* So far as God *takes pleasure* in what is good, he is called *holy ;* so far as he *exhibits* this pleasure, in his actual procedure in the government of the world, he is called *just.* The term *holiness,* accordingly, refers rather to the internal disposition of God; and *justice,* to the display or outward manifestation of this disposition.

The *justice* of God may be considered as *general* or *particular.* The *general* or *universal* justice of God is that perfection of his nature which leads him, on all occasions, to do what is right and equal, and is often expressed by the term *righteousness.* His *particular* justice consists in his perfect rectitude as a moral governor. His justice, in this sense, is either *legislative* or *judicial.*

LEGISLATIVE JUSTICE determines man's duty and binds him to the performance of it. It also defines the rewards of the obedient and the punishments of the rebellious. God has unquestionably an absolute right to the entire and perpetual obedience of his creatures; and in pursuance of this all moral agents are placed under *law*, and are subject to rewards and punishments.

JUDICIAL JUSTICE is that which respects a righteous retribution. God " will render to every man according to his deeds." Rom. ii, 6. This branch of justice is either *remunerative*, as when God rewards the obedient, or *vindictive*, as when he punishes the guilty. Rewards, properly speaking, are of *grace*, and not of debt; for God cannot be a debtor to his creatures. But since he binds himself by engagements in his law, " this do, and thou shalt live," or attaches a particular promise of reward to some duty, it becomes a part of *justice* to perform the engagement. "If we confess our sins, he is faithful and *just* to forgive us our sins." 1 John i, 9.

VINDICTIVE or PUNITIVE JUSTICE consists in the infliction of punishment. In the first place, it renders the punishment of unpardoned sin *certain*, so that no criminal shall escape; and, secondly, it graduates the exact proportion of punishment to the nature and circumstances of the offense. Both these facts are marked in numerous passages of Scripture, the testimony of which on this subject may be summed up in the words of Elihu: "For the *work* of man shall he render unto him, and cause every man to find *according* to his ways; yea, surely God will not do wickedly, neither will the Almighty pervert judgment." Job xxxiv, 12.

There are many circumstances in the administration of the affairs of the world which appear to be irreconcilable to that strict exercise of justice which is ascribed to God as our Supreme Ruler. We see, for instance, that the notoriously wicked, in some cases, enjoy a long life and great worldly prosperity, while those who are truly pious are subjects of poverty and affliction. But if we take these two facts into the account, 1, that offending man is under a dispensation of mercy, which provides for his pardon and moral renovation; and, 2, that God has " appointed a day in which he will judge the world in righteousness," a satisfactory light will be thrown upon all those cases in the Divine administration which have been thought most difficult.

The doctrine of a *future and general judgment*, which alone explains so many difficulties in the dispensations of Providence, is grounded solely on the doctrine of redemption. Under an administration of *strict justice*, punishment must follow offense without delay. This is clearly indicated in the sanction of the first law, " in the day thou eatest thereof thou shalt surely die;" a threat which would have been fully executed but for the immediate introduction of the redeeming scheme. Under such an administration no reason would seem to exist for a general judgment. This has its reason in the circumstances of trial in which men are placed by the introduction of a method of recovery. Justice, in virtue of the *atonement*, admits of the suspension of punishment for offense, of long-suffering, of the application of means of repentance and conversion, and that through the whole term of human life. But the judgment, the examination, and the public exhibition of the use or abuse of these appliances are deferred to an appointed day, in which he who now offers grace will administer justice, strict and unsparing.

However difficult it may be, without taking these things into consideration, to trace the manifestations of justice in God's moral government, or to reconcile certain circumstances with the character of a righteous governor, by their aid all difficulty is entirely removed. Indeed, the single fact of a general judgment is enough to rectify all the inequality of present dispensations were it a thousand times greater.

From these remarks respecting the nature and characteristics of Divine justice several important conclusions may be drawn.

1. It is no impeachment of a righteous government that external prosperity should be the lot of great offenders. This may be part of a gracious adminstration to bring them to repentance by *favor ;* or it may be designed to make their fall and final punishment more *marked*, and to show the light value of outward advantages, separate from holy habits and a thankful heart.

2. It is not inconsistent with the rectitude of God that the pious should be afflicted and oppressed, since their defects may require chastisement, and since, also, afflictions are made to work out for them " a far more exceeding and eternal weight of glory."

3. As the administration under which man is placed is one of *grace* in harmony with *justice*, the dispensation of what is purely matter of favor may have a great variety, without any impeachment of Divine justice. Of this fact the parable of our Lord respecting the laborers in the vineyard is a fit illustration.*

4. But with *nations* the case is very different. Their rewards and punishments, being of a civil nature, may be fully administered in this life; for, as bodies politic, they have no posthumous existence. National retribution has, therefore, in all ages, been visible and striking. In succession all vicious nations have perished ; and always by means so marked, and often so singular, as to bear upon them a broad and legible *punitive* character.

§ 11. *The Holiness of God.*

Holiness, considered as an attribute of God, is his *perfect moral purity*. It is that perfection of his nature by which he is infinitely averse to all moral evil, and inclined to love all that is good and right. The

---

* See Matt. xx, 1–16.

holiness of God, then, implies the absence of all moral impurity and imperfection, and the possession, in an infinite degree, of all that is morally pure, lovely, and excellent.

It may be proper to remark, that the term *holy*, when applied to God, is sometimes used to signify *august* and *venerable*. Thus, when the Psalmist pronounces his name to be "Holy and Reverend," the second epithet may be understood to be exegetical of the first. And when he says that "his *holy arm* hath gotten him the victory," there is no direct reference to *moral excellence*, but to majestic force, to irresistible power. The command to "sanctify the Lord," is a command to treat him with the most profound reverence, and is thus explained by Isaiah: "Sanctify the Lord God of hosts himself, and let him be your fear, and let him be our dread." Isa. viii, 13. He is a Being separated or distinguished from all other beings by his infinite excellence, as sacred things are separated from things that are common. He is possessed of every perfection, intellectual and moral, in the highest possible degree, and is, therefore, entitled to the veneration of angels and of men.

But while the holiness of God does certainly suggest, in many instances, the idea of *greatness* or *majesty*, it is equally certain, that in others it is expressive of the purity of his nature. This is obviously the case in the following passage: "As he which hath called you is *holy*, so be ye holy in all manner of conversation, because it is written, Be ye holy, for I am *holy*." 1 Pet. i, 13. There would be no force in the exhortation if the holiness ascribed to God were not of the same nature as that which is required of us; for the former is referred to as the reason and pattern of the latter. Hence, when we call God *holy*, we mean that there are in his nature certain moral qualities or principles analogous to those on account of which men are pronounced holy, that he is perfectly free from the slightest taint of moral pollution, and that his will is always conformable to the rectitude of his nature, so that he invariably hates sin and loves righteousness.

The holiness of God is commonly regarded as an attribute distinct from all his other perfections; but this, we think, is a mistake. Holiness is a complex term, and denotes, not so much a particular attribute, as that *general character* of God which results from all his moral perfections. The holiness of a man is not a distinct quality from his virtuous dispositions, but signifies the state of his mind and heart as influenced by these. When we proceed to analyze his holiness, or to show in what it consists, we say that he is a devout man, a man of integrity, a man faithful to all his engagements and conscientious in all his relative duties, a man who abhors sin and loves righteousness. In like manner, the holiness of God is not, and cannot be, something different from the moral perfections of his nature, but is the general term under which all these perfections are comprehended.

The holiness of God is proved,

1. From the Scriptures.

"Ye shall be holy, for I the Lord your God am *holy.*" Lev. xix, 2. "Exalt the Lord our God, and worship at his holy hill; for the Lord our God is *holy.*" Psa. xcix, 9. This attribute was the subject of praise to the seraphim who surrounded the throne of Jehovah when he appeared in the temple to the prophet Isaiah. "And one cried unto another, and said, Holy, holy, holy is the Lord of hosts; the whole earth is full of his glory." Isa. vi, 3. It is said in the Apocalypse, of the four living creatures, that "they rest not day and night, saying, Holy, holy, holy, Lord God Almighty." Rev. iv, 8.

2. From the Moral Nature with which Man was endowed at his Creation.

Man was not only made a living soul, and endowed with intellectual powers, but there was impressed upon him the image of his Maker, consisting in the perfect rectitude of his mind, in the order and harmony of his faculties, and in pure and heavenly affections. Thus man, in his primitive state, was resplendent with the glory of God's moral excellence. This state he might have retained; for, to suppose that his power was not adequate to his circumstances, would be to make God the author of sin. The fall of man was not owing to the want of anything which God ought to have done for him, but he voluntarily yielded to temptation, disregarding the considerations which would have counteracted its influence.

3. From the Nature and Design of the Law which was originally given to Man.

As to the *nature* of this law, it is pure and holy. It forbids sin in all its modifications: in its most refined as well as in its grossest forms, the taint of the mind as well as the pollution of the body, the secret approbation of sin as well as the external act, the transient look of desire, and every irregular emotion. While it commands us to place a guard upon the avenues by which temptation might enter, it enjoins the strictest care of the heart, and calls upon us to destroy the seed before it has grown. "The law is holy, and the commandment holy." Rom. vii, 12.

The *design* of the law was to retain man in a state of innocence and purity. It was sanctioned by promises and threatenings, and thus, while it taught him his duty, it actuated him to obedience by the hope of reward, and deterred him from sin by the fear of punishment. In this, therefore, we see a proof both of God's care for man and of his regard to holiness.

4. From the indications of Providence in the government of the Moral World.

Let us here notice, in the *first* place, the natural checks which God has placed upon sin, and the natural encouragements which he has held out to the practice of virtue, for in these we clearly perceive his regard to the interests of holiness. It is certain that various affections and actions have been enjoined upon all rational creatures under the general name of *righteousness*, and their contraries have been prohibited. It is also a matter of constant experience and observation, that the good of society is promoted only by what is commanded, and injured by what is forbidden; and that every individual derives, by the very law of his nature, benefit and happiness from rectitude, and injury and misery from vice. This constitution of human nature is, therefore, an indication that the Maker and Ruler of men formed them with the intent that they should avoid vice and practice virtue; and that the former is the object of his aversion, the latter of his regard.

We notice, *secondly*, that God has manifested his holiness, and his infinite abhorrence of sin, by the exercise of his punitive justice. When angels rebelled against him they were cast down to hell. When our first parents disobeyed the Divine command they were expelled from Paradise. When the antediluvian world sinned against God he overwhelmed them in the waters of the deluge. Upon Sodom and Gomorrah he rained down fire and brimstone; and when his chosen people indulged in vice, or forsook his worship, he delivered them into the hands of their enemies. Truly, then, God is *holy*.

5. FROM THE WORK OF REDEMPTION.

It is this that dispelled the cloud which sin had spread over the character of God, revealing him in all his glory as the moral governor of the world. In the person of the Redeemer we have an exemplification of that holiness in which man was created, and to which he must be restored, in order that he may be admitted to eternal life. In the sufferings and death of Christ, as an atonement for sin, we have a demonstration both of the inflexible justice of God and of his infinite compassion toward the guilty. The immediate design of the atonement was to meet the claims of God's holy law; but the ultimate design was to restore men to that state of holiness from which they had fallen. The means were of the most wonderful and unexpected kind—the substitution and sufferings of a Divine person—the obedience and crucifixion of the Lord of glory. He "gave himself for us, that he might redeem us from all iniquity, and purify unto himself a peculiar people, zealous of good works." Titus ii, 14. It follows, therefore, that holiness must be infinitely acceptable to God, and that he is an infinitely holy being, since he resorted to this extraordinary method of re-establishing holiness in our world.

§ 12. *The Goodness of God.*

In the investigation of this Divine attribute it will be proper, in the first place, to make some general observations explanatory of its *nature ;* and, secondly, to adduce the *proofs* by which the goodness of God is established.

I. The Nature of the Divine Goodness.

Goodness, when it is considered as a distinct attribute of God, signifies *benevolence,* or a disposition to communicate happiness. From an inward principle of good-will, God exerts his omnipotence in diffusing happiness through the universe in proportion to the different capacities with which he has endowed his creatures, and according to the direction of his infinite wisdom. Here we may observe,

1. *That the goodness of God, according as it terminates upon different objects, admits of different denominations.* When it confers happiness without merit, it is called *grace;* when it commiserates the distressed, it is *pity;* when it supplies the indigent, it is *bounty;* when it bears with offenders, it is *patience* or *long-suffering;* and when it pardons the guilty, it is *mercy.* These, therefore, are not to be regarded as distinct attributes of God, but as various modes according to which he manifests his *goodness* to his creatures.

2. *That goodness in God is represented as goodness of* NATURE, as one of his essential perfections, and not as an accidental or occasional affection. He is thus set infinitely above the imaginary gods of the heathen, whose benevolence was occasional, limited, and often disturbed by contrary passions. Such were the best views of pagans; but to us a being of a far different character is manifested as our Creator and Lord. One of his appropriate and distinguishing names, as proclaimed by himself to Moses, signifies, " *The gracious One,*" and imports *goodness* in the *principle;* and another, " *The all-sufficient and all-bountiful pourer forth of all good,*" and expresses goodness in *action.*

3. *That the goodness of God is* EFFICIENT *and* INEXHAUSTIBLE. It reaches every fit case, it supplies all possible want, and endures forever. As the sun sheds his rays upon the surrounding worlds, and enlightens and cherishes the whole creation without being diminished in splendor, so God imparts without being exhausted, and though ever giving, has yet infinitely more to give.

4. *That God* TAKES PLEASURE *in the exercise of his goodness.* It is not reluctantly or coldly imparted, nor is it stintedly measured out. He "is rich unto all that call upon him." He "giveth to all men liberally, and upbraideth not." He is ready to do for us "exceeding abundantly above all that we ask or think." It is under these views that the Scriptures afford so much encouragement to *prayer,* and lay so strong a ground for absolute *trust* in God. His goodness throws a mild and tranquilizing luster over the majestic attributes of his nature, and presents them to us under a friendly aspect. It enables us to regard him not only as a Sovereign, but as a Father. It causes us to feel emotions of gratitude and love, rising in harmony with sentiments of veneration, and encourages us to supplicate his favor and submit to his control.

II. Proofs by which the Goodness of God is established.

These are so numerous that they cannot all be adduced, nor will our limits allow us to pursue the argument to any great length. The most that we can do is to present a few of the most obvious proofs in support of the Divine goodness. We may argue it,

1. *From the plain and positive declarations of Scripture.*—When Moses prayed, "I beseech thee, show me thy glory," Jehovah replied, "I will make all my goodness pass before thee," as if he accounted this attribute most glorious to himself. Thus he proclaimed his own name: "The Lord, the Lord God, merciful and gracious, long-suffering, and abundant in goodness and truth." Exod. xxxiv, 6. This description of the Divine character is confirmed throughout the whole system of revelation. "O give thanks unto the Lord, for he is good; for his mercy endureth forever." 1 Chron. xvi, 34. "The earth is full of the goodness of the Lord." Psa. xxxiii, 5. "O taste and see that the Lord is good." Psa. xxxiv, 8. "For thou, Lord, art good, and ready to forgive, and plenteous in mercy unto all them that call upon thee." Psa. lxxxvi, 5. "The Lord is good to all; and his tender mercies are over all his works." Psa. cxlv, 9.

2. *From the fact of creation.*—When we consider God as possessing in himself all possible perfection and felicity, and as being independent of all creatures, we may ask, What motive could have induced him to exert his power in giving life to so many orders of beings, and in fitting up the earth to be a convenient habitation for them, but pure and unmixed goodness—a desire to communicate happiness to other beings? He did not perform the work of creation by a necessity of nature, as the sun gives light, or as a fountain pours out its waters; but in consequence of counsel and design. As a free agent, he exerted his power to such an extent, and in such a variety of ways, as seemed agreeable to himself. Of the counsels of God we are not competent judges, and it would, therefore, be presumptuous in us to affirm that benevolence was the *only* motive to the work of creation; but we are safe in concluding that the diffusion of happiness was its *primary* design. What other idea is suggested by the contemplation of a system so regular and beautiful in all its parts, and teeming with life and enjoyment? Had not the nature of God been communicative he would have remained alone; but now he beholds from his throne a scale of beings, ascending from the insect to the archangel, all rejoicing in conscious existence, and partaking of the riches of his liberality.

3. *From the state in which living creatures are made.*—They are relatively perfect; that is, they are all perfectly fitted for their various places in creation, their peculiar modes of life, and the purposes which they were designed to serve. They possess everything that is necessary for the preservation of life, for defense, for the procuring of food, and for motion from place to place. Had we found living creatures

that were destitute of any of those members and organs of sense on which their safety and comfort depended, as birds without wings, fishes without fins, or beasts without legs, we might have supposed that the Creator intended them to languish in misery and perish; but the contrary conclusion must be drawn from the provision which has been evidently made for the comfortable subsistence of animated nature. He who has bestowed life has rendered it a gift worthy of himself, by associating with it a variety of conveniences and pleasures.

4. *From the abundant provision which God has made for the wants of his creatures.*—"The eyes of all wait upon thee; and thou givest them their meat in due season. Thou openest thine hand, and satisfiest the desire of every living thing." Psa. cxlv, 15, 16. With the care and bounty of a father, he provides for all the members of his family. The various species of animals differ from one another as much in their taste as in their form. The food that sustains one will not nourish another; and what one eagerly seeks another rejects with disgust. Substances offensive to *our* senses, and which if taken into our stomachs would be noxious, furnish wholesome and delicious nutriment to creatures differently constituted. Thus God manifests his goodness in providing for every living creature its appropriate aliment; for, though the guests at the table of Providence have no community of interests and feelings, yet they all find suitable entertainment. Not one of them goes away disappointed, for our "heavenly Father feedeth them."

5. *From the variety of natural pleasures which God has provided for the animal creation.*—Every creature capable of happiness, that comes immediately from the forming hand of God, is placed in circumstances of positive felicity; and by associating happiness with animal existence he has made life truly a blessing, and has acted in the character of benevolence. There seems, indeed, to be a high degree of pleasure attached to simple existence, as we may judge from the lively motions of young animals. These motions appear to have no specific object, as the friskings of a lamb, for example, but to proceed from an indescribable satisfaction which animals experience in the possession of life and activity. The goodness of God is farther displayed in the pleasures which animals derive from the gratification of their natural appetites, and from pursuing their instinctive propensities. When in summer the air is filled with myriads of insects, which are almost constantly on the wing, wheeling in sportive circles, we have an evidence of the delight with which they pass their transitory duration, and a proof of the Divine beneficence. Their enjoyment is merely sensitive, but it is the only kind of which they are capable; and it is goodness, rich in its treasures and minute in its attentions, which thus adapts itself to every living nature.

What has been said relates chiefly to the condition of the lower animals; but we will now proceed to argue the goodness of God,

6. *From his dispensations to Man.*—As this is a subject of vast extent, the reader will at once perceive that we can only present a hasty sketch of the argument, leaving him to fill up the outline by his own reflections.   Let us then notice,

(1.) *Man's original state and condition.*—Though created last, he was not least.   A high rank was assigned to him in the scale of being. As to his body, it was " fearfully and wonderfully made."   In his *intellectual* powers he was placed infinitely above every other terrestrial creature.   He possessed understanding and reason, and had a knowledge of himself and his Maker, and of the various relations which subsisted between them.   He was also endowed with a *moral* nature, with innate rectitude, a love of holiness, and a strong desire to know and serve God.   He therefore enjoyed, under the smile of his Maker, a felicity incomparably greater, both in kind and degree, than that of the inferior creatures.   The *place* of his abode corresponded with the dignity of his character and with the peculiarities of his constitution.   In the garden of Paradise, which the hand of God prepared for man, there was nothing wanting that could minister to his good or afford him comfort—all was beauty, and melody, and delight.

Again, God placed man under moral government.   He gave him a good and holy law, promising to reward his obedience with everlasting felicity.   Obedience, indeed, was a debt which he owed his Creator; so that, though he had fulfilled the whole law, he should have had no claim to remuneration.   True, man lost the noble prize which was set before him; but that event does not in any degree obscure the evidence of benignity in God, from which the promise of it proceeded.   Even at this distance we ought to look back with grateful emotions upon the hope which animated our first progenitor in the commencement of his career, and the blessedness which might have descended as an inheritance to his children.   Now, if we look at these facts, either separately or taken together, we will be forced to the conclusion that God intended the happiness of man, and that, therefore, he is rich in goodness.   But we may look at man,

(2.) *In his present fallen condition.*—When he transgressed the law of his Creator a dispensation of unmixed wrath might have commenced. And when for wise reasons God suspended the infliction of the threatened penalty, and permitted the offender to live, he might have doomed him and his posterity to a life of extreme misery; but we find it far otherwise.   Though our world is a world of sinners, yet it is one in which the goodness of God is gloriously displayed.   It is especially for man that the sun pours out a flood of light and genial heat; that the earth is endowed with unceasing powers of fertility; and that life and health are borne upon the wings of the wind.   What a delightful view of the Divine goodness is given by the regular succession of the seasons, the opening buds and blossoms of spring, the luxuriant growth of summer, and the matured fruits and rich harvests of autumn! Surely God has not left "himself without witness, in that he did good, and gave us rain from heaven, and fruitful seasons, filling our hearts with food and gladness." Acts xiv, 17.

The goodness of God appears also in the provision which he has made for the gratification of our senses. We experience that food not only satisfies the appetite of hunger and nourishes our bodies, but also gratifies our taste. Now this pleasure is not at all necessary to the great design of food. It might be perfectly tasteless, without any diminution of its nutritive quality; but the taste is superadded by our Maker to render it pleasant as well as useful, and clearly shows his attention to our animal comfort. The same conclusion may be drawn from the gratification of other senses. There is beauty prepared for the eye, music for the ear, and sweet perfumes for the sense of smelling. But why is it that we are thus so agreeably affected by natural objects? Not because it renders them more useful, but more attractive; not because it sustains life, but imparts to it a higher relish.

It is here urged, as an objection to the doctrine which we have advocated, that the globe, as the residence of man, has its inconveniences and positive evils. This is admitted. It has its extremes of cold and heat; its earthquakes, volcanoes, tempests, and inundations: its sterility in some places, which wears down man with labor; and its exuberance of vegetable and animal life in others, which generates diseases, or gives birth to annoying and destructive animals. The diseases of the human race, their general poverty, their universal sufferings and cares, and their short life and painful dissolution, must all be acknowledged.

It was to account for such evils as these that the ancient philosophers supposed the world to be governed by two contrary deities. They could not see how a benevolent being could be the author of natural evil, and hence they ascribed everything of this kind to an evil god. We, however, who enjoy the light of the Scriptures, can solve this question without difficulty. We acknowledge that there are real evils in the world; but we contend that their existence is not inconsistent with the benevolence of the Author of nature, because the world in which they are found is inhabited by sinful beings. Physical evil is the consequence of moral evil. Had man continued in his original state, natural evil would be unaccountable; but no one who believes that God is just can wonder that suffering should be the attendant of guilt. God is holy as well as benevolent, and his goodness ought to be considered, not as a disposition to confer happiness indiscriminately, but to confer it upon proper objects. We are placed under a mixed dispensation of mercy and judgment. God exercises much patience and long-suffering toward men, but he also gives tokens of his displeasure; and the true ground of surprise is, not that there is a portion of evil in their lot, but that there is so much good; because they deserve the former, but are altogether unworthy of the latter.

But with all the evils which belong to our condition, we cannot but acknowledge that physical good greatly preponderates. In general the days of health are many, and those of pain and sickness few. Enjoyment of one kind or other is within the reach of all; and even in conditions which seem to be most unfavorable to it, there are sources of satisfaction of which others are not aware. The poor have their pleasures as well as the rich; the laboring classes as well as those who are living at ease. All esteem existence a blessing, and suicide is committed only when the mind is diseased, or when the instinctive love of life is overcome by the extremity of pain, or the dread of some intolerable evil. The state even of fallen man bears ample testimony to the goodness of his Maker. It is, upon the whole, a happy world in which we live, although it is a world of sinners. God displays before our eyes the riches of his goodness, forbearance, and long-suffering.*

There are two other considerations which ought not to be overlooked in this connection. The *first* is, that positive evils are mitigated by various alleviations, and are often connected with beneficent ends. The necessity of *labor* obliges us to occupy time usefully, which is both a source of enjoyment and a preventive of much evil. *Familiarity* and *habit* render many circumstances tolerable which at first sight we conceive to be necessarily the sources of wretchedness. Pain teaches vigilance and caution, and renders its remission in returning health a source of higher enjoyment; while the process of mortal diseases mitigates our natural horror of death. In all this there is surely an ample proof and an adorable display of the Divine goodness.

The second consideration is, that man himself is chargeable with far the largest share of the miseries of the present life. View men *collectively*. Sin, as a *ruling habit*, is not necessary. The means of repressing its inward motions, and of restraining its outward acts, have been furnished to all mankind; and if the miseries which are the effects of voluntary vice were all removed, comparatively few would remain in the world. Oppressive governments, private wrongs, wars, jealousies, intemperance, and all their consequent evils, would disappear.

But besides the removal of so many evils, how greatly would the sum of positive happiness be increased! Peace, security, and industry would cover the earth with fruits in sufficient abundance for all. Intellectual improvement would yield the pleasures of knowledge. Arts would multiply the comforts, and mitigate many of the most wasting toils of life. General benevolence would unite men in warm affections and friendships, productive of innumerable reciprocal offices of kindness, and piety would crown all with the pleasures of pure devotion, remov-

* See Dick's Theology, Lecture 24..

ing every annoying passion and tormenting fear, and inspiring its subjects with a blissful hope of a better state of being. All this is *possible*.
If it is not *actual*, it is the fault of the human race, not of their Maker;
and his goodness is not to be questioned because they are perverse.
We may direct our attention,

(3.) *To what God has done for Man's recovery.*—It is in the plan of
human redemption, that he has most gloriously evinced the perfection of
his goodness—goodness beyond all calculation, immense and infinite!
It is on this subject, more than on any other, that we are constrained to
cry out in profound admiration, "*God is love.*" The whole scheme
originated from this source, and every part of it declares "the exceeding riches of his grace, in his kindness toward us, through Christ Jesus."
Eph. ii, 7.

It is impossible to set a *proper* estimate upon the goodness of God,
as manifested in the work of human redemption; but if we would
make any considerable approach toward it we must consider, 1. The
gift bestowed: "He gave his only begotten Son." John iii, 16. 2. The
manner in which Christ effected our redemption: "He took upon him
the form of a servant, and was make in the likeness of men; and being
found in fashion as a man, he humbled himself, and became obedient
unto death, even the death of the cross." Phil. ii, 7, 8. 3. The depth of
misery from which we were rescued: "Christ hath redeemed us from
the *curse of the law*." Gal. iii, 13. 4. The height of bliss to which we
are raised: "peace with God" here, and "everlasting life" hereafter.
And, 5. The means which are still in operation to bring men to the
enjoyment of this great salvation, the institutions of the Gospel, and
the saving influences of the Holy Spirit. Who can take a survey of this
wonderful system of human recovery and call in question the goodness
of God?

Such are the adorable perfections of the ever-blessed God, which are
distinctly revealed to us in his Word; but in addition to these there
are other excellences, ascribed to him in a more general way, which
serve to heighten our conceptions of his character, and to set before the
humbled and awed spirit of man an overwhelming height and depth of
majesty and glory.

God is PERFECT. We are thus taught to ascribe to him every natural
and moral excellence which we can conceive. Every attribute in him
is perfect in its *kind*, and is the most elevated of its kind. It is perfect
in its *degree*, not falling in the least below the standard of the highest
excellence either in our conceptions, or those of angels, or in the possible nature of things.

God is ALL-SUFFICIENT. This is another of those declarations of
Scripture which exalt our views of God into a mysterious, unbounded,
and undefined amplitude *from himself*, eternally rising out of his own

perfection, *for himself*, so that he is ALL to himself, and depends upon no other being, and *for all that communication*, however large and however lasting, on which the whole universe depends. The same vast thought is expressed by St. Paul in the phrase, "ALL IN ALL."

God is UNSEARCHABLE. All that we see or hear of him is but a faint and shadowy manifestation. Beyond the highest glory there is yet an unpierced and unapproachable light, a track of intellectual and moral splendor, untraveled by the thoughts of the adoring spirits who are nearest his throne. "Canst thou find out the Almighty unto perfection?" Job xi, 7. "Great is the Lord, and greatly to be praised, and his greatness is unsearchable." Psa. cxlv, 3.

We cannot close this chapter in a more suitable manner than in the adoring language of the psalmist: "*Blessed* be the *Lord God*, the God of Israel, who only doeth wondrous things. And *blessed* be his glorious *name* forever: and let the whole earth be filled with his *glory; Amen, and Amen*. Psa. lxxii, 18, 19.

CHAPTER III.

THE TRINITY IN UNITY.

WE now approach this great mystery of our faith, the doctrine of the *Trinity*, for the declaration of which we are exclusively indebted to the Sacred Scriptures. Not only is it incapable of proof *à priori*, but it derives no direct confirmatory evidence from the existence and wise and orderly arrangement of the works of God. It stands, however, on the unshaken foundation of his own word, that revelation which he has given of himself in both Testaments; and if we see no traces of it in the works of creation, as we do of his existence and perfections, the reason is, that creation in itself could not be the medium of manifesting or of illustrating it.

Among the leading writers in defense of the Trinity there are some shades of difference in opinion as to what constitutes the *Unity* of the three persons in the Godhead. The scheme which seems to comport most exactly with Scripture is that of Bishop Pearson, with whom Bishop Bull and Dr. Owen also agree. It is thus expressed by Dr. Doddridge: "Though God the Father is the fountain of the Deity, the whole Divine nature is communicated from the Father to the Son, and from both to the Spirit, yet so as that the Father and the Son are not separate, nor separable from the divinity, but do still exist in it, and are most intimately united to it."

The term *person* signifies in ordinary language an intelligent being.

Two or more persons, therefore, in the strict philosophical sense, would be two or more distinct intelligent beings. If the term *person* were so applied to the Trinity in the Godhead a plurality of gods would follow; while if taken in what has been called a *political* sense, personality would be no more than *relation*, arising out of office. Personality in God is, therefore, not to be understood in either of the above senses if we pay respect to the testimony of Scripture. God is *one being*. But he is more than one being in three *relations;* for *personal acts*, such as we ascribe to distinct persons, and which most unequivocally characterize personality, are ascribed to each person of the Trinity. The Scripture doctrine therefore is, that the persons are not *separate*, but distinct, and that they are so united as to be but *one God*. In other words, that the Divine nature exists under the personal distinction of Father, Son, and Holy Ghost, and that these three have equally, and in common with one another, the nature and perfections of supreme divinity. This appears to be the true simple doctrine of the Trinity, when stripped of refined and learned distinctions. As to the *manner* in which three persons are united in the Godhead, it is granted to be incomprehensible; but so is God himself, as is also every essential attribute of his nature.

It is objected by some that the term *person* is not used in the Scriptures, and that, therefore, we should not employ it in connection with this subject. To such it may be sufficient to reply, that if what is clearly taught in Scripture is compendiously expressed by this term, and cannot so well be expressed, except by an inconvenient periphrasis, it ought to be retained. But is there not a scriptural warrant for the term itself? Our translators so concluded when in Heb. i, 3, they called the Son "the express image" of the Father's "*person.*" The original word is ὑποστασις, which signifies substance, essence, being; something of which we can say, it is, in opposition to mere appearance, and was understood by the Greek fathers to signify a *person*, though not exclusively so used.

The sense of ὑποστάσις in this passage must be considered, by all who allow the divinity of the Son of God, as fixed by the apostle's argument. For the Son being called "the express image" of the Father, a *distinction* between the Son and the Father is thus unquestionably expressed; but if there is but *one* God, and if the Son is Divine, the distinction here expressed cannot be a distinction of essence, and must, therefore, be a *personal* distinction.

Having made these preliminary remarks, we are now prepared to enter upon a more particular investigation of the doctrine of the Trinity. We will consider, *first*, its vast importance in the system of revealed truth; and, *secondly*, the Scripture proofs by which it is established.

§ 1. *The Importance of the Doctrine.*

To consider the importance of the doctrine of the Trinity is the more necessary because it has been represented as of little consequence, or as a matter of useless speculation. Thus Dr. Priestley: "All that can be said for it is, that the doctrine, however improbable in itself, is necessary to explain some particular texts of Scripture; and that, if it had not been for those particular texts we should have found no want for it."* That the reader may see the importance of this revealed doctrine, he is requested to weigh the following considerations:

1. THE KNOWLEDGE OF GOD IS FUNDAMENTAL TO RELIGION; and as we know nothing of him but what he has revealed, and as these revelations have all *moral ends*, and are designed to promote *piety*, and not to gratify *curiosity*, all that he has revealed of himself in *particular* must partake of that character of fundamental importance which belongs to the knowledge of God in the aggregate. Nothing, therefore, can disprove the fundamental importance of the Trinity in Unity but that which will prove that it is not a doctrine of Scripture.

2. IT ESSENTIALLY AFFECTS OUR VIEWS OF GOD AS THE OBJECT OF OUR WORSHIP, whether we regard him as one in essence and one in person, or admit that in the unity of the Godhead there are three equally Divine persons. These are two very different conceptions, both of which cannot be true. The God of those who deny the Trinity is not the God of those who worship the Trinity in Unity, so that either the former or the latter worship a being which does not exist; and, so far as it respects any *reality* in the object, they might as well worship a pagan idol.

But as the *object* of our worship is affected by our respective views on this great subject, so also is its *character*. For if the doctrine of the Trinity is true, then those who deny it do not worship the God of the Scriptures, but a fiction of their own framing, and are, therefore, guilty of idolatry. If it is false, Trinitarians, by paying Divine honors to the Son and to the Holy Ghost, are equally guilty of idolatry, though in another mode. The importance of the doctrine must, therefore, be obvious to all.

3. THE DOCTRINE OF THE TRINITY HAS AN INTIMATE CONNECTION WITH THE SUBJECT OF MORALS. What is morality but conformity to the Divine law, which law must take its character from that of its Author? The Trinitarian scheme is essentially connected with the doctrine of atonement, which depends on the divinity of Christ. It acknowledges the fallen and helpless condition of man, the exceeding sinfulness of sin, and the inflexible justice of God. The Unitarian theory necessarily excludes atonement, and regards sin as a matter of

---

* History of "Early Opinions."

comparatively trifling moment. It supposes that God is not strict to punish sin, and that if punishment does follow it will not be eternal. Whether, under these soft and easy views of the law of God, and of the evil of transgression, morals can have an equal sanction, or human conduct be equally restrained, are points too obvious to be argued.

But we must not forget that faith in the testimony of God is an essential part of morality. To *believe* is so much a Divine *command* that the highest sanction is connected with it. "He that believeth shall be *saved;* and he that believeth not shall be *damned.*" It is, therefore, an act of *duty* to believe, because it is an act of *obedience;* and hence St. Paul speaks of "the obedience of faith." It is of the utmost importance, then, that we should know what God has revealed as the object of our faith, since the rejection of any revealed truth must certainly be visited with punishment; the *law of faith* having the same authority and the same sanction as the *law of works.* Thus we see the connection of this doctrine with Christian morality, and, consequently, its great value.

4. *But the importance of the doctrine of the Trinity may be finally argued* FROM THE MANNER IN WHICH A DENIAL OF IT WOULD AFFECT THE CREDIT OF THE HOLY SCRIPTURES. Dr. Priestley allows that this doctrine "is necessary to explain some particular texts of Scripture." This fact alone is sufficient to mark its importance and to establish its truth, especially as it can be shown that these "*particular* texts" comprehend a very large portion of the sacred volume. If the doctrine of a Trinity of Divine persons in the Godhead is true, the style and manner of the Scriptures are in perfect accordance with the facts in the case; but if the Son and the Holy Spirit were creatures, then would the language of the sacred books be most deceptive and dangerous. It would be so well adapted to lead men to the belief of falsehood, even in fundamental points, and to idolatry itself, that " abominable thing" which the Lord hates, that they would lose all claim to be regarded as a revelation from the God of truth, and ought rather to be shunned than studied.

If the doctrine of the Trinity is denied, how is it to be accounted for, that in the Old Testament God should be spoken of in plural terms, and that this plurality should be restricted to *thee?* How is it that the very name *Jehovah* should be given to each of them, and that repeatedly on the most solemn occasions? How is it that the incarnate Messiah should be invested with the loftiest attributes of God; and that acts and characters of unequivocal divinity should be ascribed to the *Holy Spirit* also? How is it that in the New Testament the name of God should be given to both, and that without any intimation that it is used in an inferior sense? How is it that, in the very form of initiation by baptism into the Church of Christ, the ordinance, which itself is a public and solemn profession of faith, is to be performed in the *one name* of Father, Son, and Holy Ghost? This, if Socinianism were true, would be to administer baptism in the name of one God and two *creatures;* as though the very door of entrance into the Christian Church should have been purposely made the gateway into the temple of idolatry!

§ 2. *The Scripture Proofs.*

In deducing from the sacred volume the doctrine of a Trinity of Divine persons in the Unity of the Godhead, our attention will be directed to the important fact,

1. THAT THE ONE JEHOVAH OF THE BIBLE IS FREQUENTLY DESIGNATED BY PLURAL APPELLATIONS, AND PLURAL FORMS OF SPEECH.

The very first name under which he is made known to us as the Creator of the world is in the plural form. " In the beginning אלהים," ELOHIM, *the Gods*, " created the heavens and the earth." Gen. i, 1. That the word is plural, is made certain by its being often joined with adjectives, pronouns, and verbs plural. But when it can mean nothing else than the true God, it is usually joined in its plural form with a singular verb; as ברא אלהים, BARA ELOHIM, *the Gods created*.

This name is plural throughout the whole first chapter of Genesis, where it is so often employed, and in a thousand other places. In fact, it is rarely used in the singular אלה, ELOAH. The plural is preferred even when the design is to assert, in the most solemn manner, the Unity of God. Thus, " Hear, O Israel, the Lord אלהינו," ELOHAYNU, *our Gods*, " is one Lord." Deut. vi, 4. But this is not the only name which is applied in its plural form to the Divine Being. " If I be אדונים," ADONIM, *Masters*, " where is my fear?" Mal. i, 6. " Remember את בוראיך," ETH BOREKA, *thy Creators*, " in the days of thy youth." Eccl. xii, 1. " For בעליך עשיך," BOALAIK OSAIK, *thy Makers is thy husbands*. Isa. liv, 5.

Other plural forms of speech also occur when the ONE true God only is spoken of. " And God said, Let *us* make man in *our* image, after *our* likeness." Gen. i, 26. " And the Lord God said, Behold, the man is become as *one of us*." Gen. iii, 22. These instances need not be multiplied ; they are common forms of speech in the sacred Scriptures, which no criticism has been able to resolve into mere idioms, and which only the doctrine of a plurality of persons in the Unity of the Godhead can satisfactorily explain.

This argument, however, does not contain the strength of the case ; for if these plural titles and forms of expression were blotted out, the evidence of a plurality of Divine persons in the Godhead would still remain in its strongest form. This evidence is found in the fact,

2. THAT THE SCRIPTURES SPEAK OF THREE PERSONS, AND THREE PERSONS ONLY, UNDER DIVINE TITLES.

It is a remarkable fact, that while the Scriptures maintain, as their leading principle, that there is but ONE God, they so frequently speak of *three* persons, to each of whom they ascribe the peculiar attributes of divinity. This being once established, it may be asked which of the hypotheses, the Orthodox, the Arian, or the Socinian, agrees best with what the Scriptures so plainly teach upon this subject; and whether those who confide in the testimony of God, rather than in the opinions of men, have not sufficient reason to distinguish their faith from the unbelief of others by avowing themselves *Trinitarians.**

(1.) *This doctrine is indicated in that solemn form of benediction in which the Jewish high priests were commanded to bless the children of Israel,* and which singularly answers to the apostolic benediction that so appropriately closes the solemn services of Christian worship. It is given in Num. vi, 24–27 :

> "Jehovah bless thee, and keep thee;
> Jehovah make his face to shine upon thee, and be gracious unto thee;
> Jehovah lift his countenance upon thee, and give thee peace."

If the three members of this form of benediction be attentively considered, they will be found to agree respectively to the three persons of the Trinity, taken in the usual order of Father, Son, and Holy Ghost. The first member of the formula expresses "the love of God," the Father of mercies and Fountain of all good; the second well comports with the redeeming and reconciling "grace of the Lord Jesus Christ;" and the last is appropriate to the purity, consolation, and joy which are received from "the communion of the Holy Ghost."

The connection of certain blessings in this form of benediction with the Jehovah, mentioned three times distinctly, and those which are represented as flowing from the Father, Son, and Holy Ghost in the apostolic form, would be a singular coincidence if it even stood alone; but the light of the same eminent truth breaks forth from other partings in the clouds of the early morning of revelation. Hence,

(2.) *The inner part of the Jewish sanctuary was called the* HOLY OF HOLIES, that is, the holy place of the *Holy Ones.* The number of these is indicated, and limited to *three,* in that celebrated vision of Isaiah which took place in the very abode of the *Holy Ones.* Before them the seraphim vailed their faces, " and one cried unto another, and said, Holy, holy, holy is the Lord of hosts." Isa. vi, 3. Here let it be observed, that this *trine* act of adoration, which has been supposed to mark a plurality of persons in the object of it, is answered by a voice from the excellent glory which overwhelmed the mind of the prophet, responding in the same language of plurality in which the doxology of the seraphim is expressed. " Also I heard the voice of the Lord, saying, Whom shall I send, and who will go for us ?"

But this is not the only evidence that the *persons* who were addressed,

* The word τριας, *trinitas,* came into use in the second century.

each by his appropriate and equal designation of *holy*, were the *three* Divine substances in the Godhead. The Being addressed is the "Lord of hosts." This phrase, all acknowledge, designates the Father; but the Evangelist John, in manifest reference to this same transaction, observes, "These things said Esaias, when he saw his (Christ's) glory and spake of him." John xii, 41. In this vision, therefore, we have the *Son* also, whose glory on this occasion the prophet beheld; and St. Paul bears testimony to the presence of the Holy Spirit. "Well spake the *Holy Ghost* by Esaias the prophet unto our fathers, saying, Go unto this people and say, Hearing ye shall hear, and shall not understand; and seeing ye shall see, and shall not perceive." Acts xxviii, 25, 26. These words, quoted from Isaiah, the apostle declares to have been spoken by the Holy Ghost; but Isaiah tells us, that they were spoken on this very occasion by the "Lord of hosts."

Now let all these circumstances be placed together—THE PLACE, the holy place of the Holy Ones; the repetition of the homage, THREE times Holy, holy, holy; the ONE Jehovah of hosts, to whom it was addressed; the plural pronoun used by this ONE Jehovah, US; the declaration of St. John, that on this occasion Isaiah saw the glory of CHRIST; and the testimony of St. Paul, that the Lord of hosts who spoke on that occasion was the HOLY GHOST; and the conclusion will not be without most powerful authority, both circumstantial and declaratory, that the adoration Holy, holy, holy, referred to the Divine *three* in the one essence of the Lord of hosts. Accordingly, in the book of Revelation, where "*the Lamb*" is associated with the Father as the object of *equal* homage, the *living creatures*, corresponding to the seraphim of the prophet, are heard in the same strain, and with the same *trine* repetition, saying, "Holy, holy, holy, Lord God Almighty, which was, and is, and is to come." Rev. iv, 8.

(3.) *The prophet Isaiah makes this threefold distinction and limitation.* "And now the *Lord God*, and his Spirit, hath sent *me*." Isa. xlviii, 16. The words are manifestly spoken by Messiah, who declares himself to be sent by the *Lord God*, and by his *Spirit*. Some render it, hath sent *me* and his *Spirit*, the latter term being also in the accusative case. This strengthens the application by bringing the phrase nearer to that which is so often used by our Lord when he speaks of *himself* and the *Spirit* as being sent by the Father.

Again, "I am with you, saith the *Lord of hosts*: according to the word that I covenanted with you when ye came out of Egypt, so *my Spirit* remaineth among you; fear ye not. For thus saith the Lord of hosts; I will shake all nations, and the Desire of all nations shall come." Hag. ii, 4–7. Here also we have three persons distinctly mentioned, the *Lord* of hosts, his *Spirit*, and the *Desire* of all nations.

(4.) *This doctrine is most explicitly taught in the New Testament.* The passages commonly adduced are familiar to all: "Baptizing them

in the name of the *Father*, and of the *Son*, and of the *Holy Ghost*."
Matt. xxviii, 19.   " The grace of the *Lord Jesus Christ*, and the love of
God, and the communion of the *Holy Ghost*, be with you all." 2 Cor.
xiii, 14.   There are other passages in which the sacred *three*, and *three*
only, are thus collocated as objects of *equal* trust and honor, and as
being *equally* the *fountain* and *source* of grace and benediction.   But
the strongest proof which the Scriptures afford of the doctrine of the
Trinity is in the fact,

3. THAT IN NUMEROUS INSTANCES TWO PERSONS ARE SPOKEN OF AS
BEING ASSOCIATED WITH GOD IN HIS PERFECTIONS.

We have now shown that while the Unity of God is to be considered
a fundamental doctrine of the Scriptures, the very names of God, as
given in the revelation which he has made of himself, have plural forms,
and are connected with plural modes of speech; that other indications
of plurality are given in various passages; and that this plurality is
restricted to *three*.   On those texts, however, which in their terms
denote a plurality and a Trinity, we do not wholly or chiefly rely.   There
are multiplied instances in which *two* distinct persons are spoken of,
sometimes connectedly and sometimes separately, as being associated
with God in his incommunicable perfections, and as performing works
of unequivocal Divine majesty and infinite power; and thus that *triunity*
of the Godhead is manifested which the Church has, in all ages, adored
and magnified.   This, then, is the great proof upon which the doctrine
mainly rests.   The first of these two persons is the *Son*, the second the
Holy Spirit.

(1.) *Of the* SON, *it may be observed that he is invested with all the
titles and attributes of God;* that he is eminently known, both in the
Old Testament and in the New, as the Son of God; that he became
incarnate in our nature, and wrought miracles by his own power; that
he authoritatively forgave sin; that he is seated upon the throne of the
universe, in the possession of all power in heaven and in earth; that he
is worshiped both by men and angels; and that he will raise the dead
at the last day, judge the world, and, finally, determine the everlasting
state of the righteous and the wicked.

(2.) *As to the Divine character of the Holy Spirit, it is equally explicit.*
To him also are ascribed the names, the attributes, and the works of
Jehovah; and, finally, he is associated with the Father and the Son in
the Christian form of baptism, and in the apostolic form of benediction,
as being, equally with them, the source and fountain of grace and blessedness.   These decisive points we shall soon proceed to establish by
express declarations both of the Old and the New Testament.   When
that is done, the argument will then be, that as, on the one hand, there
is but ONE GOD; and as, on the other, *three persons* are, in unequivocal
language, and by unequivocal circumstances, declared to be *Divine;*
therefore, these THREE PERSONS ARE ONE GOD.   This is the only con-

clusion that can harmonize the declarations of Scripture on this important subject.

Thus the Trinity is asserted, but the Unity of God is not obscured;
while his Unity is confessed without a denial of the Trinity. It is not,
however, the Socinian notion of Unity. Theirs is the Unity of *one*,
ours the Unity of *three*. Nor do we believe, as they seem to suppose,
that the Divine Essence is *divisible*, or that it is *participated* by three
persons, and *shared among* them; but that it is wholly and undividedly
possessed by each. Whether, therefore, we address our prayers and
adorations to the Father, the Son, or the Holy Ghost, we address *the
same adorable Being, the one living and true God.*

A few remarks on the *difficulties* in which the doctrine of the Trinity
is supposed to involve its advocates may properly close this chapter.

Mere difficulty in conceiving of what is wholly proper and peculiar to
God forms no objection to a doctrine. It is more rationally to be considered as a presumption of its truth, since in the nature of God there
must be mysteries far above the reach of the human mind. All his
natural attributes, though of some of them we have images in ourselves,
are utterly incomprehensible; and the *manner* of his existence cannot
be less so. All attempts, however, to show that the doctrine implies a
contradiction have failed. A contradiction is only where two contraries
are predicated of the *same thing*, and in the *same respect*. Let this be
kept in view, and the sophism of our opponents will be easily detected.
They urge that the same thing cannot be *three* and *one;* that is, if the
proposition has any meaning at all, not in the *same respect*. The three
persons cannot be one *person*, nor can the one *God* be three *Gods*. But
it is no contradiction to say that in *different respects* the three may be
one; that is, that in respect to *persons* they may be *three*, and in respect
to *Godhead*, *essence*, or *nature*, they may be *one*.

As for *difficulties*, we shall certainly not be relieved by running either
to the Arian or the Socinian hypothesis. The one ascribes the creation
and government of the world, not to the Deity, but to a *creature;* for
however exalted the Arian inferior Deity may be, he is a creature still.
The other makes a mere man the creator of all things; for whatever is
meant by the Word that " was made flesh," he is the very same Word
by whom " all things were made."

CHAPTER IV.

THE DIVINITY OF CHRIST.

THE result of our observations on the doctrine of the Trinity is, that there are three persons in the Divine Essence, or that the Father, Son, and Holy Ghost are the same in substance, and equal in power and glory. If we have succeeded in proving that a Trinity is revealed in the Scriptures, we might proceed without delay to the consideration of other subjects, fully assured that he who redeemed us with his own blood, and he who is the Author of our holiness and consolation, are not to be ranked among creatures, but are entitled to the same religious honor which is due to the Father. There are, however, various considerations which point out the propriety of suspending our progress, and of engaging in a more minute inquiry into the divinity of the Son and of the Holy Spirit.

The Supreme Divinity of our Lord Jesus Christ will be made the subject of this chapter. In proof of this doctrine we will proceed to show that he existed previous to his incarnation; that he was the Jehovah of the Old Testament; that to him are ascribed Divine titles, Divine attributes, and Divine works; and that he is the object of Divine worship.

§ 1. *The Pre-existence of Christ.*

By establishing, on scriptural authority, the pre-existence of our Lord, we take the first step in the demonstration of his absolute divinity. His pre-existence, indeed, simply considered, does not evince his Godhead, and is not, therefore, a proof against the *Arian* hypothesis; but it destroys the *Socinian* notion, that he was a *mere man.* To prove that he existed prior to his incarnation, it will only be necessary to weigh the following scriptural propositions.

1. HE WAS BEFORE JOHN THE BAPTIST.—"He that cometh after me is preferred before me, for *he was before me.*" John i, 15.

The Socinian exposition is: "The Christ, who is to begin his ministry after me, has, by the Divine appointment, been preferred before me, because he is my chief or principal." Thus they interpret the last clause, "For he was before me," in the sense of *dignity,* and not of *time ;* though St. John uses the same word to denote priority of time in several places in his Gospel.* The verb in this clause sufficiently fixes πρῶτός in the sense of priority of time. Had it referred to the

* See in the original, John viii, 7; xv, 18; xx, 4, 8.

rank and dignity of Christ it would not have been ην, "he WAS," but εστι, "he IS before me."

2. HE WAS BEFORE ABRAHAM.—Thus our Lord declared: "Before Abraham was, I am." John viii, 58.

Whether the verb ειμι, "*I am,*" may be understood to be equivalent to the incommunicable name *Jehovah,* shall be considered in another place. The obvious sense of the passage is, Before Abraham was, or was born, I was in existence. Our Lord had declared that Abraham rejoiced to see his day. "Then said the Jews unto him, Thou art not yet fifty years old, and hast thou seen Abraham?" To this he solemnly replied, "Verily, verily, I say unto you, before Abraham was, I am." I had priority of existence, with a continuation of it to the present time. Nor did the Jews mistake his meaning, but being filled with indignation at so manifest a claim to divinity, "they took up stones to stone him."

How, then, do the Socinians dispose of this passage? The two hypotheses on which they have rested, for one would not suffice, are, *first,* "that Christ existed before Abraham had become, according to the import of his name, the Father of many nations; that is, before the Gentiles were called." But this was as true of the Jews with whom Christ was conversing as it was of himself. The *second* is: "Before Abraham was born, I am *he;* that is, the Christ, in the destination and appointment of God." But this was not declaring anything that was peculiar to Christ; since the existence, and the part which every one of his hearers was to act, were as much in the destination and appointment of God as his own. These opinions, therefore, are too absurd to require a formal refutation.

3. CHRIST CAME DOWN FROM HEAVEN.—Thus he declares: "I am the living bread which came down from heaven." John vi, 51. "No man hath ascended up to heaven, but he that came down from heaven, even the Son of man, which is in heaven." John iii, 13. Socinius and his early disciples, in order to account for these phrases, supposed that Christ, between the time of his birth and entrance upon his office, was translated to heaven, and remained there some time, that he might see and hear what he was to publish to the world. But modern Socinians, finding the unreasonable position of their elder brethren to be entirely destitute of proof, resolve the whole into *figure.* They tell us that our Lord's words do not necessarily imply a literal ascent and descent, but merely "that he alone was admitted to an intimate knowledge of the Divine will, and was commissioned to reveal it to men."*

In these passages, which so clearly teach the pre-existence of Christ, there are two phrases to be accounted for: *ascending into heaven,* and *coming down from heaven.* If to be "admitted to an intimate knowledge of the Divine will" were the sense of the former, it would not

* BELSHAM'S "Calm Inquiry."

be true that "*no man*" had thus ascended but "the Son of man;" since Moses and all the prophets in succession had been admitted to a knowledge of the Divine counsels, and had been commissioned to reveal them to men. Allowing, therefore, the principle of the Socinian gloss, it is totally inapplicable to the texts in question, and is, in fact, directly refuted by them.

But their principle of interpretation is false. For, whatever the phrase, *ascending into heaven*, may be supposed to signify, *coming down from heaven* must signify the opposite if we abide by the figure. But the latter phrase, they say, means, "to be commissioned to reveal the will of God to man."* If so, the two phrases, which are manifestly opposed to each other, lose all their opposition in the interpretation, which is sufficient to show that it is, as to both, entirely gratuitous, arbitrary, and contradictory. Now, allowing Socinians all they wish to establish as to the first clause—that *to go up into heaven* means *to learn and become acquainted with the counsels of God*—what must follow if they were to reason justly upon their own principles? Plainly this: that *to come down from heaven* being precisely the opposite of the former, must mean *to unlearn or to lose the knowledge of those counsels.*

Another passage which may be quoted in this connection is John vi, 62. Our Lord had told the Jews that he was the bread of life which "*came down from heaven.*" This they understood *literally*, and therefore asked: "Is not this the son of Joseph, whose father and mother we know? how is it, then, that he saith, *I came down from heaven.*" His disciples, too, so understood his words, for they also "murmured." But our Lord, so far from removing that impression, strengthens the assertion, and makes his profession a stumbling-block still more formidable. "Doth this offend you? What and if ye shall see the Son of man ascend up WHERE HE WAS BEFORE?" The occasion, therefore, fixes the sense of the passage beyond all perversion.

4. CHRIST CLAIMS A GLORIOUS EXISTENCE ANTECEDENT TO THE WORLD. —" And now, O Father, glorify thou me with thine own self, *with the glory which I had with thee before the world was.*" John xvii, 5. Whatever this glory was, it was possessed by Christ "before the world was;" or, as he afterward expresses it, "before the foundation of the world." But if he was with the Father, and had a glory with him "before the world was," then had he an existence, not only before his incarnation, but before the very "foundation of the world."

The Socinian gloss is, "The glory which I had with thee, in thy immutable decree, before the world was, or which thou didst decree before the world was, to give me." But the words rendered "which I had with thee" cannot bear any such sense, and the occasion was too peculiar to admit of any mystical, forced, or para-

* BELSHAM'S "Calm Inquiry."

bolic modes of speech. It was in the hearing of his disciples, just before he went out into the garden, that these words were spoken. There, in a solemn act of devotion, he declares to the Father that he had a glory with him before the world was, and prays that he might be reinstated in that former glory. The language is so explicit, that if there were no other proof in the whole New Testament of the pre-existence of Christ, this single passage would establish it.

Whatever, therefore, the true nature of our Lord Jesus Christ may be, we have at least discovered, from testimonies which no criticism and no unlicensed and paraphrastic comments have been able to shake or obscure, that he had an existence previous to his incarnation, and previous to the very " foundation of the world."

§ 2. *Christ, the Jehovah of the Old Testament.*

In reading the Scriptures of the Old Testament, it is impossible not to mark with serious attention the frequent visible appearances of God to the patriarchs and prophets, and, what is still more singular, his visible residence in a cloud of glory, both among the Jews in the wilderness, and in their sacred tabernacle and temple. The fact of such appearances cannot be disputed, and in order to point out its bearing upon the divinity of Christ it will be necessary to establish three propositions, namely:

1. THE PERSON WHO MADE THESE APPEARANCES WAS TRULY A DIVINE PERSON.—The proofs of this are, that he bears the name of Jehovah, God, and other Divine appellations; and that he dwelt among the Israelites as the object of their supreme worship.

(1.) *He bears the name of Jehovah and God.*—When the angel of the Lord found Hagar in the wilderness, " she called the name of *Jehovah* that spake unto her, Thou God seest me." Gen. xvi, 13. One of the three persons in human form who appeared to Abraham in the plains of Mamre is called Jehovah. "And JEHOVAH said, Shall I hide from Abraham that thing which I do?" Two of the three departed, but he to whom this high appellation is given remained; for "Abraham stood yet before JEHOVAH." This Jehovah is also called by Abraham "the Judge of all the earth," and the account of the solemn interview is thus given by the sacred historian: " The Lord (JEHOVAH) went his way, as soon as he had left communing with Abraham." Gen. xviii, 33.

This Divine person appeared to Jacob on several occasions. After one of these manifestations he said, "Surely the Lord (JEHOVAH) is in this place;" and after another, "I have seen God face to face." Gen. xxviii, 16; xxxii, 30. The same Jehovah was made visible to Moses, and gave him his commission. "God said unto Moses, I AM THAT I AM: and he said, Thus shalt thou say unto the children of Israel,

I am hath sent me unto you." Exod. iii, 14. The same Jehovah went before the Israelites in a pillar of cloud by day, and in a pillar of fire by night; and by him the law was given, amid terrible displays of power and majesty, from Mount Sinai. "Did ever people hear the voice of *God* speaking out of the midst of the fire, as thou hast heard, and live?" Deut. iv, 33.

(2.) *This Jehovah dwelt among the Israelites as the object of their supreme worship.*—He commanded them to build him a sanctuary, that he might reside among them; and when it was erected he took possession of it in a visible form, which was called "the glory of the Lord." There the SHECHINAH, the visible token of the presence of Jehovah, rested above the ark. There he was consulted on all occasions, and there he received their worship from age to age. Both in their tabernacle and temple services he was constantly celebrated as JEHOVAH, the God of Israel, the God of their fathers, and the object of their own exclusive *hope* and *trust*.

To this it is objected, that this personage is also called " the ANGEL of the Lord." This is true; but if "the angel of the Lord" is the same person as he who is called Jehovah, the same as he who gave the law in *his own name*, then it is clear that the term "angel" does not, in this application of it, indicate a created being, that it is not a designation of *nature* but of *office*, and that it is not inconsistent with absolute divinity.

It will be easy to show that Jehovah and "the angel of the Lord," when used in this eminent sense, denote the same person. Jacob says, "The angel of God spake unto me in a dream, saying, I am the God of Bethel." Gen. xxxi, 11, 12. Upon his death-bed he calls this same Divine person both *God* and *Angel*. "The *God* which fed me all my life long unto this day, the angel which redeemed me from all evil, bless the lads." Gen. xlviii, 15, 16. The prophet Hosea says of Jacob that "He had power with *God;* yea, he had power over the *angel*, and prevailed. He found him in Bethel, and there he spake with us; even the *Lord God of hosts*." Hos. xii, 3–5. Here the same person is called God, Angel, and Lord God of hosts. "The *angel of the Lord* called unto Abraham out of heaven the second time, and said, By myself have I sworn, saith the *Lord*, (JEHOVAH,) for because thou hast done this thing." Gen. xxii, 15, 16. It was the *angel of the Lord* that appeared to Moses in a flame of fire, but it was this same angel that said to him, "I am the *God* of thy father, the *God* of Abraham, the *God* of Isaac, and the *God* of Jacob." Exod. iii, 6. St. Stephen, in alluding to this part of the history of Moses, in his speech before the council, says, "There appeared to him in the wilderness of Mount Sinai *an angel of the Lord* in a flame of fire," showing that this phraseology was in use among the Jews in his day, and that this angel was regarded as the Jehovah who gave the law; for he adds, Moses "was in the

Church in the wilderness, with the *angel* which spoke to him in Mount Sinai."

These Scriptures prove, beyond the shadow of a doubt, that the angel of Jehovah is constantly represented as Jehovah himself, and, therefore, as a Divine person. Those, however, who deny the divinity of our Lord, endeavor to evade the force of this argument, according to their respective creeds. The Arians, who think the appearing angel to have been Christ, but who yet deny his being Jehovah, assume that this glorious but created being personated the Deity, and as his embassador and representative, spoke by his authority, and took his name.

The answer to this is, that though embassadors speak in the name of their masters, they do not apply the names and titles of their masters to themselves; that *created* angels, mentioned in Scripture as appearing to men, declare that they were sent by God, and never personate him; that the prophets uniformly acknowledge their commission to be from God; that God himself asserts, "Jehovah is my name, and my glory *will I not give to another;*" and yet, that the appearing angel calls himself, as we have seen, by this incommunicable name in almost innumerable instances; and that he claims and receives the *exclusive* worship both of the patriarchs, to whom he occasionally appeared, and the Jews, among whom he visibly resided for ages. To suppose him therefore to to be a created being, is to suppose the religion of the Bible to be a system of idolatry.

If the Arian account of the angel of Jehovah is untenable, the Socinian notion will be found to be equally unsupported, and indeed ridiculous. Dr. Priestley assumes the marvelous doctrine of "occasional personality," and thinks that "in some cases angels were nothing more than *temporary appearances,* and no permanent beings, the mere organs of the Deity, assumed for the purpose of making himself known." He speaks therefore of "a power occasionally emitted, and then taken back again into its source;" of this power being vested with a *temporary personality,* and thinks this possible! Little cause had the doctor and his adherents to talk of the mystery and absurdity of the doctrine of the Trinity, who can make a *person* out of a *power,* emitted and then drawn back again to its source; a *temporary person,* without individual subsistence! The wildness of this fiction is its own refutation. But that the angel of Jehovah was not this temporary occasional person, is made evident by Jacob's calling him the angel of the Lord who had fed him all his life long; and by this also that the same *person* who was called by himself and by the Jews "the God of Abraham, of Isaac, and of Jacob," was the God of the chosen people in *all* their generations.

Mr. Belsham's theory is that "the angel of the Lord was the visible symbol of the Divine presence;" and this opinion commonly obtains among Socinians. This notion, however, involves a whole train of absurdities. The phrase, the "angel of Jehovah," is not accounted for by a visible symbol, unless that symbol be considered as distinct from Jehovah. We have then the name Jehovah given to a cloud, a light, a fire. The fire is the *angel of the Lord*, and yet the angel of the Lord calls to Moses *out of the fire*. This visible symbol says to Abraham, "By MYSELF I have sworn," for these are said to be the words of the angel of Jehovah; and this angel, the visible symbol, spake to Moses on Mount Sinai. Such are the absurdities which flow from error! Most clearly, therefore, is it determined on the testimony of several Scriptures, and by necessary induction from the circumstances attending the numerous appearances of the angel of Jehovah in the Old Testament, that the person thus manifesting himself, and thus receiving supreme worship, was not a created angel, as the Arians would have it, nor an *atmospheric appearance*, the theory of modern Socinians, but that he was a DIVINE PERSON.

2. THIS DIVINE PERSON WAS NOT GOD THE FATHER.—We do not claim that the Father never manifested himself to men, as distinct from the Son; for this is contradicted by Scripture testimonies.* It is amply sufficient for the argument with which we are now concerned to prove that the angel of the Lord, whose appearances are so often recorded, is *not* the Father. This is clear from his appellation *angel*, with respect to which there can be but two interpretations. It is either a name descriptive of *nature* or of *office*. In the first view it is generally employed in the sacred Scriptures to designate one of an order of intelligences superior to man, but still *finite* and *created*. We have, however, already proved that the angel of the Lord is not a *creature;* and he cannot therefore be called an angel with reference to his *nature*.

The term must then be considered as a term of *office*. He is called the *angel* of the Lord because he was the *messenger* of the Lord— because he was *sent* to do his will and to be his visible image and representative. His office, therefore, under this appellation, was ministerial; but ministration is never attributed to the Father. He who was *sent* must be a distinct person from him *by whom* he was sent; the *messenger* from him whose *message* he brought, and whose will he performed. The angel of Jehovah is therefore a different person from the Jehovah whose messenger he was; and yet the angel himself is Jehovah, and, as we have proved, truly Divine. Thus does the Old Testament most clearly reveal to us, in the case of Jehovah and the angel of Jehovah, *two Divine persons*, while it still maintains its great fundamental principle, that there is but *one God*.

3. THE DIVINE PERSON SO OFTEN CALLED THE ANGEL OF THE LORD WAS THE PROMISED MESSIAH, *and is consequently* THE LORD AND SAVIOUR OF THE CHRISTIAN CHURCH.—We have seen that it was the angel of

* See Exod. xxiii, 20; Matt. iii, 17; xvii, 5.

13

the Lord who gave the law to the Israelites, and that in his *own name*, though still an *angel*, a *messenger* in the transaction; being at once servant and Lord, angel and Jehovah—circumstances which can only be explained on the hypothesis of his divinity, and for which neither Arianism nor Socinianism can give any solution. He was therefore the person who made the Mosaic covenant with the children of Israel. But the prophet Jeremiah says that the *new* covenant with Israel was to be made by the same person who had made the old. "Behold, the days come, saith the Lord, that *I will make* a new covenant with the house of Israel, and with the house of Judah; not according to the covenant that *I made* with their fathers, in the day that I took them by the hand, to bring them out of the land of Egypt." Jer. xxxi, 31, 32. The angel of Jehovah, who led the Israelites out of Egypt and gave them their law, is here plainly introduced as the author of the new covenant. But this new covenant, as we learn from the Epistle to the Hebrews,* is the Christian dispensation; and if Christ is its author, the Jehovah of the Old Testament and Christ of the New are the same Divine person.

Equally striking is the celebrated prediction of Malachi, the last of the Jewish prophets: "Behold, I will send my messenger, and he shall prepare the way before me; and the Lord, whom ye seek, shall suddenly come to his temple, even the messenger of the covenant whom ye delight in; behold, he shall come, saith the Lord of hosts." Mal. iii. 1. Here the prophet describes the coming Messiah, not only as the messenger of the covenant, but also as the Lord and Owner of the Jewish temple; and, consequently, as a Divine prince or governor—he shall "come to *his temple*." The Lord of any temple is the divinity to whose worship it is consecrated. The temple at Jerusalem, of which the prophet here speaks, was consecrated to the true and living God; and we have therefore the express testimony of Malachi that the Christ, the Deliverer, whose coming he announced, was no other than the Jehovah of the Old Testament.

This prophecy is expressly applied to Christ by St. Mark. "As it is written in the prophets, Behold, I send my messenger before thy face, which shall prepare thy way before thee." Mark i, 2. It follows from this that Jesus Christ is the Lord, the Lord of the temple, the messenger of the covenant mentioned in the prophecy. The appearing Jehovah of the Old Testament was the *King* of the Jews; their temple was HIS, because he resided in it; and he was the *messenger* of *their covenant*. But as all these characters are ascribed to Jesus Christ, the identity of the persons cannot be mistaken. One coincidence is singularly striking. It has been proved that the Angel Jehovah had his residence in the Jewish tabernacle and temple, and that he took possession of both at their dedication, suddenly filling them with his glory. On one occasion Jesus himself, though in his state of humiliation, came

* Heb. viii, 8–13.

in public procession to the temple at Jerusalem, and called it *his own ;* thus at once declaring that he was the ancient and rightful Lord of the temple, and appropriating to himself this eminent prophecy.

It would be easy to multiply quotations in which the name Jehovah and other Divine titles are applied to the Messiah; and to show, moreover, that these very passages are applied, in the New Testament, to our Lord Jesus Christ. We will, however, notice only two others. The first is Isaiah xl, 3 : " The voice of him that crieth in the wilderness, Prepare ye the way of the LORD, (JEHOVAH,) make straight in the desert a highway for our GOD." This prediction is applied, in the Christian Scriptures, to John the Baptist, as the harbinger of Christ; and it is, therefore, evident that our Lord is the person whom the prophet calls JEHOVAH and " *our* GOD."

The other passage is 1 Cor. x, 9 : " Neither let us tempt Christ, as some of them (that is, the Jews in the wilderness) also tempted, and were destroyed of serpents." The pronoun *αυτὸν, him,* must be understood after " tempted," as referring to Christ just before mentioned. The Jews in the wilderness are here said to have tempted some person; and to understand by that person any other than Christ, who is just before mentioned, is against all grammar, which never allows, without absolute necessity, any other accusative to be understood with the verb than that of some person or thing previously mentioned in the same sentence. The conjunction *και, also,* establishes this interpretation beyond a doubt. Neither let us tempt CHRIST as some of them ALSO tempted—tempted whom? The obvious answer is, *Christ.* If, therefore, the Israelites tempted Christ in the wilderness he is the Jehovah of the Old Testament.

It has now been established that the Angel Jehovah and Jesus Christ our Lord are the same person; and this is the first great argument by which his divinity is proved. He not only existed before his incarnation, but is seen at the head of the religious institutions of his Church up to the earliest ages. In every manifestation of himself he has given evidence that he " thought it not robbery to be equal with God." No name is given to the Angel Jehovah which is not given to Jehovah Jesus. No attribute is ascribed to the one which is not ascribed to the other. The worship which was paid to the one by patriarchs and prophets was paid to the other by evangelists and apostles ; and the Scriptures declare them to be the same august person, *the Redeeming Angel, the Redeeming Kinsman, and the Redeeming* GOD.

§ 3. *Divine Titles ascribed to Christ.*

The next argument in support of the divinity of Christ is drawn from the titles which are ascribed to him in the sacred volume. If they are such as can designate a Divine Being, and a Divine Being *only,* then is

Christ truly Divine. To deny this conclusion would be to charge the word of truth with direct deception, and that, too, in a fundamental article of religion. This is our argument, and we will proceed to the illustration. Our attention will be directed to only four of the Divine titles which are ascribed to our Lord. These are, *Jehovah*, *Lord*, *God*, and *King of Israel*.

1. JEHOVAH.—That this name is applied to the Messiah in many passages of the Old Testament is admitted even by our opponents. But Dr. Priestley attempts to destroy the force of the argument deduced from this fact, by alleging that "several things in the Scriptures are called by the name of Jehovah; as, Jerusalem is called Jehovah our righteousness."* It is, however, a miserable pretense to meet this argument by asserting that the name Jehovah is sometimes given to places. It is so, but only in composition with some other word; as Jehovah-Jire, Jehovah-Nissi, Jehovah-Shallum. Such names are used, not as descriptive of particular localities, but as *memorials* of events connected with them, which mark the interposition and character of Jehovah himself. Thus: "Jehovah-Jire," *the Lord will see* or *provide*, referred to HIS interposition to save Isaac, and probably to the *provision* of the sacrifice of Christ. Nor is it true that Jerusalem is called "Jehovah our righteousness." The parallel passage clearly shows that this is the name, not of Jerusalem, but of "THE BRANCH."† No instance can be given in which a created being is called Jehovah in the Scriptures, or was so called among the Jews. The peculiar sacredness attached to this name among them was a sufficient guard against such an application of it in their common language; and as for the Scriptures, they explicitly represent it as peculiar to divinity itself. "I am JEHOVAH, that is my name, and my glory will I *not* give to *another*." Isa. xlii, 8. "Thou, whose NAME ALONE is JEHOVAH, art the Most High above all the earth." Psa. lxxxiii, 18.

We see, then, that this is the peculiar and appropriate name of God, that name by which he is distinguished from all other beings, and which imports perfections so exclusively belonging to the living and true God that it cannot, in truth, be applied to any other being. This name, however, is *solemnly* and *repeatedly* given to the *Messiah ;* and, unless we can suppose Scripture to contradict itself, by making that a peculiar name of God which is not peculiar to him, and by establishing an inducement to that idolatry which it so sternly condemns, then this adorable name itself declares the absolute divinity of him who is invested with it.

2. LORD.—Our Lord's disciples not only applied to him those passages of the Old Testament in which the Messiah is called Jehovah, but they saluted and worshiped him by the title κυριος, LORD, which is of precisely the same original import. We admit that it is sometimes

* History of "Early Opinions."   † Jer. xxiii, 5, 6; xxxiii, 16.

used as the translation of other names of God, which import simply dominion, and that it is applied also to merely human masters and rulers; but, in its *highest sense*, it is universally allowed to belong to God. If in this *highest sense* it is applied to Christ, then are we to regard it as denoting true and absolute divinity.

The *first* proof of this is, that both in the Septuagint and by the writers of the New Testament, κύριος is the term by which the name Jehovah is translated. In all those passages, therefore, in which the Messiah is called by that peculiar title of divinity, we have the authority of the LXX for applying it in its full and highest signification to Jesus Christ, who is that Messiah. Accordingly, the New Testament writers apply this appellation to their Master when they quote these prophetic passages as fulfilled in him. They found it used in the Greek version of the Old Testament, in its *highest possible import*, as a rendering of Jehovah. Had they thought Jesus to be less than God, they could not have given him a title which would have misled their readers, unless they had intimated that they did not use it as a title of divinity, but in its lowest sense, as a term of merely human courtesy, or at most, of human dominion. But we have no such intimation; and, if they wrote under Divine inspiration, it follows that they used it as being fully equivalent to the title JEHOVAH itself, as their quotations will show.

St. Matthew quotes, and applies to Christ, Isaiah xl, 3: "The voice of one crying in the wilderness, Prepare ye the way of the LORD, κυρίου." The other Evangelists make the same application of it, representing John as the herald of Jesus, the Jehovah of the prophet, and their κύριος, *Lord*. On this point St. Paul also adds his testimony, Romans x, 13: "Whosoever shall call on the name of the LORD (κυρίου) shall be saved," which is quoted from Joel ii, 32: "Whosoever shall call on the name of JEHOVAH shall be delivered."

But, *secondly*, even when the title κύριος, LORD, is not employed as the rendering of the name JEHOVAH, but is used as a common appellation of Christ, it is so connected with other terms, and with circumstances which clearly imply divinity, as to afford additional proof that the disciples themselves considered it as a Divine *title*, and intended that it should be so understood by others. It is put *absolutely*, and by way of *eminence*, "THE LORD." Christ is called by St. Luke "the LORD GOD;" and Thomas adoringly addresses him, "My LORD and my GOD." When κύριος is used to express dominion, that dominion is represented as *absolute* and *universal*, and therefore *Divine*. Hence Peter declares of Jesus Christ that "he is (κύριος) LORD of all." Acts x, 36.

3. GOD.—That this title is ascribed to Christ, even the adversaries of his divinity are obliged to confess. It is indeed said, that the term is sometimes used in an inferior sense; but this proves nothing against the Deity of Christ, for it must still be allowed that it is *generally* used in

Scripture to designate the Divine Being. The question is, therefore, limited to this: Is our Lord called *God* in the highest sense of that appellation?

Before we proceed to the examination of this question, it will be necessary to show that the term *God*, in its highest sense, involves the idea of absolute divinity. This has been denied by Sir Isaac Newton and Dr. Samuel Clarke, who considered it a *relative* term, importing nothing more than dominion. But if we trace the Scripture notion of what is *truly* and *properly* God, we shall find it made up of these several ideas: infinite wisdom, invincible power, immutability, all-sufficiency, and the like. These are the foundation of *dominion*, which is a secondary consideration; but it must be nothing less than dominion *supreme*, which will accord with the Scripture notion of *God*. It is not merely that of a *ruler*, a *governor*, a *lord*, or a *protector;* but a *Sovereign* Ruler, an *Omniscient* and *Omnipresent* Governor, an *Almighty* Lord, an eternal, immutable, and all-sufficient *Creator*, *Preserver*, and *Protector*. Whatever falls short of this is not *properly* God, in the Scripture import of that term, and cannot be so denominated, except by way of figure.

If *God* were merely a relative term, having reference to *subjects*, it would necessarily follow, either that some of those subjects had an eternal existence, or that there was a time when there was no God. We have, however, the express testimony of Divine truth, that it is not dominion *only*, but absolute divinity, that is designated by the term. Thus, "Before the mountains were brought forth, or ever thou hadst formed the earth or the world, even from everlasting to everlasting, thou art GOD." Psa. xc, 2. Here the term *God* is applied to that eternal Being who "formed the earth and the world." He is declared to be GOD "from everlasting," and consequently before any creature existed, and so before he had any *subjects*, or exercised any *dominion*.

The import of the term GOD, in its highest sense, being thus shown to include all the excellences and glories of the Divine nature, if in this sense it is ascribed to Christ, it will prove, not as Arians would have it, his *dominion* only, but his divinity. Nor will it set aside this conclusion to say, that men are sometimes called gods; for in the New Testament the term God is never applied in the singular to any man.

Let us then adduce a few passages of Scripture in which this appellation is applied to Jesus Christ. Matt. i, 23: "Behold, a virgin shall be with child, and shall bring forth a son, and they shall call his name EMMANUEL, which being interpreted is, GOD with us."

John i, 1: "In the beginning was the WORD, and the WORD was with GOD, and the WORD was GOD."

John xx, 28: "And Thomas answered and said unto him, My Lord and my GOD."

Romans ix, 5: "And of whom, as concerning the flesh, Christ came, who is over all, GOD blessed forever."

Titus ii, 13: "Looking for that blessed hope, and the glorious appearing of the great GOD and our Saviour Jesus Christ."

Hebrews i, 8: "But unto the Son he saith, Thy throne, O GOD, is for ever and ever."

1 John v, 20. "And we are in him that is true, even in his Son Jesus Christ. This is the true GOD, and eternal life."

4. KING OF ISRAEL.—This title has an allusion to Christ's pre-existence, and to his sovereignty over Israel under the law. It has been already established that the "*Jehovah*," "the *Holy One of Israel*," "the *Lord of hosts*," "the *King of the Jews*" of the Old Testament, is not the Father, but another Divine person, who, in the New Testament, is affirmed to be *Jesus Christ*. This being the view of the sacred writers of the evangelical dispensation, it is evident that they could not use the appellation " KING OF ISRAEL " in a lower sense than that in which it stands in the Old Testament, and it is equally evident that the Jews understood it to imply divinity.

Nathanael, upon a satisfactory proof of Christ's Messiahship, exclaimed, "Thou art the Son of God, thou art the KING OF ISRAEL." John i, 49. While our Saviour hung upon the cross, the chief priests, the scribes, and the elders said, "If he be the KING OF ISRAEL, let him now come down from the cross, and we will believe in him." Matt. xxvii, 42.

§ 4. Divine Attributes are ascribed to Christ.

Having considered the import of some of the titles applied to our Lord in the Scriptures, and having proved that they imply divinity, we may next consider the *attributes* which are ascribed to him. If, to names and lofty titles which imply divinity, we find added attributes never given to creatures, and from which all creatures are excluded, the Deity of Christ will be established beyond reasonable controversy. No argument can be more conclusive than this. Of the essence of Deity we know nothing, but that he is a Spirit. He is made known to us by his attributes, and it is from them we learn that there is an *essential* distinction between him and his creatures. He has attributes which they have not, and those which they have in common with him he possesses in an absolutely perfect degree. From this it follows, that HIS is a *peculiar* nature, a nature *sui generis*, to which no creature can possibly approximate. Should, then, these same attributes be found ascribed to Christ as explicitly and literally as to the Father, it will follow of necessity that, the attributes being the same, the essence must be the same, and that this essence is the exclusive nature of the θεοτης, or Godhead.

Of the peculiar attributes of Deity which are ascribed to Jesus Christ we may notice,

1. ETERNITY.—Isaiah calls him "The mighty God, the *Everlasting Father*, the Prince of Peace." Isa. ix, 6. The phrase "Everlasting Father" is variously rendered by the best orthodox critics; but every rendering is consistent with the application of a positive eternity to the Messiah, of whom this is evidently a prediction. Christ declares of himself, "I am THE FIRST and THE LAST;" and again, "I am Alpha and Omega, the beginning and the ending, saith the Lord, which is, and which was, and which is to come, the Almighty." Rev. i, 8, 17. Now, it is by these very terms that the eternity of God is declared. "Before me there was no God formed, neither shall there be after me." Isa. xliii, 10. "I am the first, and I am the last; and besides me there is no God." Isa. xliv, 6. These titles clearly indicate that the Being to whom they properly belong had no beginning, and will have no end; and as they are explicitly and absolutely claimed by Christ, they are proofs of his eternity.

2. OMNIPRESENCE.—Our Lord declares himself to be, at the same time, both in heaven and upon the earth; which is surely a property of divinity alone. "No man hath ascended up to heaven, but he that came down from heaven, even the Son of man which is in heaven." John iii, 13. Again, "Where two or three are gathered together in my name, *there am I in the midst of them*." Matt. xviii, 20.

How futile is the Socinian comment on this text, that this promise is to be "limited to the apostolic age!" Were that even granted, what would the concession avail? In that age the disciples met in the name of their Lord many times in the week and in many parts of the world at the same time. He, therefore, who could be "in the midst of them," whenever and wherever they assembled, must be *omnipresent*. The text is as literal a declaration of Christ's presence everywhere with his true worshipers, as that similar promise of Jehovah to the Israelites: "In all places where I record my name, I will come unto thee, and I will bless thee." Exod. xx, 24. At the very moment, too, of Christ's ascension, and when, as to his bodily presence, he was about to leave his disciples, he promised still to be with them, calling their attention to this promise by an emphatic exclamation: "Lo, I AM WITH YOU ALWAY, even to the end of the world." Matt. xxviii, 20.

3. OMNISCIENCE.—This is an attribute which cannot be ascribed to a creature; for though it may be difficult to say how far the knowledge of the highest order of intelligent creatures may be extended, yet there are two kinds of knowledge which God solemnly and exclusively claims as peculiar to himself. The *first* is a perfect knowledge of the thoughts and purposes of the human heart. "I the Lord search the heart, I try the reins." Jer. xvii, 10. "Thou, even thou only, knowest the hearts of all the children of men." 1 Kings viii, 39. This knowledge is

attributed to our Lord, and claimed by him; not, however, as a super-natural *gift*, but as an original attribute.   Hence St. John declares that "HE KNEW ALL MEN, and needed not that any should testify of man; for HE KNEW WHAT WAS IN MAN." John ii, 24, 25.   After his exaltation he claimed this prerogative, in the full style and majesty of the Old Testament Jehovah.   "And all the Churches shall know that *I am he which* SEARCHETH THE REINS AND HEARTS." Rev. ii, 23.

The *second* kind of knowledge, to which reference has been made, is the knowledge of *futurity;* which is so peculiar to Deity that God distinguishes himself from all the false divinities of the heathen by this circumstance alone.   "I am God, and there is none else; I am God, and there is none like me; declaring the end from the beginning, and from ancient times the things that are not yet done." Isa. xlvi, 9, 10.   This kind of knowledge is also ascribed to Christ.   All the predictions which he uttered are in proof that he possessed this attribute; for they are nowhere referred to *inspiration*, the source to which all the prophets and apostles ascribed their prophetic gifts, but resulted from his own prescience.   He "*knew from the beginning* who they were that believed not, and who should betray him." John vi, 64.

4. OMNIPOTENCE.—This also is peculiar to the Godhead; for, though power may be communicated to a creature, yet a finite capacity must limit the communication; nor can it exist in an infinite degree any more than wisdom, except in an infinite nature.   Christ claims "all power in heaven and in earth;" and in Rev. i, 8, he is expressly styled "THE ALMIGHTY."   To the Jews he said, "What things soever he [the Father] doeth, THESE ALSO DOETH THE SON LIKEWISE." John v, 19.

Thus we have seen that the Scriptures ascribe to our Lord Jesus Christ *Eternity, Omnipresence, Omniscience,* and *Omnipotence*—attributes which prove him to be "The true God;" and we may now close the argument with his own remarkable declaration: "ALL THINGS which the Father hath ARE MINE." John xvi, 15.   If the Son possess all things that belong to the Father, then he possesses all the attributes and perfections of the Father, and must necessarily be of the same nature, substance, and Godhead.

§ 5. *Divine Works are ascribed to Christ.*

This argument is confirmatory of the foregoing; for if acts have been done by Christ which, in the nature of things, cannot be performed by any creature, however exalted, then must he be truly God.   That such works are ascribed to him in the Holy Scriptures, we will now proceed to show.

1. CREATION.—The Socinians themselves acknowledge that the production of things out of nothing is possible only to Divine power; and they, therefore, attempt to prove that the creation of which Christ is

said to be the author, is a *moral* creation. To correct this error it is only necessary to exhibit two or three passages of Scripture which evidently ascribe to him the whole physical creation. St. John affirms, in the introduction of his Gospel, that " all things [without limitation or restriction] were made by" the Divine Word; and that " without him was not *anything* made that was made." If he had reference to a *moral*, and not a *physical* creation, he could not have expressed himself in this manner without intending to mislead: a supposition which is equally contrary to his piety and to his inspiration. His meaning must, therefore, be, that there is no created object which had not Christ for its creator.

But the apostle shows most clearly that the physical creation was the work of Christ, by asserting that "THE WORLD WAS MADE BY HIM;" that world into which he came as " the light;" that world *in* which he was when he was made flesh ; that *world* which " knew him not." It matters nothing to the argument whether " the world" be understood of men or of the material world. On either supposition " the world was made by him," and the creation was, therefore, *physical.* In neither case could the creation be a *moral* one, for the *material* world is incapable of a moral renewal; and the world which " knew not" Christ, if understood of *men*, was not renewed by a moral creation, but was unregenerate.

Another passage, equally explicit in ascribing to Christ the physical creation, is found in Heb. i, 2 : " By whom also HE MADE THE WORLDS." " God," says the apostle, " hath in these last days spoken unto us by his SON, whom he hath appointed heir of all things;" and he then proceeds to give *farther* information in regard to the nature and dignity of the personage thus denominated the " SON" and " HEIR." In order to prove him greater than angels, who are the greatest of all created beings, the apostle declares that " by him also God made the worlds." That the term " worlds" is here to be understood of the material universe, is evident from Heb. xi, 3 : " Through faith we understand that the WORLDS were framed by the word of God, so that things which are seen were not made of things which do appear:" words which can only be understood of the physical creation.

Another consideration which fixes the meaning of the clause, " by whom also he made the worlds," is, that in the same chapter the apostle reiterates the doctrine of the creation of the world by Jesus Christ. " But unto THE SON he saith," not only, " Thy throne, O God, is for ever and ever;" but also, " Thou, Lord, [Jehovah,] in the beginning hast laid the foundation of the earth; and·the heavens are the works of thine hands." This language is, beyond all controversy, addressed to Christ, and will forever attach to him, on the authority of inspiration, the title of " *Jehovah*," and array him in all the majesty of creative power and glory.

The only additional passage which it is necessary to adduce, in order to show that Christ is the creator of all things, and that the creation of which he is the author is not a *moral* but a *physical* creation; not the framing of the Christian dispensation, but the forming of the whole universe of creatures out of nothing, is Colossians i, 16, 17: "For by him were all things CREATED, that are in heaven, and that are in earth, visible and invisible, whether they be thrones, or dominions, or principalities, or powers; all things were created BY him and FOR him; and he is BEFORE all things." The terms here employed are an abundant refutation of the notion, that the creation mentioned is to be understood in a *moral* sense. The objects created are " all things in heaven and in earth ;" and lest immaterial beings should be thought to be excluded, the apostle adds, "visible and invisible." And, lest things *invisible* should be understood of *inferior* angels only, to the exclusion of those of the higher orders, the apostle becomes still more particular, and adds, " whether they be thrones, or dominions, or principalities, or powers ;" terms by which the Jews expressed the different orders of angels, and which are thus employed in the Scriptures.* The passage shows, moreover, that in the creation of all things Jesus Christ was both the *efficient* and the *final* cause, and not merely the *instrumental* cause, working by and for another. " All things were created BY him and FOR him."

2. PRESERVATION.—The sacred Scriptures declare that Jesus Christ is the preserver of all things as well as their creator, for "by him all things CONSIST," (συνεστηκε, *sunesteke*,) are kept together, or preserved from falling into confusion or annihilation. This is surely a Divine work; nor could it be said, consistent with reason and piety, that the universe is sustained by a created being. The same doctrine is taught in Heb. i, 3, where Christ is spoken of as " *upholding all things* by the word of his power." Τὰ πάντα (*ta panta*) signifies the universe, which the Son of God bears up, or sustains, by his almighty word. If, then, to preserve the created universe is the work of JEHOVAH, as the Scriptures declare,† and if this work is ascribed to our Lord, there can remain no doubt whatever that he also is JEHOVAH.

3. THE FORGIVENESS OF SINS.—This is unquestionably one of the peculiar acts of God. In the manifest reason of the thing, no one can forgive but the party offended; and, as sin is the transgression of the law of God, he alone is the offended party, and, therefore, he only can forgive. *Mediately* others may *declare* his pardoning acts, or the conditions on which he proposes to forgive; but *authoritatively*, there can be no actual forgiveness of sins but by God himself.

But Christ forgives sins by his own authority, and therefore he is God. One single passage will prove this. " He said to the sick of the palsy, Son, be of good cheer, *thy sins be forgiven thee*." Matt. ix, 2.

* See Eph. i, 21; Col. ii, 10.   † Neh. ix, 6; Psa. xxxvi, 6.

The scribes understood that he did this *authoritatively*, and that he thereby assumed a Divine prerogative. They, therefore, said among themselves, "This man blasphemeth." What then was the conduct of our Lord on that occasion? Did he admit that he only ministerially *declared*, in consequence of some revelation, that God had forgiven the sins of the paralytic? On the contrary, he performed a miracle to prove that the very right which they disputed was vested in him. "That ye may KNOW that the Son of man hath power on earth to forgive sins, then saith he to the sick of the palsy, Arise, take up thy bed, and go unto thine house." Matt. ix, 6.

4. THE RAISING OF THE DEAD.—It will be acknowledged by all, that to raise the dead is a Divine work. He only who first framed the human body, and connected with it a living spirit, can restore that body again to life, and bring back the soul from the invisible world to its original abode. It is "God who quickeneth the dead." Rom. iv, 17. But this power is claimed by Jesus Christ: "As the Father raiseth up the dead, and quickeneth them; even so the Son quickeneth whom he will." John v, 21. Here Christ explicitly assumes equal power with the Father, and the same uncontrolled and sovereign exercise of it in the restoration of life. This power was exerted by our Lord, while he sojourned upon the earth, in raising to life the daughter of Jairus, the widow's son, Lazarus, and others; but it will be more gloriously displayed at the end of time, in restoring to life the millions of the human race who shall then be sleeping in the dust. "The hour is coming, in which all that are in the graves shall hear his voice, and shall come forth." John v, 28, 29.

It may be objected that this work is not a decisive proof of divinity, because the dead were raised by some of the prophets and by the apostles of our Lord. To this it is only necessary to reply, that the prophets raised the dead *in the name* of the God of Israel, and the apostles *in the name* of Jesus Christ; but he performed this miracle of power in his own name, and spoke of himself in terms which no prophet or apostle would have dared to employ: "I am the resurrection and the life; he that believeth in me, though he were dead, yet shall he live." John xi, 25.

5. THE FINAL JUDGMENT IS ASCRIBED TO CHRIST.—The Scriptures declare that "the *Lord* (JEHOVAH) is our Judge," and that "every one of us shall give account of himself to *God*;" but they declare also, that "we must all appear before the judgment-seat of *Christ*;" that "before him shall be gathered all nations;" and that "he shall separate one from another, as a shepherd divideth his sheep from the goats."* To him who will pronounce the final sentence omniscience is necessary as well as omnipotence to execute it; for it will proceed not merely upon the external actions of men, but upon their motives and their

* See Isa. xxxiii, 22; Rom. xiv, 12; 2 Cor. v, 10; Matt. xxv, 32.

thoughts, which are known to him alone who searches the heart. Christ will indeed act in concurrence with the Father, who is hence said to judge the world by him; but this high office necessarily supposes him to be truly God.

§ 6. *Divine Worship is paid to Christ.*

It will be our business in this section, *first*, to establish the fact that Jesus Christ is the object of worship; and *secondly*, to consider the bearing which this fact has upon the doctrine of his Supreme Divinity.

1. CHRIST IS THE OBJECT OF WORSHIP.—Of this fact there are numerous proofs in the sacred Scriptures, a few of which we will notice.

(1.) *He was worshiped by his disciples prior to his ascension to heaven.*—"When he was come down from the mountain, great multitudes followed him; and behold, there came a leper and WORSHIPED HIM, saying, Lord, if thou wilt, thou canst make me clean." Matt. viii, 1, 2. When Jesus said to the man whom he had previously cured of blindness, "Dost thou believe on the Son of God? he answered and said, Who is he, Lord, that I might believe on him? And Jesus said unto him, Thou hast both seen him, and it is he that talketh with thee. And he said, Lord, I believe; and he WORSHIPED HIM." John ix, 35–38. He worshiped Christ, be it observed, under the character, "Son of God," a title which the Jews regarded as implying actual divinity. The worship paid by this man must, therefore, in its intention, have been supreme, for it was offered to a person who was acknowledged to be Divine, "the Son of God." Again, when the disciples, fully yielding to the demonstration of our Lord's Messiahship, arising out of a series of splendid miracles, recognized him *also* under his personal character, "they WORSHIPED HIM, saying, Of a truth thou art the Son of God." Matt. xiv, 33.

It is admitted that the word προσκυνέω, (*proskuneo,*) *to worship*, is sometimes used to express that lowly reverence with which, in the East, it has been always customary to salute persons of rank, and especially rulers and sovereigns; but it is frequently used to express also the worship of the Supreme Jehovah. Whether, then, it denotes an act of civil respect or of Divine adoration, the circumstances of the case must determine.

Our Lord could not have received the worship which was paid to him in the character of a civil governor. He had cautiously avoided the least intimation that he had any civil pretensions, or that his object was to make himself a king; and, therefore, to have suffered himself to be saluted with the homage proper to civil governors would have been a marked inconsistency. Nor could he have received it in compliance with the custom of the Jewish Rabbins, who exacted great external reverence from their disciples, for he sharply reproved their haughtiness, and their love of adulation and honor. The circumstances, then, which accompany these instances make it evident that the worship which the disciples paid to Christ was of the highest order—they *worshiped him as* GOD.

(2.) *Christ was worshiped by his disciples subsequent to his resurrection and ascension.*—When "he was parted from them, and carried up into heaven, they WORSHIPED HIM." Luke xxiv, 51, 52. Here the act must necessarily have been one of Divine adoration, since it was performed *after* "he was parted from them," and, therefore, it cannot be resolved into the customary token of *personal* respect paid to superiors, which was always exhibited in their *presence.*

When the apostles were assembled to fill the place of Judas, the lots being prepared " they prayed, and said, Thou, Lord, which knowest the hearts of all men, show whether of these two thou hast chosen." Acts i, 24. That this prayer was addressed to Christ is clear, from its being his special prerogative to choose his own apostles. They are, therefore, styled "apostles," not of the Father, but " of Jesus Christ." Here, then, is a direct act of worship, because it is an act of prayer, and our Lord is addressed as one who knows " the hearts of all men."

When Stephen, the protomartyr, was stoned, he prayed, "LORD JESUS, RECEIVE MY SPIRIT;" and again, "LORD, LAY NOT THIS SIN TO THEIR CHARGE." Acts vii, 59, 60. In the former petition he acknowledges Christ to be the disposer of the eternal states of men; in the latter, he acknowledges him to be the governor and judge of men, having power to remit, pass by, or visit their sins. These are so manifestly Divine acts that Stephen must have prayed to Christ, believing him to be truly GOD.

St. Paul, in that affliction which he metaphorically describes by " a thorn in the flesh," "besought the Lord thrice, that it might depart from" him; and the answer shows that "*the Lord*" to whom he addressed his prayer was CHRIST; for he adds, " And he said unto me, My grace is sufficient for thee: for my strength is made perfect in weakness. Most gladly therefore will I rather glory in my infirmities, that the POWER OF CHRIST may rest upon me." 2 Cor. xii, 7–9. The invoking of Christ was not only practiced by the apostle himself, as several passages show ;* but is adduced by him as a distinctive characteristic of Christians, so that among all the primitive Churches this practice must have been universal. " Unto the Church of God which is at Corinth, with all that IN EVERY PLACE CALL UPON THE NAME OF JESUS CHRIST our Lord." 1 Cor. i, 2.

To these instances are to be added all the *doxologies* to Christ, in common with the Father and the Holy Spirit, and all the *benedictions* made in his *name* in common with theirs, for all these are forms of wor-

* See 2 Thes. ii, 16, 17 ; 2 Tim. iv, 22.

ship. The first consist of ascriptions of equal and Divine honors, with grateful recognitions of the Being addressed as the author of benefits received. The following may be given as a few out of many instances: "But grow in grace, and in the knowledge of our Lord and Saviour Jesus Christ. To him be GLORY, both now and for ever. Amen." 2 Pet. iii, 18. "Unto him that loved us, and washed us from our sins in his own blood, and hath made us kings and priests unto God and his Father, to him be GLORY and DOMINION for ever and ever. Amen." Rev. i, 5, 6. When we consider the serious and reverential manner in which these doxologies are introduced, and the superlative praise which they convey, so far surpassing what humanity can deserve, we must suppose that the Being to whom they refer is really Divine. The ascription of eternal glory and everlasting dominion, if addressed to any creature, however exalted, would be idolatrous and profane.

Benedictions are blessings solemnly pronounced upon persons in the name of God, and were derived from the practice of the Jewish priests, and the still older patriarchs, who blessed others in the name of Jehovah, as his representatives. These are so regular in their form as to make it clearly appear that the apostles constantly *blessed* the people *ministerially* in the name of Christ as one of the blessed Trinity. "Grace to you, and peace from God our Father, and the Lord Jesus Christ." Rom. i, 7. "The grace of the Lord Jesus Christ, and the love of God, and the communion of the Holy Ghost, be with you all." 2 Cor. xiii, 14.

In answer to the Socinian perversion, that these are mere "wishes," or "expressions of good-will," it may be observed that this objection overlooks, or notices very slightly, the main point on which the whole question turns, the *nature* of the blessings sought, and consequently, the *qualities* which they imply in the Person who is desired to bestow them. The blessings sought are *grace, mercy,* and *peace;* which are the highest gifts that Omnipotent Benevolence can bestow, or a dependent nature receive. To desire such blessings, either in the mode of direct address, or in that of precatory wish, from any being who is not possessed of omnipotent goodness, would be absurd, and sinful in the highest degree.

(3.) *The worship of Christ is practiced among heavenly beings.*— "When he bringeth in the first-begotten into the world, he saith, And let ALL THE ANGELS OF GOD WORSHIP HIM." Heb. i, 6. The Apocalypse, in its scenic representations, exhibits Christ as, equally with the Father, the object of the worship of angels and glorified saints; placing every creature in the universe, except the inhabitants of hell, in prostrate adoration at his feet. "And every creature which is in heaven and on the earth, and under the earth, and such as are in the sea, and all that are in them, heard I saying, Blessing, and honor, and glory, and power, be unto him that sitteth upon the throne, AND UNTO THE LAMB forever and ever." Rev. v, 13. Having now established the fact, that Jesus Christ is the object of *worship*, we will proceed to consider,

2. THE BEARING WHICH THIS FACT HAS UPON THE DOCTRINE OF HIS SUPREME DIVINITY.—To perceive this clearly, we should first inquire into the religious principles and practice of the early disciples of our Lord. As to their religious principles, they were Jews; and Jews, too, of an age in which their nation had shaken off its idolatrous propensities, and which was distinguished by its zeal against all worship or religious trust of which any creature was the object. The great principle of the law was, "Thou shalt have no other gods before (or *beside*) me."* It was, therefore, commanded by Moses, "Thou shalt fear the Lord thy God, and *him* shalt thou serve;"† which words are quoted by our Lord in his temptation, when solicited to worship Satan, so as to prove that to *fear* God and to *serve* him are expressions which signify *worship*, and that all other beings but God are excluded from it. "Thou shalt WOR-SHIP the Lord thy God, and him *only* shalt thou serve." Luke iv, 8. Accordingly, we find the apostles teaching and practicing this as a first principle of their religion.

St. Paul charges the heathen with not *glorifying* God when they *knew* him, and with worshiping and serving "the *creature* more than (or *besides*) the Creator." Rom. i, 25. Again, when he mentions it as one of the crimes of the Galatians, previous to their conversion to Christianity, that they "did service unto them which by *nature* are no gods," he plainly intimates that no one has a title to religious *service* but he who is by *nature* God; and if so, he himself could not have worshiped Christ had he not believed him to be truly Divine.

The *practice* of the apostles was in strict accordance with this principle. Thus, when worship was offered to Peter by Cornelius, who certainly did not take him to be God, he forbade it. So also Paul and Barnabas prevented the people at Lystra from offering to them religious honors with expressions of horror. An eminent instance is recorded, also, of the exclusion of all creatures, however exalted, from the honor of religious worship, in Rev. xix, 10, where the angel refused to receive so much as even the outward act of adoration. His language is, "See thou do it not: *worship God*," clearly intimating thereby that all acts of religious worship are to be appropriated to God alone.

From the known and avowed religious sentiments, then, of the apostles, both as Jews and as Christians, as well as from their practice, it follows that they could not have paid religious worship to Christ, a fact which has already been established, unless they had considered him as a Divine person, and themselves as bound on that account, according to his own words, to *honor the* SON, *even as they honored the* FATHER. It is the testimony of St. Paul that he, "being in the form of God, thought it not robbery to be equal with God,"—a passage which inci-

* Exod. xx, 4.   † Deut. x, 20.

dentally teaches the Godhead of Christ, and which cannot be reconciled to any hypothesis that excludes his essential Deity.

Arians devised the doctrine of *supreme* and *inferior* worship, and a similar distinction was maintained by Dr. Samuel Clarke, to reconcile the worship of Christ with his semi-Arianism. The same sophistical distinction is resorted to by Roman Catholics to vindicate the worship of angels, the Virgin Mary, and departed saints. But it is a sufficient refutation of this theory,

(1.) *That it has no countenance in the Sacred Scriptures.*—We often read of prayer; but there is not a word respecting absolute and relative, supreme and inferior prayer. We are commanded to pray fervently and incessantly, but never to pray sovereignly or absolutely. Nor have we any rules left us about raising or lowering our intentions, in proportion to the dignity of the object.

(2.) *That the Scriptures are directly opposed to it.*—Sacrifice was a mode of worship required under the law, and was doubtless not more solemn in its character than the exercise of prayer; but it is said, "He that sacrificeth unto any god, save unto the Lord only, he shall be utterly destroyed." Exod. xxii, 20. Now suppose any person, considering that this law referred only to absolute and sovereign sacrifice to God, had sacrificed to other gods, and had been convicted of it before the judges. His apology for the act must have run thus: "I did, indeed, sacrifice to other gods, but it was not absolute or supreme sacrifice, which is all that the law forbids. I considered the gods to whom I sacrificed as inferior beings, and I offered them, therefore, only a relative and inferior service; reserving all sovereign sacrifice to the Supreme God of Israel." But is it likely that such an apology would have saved him from the penalty of the law? If it would not, which we think is evident, then the law appropriated all sacrifice to God.

Such being the case with respect to sacrificial worship, we may ask, What is there so peculiar in invocation and adoration that they should not be governed by the same law? Why should not absolute and relative prayer and prostration appear as absurd as absolute and relative sacrifice? They are, like the other, acts of religious worship, and are appropriated to God in the same manner, by the same laws, and upon the same grounds and reasons. We are not at liberty to fix what signification we please to the acts of religious worship, making them high or low at discretion; for God himself has determined their signification to be supreme by claiming to be their only lawful object. It follows, therefore, that we can never use them in any other sense without being guilty of profaneness or idolatry.

CHAPTER V.

THE SONSHIP OF CHRIST.

THAT the title "SON OF GOD" is applied to Jesus Christ is not denied. His disciples, occasionally before and frequently after his resurrection, gave him this appellation, and he assumed it himself. The question, therefore, is, In what sense is this title to be understood? In answering this question we will, *first*, notice several false theories that have been adopted respecting the Sonship of Christ; *secondly*, adduce the testimony of Scripture in support of the doctrine that the title "Son of God" is a designation of his Divine nature; and, *thirdly*, make some remarks on the importance of maintaining the orthodox view upon this subject.

I. WE ARE TO NOTICE SEVERAL FALSE THEORIES THAT HAVE BEEN ADOPTED RESPECTING THE SONSHIP OF CHRIST.

1. Various attempts have been made to restrict the title "Son of God" to the mere humanity of our Saviour, and to rest its application upon his *miraculous conception*. It is true that this opinion is held by some who hesitate not to acknowledge that Jesus Christ is a Divine person; but, by denying his Deity as "THE SON OF GOD," they both depart from the faith of the early Christian Church, and give up to Socinians the whole argument for the divinity of Christ, which is founded upon that eminent appellation.

Those who think that it was assumed by Christ, and given to him by his disciples because of his miraculous conception, are obviously in error. Our Lord, when he adopted the appellation, never urged his miraculous birth as a proof of his Sonship; but when he called God his Father, he grounded the proof of his claim upon the *miracles* which he performed. The Jews clearly conceived that, in making this profession of Sonship with reference to God, he assumed a Divine character, and made himself "*equal with God.*" They, therefore, took up stones to stone him.

Nor did the disciples themselves give him this title with reference to his conception by the Holy Ghost. Certain it is, that Nathanael did not know the circumstances of his birth, for he was announced to him by Philip as Jesus of *Nazareth*, "the *Son* of *Joseph ;*" and he, therefore, asked, "Can any good thing come out of *Nazareth ?*" He did not know but that Jesus was the son of Joseph; he knew nothing of his being born in Bethlehem; and yet he confessed him to be "THE SON OF GOD" and "the KING OF ISRAEL."

It may also be observed that in the celebrated confession of Peter,

"Thou art the Christ, the Son of the living God," there is no reference at all to our Lord's miraculous conception. Nor did this form any part of the ground on which he confessed " the *Son of Man* " to be the "Son of God;" for our Lord replied, "Flesh and blood hath not revealed this unto thee, but my Father which is in heaven." Peter had, therefore, been taught the doctrine of the Sonship of Christ by a special revelation from God the Father, an unnecessary thing, certainly, if the miraculous conception had been the only ground of that Sonship; for the evidence of that fact might have been collected from Christ and his virgin mother.

2. This ground, therefore, not being tenable, it has been urged that "Son of God" was simply an appellation of Messiah, and is, consequently, an *official*, and not a *personal* designation. Against this, however, the evangelic history affords decisive proof.

That the Messiah was the Jehovah of the Old Testament has been shown in a former chapter; and this is to be regarded as the faith of the ancient Jewish Church. But it is certain that at the period of our Lord's advent the great body of the Jews had given up the Divine character of the Messiah, and held the opinion that he was to be a *temporal monarch*. The true doctrine was retained only among the faithful few, as Simeon, who expressly ascribed divinity to the Messiah, and Nathanael, who connected "Son of God " and "King of Israel" together, one the designation of the Divine *nature*, the other of the *office* of the Messiah.

Three things are therefore clear, from the writings of the Evangelists : 1. That the Jews recognized the existence of such a being as the " Son of God."   2. That they regarded it blasphemy for any created being to claim this designation.   3. That for a person to profess to be the Messiah simply was not considered blasphemy, and did not exasperate the Jews. Our Lord certainly professed to be the Messiah; many of the Jews also, at different times, believed on him *as such;* and yet these same Jews were not only offended, but took up stones to stone him as a blasphemer when he declared himself to be the "Son of God."   We cannot, therefore, account for the use of this title among the Jews of our Lord's time, whether by his disciples or his enemies, by considering it as synonymous with Messiah. The Jews regarded the former as *necessarily* involving a claim to divinity, but not the latter; and the disciples did not conceive that they fully confessed their Master by calling him the Messiah without adding to it his higher designation. "Thou art Christ," said Peter; but he immediately added, " The Son of the Living God."   So Nathanael, under the influence of a recent proof of his omniscience, and, consequently, of his divinity, salutes him, first, as the "Son of God," and then as Messiah, "the King of Israel."

We conclude, therefore, that the title "Son of God," as it is applied to Jesus Christ, is a *personal* designation, and not one of office; that it was *essential* in him to be a Son, and only *accidental* that he was the Messiah; that he was the first by *nature*, the second by *appointment;* and that, in constant association with the name *Son*, as given to him alone, and in a sense which shuts out all creatures, however exalted, are found ideas and circumstances of full and absolute divinity.

3. Another opinion is, that the title "*Son of God*" is applied to Christ because God raised him from the dead. Those who adopt this theory rest it mainly on a passage in the second Psalm: "The Lord hath said unto me, Thou art my Son; this day have I begotten thee." They suppose that the *day* spoken of in the text is the day of Christ's resurrection, and interpret his being "begotten" of the Father as denoting the act of raising him from the dead, thus making his resurrection the ground of his Sonship.

From apostolic authority we know that the "*Son*" here represented as speaking is Christ, for to him this passage is explicitly applied at least twice in the New Testament.* But he is so frequently called the Son, when there is no reference to his resurrection, that this cannot be the ground of that relation. This point, however, may be settled by the following considerations:

(1.) It is clearly indicated in the Scriptures that Christ raised himself from the dead by his own power. He explicitly declared, when speaking of his *life*, "I have power to lay it down, and I have power to take it again." John x, 18. Accordingly he said to the Jews, "Destroy this temple, and in three days *I will raise it up*." John ii, 19. Hence it would follow, if the preceding interpretation were true, that our Lord begat himself, and is therefore his own son, which is absurd.

(2.) He was declared from heaven to be the beloved Son of the Father at his very entrance upon his public ministry, and, consequently, before his resurrection. " And lo, a voice from heaven, saying, This is my beloved *Son*, in whom I am well pleased." Matt. iii, 17.

(3.) St. Paul tells us (Rom. i, 4) that the resurrection of Christ was the DECLARATION of his Sonship, and not the ground of it— "DECLARED to be the Son of God with power, by the resurrection from the dead." This was, therefore, the declaration of an *antecedent* Sonship.

(4.) The titles and honors ascribed in this Psalm to the extraordinary person who is the chief subject of it far transcend what the Scriptures ascribe to any mere creature. He is the Lord's *Anointed*, the *King of Zion*, and the rightful *Sovereign of the nations*. Accordingly, kings and judges of the earth are exhorted to " kiss the Son;" and all are pronounced blessed who "*put their trust in him*." This is surely an unequivocal declaration of divinity; for it is written, " Cursed be the man that trusteth in man and maketh flesh his arm." Jer. xvii, 5.

* See Acts xiii, 33; Heb. i, 5.

(5.) It is also to be noted that St. Paul employs the very passage under consideration to prove that Christ is superior to angels: "For unto which of the angels said he at any time, Thou art my Son, this day have I begotten thee?" Heb. i, 5. The force of this argument lies in the expression "begotten," importing that the person addressed is the Son of God, not by creation, but by generation. Christ's pre-eminence over the angels is here stated to consist in this, that whereas they were *created*, he was *begotten;* and the apostle's reasoning would be fallacious if the expression did not intimate a proper and peculiar filiation. The argument shows, therefore, that the title SON, which is given to the Messiah in this Psalm, implies real divinity.

‧Having noticed and refuted some of the false theories respecting the Sonship of Christ, we will now proceed,

II. To ADDUCE THE TESTIMONY OF SCRIPTURE IN SUPPORT OF THE DOCTRINE THAT THE TITLE "SON OF GOD" IS A DESIGNATION OF HIS DIVINE NATURE.

We will direct our attention,

1. *To a few passages in the Old Testament in which a Divine Son is spoken of.*—We have seen that the term *Son*, in the second Psalm, is applied to Jesus Christ, and that it denotes real divinity. To this we may add Prov. viii, 22, in which Solomon introduces, not the personified, but the *personal* wisdom of God, under the same relation of a Son, and in that relation ascribes to him Divine attributes. "The Lord possessed me in the beginning of his way, before his works of old. I was set up (appointed) from everlasting, from the beginning, or ever the world was. When there were no depths I was brought forth," or *born*. Here, from a consideration of the excellence of wisdom in the abstract, there is an easy transition to that of its infinite Source; and hence the inspired writer proceeds to delineate a Divine Being, who is portrayed in colors of such splendor and majesty as can be attributed to no other than the eternal Son of God.

To say of wisdom, as an attribute, that God possessed it in the beginning of his way, is certainly too trifling an observation to be attributed to the wise monarch of Israel. In what way can it be predicated of a quality that it was set up or appointed from everlasting? But every attribute which is here ascribed to wisdom is strictly applicable to the divine *Logos*, who "was in the beginning with God," and in whom "dwelleth all the fullness of the Godhead bodily."

The eternal Sonship of Jesus Christ is most unequivocally expressed in the prophecy of Micah: "But thou, Bethlehem Ephratah, though thou be little among the thousands of Judah, yet out of thee shall he come forth unto me that is to be Ruler in Israel; whose goings forth have been from of old, from everlasting;" or, as it is in the margin, "from the days of eternity." Micah v, 2. There is here ascribed to the person spoken of a twofold birth or going forth. By a natural birth he was to come forth from Bethlehem of Judah; but by another and higher birth he had been "from the days of eternity."*

This passage is so signal a description of Christ, the eternal Son of God, who assumed our nature and was born in Bethlehem, that it evidently belongs to him, and to no other being; and it is so decidedly indicative of that peculiar notion of his divinity, which is marked by the term and the relation of SON, that Socinians have resorted to the utmost violence of criticism to escape its powerful evidence. Dr. Priestley says "that it may be understood concerning the promises of God, in which the coming of Christ was signified to mankind from the beginning of the world."

To this we reply that the word which is rendered "goings forth" never signifies the work of God in predicting future events, but is often used to express natural birth and origin. It is unquestionably so used in the preceding clause, and cannot be taken in a different sense in that which immediately follows, and especially when a clear antithesis is marked and intended. He was born in time, but was not, on that account, merely human; for though born in Bethlehem, his "goings forth," his production, his heavenly birth or generation, was from *everlasting*.

Others refer the phrase, "his goings forth," to the purpose of God that Christ should come into the world; but this is too absurd to need refutation. It would be mere trifling solemnly to affirm of the Messiah what is just as true of every other man born into the world. This passage is, therefore, an irrefutable proof of the faith of the ancient Jewish Church, both in the divinity and the Divine Sonship of the Messiah.

The same relation of SON, in the full view of Supreme Divinity, and where no reference appears to be had to the office and work of the Messiah, is found in Prov. xxx, 4: "Who hath ascended up into heaven, or descended? who hath gathered the wind in his fists? who hath bound the waters in a garment? who hath established all the ends of the earth? what is his name, and what is his SON's name, if thou canst tell?" Here the Deity is contemplated, not in his redeeming acts, but in his works of creation and providence, managing at will and ruling the operations of nature; and yet, even in these peculiar offices of divinity alone, he is spoken of as having a SON, whose "name," that is, according to the Hebrew idiom, whose *nature* is as *deep, mysterious*, and *unutterable* as *his own*. "What is HIS name, and what is his SON's name; canst thou tell?"

It was thus that the Scriptures of the Old Testament furnished the Jews with the idea of a personal Son in the Divine nature. They were

---

* The word רצי, YATZA, *to come forth*, is frequently used in reference to *birth*, or *generation*, as in Gen. xvii, 6; 2 Kings xx, 18; and so the Jews understood it, when they replied to the inquiry of Herod in regard to the place where Christ should be born, by quoting this very passage. According to a common Hebraism in order to denote *eminency*, the word for birth, which is rendered "goings forth," is used in its plural form.

not only acquainted with the phrase "Son of God," but in a good degree they understood its true import. Nor is it any objection to this, that among their ancient writers it was sometimes applied to the Messiah. It is granted that the Messiah is the Son of God; but that the phrase *Son of God* ceases, on that account, to be a personal designation, or that it imports the same as *Messiah*, is what we deny. David was the son of Jesse and the king of Israel. He, therefore, who was king of Israel was the son of Jesse; but the latter is the *personal*, the former only the *official* description. The latter marks his origin and family; for before he was king of Israel he was the son of Jesse. In like manner "Son of God" marks the *natural* relation of the Messiah to God, and the term *Messiah* his *official* relation to men. This relation to God subsists not in the human, but in the *higher* nature of the Messiah; and this higher nature being proved to be Divine, it follows that the phrase "Son of God," as applied to Jesus Christ, is a title of absolute divinity, importing his participation in the very nature and essence of God.

2. *The same ideas of a* Divine Sonship *are suggested by almost every passage in which the phrase occurs in the New Testament.*—When Jesus was baptized "the heavens were opened unto him, and he saw the Spirit of God descending like a dove, and lighting upon him; and lo, a voice from heaven, saying, This is my beloved Son, in whom I am well pleased." Matt. iii, 16, 17. The circumstances of this testimony are of the most solemn and impressive kind, and there can be no rational doubt but that they were designed authoritatively to invest our Lord with the title "Son of God" in its fullest sense—rendered stronger and more emphatic by the epithet "*beloved*," and by the declaration that in him the Father was "*well pleased.*" It is evident that the title was applied to him on grounds independent of the circumstances of his *birth*, or of his *official relation* to men; and that he was in a higher *nature* than his human, and for a higher reason than an *official* one "the Son of God." Accordingly, as soon as John the Baptist had heard the testimony of the Father respecting our Lord, and had seen the descent of the Holy Spirit upon him, he declared him to be "the Son of God."

To the transaction at his baptism our Lord himself adverts in John v, 37: "And the Father himself, which hath sent me, hath borne witness of me." He had just adverted to the evidence of his divinity arising from his miraculous works, and, in addition to this, he introduces that distinct personal testimony of the Father which was given at his baptism. Now, the witness of the Father on that occasion is that Christ is his "*beloved* Son;" and it is remarkable that our Lord introduces this testimony of the Father at a time when his claim to be the Son of God was a matter of dispute with the Jews. They denied that God was his Father in the high sense in which he was obviously to be understood; and "they sought to kill him, because he had said that

God was his Father, *making himself equal with God.*" What then, in this case, was the conduct of our Lord? He reaffirmed his Sonship even in this very objectionable sense, claiming the power to perform the works of God, to raise the dead, and to exercise all judgment, and the right to be honored of all men, "even as they honor the Father."*

The epithet "ONLY BEGOTTEN," which several times occurs in the New Testament, affords further proof of the Sonship of Christ in his Divine nature. One of these instances *only* need be selected: "The Word was made flesh, and dwelt among us, and we beheld his glory, the glory as of the ONLY BEGOTTEN of the Father, full of grace and truth." John i, 14. If the term "only begotten" referred to Christ's miraculous conception, then the glory "as of the only-begotten" must be a glory of the human nature of Christ only, for that alone was capable of being thus conceived. This, however, is clearly contrary to the scope of the passage, which does not speak of the glory of that nature which the Word assumed, but of the glory of the WORD HIMSELF, who is here said to be the "only-begotten of the Father." It is, therefore, the glory of his Divine nature that is here intended.

It is also clear that the miraculous conception of Christ could not constitute him a Son, except as it consisted in the immediate formation of his manhood by the power of God; but, in this respect, he was not the "*only-begotten,*" not the *only Son*, because Adam was thus also immediately produced, and for this very reason is called by St. Luke "the son of God." The note in the Socinian version tells us, "that this expression," only-begotten, "does not refer to any particular mode of derivation or existence; but is used to express merely a higher degree of *affection*, and is applied to Isaac, though Abraham had other sons." Isaac, however, was so called because he was the only child which Abraham had by his wife Sarah; and this instance is therefore against the Socinian theory. It would be easy to show that μονογενης, *only-begotten*, does not anywhere import the affection of a parent, but the peculiar relation of an *only son*, and as this peculiarity does not apply to the production of the mere humanity of our Lord, the first man being in this sense, and for this very reason, a "son of God," the epithet must be applied to his Divine nature, in which alone he is at once *naturally* and *exclusively* "the SON OF THE LIVING GOD."

Those passages which declare that "all things were made by" the SON,† and that "God *sent* his Son into the world,"‡ may be considered as declarations of a Divine Sonship. The former imply that the CREATOR was a SON at the very period of creation, and the latter, that he was the SON OF GOD before he was *sent* into the world; and thus both will prove that this relation is independent of his incarnation, or of his official appointment as Messiah.

---

* See John v, 18–29.   † See John i, 3; Col. i, 16; Heb. i, 2.
‡ See John iii, 17; Gal. iv, 4: 1 John iv, 9, 10, 14.

The only plausible objection to this is, that a person may be said to perform actions under a title which he subsequently receives. Thus we ascribe the "*Principia*" to *Sir* Isaac Newton, though that work was written before he received the honor of knighthood. Accordingly, we are told by those who allow the divinity of Christ, while they deny his Divine Sonship, that the sacred writers ascribed creation and other Divine acts to the Son merely by an interchange of appellations between his human and his Divine nature; meaning thereby, that they were done by that same Divine Person who, in consequence of his incarnation and miraculous conception, became the Son of God. Thus it is said that "the Lord of glory" was crucified, and that God purchased the Church "with his *own blood.*" So, also, in familiar style, we speak of the divinity of Jesus, and of the Godhead of the Son of Mary.

To this our reply is, that though an interchange of appellations is acknowledged, yet even this supposes that some of them are designations of our Lord's Divine nature, while others describe the nature which he assumed. But the simple circumstance of such an interchange will no more prove the title Son of God to be a human designation than it will prove Son of Mary to be a *Divine* one. If "Son of God" does not relate to the divinity of our Lord, then, as God, he has no distinctive name in all the Scriptures. The title "God" does not distinguish him from the other persons of the Trinity, and the term "word" stands in precisely the same predicament as "Son;" for the same kind of criticism may reduce it to merely an *official* appellative.

But the notion that the title "Son of God" is an appellation of the human nature of our Lord, and that it is applied to him in his Divine character merely by a customary interchange of designations, is an assumption which cannot be proved; while all those passages which connect the title "*Son,*" immediately and by way of eminence, with his divinity, remain wholly unaccounted for on this theory, and are therefore contrary to it. It is evident, that in direct relation to his Divine nature, and without reference to any other circumstance, he claimed God as his Father. When he said to the Jews, "My Father worketh hitherto and I work," they understood him to assert that in this high sense "God was his Father, [πατερα ιδιον, HIS OWN PROPER FATHER,] making himself EQUAL with God." John v, 17, 18. And when our Lord said, "I and my Father ARE ONE," the "Jews took up stones to stone him," saying, "For a good work we stone thee not, but for blasphemy; and because thou, being a man, makest thyself God." John x, 31–33.

His unequivocal answer to the direct question of the Jewish council, when he was on his trial before them, is also in point here. "Then said they all, Art thou then the Son of God? And he said unto them, Ye say that I am." Luke xxii, 70. The obvious meaning of our Lord's reply is, *I am that*, or *what ye say ;* thus declaring that, in the very sense in which they put the question, he was the Son of God. But in confessing himself to be in that sense the SON, he did more than claim to be the Messiah, for the counsel judged him to be guilty of blasphemy, and therefore worthy of death; a charge which could not lie against any one, by the Jewish law, for professing to be the Messiah. His blasphemy was alleged to consist in his making himself "THE SON OF GOD," which was, in their view, an assumption of positive divinity; and the conduct of our Lord shows that they did not mistake his intention, for he suffered them to proceed against him without lowering his claims or correcting their opinion.

The whole argument of the apostle in the first chapter of Hebrews is designed to prove that our Lord is superior to angels, and he adduces, as conclusive evidence on this point, that to none of the angels did God ever say, "Thou art my SON, this day have I begotten thee." He argues, therefore, on this very ground of *Sonship* that Christ is superior to angels; that is, superior in *nature* and in *natural relation* to God; for in no other way is the argument conclusive. He has his title SON by way of INHERITANCE; that is, by *natural* and *hereditary* right. "He hath by *inheritance* obtained a more excellent name than they;" that is, by his being OF the Father, and therefore by virtue of his Divine filiation. Angels may be, in an inferior sense, the sons of God by *creation;* but they *cannot inherit* that title for this plain reason, that they are *created,* not *begotten;* while our Lord inherits "the more excellent name" because he is *begotten,* not *created.* "For, unto which of the angels said he at any time, Thou art my SON, this day have I BEGOTTEN thee?" The same ideas of absolute divinity connect themselves with this title throughout the chapter. "The SON," by whom "God hath in these last days spoken unto us," is "the brightness of his glory and the express image of his person;" but it is only to the Divine nature of our Lord that these expressions can refer.

As in none of these passages the title "Son of God" can possibly be considered as a designation of his human nature or office, so we find proof of equal force that it is used even by way of *opposition* and *contradistinction* to the inferior nature. Thus St. Paul says of the "Son Jesus Christ" that he "was made of the seed of David according to the flesh; and declared to be the Son of God with power, according to the Spirit of holiness, by the resurrection from the dead." Rom. i, 3, 4. A very few remarks will be sufficient to point out the force of this passage. The apostle is speaking not of what Christ is officially, but of what he is personally and essentially, for the truth of all his official claims depends upon the truth of his personal ones. If he is a Divine person he is everything else that he assumes to be. He is, therefore, considered by the apostle in his twofold nature. As a man he was "of the seed of David according to the flesh;" but in a superior nature he was "declared to be the Son of God." That an opposition is expressed between what Christ is "according to the flesh," and what he is according to a higher nature, must be allowed, or else there is no force in the apostle's observation; and it must be equally clear that the nature put in *opposition* to Christ's fleshly nature can be no other than his Divine nature, which the apostle calls "the SON OF GOD."

We also learn, from Romans viii, 3, that God sent "his own Son in the likeness of sinful flesh." The person who is here entitled the SON was sent "in the likeness of sinful flesh;" but in what other way could he have been sent if he were *Son* only as a *man?* It is, therefore, most clearly intimated that he was a SON before he was sent, and that FLESH was the nature which the Son *assumed*, but not the nature in which he was "the Son of God."

With the same idea of the absolute divinity of the SON, as distinguished from his humanity, the apostle applies that lofty passage from the forty-fifth psalm. "But unto the Son he saith, Thy throne, O God, is for ever and ever." Heb. i, 8. It is allowed by all who hold the Deity of Christ that he is here addressed as a being composed of two natures, Divine and human. As man, he is anointed "with the oil of gladness," and elevated above his "fellows;" while the stability of his throne, and the unsullied justice of his government, declare his GODHEAD. He is, however, called the SON; but this term could not characterize the being here introduced, unless it agreed with his higher and Divine nature. The SON is addressed—that Son is addressed as GOD, and as God whose throne is *for ever and ever*.

Thus we think it fully established, that the title "SON OF GOD" is not given to Christ on account of his miraculous conception; that it is not an appellative of his human nature, occasionally applied to him by metonymy, when Divine acts and relations are spoken of, as any other human title might be applied; that it is not ascribed to him simply because of his assuming our nature, as is supposed by some who admit the divinity of our Lord but deny his eternal filiation; and that the use of the title cannot be fully explained by any *office* with which he is invested, or any *event* in his mediatorial undertaking. It follows, therefore, that it is a title characteristic of his mode of existence in the Divine essence, and of the relation which exists between the first and the second person in the ever blessed Trinity.

It only remains for us now,

III. TO MAKE SOME REMARKS ON THE IMPORTANCE OF MAINTAINING THE ORTHODOX VIEW RESPECTING THE SONSHIP OF JESUS CHRIST.

It is granted that some divines, truly decided on the question of our Lord's divinity, have rejected the Divine Sonship; but in this they have gone contrary to the judgment of the Church of Christ in all ages, and would certainly have been ranked among heretics in her earliest and purest times. This consideration alone is worthy of attention, and ought to induce caution; but there are many considerations to show that points of great moment are involved in the denial or maintenance of the doctrine in question. A few of these we will present in the following remarks:

1. The loose and general manner in which many passages of Scripture, which speak of Christ as a Son, must be explained by those who deny the Divine filiation of Christ, seems to sanction principles of interpretation which would be highly dangerous, or rather absolutely fatal, if generally applied to the Scriptures.

2. The denial of the Divine Sonship destroys all *relation* among the persons of the Godhead. No other relation of the Divine persons is mentioned in Scripture except those which are expressed by *paternity*, *filiation*, and *procession*. If these *natural* relations are removed, we must then conceive of the *persons* in the Godhead as perfectly independent of each other, a view which is incompatible with the *unity* of the Divine *essence*.

3. It is the doctrine of the Divine paternity only which preserves the Scripture idea that the Father is the *fountain* of deity, and as such, the *first*, the *original*, the *principle*. He must have read the Scriptures to little purpose who does not perceive that this is their constant doctrine—that "OF him are all things;" that though the Son is Creator, yet BY the Son the Father made the worlds, and that "as the Father hath life in himself, so hath he given to the Son to HAVE LIFE IN HIMSELF," which can only refer to his Divine nature, nothing being the source of life in itself but what is *Divine*. But where the essential paternity of the Father and the correlative filiation of the Son are denied, these Scriptural representations have no foundation in fact, and are incapable of interpretation.

4. The perfect EQUALITY of the Son with the Father, and, at the same time, the SUBORDINATION of the Son to the Father, are to be equally maintained only by the doctrine of the Divine Sonship. Deny this, and the Son might as well be the *first* as the *second* person in the Godhead, and the *second* as well as the first. The Father might have been *sent* by the Son without incongruity, or either of them by the Holy Spirit. These are most absurd and repulsive conclusions, which the doctrine of the Sonship avoids, and thus proves its accordance with the Holy Scriptures.

5. A denial of the Divine filiation of Christ is derogatory to the *love* of the Father in the gift of his Son. It insensibly runs into the Socinian heresy, and restricts the Father's love to the gift of a *mere man*, if the Sonship of Christ is only *human;* and in that case, the permission of the sufferings of Christ was no greater manifestation of God's love to the world than if he had permitted any other good man to die for the benefit of his fellow-creatures.

CHAPTER VI.

THE PERSON OF CHRIST.

In the present day the controversy respecting the person of Christ is almost wholly confined to the question of his divinity; but in the early ages of the Church it was necessary to establish his proper humanity. The denial of this seems to have existed as early as the time of St. John, who, in his epistles, excludes from the pale of the Church all who denied that "Christ is come in THE FLESH." As his Gospel, therefore, proclaims his Godhead, so his epistles defend also the doctrine of his humanity.

As the Divine nature of Christ has been fully established, it is only necessary in this chapter to prove his true humanity, and to show that the two natures, the human and the Divine, are united in *one person*. But before we proceed to the discussion of these points it will be proper for us to notice, very briefly,

I. A FEW OF THE LEADING ERRORS WHICH HAVE BEEN MORE OR LESS DISSEMINATED IN THE CHURCH RESPECTING THE PERSON OF CHRIST.—These have related both to his human and his Divine nature.

1. *Errors in regard to the human nature of our Lord.*—The *Gnostics* denied the real existence of the *body* of Christ. The things which the Scriptures attribute to his human nature they did not deny, but affirmed that they took place in appearance only. The source of this error appears to have been a philosophical one. Both in the Oriental and Greek schools it was a favorite notion, that whatever was joined to *matter* was necessarily contaminated by it; and that the highest perfection of this life was abstraction from material things, and in another, a total and final separation from the body.

While the Gnostics denied the real existence of the *body* of Christ, the *Apollinarians* maintained that his body was endowed with a sensitive and not with a rational soul, and that the Divine nature supplied the place of the intellectual principle in man. Thus both these views denied to Christ a proper humanity, and both were, accordingly, condemned by the general Church.

Even among those who held the union of the Divine and the human nature in Christ, which in theological language is called the *hypostatical* or *personal* union, several distinctions were also made which led to a diversity of opinion. The *Nestorians* acknowledged two *persons* in our Lord, mystically and more closely united than any human analogy can explain. The Monophysites contended for one person and one nature, the two being supposed to be, in some mysterious manner, confounded. The Monothelites two natures and one will.

2. *Errors respecting the Divine Nature of Christ.*—Among the various errors of this class, which formerly sprung up in the Church, three only can be said to have much influence in the present day, Arianism, Sabellianism, and Socinianism. The two former are now almost entirely merged into the last, whose characteristic tenet is the simple humanity of Christ. Arius, who gave his name to the first, seems to have wrought some of the floating errors of previous times into a kind of system, which, however, underwent various modifications among his followers. The distinguishing tenet of this system was that Christ was the first and most exalted of creatures; that he was produced in a peculiar manner, and endowed with great perfections; that by him God made the worlds; that he alone proceeded immediately from God, while other things were produced mediately by him; and that all things were put under his administration.

The semi-Arians divided from the Arians, but still differed from the orthodox in refusing to admit that the Son was ὁμοούσιος, or of the *same substance* with the Father; but they acknowledged him to be ὁμοιούσιος, or of a *like* substance with the Father. It was only in appearance, however, that they came nearer to the truth than the Arians themselves, for they contended that this *likeness* to the Father in essence was not by *nature*, but by peculiar privilege. In their system, therefore, Christ was but a creature.

A still further refinement on this doctrine was advocated by Dr. Samuel Clarke. His theory was that there is one Supreme Being who is the Father, and two subordinate, derived, and dependent beings. But he objected to call Christ a creature, thinking him something between a created and a self-existent nature. This hypothesis, however, still implies, unless an evident absurdity be admitted, that Christ is a created being.

The *Sabellian* doctrine stands equally opposed to Trinitarianism and to the Arian system. It asserts the divinity of the Son and the Holy Spirit against the latter, and denies the personality of both in opposition to the former. Sabellius taught that the Father, Son, and Holy Ghost are only denominations of one hypostasis; in other words, that there is but one person in the Godhead, and that the Son and the Holy Spirit are virtues, emanations, or functions only; that under the Old Testament God delivered the law as Father; under the New dwelt among men, or was incarnate as the Son; and descended on the apostles as the Holy Spirit. In the early ages they were often called *Patripassians*, because their scheme, by denying a real Sonship, obliged them to acknowledge that it was the Father who suffered for the sins of men.

On the refutation of these errors it is not now necessary to dwell, both because they have at present but little influence, and chiefly because both are involved in the Socinian question, and are decided by the establishment of the scriptural doctrine of a Trinity of Divine persons in the Unity of the Godhead. If Jesus Christ is the Divine Son of God; if he was "sent" from God and "returned" to God; if he distinguished himself from the Father both in his Divine and human nature, saying, as to the former, "I and my Father are ONE," and as to the latter, "My Father is GREATER than I;" if there is any meaning at all in his declaration, that "no man knoweth the Son but the Father, neither knoweth any man the Father save the Son," words which cannot, by any possibility, be spoken of *official* distinction, or of an *emanation* or *operation;* then all these passages prove a real personality, and are incapable of being explained by a *modal* one. This is the answer to the Sabellian opinion; and as to the Arian hypothesis, it falls, with Socinianism, before that series of proofs which has already been adduced from the Scriptures to establish the eternity of our Lord, his consubstantiality and coequality with the Father, and, consequently, his Supreme Divinity. But,

II. WE ARE TO PROVE THAT OUR LORD WAS TRULY MAN AS WELL AS GOD.

That he assumed *humanity*, in the full and proper sense of that term, is, we think, abundantly evident from the following considerations :

1. *The prophets who predicted the coming of the Messiah often spoke of him as a Man.* Hence he is represented as being the seed of the woman;* the seed of Abraham;† a prophet like unto Moses;‡ and "the son of David."§

2. *He is called a* MAN, *and the* SON OF MAN, *in a multitude of instances.*—He is designated by the latter appellation no less than seventy-one times in the sacred Scriptures. In sixty-seven of these instances the title is employed by our Lord *himself*, once by *Daniel*, once by *St. Stephen*, and twice by *St. John*. It must surely be acknowledged that in giving this appellation to himself he disclosed his true character, and that he was therefore, in reality, what he called himself, *the Son of Man*. When spoken of as a man he is ascribed with just such characteristics as belong to other men, those only excepted which involve error or sin. He is exhibited as meek, lowly, and dutiful to his parents; as hungering, thirsting, and being weary; as sustained and refreshed by food, drink, and sleep; as the subject of temptations, infirmities, and afflictions; as weeping with tenderness and sorrow; and, in general, as having all the innocent characteristics of our nature.

3. *The history of the birth, life, and death of our Lord is unanswerable proof that he was really Man.*—He was born, he lived, and he died essentially in the same manner as other men. He "increased in wisdom

* Gen. iii, 15.   † Gen. xxii, 18.   ‡ Deut. xviii, 15.   § Matt. xxii, 42.

and stature;" wrought with his hands; ate, drank, slept; suffered on the cross; gave up the ghost, and was buried, as other men.

4. *The humanity of Christ is argued at large and proved by St. Paul in the second chapter of Hebrews.*—In the passage containing this argument are the following declarations: "Forasmuch then as the children are partakers of flesh and blood, he also himself likewise took part of the same;" and again, "in all things it behooved him to be made like unto his brethren." That Christ had a human body cannot be denied. It is equally undeniable that to increase in wisdom, to be sorrowful, to be tempted, to be obedient to parents, together with many other things of a similar nature, cannot be attributed either to *God* or to *a mere human body*, but are appropriate characteristics of *the human soul*. Christ, therefore, possessed a human *soul* as well as a human body, and was perfectly *man;* or, as it is very properly expressed in the Shorter Catechism, he "became man by taking to himself a true body and a reasonable soul."

While we maintain the integrity of Christ's human nature, we admit that he assumed it with all its *innocent infirmities*. He was not subject to any of the *sinful* infirmities of man, nor was there any stimulus or incentive to sin in the constitution or temperament of his body. The Scriptures declare that he was "without sin;" that "in him is no sin;" and that, though he came "in the likeness of sinful flesh," he was "holy, harmless, undefiled," and "separate from sinners." Nor does it appear that he was subject to any of those bodily diseases which are the portion of man. Infirmities of this kind would have discommoded him in the discharge of his duty, and he was exempted from them on account of his personal purity. But he was subject to hunger and thirst, to cold and heat, to pain of body arising from external injuries, and to distress of mind, from various causes. Against all such annoyances he might have been defended by the order of Omnipotence; but this would not have accorded with the design of his mission. He submitted to our infirmities that he might acquire an experimental knowledge of our sufferings, both corporeal and mental, and that we might be more fully assured of his sympathy. "We have not a high priest which cannot be touched with the feeling of our infirmities; but was in all points tempted like as we are." Heb. iv, 15.

III. WE ARE TO SHOW THAT THE HUMAN AND THE DIVINE NATURE OF OUR LORD ARE UNITED IN ONE PERSON.

The true sense of Scripture appears to have been very accurately expressed by the Council of Chalcedon, in the fifth century, that in Christ there is *one person*, in the unity of person *two natures*, the Divine and the human; and that there is no change, or mixture, or confusion of these two natures, but that each retains its own distinguishing properties. With this agrees the Athanasian Creed; and the Church of England professes, in her second article, that "The Son, which is the word of the Father, begotten from everlasting of the Father, the very and eternal God, of one substance with the Father, took man's nature in the womb of the blessed Virgin of her substance; so that two whole and perfect natures, that is, the Godhead and manhood, were joined together in one person, never to be divided, whereof is one Christ, very God and very man."

Whatever objections may be raised against these views by the mere reason of man, unable to comprehend mysteries so high, but often bold enough to impugn them, they certainly exhibit the doctrine of the New Testament on this important subject though expressed in different terms. That Christ is very God has been fully proved, and that he became truly man no one can reasonably deny. That he is but *one person* is sufficiently clear from these considerations: 1. That no distinction into two was ever made by himself or by his apostles. 2. That actions peculiar to the Godhead are sometimes ascribed to him under his human appellations; and, 3. That actions and sufferings peculiar to humanity are also predicated of him under Divine titles.

That in him there is no confusion of the two natures is evident from the absolute manner in which both are spoken of in the Scriptures. His Godhead was not deteriorated by uniting itself with a human body, for he "is the true God;" nor was his humanity, while on earth, exalted into properties which made it differ in kind from the humanity of his creatures; for, "as the children were partakers of flesh and blood, he also took part of THE SAME." If the Divine nature in him had been imperfect it would have lost its essential character, for it is essential to Deity to be perfect; if any of the essential properties of human nature had been wanting he would not have been man; and if the Divine and the human nature had been mixed or confounded in him he would have been neither God nor man. Nothing was deficient in his divinity, nothing in his humanity, and yet he is *one Christ.*

It is only in the light of these two circumstances, *the completeness of each nature* and *the union of both in one person,* that the testimony of God concerning his Son can be consistently explained. Some things which are spoken of Christ relate to his Divine, others to his human nature; and he who takes with him this principle of interpretation will seldom find any difficulty in apprehending the sense of the sacred writers, though the subjects themselves may be inscrutable.

1. Does any one ask, for instance, If Jesus is truly GOD how could he be born and die? how could he be subject to law? how could he grow in wisdom and stature? how could he be tempted, or stand in need of prayer? how could his soul be "exceeding sorrowful even unto death?" how could he purchase the Church with "his own blood?" The answer is, that he was also MAN.

But if, on the other hand, it be a matter of surprise that a VISIBLE MAN should heal diseases at his will, and by his own power, still the winds and the waves, know the thoughts of men, authoritatively forgive sins, be with his disciples, wherever two or three are met in his name, claim universal homage from all creatures, and be associated with the Father in solemn ascriptions of glory and thanksgiving: what is the answer? The *only* one explanatory of all these statements is, that our Lord Jesus Christ is GOD as well as MAN. But,

2. The *union* of the two natures of Christ in *one person* is as essential as the completeness of each nature to the full exposition of the Scriptures. Without it many passages lose all force, because they lose all meaning. In what possible sense could it be said that "THE WORD was made FLESH" if no such personal unity existed? Without the hypostatical union, how could the argument of our Lord be supported, that the Messiah is both David's SON and David's LORD? If this is asserted of *two persons*, then the argument is gone; if of *one*, then two natures, one which had authority as *Lord*, and the other capable of natural descent, were united in one person.

By this doctrine we also learn how it was that "the Church of God" was "purchased with his OWN BLOOD." Even if we concede the genuine reading to be "the Lord," instead of "God," the concession yields nothing to the Socinians, unless the term *Lord* were a human title, which has already been disproved; and unless a mere *man* could be "Lord both of the dead and living," could wield universal sovereignty, and be entitled to universal homage. If, then, the title "LORD" be an appellation of Christ's superior nature, in no other sense could it be said that the Church was "purchased with HIS OWN blood" than by supposing the existence of that union which we call personal, a union which alone distinguished the sufferings of Christ from those of his martyred followers, gave to his sufferings a merit which theirs had not, and made his blood capable of PURCHASING the Church.

Again: "Who being the brightness of his glory, and the express image of his person, and upholding all things by the word of his power, when he had BY HIMSELF purged our sins, sat down on the right hand of the Majesty on high." Heb. i, 3. To this passage, also, the hypostatical union is the only key. Of whom does the apostle speak when he says, "when he had BY HIMSELF purged our sins," but of HIM who is "the brightness of" the Father's glory, "and the express image of his person?" HE "BY HIMSELF purged our sins;" yet this was done by the shedding of his blood. In that higher nature, however, he could not suffer death, and nothing could make the sufferings of his humanity a purification of sins BY HIMSELF but such a union of the two natures as should constitute one person. For, unless this be allowed, either the characters of divinity in this passage are characters of a being merely human, or else Christ's higher nature was capable of suffering death; or, if not, the purification was not made by HIMSELF, which yet the text affirms.

Another passage of Scripture which may be noticed in this connection is Col. i, 14, 15: "In whom we have redemption through HIS blood, even the forgiveness of sins: WHO is the image of the invisible God, the first-born of every creature." In this passage the lofty description which is given of the person of Christ stands in immediate connection with the mention of the efficacy of "his blood," and is to be considered as the reason why, through that blood, redemption and remission of sins became attainable. Thus, "without shedding of blood" there could be "no remission;" but the blood of Jesus only is thus efficacious, who is "the image of the invisible God," the "Creator" of all things. His blood it could not be but for the hypostatical union, and it is equally true that were it not for this union he could not have had any blood to shed; because, as "the image of the invisible God," that is, God's equal, or God himself, he was incapable of death.

Thus it is by the union of the Divine and the human nature in one person that our Lord is qualified to be the Saviour of the world. He became man that, with the greatest possible advantage to us, he might teach us the nature and the will of God; that his life might be our example; that his acquaintance with human infirmities might assure us of his sympathy; that by suffering on the cross he might atone for our sins; and that in his glorious reward we might behold both the earnest and the pattern of ours.

But had Jesus been *only* a man, or had he been even one of the spirits that surround the throne of God, he could not have accomplished the work of human redemption. For, the entire obedience of every creature being due to the Creator, no part of that obedience can be placed to the account of other creatures so as to supply the defects of their service, or to rescue them from deserved punishment. But the Scriptures declare that the Redeemer who appeared upon earth as *man* is also *God*, mighty to save; and by this revelation we are taught that the efficacy of his interposition in our behalf depends upon the hypostatical union.

CHAPTER VII.

PERSONALITY AND DEITY OF THE HOLY GHOST.

The discussion of this point of Christian doctrine may be included in much narrower limits than those which have been assigned to the divinity of Christ, because many of the principles on which it rests have been already closely considered, and because the Deity of the Holy Spirit, in several instances, inevitably follows from that of the Son. It will, however, be necessary to show that the Holy Ghost is a PERSON, and that he is GOD.

As to the *manner* of his being, the Orthodox doctrine is, that as Christ is God by an eternal *filiation*, so the Holy Spirit is God by *procession* from the Father and the Son; which procession rests on direct scriptural authority. It is expressly asserted that the Holy Ghost proceeds from the Father. "But when the Comforter is come, whom I will send unto you from the Father, even the Spirit of truth which *proceedeth from the Father*, he shall testify of me." John xv, 26. And though the Scriptures do not expressly declare that the Holy Ghost proceeds from the Father *and the Son*, yet they evidently teach that doctrine. Because he proceeds from the Father, he is called the Spirit of the Father and the Spirit of God.* But the same Spirit is also called the Spirit of the Son and the Spirit of Christ;† and, therefore, there must be the same reason presupposed in reference to the Son as is expressed in reference to the Father. If the Holy Ghost is called the Spirit of the Father because he proceeds from the Father, it will follow that he is called the Spirit of the Son because he proceeds also from the Son.

Again, because the Holy Ghost proceeds from the Father he is spoken of as being *sent* by the Father. "The Comforter, which is the Holy Ghost, whom the *Father will send* in my name, he shall teach you all things." John xiv, 26. But the same Spirit which is sent by the Father is also sent by the Son, as he said, "When the Comforter is come, *whom I will send* unto you." As, therefore, the Scriptures expressly declare that the Holy Spirit proceeds from the Father, so do they also virtually teach that he proceeds from the Son.

ARIUS regarded the Spirit not only as a creature, but as created by Christ; thus making him the creature of a creature. Some time afterward his personality was wholly denied by the Arians, and he was considered as the *exerted energy* of God. This appears to have been the notion of Socinus, and, with occasional modifications, has been adopted by his followers. They sometimes regard him as an *attribute*, and at others they resolve the passages in which he is spoken of into a figure of speech.

Having made these preliminary remarks, we will proceed to establish the proper Personality and Deity of the Holy Ghost.

I. HIS PERSONALITY.

With respect to the Personality of the Holy Ghost, it may be observed,

1. *That it follows from the mode of his subsistence in the Sacred Trinity.*—He proceeds from the Father and the Son, and, therefore, cannot be either. To say that an *attribute* proceeds or comes forth from God would be a gross absurdity. Accordingly, our Lord most clearly represents the Holy Ghost as the third *person* of the Divine

---

* See Matt. x, 20; 1 Cor. ii, 12.   † See Rom. viii, 9; Gal. iv, 6.

essence, and as distinguished *personally* from the Father and the Son. His language is, "I will pray the Father, and he shall give you another Comforter, that he may abide with you forever." This "Comforter," said he, "is the Holy Ghost, whom the Father will send in my name." John xiv, 16, 26. Here he calls the *first* person, most expressly and undeniably, "the Father," and the *third* person, as expressly, "the Holy Ghost." It is, therefore, most evident, and beyond even the possibility of a doubt, that he does not, by these two appellatives, mean one and the same Divine person.

2. *That many Scriptures are wholly unintelligible, and even absurd, unless the Personality of the Holy Ghost is allowed.*—Those who understand the phrase as ascribing merely a figurative personality to the *energy* or *power* of God, reduce such passages as the following to an utter want of meaning: "God anointed Jesus of Nazareth with the Holy Ghost and with power;" that is, with the *power of God* and with power. "That ye may abound in hope, through the power of the Holy Ghost;" that is, through the power of *the power of God.* "It seemed good to the Holy Ghost," that is, to *the power of God*, "and to us."

3. *That in some passages in which the Holy Ghost is spoken of personification of any kind is impossible.*—The reality, which this supposed figure of speech is said to represent, is either an attribute of God, or else the doctrine of the Gospel. Let this theory, then, be tried upon a few passages. "He (the Spirit) shall not speak of *himself*, but whatsoever he shall *hear*, that shall he speak." What attribute of God can here be personified? And if the doctrine of the Gospel be arrayed with personal attributes, where is there an instance of so monstrous a prosopopæia as this passage would present? the doctrine of the Gospel not speaking "of himself," but speaking "whatsoever he shall hear!" "The Spirit maketh intercession for us." What Divine attribute is capable of interceding, or how can the doctrine of the Gospel intercede?

Personification, too, is the language of poetry, and takes place naturally only in excited and elevated discourse; but if the Holy Ghost is a personification, we find it in the New Testament, in the cool and ordinary strain of mere narration and argumentative discourse, and in the most incidental conversations.*

4. *That there have been distinct symbolical representations of the Holy Ghost.*—At the baptism of our Lord, while the Father, by an audible voice declared, "This is my beloved Son," the Spirit "descended like a dove, and lighted upon him." Matt. iii, 16, 17. And on the day of Pentecost also, the communication of the Spirit to the apostles was represented by "cloven tongues like as of fire." Acts ii, 3. St. Peter's exposition of this miracle proves that the Spirit, though act-

* See Acts viii, 29; xix, 2.

ing in union with the Father and the Son, was yet a different person. "This Jesus," said he, "being by the right hand of God exalted, and having received of the Father the promise of the Holy Ghost, hath shed forth this which ye now see and hear." Acts ii, 33.   These appearances, we allow, were merely emblematical of the Spirit's operations, and cannot convey to us any adequate conception of his real nature, or the mode of his existence, but they are nevertheless strong indications of his distinct personality.

5. And finally, *that the Holy Ghost is a person, and not an attribute, is proved by the use of masculine pronouns and relatives in the Greek of the New Testament*, in connection with the neuter noun πνευμα, Spirit, and by so many distinct personal acts being ascribed to him ; as, to come, to go, to be sent, to teach, to guide, to comfort, to make intercession, to bear witness, to give gifts, "dividing them to every man as HE WILL," to be vexed, grieved, and quenched.   These cannot be applied to the mere fiction of a person, and they therefore establish the true personality of the Holy Spirit.

II. THE DEITY OF THE HOLY SPIRIT.

That the Holy Spirit is really God, admits of so little doubt that his divinity is acknowledged even by many who deny his personality. But to place this doctrine in as clear a light as possible, we will adduce the leading arguments by which it is supported.   And,

1. *The names which are applied to the Holy Spirit clearly indicate his Divine character.*—He is denominated GOD.   "Why hath Satan filled thine heart to lie to the Holy Ghost?   Thou hast not lied unto man, but unto God." Acts v, 3, 4.   The spiritual gifts which the Corinthians received are all declared to be the work of "that self-same Spirit ;" and yet concerning these operations St. Paul as expressly asserts, that "it is the same *God* which worketh all in all." 1 Cor. xii, 6–11.   Moreover, to be "born of the Spirit," and to be "born of God," are convertible phrases.*   He is also called LORD.   "Now the Lord is that Spirit." 2 Cor. iii, 17.

2. *The Attributes which are ascribed to him proclaim his Divinity.*— ETERNITY is his, for he is called "the Eternal Spirit." Heb. ix, 14.   He is OMNIPRESENT.   "Your body," says the apostle, "is the temple of the Holy Ghost which is in you." 1 Cor. vi, 19.   And again, "As many as are led by the Spirit of God, they are the sons of God." Rom. viii, 14. Now, as all true Christians are temples of the Holy Ghost, and are led by him, he must be present with them at all times and *in all places.*   He is also OMNISCIENT ; for, "the Spirit searcheth all things, yea, the deep things of God." 1 Cor. ii, 10.   The moral attributes of God are also given to him.   HOLINESS, which includes all in one : the HOLY Ghost is his eminent designation.   GOODNESS : "Thy Spirit is good."   GRACE : he is "the Spirit of Grace."   TRUTH also, for he is "the Spirit of Truth."

* See John iii, 5, 6, 8; 1 John v, 1, 4, 18.

3. *His works are unequivocal attestations of his Divinity;* for they are such as no finite being can perform.

(1.) Creation *is ascribed to him.* "He garnished the heavens," and "moved upon the face of the waters," to reduce the chaotic mass to order, and to impregnate dead matter with life and animation.* Nor is it an objection to the argument, that creation is ascribed to the Father, and also to the Son, but a confirmation of it, for that creation should be effected by all the three persons of the Godhead, so that each should be a *Creator*, and, therefore, a *Divine Person*, can be explained only by their unity in one essence. If the Spirit of God were a mere influence or attribute he could not be a *Creator*, distinct from the Father and the Son. But that creation is ascribed to him is evident, not only from the passages just quoted, but also from the language of the Psalmist: "By the Word of the Lord were the heavens made, and *all the host of them by the* BREATH (Heb. Spirit) *of his mouth.*" Psa. xxxiii, 6. This is further confirmed by Job xxxiii, 4 : " The Spirit of God hath made me, and the BREATH *of the Almighty* hath given me life." Here, the latter clause is obviously exegetical of the former, and the whole text proves, that in the patriarchal age believers in the true religion ascribed creation to the Spirit, as well as to the Father ; and that one of his appellations was "the Breath of the Almighty." But as we have seen him acting in the material creation, so he is the author of the *new creation*, which is as evidently a work of Divine power as the former.

(2.) Preservation, *which has been well denominated a continued creation*, is also ascribed to the Holy Spirit.—This is beautifully presented in the following passage : "Thou sendest forth thy Spirit, they are created, (or *reanimated*,) and thou renewest the face of the earth." Psa. civ, 30. It cannot here be meant that the Spirit, by which the generations of animals are perpetuated, is *wind;* nor can the term denote a mere attribute of God, for the Scriptures nowhere teach that he *sends forth* his attributes to renew the face of the earth.

(3.) *It belongs to the Spirit to* raise the dead.—"It is the Spirit," said our Lord, "that quickeneth." John vi, 63. Peter testifies that Christ was "put to death in the flesh, but quickened by the Spirit." 1 Peter iii, 18. St. Paul assures us that at the last day our scattered dust shall be collected and reanimated by the same Divine agent. "He that raised up Christ from the dead shall also quicken your mortal bodies by his Spirit that dwelleth in you." Rom. viii, 11.

(4.) *He is the source of* inspiration *to the prophets.*—St. Paul says that "God spake unto the fathers by the prophets." Heb. i, 1. St. Peter declares that these "holy men of God spake as they were moved by the Holy Ghost;" 2 Peter i, 21 ; and also that it was " the Spirit of Christ which was in them." 1 Peter i, 11. We may defy any Socin-

* See Gen. i, 2 ; Job xxvi, 13.

ian to interpret these three passages, by making the Spirit an influence or attribute, and thereby reducing the term Holy Ghost to a figure of speech. "*God*," in the first passage, is unquestionably God the Father, and the "holy men of God," the prophets, would then, according to this view, be moved by the influence of the Father; but according to the third passage, the source of their inspiration was "the Spirit of Christ." Thus the two passages contradict each other. Allow the Trinity in Unity, and there is no impropriety in calling the Spirit the Spirit of the Father and the Spirit of the Son, or the Spirit of either. But if the Spirit were an influence, that influence could not be the influence of two persons, one God and the other a creature. If, however, the Holy Ghost is the Spirit of the Father and of the Son, united in one essence, the passages are easily harmonized; for, in conjunction with the Father and the Son, he is the source of prophetic inspiration, and is therefore Divine.

4. The last argument for the divinity of the Holy Ghost is founded on the fact *that he is the object of supreme worship*. We are taught throughout the Scriptures to seek for the influences of the Spirit by fervent prayer; to depend upon him for the mortification of sin, and for our growth in holiness; and to yield ourselves with unfeigned submission to his direction.*

We have an example of prayer to him in the following words, which are still used in the solemn benediction of the Church: "The grace of the Lord Jesus Christ, and the love God, and the *communion of the Holy Ghost*, be with you all. Amen." 2 Cor. xiii, 14. Here the Holy Ghost is acknowledged as the source of spiritual blessings, as well as the Father and the Son, and is invoked in the same spirit of devotion. It is vain to call this merely a wish. It is as distinctly a prayer as any other that occurs in the Scriptures; and there would be no question about its nature if there were no design to evade the force of its evidence.

The form of baptism is also demonstrative of the divinity of the Holy Spirit. It is the form of *covenant* by which the sacred Three become our ONE and ONLY GOD, and we become HIS people. "Go ye, therefore, and teach all nations, baptizing them in the NAME of the FATHER, and of the SON, and of the HOLY GHOST." Matt. xxviii, 19. How is this text to be disposed of if the divinity of the Holy Ghost is denied? Does the form of baptism imply that persons are to be baptized in the name of one *God*, one *creature*, and one *attribute?* An opinion so grossly absurd is its own refutation; for, in the case before us, there can be no personification. If, then, all the Three are *persons*, is Christian baptism to be administered in the name of one *God* and two *creatures?* This would be downright idolatry. It follows, therefore, that in this single passage of Scripture we have a most convincing proof of the divinity of the *Spirit*, as well as of the Father and the Son.

* See Luke xi, 13; Rom. viii, 13, 14; Gal. v, 25.

It may also be observed in this connection that what the Scriptures declare respecting the sin against the Holy Ghost proves him to be the object of supreme worship, and therefore Divine. "But whosoever speaketh against the Holy Ghost, it shall not be forgiven him, neither in this world, neither in the world to come." Matt. xii, 32. This crime consisted in ascribing to Satan the miracles which our Lord wrought by the power of the Holy Ghost. But if to "speak against the Holy Ghost" was a sin in the proper sense, and of so malignant a kind as to place it beyond the reach of mercy, he can be no other than the very and eternal God.

It follows, therefore, in conclusion, that our regards are justly due to this DIVINE PERSON as the object of worship and trust, of prayer and blessing—duties to which we are especially called, both by the general consideration of his divinity and by that affectingly benevolent and attractive character under which he is presented to us in the holy Scriptures. In *creation* we see him moving upon the face of chaos, and reducing it to beauty and order; in *providence*, renewing the earth, garnishing the heavens, and giving life to man. In *grace* we behold him expanding the prophetic scene to the vision of the seers of the Old Testament, and making a perfect revelation of the doctrines of Christ to the apostles of the New. He reproves the world of sin, working in the human heart a secret conviction of its evil and danger. He is "the Spirit of grace and supplication;" and from him are the softened heart, the yielding will, and all heavenly desires and tendencies. He hastens to the troubled spirit of penitent men, who are led by his influences to trust in Christ, with the news of pardon; bearing witness with their spirit that they are the children of God. He helps their infirmities; makes intercession for them; inspires thoughts of consolation and feelings of peace; plants and perfects in them whatsoever things are pure, lovely, honest, and of good report; dwells in the soul as in a temple; and, after having rendered the spirit to God, without "spot, or wrinkle, or any such thing," finishes his benevolent and glorious work by raising the bodies of the saints, at the last day, to immortality and eternal life. So powerfully does "the Spirit of glory and of God" claim our love, our praise, and our obedience! Hence, in the forms of the Christian Church he has been constantly associated with the Father and the Son in equal glory and blessing; and this recognition of the Holy Spirit ought to be made in every gratulatory act of devotion, that so equally to each person of the eternal Trinity glory may be given "in the Church throughout all ages. Amen."

CHAPTER VIII.

THE DECREES OF GOD.

We have hitherto considered God with regard to his existence, his nature and attributes, and the manner of his subsisting in a Trinity of Persons; but we will now proceed to contemplate him in his *acts* or *efficiency*.

The *acts* of God are, in theological language, either *internal* or *external*. His *internal* acts are either those which belong to himself alone, as the generation of the Son, and the procession of the Holy Ghost; or those which take place in himself with respect to external objects. Such are his *decrees* "which he hath purposed in himself." Eph. i, 9.

The *external* acts of God are those exertions of his power which terminate upon his creatures. These are comprehended in his works of *creation* and *providence*.

As it is reasonable to believe that God does nothing without previous deliberation, and thence resolving upon what his infinite wisdom perceives to be best, which resolves have obtained among divines the name of *decrees*, it will be proper, before we consider his external acts, to present a scriptural view of these decrees; and to this subject our attention will be directed in the present chapter. We will *first* prove their existence, and *secondly*, inquire into their nature and properties.

I. THE EXISTENCE OF THE DIVINE DECREES.

No one who believes God to be an intelligent being, and who considers what intelligence implies, will deny that there are Divine decrees. As God knew all things that his power could accomplish, there were undoubtedly reasons which determined him to do certain things in preference to others, and his choice, which was founded upon those reasons, was his purpose or decree.

It will certainly be admitted, that God intended to create the world before he actually created it; that he intended to make man before he fashioned his body, and breathed into him the breath of life; and that he intended to govern the world according to certain laws. It will be admitted also, that when he resolved to create the world, to make man, and to establish laws physical and moral, he had some ultimate object in view. Having constructed a machine and set it in motion, he knew what would be the result; and this result was the true reason or the final cause why the machine was constructed. This intention of God is, therefore, his decree.

To this general idea of the Divine decrees it would be unreasonable to object, because it is as necessarily forced upon our mind as the idea of a purpose in the mind of a wise man previous to his entering upon any important enterprise; and with this idea the teachings of the holy Scriptures are in perfect harmony. They speak of the purpose of God, his will, his good pleasure, his determinate counsel, and his predestination. "All things work together for good to them that love God, to them who are called according to his *purpose*." Rom. viii, 28. "Paul, an apostle of Jesus Christ by the *will* of God." 2 Cor. i, 1. "Having made known unto us the mystery of his will, according to his *good pleasure* which he hath *purposed* in himself." Eph. i, 9. "Him being delivered by the *determinate counsel* and foreknowledge of God, ye have taken," etc. Acts ii, 23. "Having *predestinated* us unto the adoption of children by Jesus Christ to himself." Eph. i, 5. But it is unnecessary to multiply quotations. These Scriptures clearly prove, as do many others, that the operations of God are not the effects of necessity, but of *counsel* and *design*.

II. The Nature and Properties of the Divine Decrees.

The decrees of God may be defined to be, *his purposes or determinations respecting his creatures*. For this reason they are sometimes called the *counsel*, and sometimes the *will* of God; terms which are never applied to necessary things, but only to the determinations of free agents.

When the Scriptures represent the decrees of God as his *counsel*, the word is not to be taken in its common acceptation, as implying consultation with others; nor is it to be understood as denoting reflection, comparison, and the establishment of a conclusion by logical deduction. But the decisions of an infinite mind are instantaneous; and they are called *counsel*, to signify that they are consummately wise.

Nor are we to conclude, because the decrees of God are denominated his *will*, that they are arbitrary decisions; but merely, that in making them he was under no control, but acted according to his own sovereignty. When a man's own will is the rule of his conduct, it is in many instances capricious and unreasonable; but *wisdom* is always associated with *will* in the Divine proceedings. Accordingly, the decrees of God are said to be "the counsel of his will."

But in considering more particularly the nature and properties of the Divine decrees, it may be remarked,

1. *That they are eternal.*—This is virtually taught by the apostle when he says, "Known unto God are all his works from the beginning of the world." Acts xv, 18. The passage clearly imports, that at the commencement of time the plan was arranged according to which the works of God were to be executed. To suppose any of the Divine decrees to be made in time, is to suppose that the knowledge of God is limited; that he receives accessions to it in the progress of time, and that he forms new resolutions as new occasions require. Surely no one who believes that the Divine understanding is infinite, comprehending the past, the present, and the future, will ever assent to the doctrine of

temporal decrees. If God has any plan at all, it must be eternal; and hence St. Paul speaks of "the *eternal purpose* which he purposed in Christ Jesus our Lord." Eph. iii, 11.

2. *The decrees of God are free.*—By this we are to understand, that his determinations were not necessitated by any external cause, that he was at liberty to decree or not to decree, and to decree one thing and not another. This liberty we must ascribe to Him who is supreme, independent, and sovereign in all his dispensations. "Who hath directed the Spirit of the Lord, or being his counselor hath taught him? With whom took he counsel, and who instructed him, and taught him in the path of judgment, and taught him knowledge, and showed to him the way of understanding?" Isa. xl, 13, 14.

To deny the *freedom* of the Divine decrees is the same as to assert that they could not have been different from what they are. But are we prepared to adopt this sentiment? As well might we affirm that God could not have performed the work of creation sooner or later than he did; that he could not have made the world in any respect different from what it is; that he could not have placed man in a higher or lower degree in the scale of being; and that, when he had fallen, he could not have done otherwise than to redeem him by the death of his Son. Such a view of necessity, however, in regard either to the operations or the purposes of God, is both contrary to Scripture, and injurious to the feelings of piety, and must, therefore, be rejected.

We assert, then, that the decrees of God are *free*. No necessity can be supposed to influence the procedure of a self-existent and independent Being, except the necessity arising from his own perfections, of always acting in a manner worthy of himself. To his infinite understanding there must have appeared more than one way of doing this; and though there were doubtless reasons for the choice which he made, it would be boldness, not to be vindicated from the charge of impiety, to say that he could not have made a different choice.

3. *The decrees of God are immutable.*—This characteristic of the Divine decrees results from the infinite perfection and immutability of God; for if the least change should take place in his plans and determinations, it would be an instance of imperfection. The mutability of human purposes is owing to the uncertainty and defectiveness of human knowledge; but God knows with absolute certainty all things that ever were, now are, or ever shall be, and his purposes must therefore continue the same, amid all the changes of created things. "He is of one mind, and who can turn him?" Job xxiii, 13. "The counsel of the Lord standeth forever; the thoughts of his heart to all generations." Psalm xxxiii, 11. He declares, "My counsel shall stand, and I will do all my pleasure." Isa. xlvi, 10.

To the immutability of the Divine decrees it has been objected that the Scriptures represent God, in some cases at least, as changing his purpose. For instance, he said to King Hezekiah, "Set thine house in order ; for thou shalt die and not live." But afterward he said to him, "I will add unto thy days fifteen years." 2 Kings xx, 1, 6. Again, God commanded Jonah to say to the people of Nineveh, "Yet forty days, and Nineveh shall be overthrown." But when he saw that "they turned from their evil way," he "repented of the evil that he had said that he would do unto them ; and he did it not." Jonah iii, 10.

To meet the objection, and to reconcile these and all similar cases with the immutability of God's purposes, it is only necessary to observe, *first*, that the objector confounds two things which are essentially different, the Divine *purpose*, and the Divine *administration*. The former is nothing more than the *plan* according to which God operates as the Creator and Governor of the world ; while the latter consists in his *actual operation* in accordance with this plan. *Secondly*, that man is a free moral agent, and is, therefore, governed by laws and motives adapted to his moral constitution ; and that the purpose of God extends to the whole duration of his existence, and not merely to some particular period of it. Hence it is easy to conceive, in view of the conditionality of God's moral government and of the mutability of man, that the Divine administration respecting him may at one time be very different from what it is at another ; while in both cases it accords with the immutability of the Divine decrees.

For the sake of illustration, we may remark that the law which at one time protects a man in the possession of civil liberty may, at a subsequent period, condemn him to death. Would this imply a change in the law ? By no means. The *law* would continue the same—the only change would be in the *subject* who should incur its penalty. When man was created he was placed under a law, in obedience to which he enjoyed life in its highest sense ; but under the operation of that same law he became liable to death spiritual, temporal, and eternal. Did the law change ? No ; but man changed by disobeying it, and thus subjected himself to its curse. If, then, it is consistent with the immutability of God's *law* that the same moral agent should at one time be acquitted and at another time condemned, it may be equally consistent with the immutability of his *decrees ;* for of these his revealed will is only the formal declaration.

When, therefore, we meet with passages of Scripture in which a change of the Divine purpose seems to be indicated, as in the case of Hezekiah, or in which God is said to repent, as it is asserted of him in regard to the inhabitants of Nineveh, we must understand them to imply a change of the Divine *administration*, but not of the Divine purpose. It is to be remembered that in many of the most positive declarations of Scripture there are implied conditions. Thus, when God said to the Jewish king, "Thou shalt die, and not live," it was only the announcement of what must have been the inevitable consequence of his sickness had it not been divinely prevented. But as Hezekiah did not believe the sentence to be unconditional, he "prayed unto the Lord" and "wept sore;" and God regarded his supplications, removed his disease, and added to his "days fifteen years." So also in the case of the Ninevites the threatening was conditional, as the event clearly proves; consequently, when they "turned from their evil way" they escaped the threatened judgment.

4. *The decrees of God have been considered by theologians as either Absolute or Conditional.*

(1.) *Absolute* decrees are such as relate to those events in the Divine administration which have no dependence upon the free actions of moral creatures. These decrees are not called absolute, however, because they were made in the exercise of mere arbitrary power; but because, though made in view of wise and good reasons, the execution of them is not suspended upon any condition that may or may not be performed by moral creatures, but is to be ascribed to Divine agency. Thus, the purpose of God to create the world, to send his Son to redeem it, to bestow Gospel privileges upon one people and to deny them to another, and all his determinations of this nature, are called *absolute decrees.*

(2.) *Conditional* decrees are those in making which God had respect to the free actions of his moral creatures. Of this class are the purposes of God respecting the eternal welfare of men. They are founded upon that foreknowledge of men's moral actions which we are compelled to ascribe to God, and are never absolute, but always conditional. We must not conclude, however, as some have done, that conditional decrees are necessarily uncertain and mutable. They no more involve the idea of mutability than do those that are absolute. To the mind of God the end is as certain in one case as in the other, the only difference being in the means by which it is brought about. In *absolute* decrees God has respect to his own agency alone; in those that are *conditional*, to the agency of his free moral subjects; but in neither case can uncertainty or mutability be justly ascribed to them. God foresaw from eternity how every man would act, and whether he would comply with the conditions under which the designs of God concerning him would take effect or would reject them; and upon this perfect foreknowledge were his decrees founded. It is on this account, therefore, and this alone, that they are denominated *conditional.*

It is maintained by some that the foreknowledge of God is dependent upon his decrees. "If we allow the attribute of *prescience*," says Mr. Buck, "the idea of a decree must certainly be allowed also; for how can an action that is really to come to pass be foreseen if it be not determined? God knew everything from the beginning; but this he could not know if he had not so determined it." This notion, though advocated by high authority, we must regard as both absurd in itself and contrary to Scripture. It is absurd in itself, because it makes an essential attribute of God depend upon his efficiency. "God could not have known everything from the beginning if he had not so determined it." Thus the Divine prescience is brought into existence by an exercise of the Divine mind, in decreeing "whatsoever comes to pass." Again, if "God foresees nothing but what he has decreed, and his decree precedes his knowledge," as Piscator tells us, then it follows that, as the cause cannot be dependent on the effect, God must have made his decrees and contrived his plans independent of his knowledge, which only had an existence as the effect of these decrees. But if these conclusions are absurd, so must that doctrine be also of which they are the legitimate consequences.

This notion is, moreover, contrary to Scripture. St. Paul says, Rom. viii, 29, "For whom he did *foreknow*, he also did *predestinate* to be conformed to the image of his Son;" and St. Peter, in addressing believers, calls them " elect *according to the foreknowledge* of God the Father." 1 Peter i, 2. In these passages the decree of predestination or election is clearly founded on the foreknowledge of God. He foreknew in order to predestinate, but he did not predestinate in order to foreknow. Now as St. Paul tells the Christians at Rome that they were predestinated according to Divine foreknowledge, and St. Peter informs those in Asia Minor that they were elected in the same way, it follows either that all the elect are thus chosen, or that God pursued one plan in electing the Christians of Rome and Lesser Asia, and a different one for the rest of the world. But as the latter cannot be true, the former must be admitted. It is therefore evident that, in the order of cause and effect, the *exercise* of the Divine attributes is consequent upon their *existence;* that the plan of the Almighty is the result of his infinite knowledge; and that the decrees of his throne flow forth from the eternal fountain of his wisdom.

The conditionality of the Divine decrees, so far as they relate to the eternal destiny of men, may be argued, *first*, from the manner in which God actually saves sinners. Does he effect their salvation *unconditionally?* We answer, that he never would have saved men had not Christ died for them. This, then, is a *condition* of human salvation, the grand event on account of which God forgives sin. But does God actually save sinners without any condition *on their part?* The Bible furnishes the answer: " Except ye repent, ye shall all likewise perish." Luke xiii, 3. "He that believeth and is baptized shall be saved; but he that believeth not shall be damned." Mark xvi, 16. "If thou wilt enter into life, keep the commandments." Matt. xix, 17. The conditions, then, of eternal life are repentance, faith, and obedience. These conditions, it is true, are of a different nature from the atonement; but they are equally necessary. Hence we come to the conclusion, that, as the actual salvation of men is *conditional*, the decrees of God respecting it are *conditional* also.

It must be admitted, that the manner in which God will distribute happiness and misery in the future world is the precise mode which he eternally intended to pursue. If, then, it can be made appear that he certainly will reward men according to their works, it will follow that he eternally purposed to do so. But the Scriptures do most explicitly declare that God "will render to every man according to his deeds;" that every man shall "receive the things done in his body, according to that he hath done, whether it be good or bad;" and that "whatsoever a man soweth, that shall he also reap." Therefore, as it is certain that God will, in the world to come, treat men according to their moral conduct here, it follows that he always intended to do so; and if the decrees of God relative to men's future destiny were thus based upon their foreseen voluntary actions, they may be properly denominated *conditional*.

Secondly, the view which we have taken of this subject is further confirmed by what we know of the *character of God*. The Scriptures declare that "God is love;" that he "is good to all, and his tender mercies are over all his works;" and that he has "no pleasure in the death of him that dieth." How, then, could he have decreed to consign millions of the human family to endless perdition regardless of their conduct? Or, how could he place men under circumstances in which they must inevitably continue in sin, and then punish them in hell forever for not exercising that repentance and faith which he determined never to give them? The Scriptures assert that God is "long-suffering to usward, not willing that any should perish, but that all should come to repentance." But how could his bearing with the non-elect be properly an act of long-suffering, if he had determined to withhold forever from them that special grace by which alone they could repent, however long he might wait with them? How could the inspired apostle say that God is "not willing that any should perish," if from all eternity he had doomed, unconditionally, a large portion of the human family to endless misery? How could he assert the willingness of God "that *all* should come to repentance," if he had unconditionally determined to leave millions of our race in that moral condition in which true repentance is impossible?

Moreover, what *sincerity* could there be in the proclamation of the "Gospel to every creature," if God had determined by an absolute decree the eternal destiny of all men? The Gospel would offer a free and full salvation to those for whom no provision had been made in the redeeming plan, and life eternal to those who had been ordained to eternal death. And how can we reconcile with the *justice* and *impartiality* of God the opinion, that while he calls men into existence with a fallen and depraved nature, he should, irrespective of their conduct, elect some to everlasting life and consign others to hell? "God is no respecter of persons; but in every nation he that feareth him, and worketh righteousness, is accepted with him." How could this be said if God had made among his creatures a distinction of such incalculable magnitude and eternal duration as would be implied in the unconditional salvation of some, and unavoidable damnation of others?

The conclusion, then, of the whole matter is this: that though we ascribe to God decrees which are absolute and unconditional, yet, so far as they relate to the eternal destiny of men, they were formed in full view of men's free moral actions, and are, therefore, *conditional*. Properly speaking, however, these decrees cannot be said to depend on any thing but God himself, who perfectly knew from the beginning what would be the nature and consequences of every future occurrence.

We will close this chapter by a brief notice of the distinction which some theologians make between the revealed will of God, and what they are pleased to call his *secret* will. If this distinction were based upon the opinion, that God has plans and purposes which he has not fully revealed to mankind, it might very readily be allowed; for the Scriptures declare that " secret things belong unto the Lord our God; but those things which are revealed belong to us and to our children." Deut. xxix, 29. It is generally assumed, however, by the advocates of this distinction, that the *secret* will of God is, in many cases, directly contrary to what he has revealed in his word. For instance, God " will have all men to be saved, and to come unto the knowledge of the truth." 1 Tim. ii, 4. This is acknowledged to be his *revealed* will; but it is nevertheless contended that his *secret* will is, that many of the human race should *not* " be saved," or " come to the knowledge of the truth," but perish forever.

To this view of the secret will of God we object, for several reasons: 1. It is wholly gratuitous. There is not a single passage of Scripture which, when fairly interpreted, teaches the doctrine that the *will* of God is in any case contrary to his *word*. 2. It is absurd in itself. We can become acquainted with the purposes of God only so far as they are revealed. Of his secret or unrevealed will we can know nothing. If, therefore, we assume, in any given case, that the *secret* will of God is contrary to what he has revealed, we virtually assume that we know, by some means or other, what the secret will of God is, and consequently that it is both secret and revealed at the same time, which is a contradiction. But, 3. This opinion is dishonorable to the Divine character. It represents God as having two wills, which are in many cases contrary to one another, as declaring in the most solemn manner that he has " no pleasure in the death of him that dieth," while it is according to his *secret will* that multiplied thousands should die eternally. We conclude, therefore, that this theory is untenable, and that we can only judge of the will of God by what he has revealed.

CHAPTER IX.

OF CREATION.

HAVING considered in the preceding chapter the decrees of God, we are naturally led to speak, in the next place, of those exertions of his power which terminate upon created objects. Our attention shall be directed, in this chapter, to the work of *Creation;* which we will consider, *first*, in general, and *secondly*, in particular.

§ 1. *Of Creation in General.*

In the investigation of this part of the subject it will be proper to inquire into the *nature*, the *date*, and the *extent* of creation.

I. THE NATURE OF CREATION.

Here it is necessary to ascertain what the precise idea of creation is, or the sense in which the term *create* is to be understood, when it is employed to denote the agency of God in the production of the universe. The original word is ברא, which signifies, in its primary sense, to cause a thing to exist or spring forth from nothing. But it means also, to form a thing out of existing materials, to revive or reinvigorate, and to effect a change in our moral nature, as when a new heart is said to be created within us.

When it is said, in the first of Genesis, that "God *created* the heavens and the earth," the word is to be taken in its primary sense, as denoting the original production of matter by Almighty power; while the subsequent verses inform us by what steps God formed this mass of rude matter into that beautiful system of nature which excites the admiration of every beholder. "In the beginning," or at the commencement of time, he made out of nothing the matter of which the heavens and the earth were composed, and upon which their present form was afterward superinduced. This seems to be the natural way of explaining this part of sacred history; and according to this view, the Bible opens with an ascription to God of the act of creation in the highest sense of the term.

There is another passage of Scripture which will assist us in ascertaining the sense in which God is said to have created the world. "Through faith we understand that the worlds were framed by the word of God, so that things which are seen were not made of things which do appear." Heb. xi, 3. Here we learn that the visible creation was not formed out of pre-existent matter. For, if it had been so formed, that matter, however extended or modified, would still *appear* in the present system; but the apostle asserts, that "the things which are seen [the visible creation] were *not* made of *things which do appear*." It follows, therefore, that he virtually denies the eternity of matter, and asserts the creation of all things out of nothing, "by the word of God."

By *creation*, then, we are to understand *that act of God by which he gave existence to the world*, or to things extrinsic to himself; or, as it is commonly expressed, *by which he made the world* OUT OF NOTH-ING. Accordingly, the holy Scriptures constantly describe God as the creator of the world; not merely in regard to its present form, but of the materials themselves from which it is formed.*

The Grecian philosophers and other ancient writers, being ignorant of Divine revelation, and guided only by the wild speculations of their own imagination, had no just idea of creation in its proper sense. They insisted upon the principle, *ex nihilo nihil fit ;* and could not admit, therefore, that it was possible for God to create the world out of nothing. Accordingly they believed almost universally that matter, in a chaotic state, existed from all eternity; and that God only arranged and moulded the discordant materials, so as to bring order out of confusion, and cause the universe to appear in its harmony and beauty. With them God was merely the *builder*, and not the *creator* of the world.

It is easy to show, however, that this notion of the eternity of matter is absurd and untenable. To suppose that matter existed from eternity is to ascribe to it self-existence. For, that which existed from eternity could not have been produced by anything else. The only cause of its existence, therefore, must be in itself; and this implies that it is self-existent and independent.

Again, if matter is self-existent and independent, as its eternity clearly implies, it must exist *necessarily*. For, if the cause of its existence has always been in itself, it could not but have existed; otherwise, the necessary connection between cause and effect would be destroyed.

But if matter exists necessarily, this necessity must be the same everywhere. Consequently, upon this supposition, matter must have existed everywhere, or must have filled every portion of space, and have been infinitely extended; which is absurd, and contrary to fact.

There is another consequence which is equally absurd, that, if matter exists necessarily, that necessity must extend to all its properties. But if so, the particular *state* in which it exists must be necessary; and then, the same eternal necessity which determined the *state* of its existence must determine its *continuance* in that state. Consequently, if

---

* The phrase, *to create from nothing*, does not occur in the canonical Scriptures, though the idea itself is scriptural. It seems to have been taken from 2 Macc. vii, 28, in the Vulgate; *" ex nihilo fecit Deus cœlum et terram."*

matter had existed from eternity in a chaotic state, it must have continued in that state until now; and upon this hypothesis the worlds could not have been produced from chaotic matter.

Some have adopted the theory that the material universe has existed from eternity in its organized condition; but this hypothesis is as unreasonable as the former.   For,

1. *It is inconsistent with the nature of time, which is a succession of moments.*—"We can conceive time •to commence at any given period, and to run on *ad infinitum*, or never to come to an end; but we cannot conceive it to be actually infinite.   An infinite duration can never be made up of finite parts; because as each of those parts has an end, the sum which they compose must also have an end.   As it is impossible that an infinite succession of moments can be past, it is impossible that the universe can have existed from eternity."*

2. *The eternity of the world in its organized state is disproved by the history of arts and sciences.*—It is but reasonable to suppose that each generation would profit by the labors and experience of preceding generations, and that human society should be characterized from age to age by progressive improvement.   But we know that civilization and learning can be traced back only to a period which is but as yesterday, and that all the great and important discoveries in the arts and sciences are of comparatively recent date.   These facts strongly indicate, therefore, that only a few thousand years have elapsed since our earth and its inhabitants came into existence.

3. *Another argument against the eternity of the world in its organized state is founded on the comparatively modern date of authentic history.*—No credible history reaches further back than the period which Moses has assigned for the creation; and profane history has nothing to relate but fables and rumors till the age of Herodotus, who flourished about five hundred years before the Christian era.   These facts would be unaccountable if the earth and man had existed from eternity; for then we might readily suppose that history, either recorded or monumental, would carry us back for thousands of centuries.

Such are some of the speculations of heathen philosophers in regard to the visible creation, and of the numerous difficulties in which their theories are involved.   But if we follow the principles of philosophy in its present improved state, or rather, if we follow the Bible, to which alone our modern philosophy is indebted for its improvement, we will not admit the maxim *ex nihilo nihil fit* in reference to the creation of the world.   This maxim is indeed incontrovertible, when applied to material causes;† but it is not true, if understood of an *efficient* cause

---

* Dick's Theology, Lecture 37.

† The *material* cause of a thing is that out of which it is made.   For example, the marble out of which a statue is made is its *material* cause; but the sculptor who forms the statue is its *efficient* cause.

to which omnipotence is ascribed. Consequently, if our theory respecting God and his attributes is well established, this principle applied to him as the efficient cause of the world must be regarded as false. For, if God is omnipotent, he can from nothing produce something, or bring into existence what did not exist before. Moreover, if it is true that matter is *not necessary*, it cannot exist *of itself*, but must derive its existence from God, or depend upon him, who at first created it out of nothing.

The truth that God created from nothing everything that exists, is the uniform doctrine of the Bible; but it is a doctrine which was unknown to the ancient philosophers long after it had been taught by the writers of the Jewish Scriptures. Indeed, it is from these Scriptures that our modern philosophers have derived, however unwilling they are to confess it, all their better views upon this subject. To the sacred writers, therefore, we owe the doctrine that God gave existence to what was not.

II. The Date of Creation.

According to the Hebrew chronology, as ascertained by Archbishop Usher, the creation took place four thousand and four years before the Christian era; but according to the Septuagint, five thousand two hundred and seventy years. It is easy to determine which of these computations should be preferred. The *original*, when all the copies agree, is surely higher authority than any translation; and especially the Septuagint, which is probably the most inaccurate of all translations. Accordingly the computation of Usher has been generally received as reliable.

But here we are encountered by the pretended discoveries of modern science. The observations which geologists have made upon the structure of the earth are supposed to contradict the Mosaic account, by proving that it must have been created at a more distant period, if it was created at all; and that it must have undergone many revolutions prior to what we call the beginning. By some the Mosaic account is rejected entirely; while others suppose it to be a record, not of the original creation of the earth, but of the changes which took place upon it after some terrible convulsion. Thus, in the language of Cowper,

> "Some drill and bore
> The solid earth, and from the strata there
> Extract a register, by which we learn
> That He who made it, and revealed its date
> To Moses, was mistaken in its age."

Geologists talk much of primitive formations. They ascribe the origin of rocks to precipitation and crystallization. Looking at a piece of granite they point out the characters of aqueous or igneous fusion, and say that it was formed by the agency of water or fire, carried on through a long process, which it required ages to complete; and from such data they come to the conclusion that a much longer period was necessary to form the rocks and strata of the earth than the Scriptures assign. Thus puny mortals, with but a spark of intellect, and only a moment for observation, deem themselves fully authorized, from a mere glance at a few superficial appearances, to contradict the account which Moses gives of the world's creation. "Where wast thou," said the Almighty to Job, "when I laid the foundations of the earth? Declare, if thou hast understanding." Job xxxviii, 4.

It is easy to show that the main geological argument for the great age of the world is without any solid foundation. It is not denied that the various formations of the earth, so far as they have been examined, appear as if they had been produced by chemical laws. But is it therefore certain that they were so produced? Why may we not suppose that God created everything in agreement with the action of those natural laws which he imparted to matter, and which he evidently intended to operate in the physical world? Why may we not suppose, for instance, that rocks were at first formed so as to correspond with all the phenomena of precipitation and crystallization? No one but an Atheist will deny that this was possible; but if it was possible the argument from primitive formations, against the comparatively modern date of the earth, falls to the ground.

That there was a first man will be admitted by all who believe in the existence of a great First Cause. Now, if we had the opportunity of examining one of his bones we should doubtless perceive that it resembled, in all respects, the bones of other men; and, reasoning according to our geologists, we should conclude that its fibers were at first soft, that they gradually became cartilage, and that they finally acquired the hardness of their perfect state. But we should reason falsely, because that bone was at once made solid and firm. Could we examine the first tree that God created, we should perceive that it indicated, like any other tree, the growth of successive years. We would naturally conclude, therefore, if we had no knowledge of its history, that it had originally sprung from a seed, and that it had come to a state of maturity by the usual process; while the fact would be that it had been produced in a moment. In the former case we would have all the *apparent effects* of ossification, and in the latter, of lignification, while it is certain that these processes never took place. It follows, then, that sensible phenomena cannot alone determine the age of the world, or the mode of the earth's formation.

Some, unwilling to reject the history of Moses in regard to the origin of the world, have attempted to reconcile it with the popular theory, by supposing that the six days of creation were not natural days of twenty-four hours, but so many periods of indefinite length. They assume that the world must have been created at an earlier date than the literal interpretation of the history assigns to it, and that ages were necessary to give rise to those appearances which are observed in its structure.

To this notion we reply, *first*, that there is no necessity for such an interpretation of the days of Moses, or for supposing the original chaos to have been an immense laboratory, from which, after the operations of ages, the earth came forth as we now see it. There was a Power adequate to create it at once—a Power which formed the primeval rocks without the aid of fire or water, as it made perfect bones and perfect trees, independent of those second causes by which they are now produced. But, *secondly*, this view of the subject is objectionable because it puts a meaning upon the word day which it bears nowhere else in simple narrative, and for which there is no authority in the Bible. Indeed, when we consider the distinct manner in which the day is defined, as "the evening and the morning," if the term were not to be taken in its literal sense, we could hardly vindicate the sacred historian from an intention to mislead.

It must not be forgotten in our geological investigations that the earth was at first in all probability in a fluid state; and, also, that it must have undergone various and great changes at the time of the deluge. It is impossible to conceive the modifications which must have been produced in its structure by the breaking up of "the fountains of the great deep," and by the irresistible action of such an immense body of water as submerged the entire globe. We may not be able to answer all the objections which geologists urge against the literal interpretation of the Mosaic history; but neither can they prove that the appearances upon which they found their theories did not result from those facts.

We conclude, therefore, that the language of Moses is to be taken in its literal sense when he says, "In *six days* the Lord made heaven and earth;" and that the account which he gives of the origin of the world is the only rational theory that has ever been presented. If in any opposing scheme philosophers were generally united, their opinion would have great force; but their theories are different and contradictory. What one builds up another destroys; while the narrative of Moses stands unmoved, like a rock amid the waves of the ocean, resting on the solid basis of all the proofs by which its Divine authority is established.

Thus the heavens and the earth were created about four thousand years before the birth of Christ. The materials themselves were produced out of nothing in an instant by the power of God; but six days were employed in moulding them into that harmonious and beautiful system of nature which we call the universe. On the first day light was created; on the second the atmosphere; on the third the water was collected into lakes and seas, and the dry land appeared, which was immediately covered with grass, herbs, and trees; on the fourth the sun, the moon, and the stars became visible; on the fifth the waters and the air were replenished with inhabitants; and on the sixth terrestrial animals and man were created.

III. The Extent of the Creation.

The sacred historian, in speaking of the creation of the universe, adopts the common and obvious division of it into two parts, the *earth* and the *heavens.* The earth, indeed, is but a small part of the universe; but as it is the allotted habitation of the human race, it was proper that it should be distinctly noticed and particularly described.

All the other parts of creation are comprehended under the term *heavens,* which signifies, in the language of the Jews, the atmosphere; the region of the sun, moon, and stars; and lastly, the habitation of the blessed. The atmosphere properly belongs to the earth, and appears to have been the work of the second day, when God said, "Let there be a firmament in the midst of the waters; and let it divide the waters from the waters." Gen. i, 6. The word רקיע, which is rendered *firmament,* signifies an *expanse* or *space;* a term which very aptly denotes the atmosphere as surrounding the earth, and extending to a great distance from its surface. This is the region in which clouds and meteors are formed, and in which the water exhaled from the earth and the sea is suspended till, condensed by cold, it falls down in dew and rain.

But the term *heavens* includes the sun, moon, and stars. The sun is the great source of light to our system; and the moon, though probably created as soon as the earth, is said to have been made on the fourth day, because it then only became visible by reflecting the rays of the sun.* Under the denomination of the stars are included, not only those luminaries which are properly so called, but the planets also which belong to our system. The Bible gives no further account of these heavenly bodies than that some of them were appointed "for signs, and for seasons, and for days and years." Any additional information respecting them is derived from observation and reasoning; and though the discoveries of modern science make no part of theology, yet they are worthy of attention because they have a tendency to exalt our ideas of the power and beneficence of the Creator.

As the planets are removed from us many millions of miles, they

---

* Though the sun is the principal source of light, yet he is not the only source from which it flows. There is light produced by the ignition of combustible substances, light struck out from hard bodies by percussion or friction, phosphoric light, and electric light. As there is at present light without the sun, there may have been light without him in the beginning, as recorded by Moses; nor can we now tell whether light proceeds from his body or from his atmosphere. But, however this may be, it seems reasonable to suppose that the sun was created at the same time with the earth, though he was not made the grand repository of light until the fourth day. It is asserted that "in the beginning God created the heaven" as well as "the earth." Moreover, the earth could not have occupied its proper place in the system if it had been created before the sun, for by the latter the former is retained in its orbit. But this matter is perfectly plain if we suppose that the sun was created at the same time with the earth, and that it was not till the fourth day that he was made a luminous body; for the influence which he exerts upon the earth depends upon his solid mass, not upon his light.

would not be visible if their magnitude were not great. But how much greater must be the magnitude of the fixed stars, the distance of which from the earth is immense, when compared with that of the utmost planet which revolves around the sun! It is natural to inquire, For what purpose were these fixed stars placed in the heavens? It was surely not to give light to the earth, for their light is of but little account to us. Nor was it to mark the progress of the seasons and the revolution of the year, for this is done by the sun and the changes which take place on the face of the earth. Were they then created in vain? Shall we suppose that He who made the earth for great and benevolent purposes, and made the sun to give it light, could have created millions of suns for no assignable end? Such a conclusion would charge the God of nature with folly, and be at variance with the proofs of intelligence and design which are so amply supplied by all his other works.

The opinion, therefore, that around those suns planets revolve, the inhabitants of which rejoice in their light and are cheered by their influence, is not a mere flight of fancy, but rests upon strong grounds of belief; and while this theory vindicates the wisdom of God, it leads us to admire his infinite goodness, which diffuses life and happiness far beyond the reach of the eye or even the range of imagination. Thus the universe presents itself to our view in all its magnificent and immeasurable extent; and while we raise our thoughts to Him who spoke it into being, we are constrained to exclaim, "O Lord, how manifold are thy works! in wisdom hast thou made them all." Psa. civ, 24.

But in the last place the term *heavens* includes that region of peace, and purity, and joy, where God manifests himself in all his glory to his perfect creatures. This must be a *place*, because human beings now dwell in it, and because it is to be the abode of the righteous after the resurrection. Jesus said to his disciples, "I go to prepare a *place* for you. And if I go and prepare a *place* for you, I will come again and receive you unto myself; that *where* I am, *there* ye may be also." John xiv, 2, 3. This is sometimes called the *third* heaven, of which the holy of holies in the Jewish tabernacle and temple was an interesting type. Where this place is, however, cannot be determined, and conjectures respecting its location are more curious than edifying.

§ 2. *Of Creation in Particular.*

Creation, considered particularly, respects those *intelligent* and *moral* beings whom God has brought into existence. They are comprehended in two general classes, *angels* and *men*. As the Bible furnishes some account of both these classes of beings, we will endeavor to ascertain, to some extent, the important information which is thus placed within our reach. But as the doctrines respecting man will constitute a separate book, we will confine our remarks, in this section, to that class of created intelligences called ANGELS.

The word ANGEL is derived from the Greek αυγελος, and is a name not of *nature*, but of *office.* It corresponds with מלאך in Hebrew, and literally signifies a messenger, or one sent on an embassy. The term is sometimes applied to men who are invested with authority over others, as "the Angels of the seven Churches," who were probably their bishops or presidents; but it is generally used in Scripture to designate a superior order of intelligences who inhabit the heavenly world.

That there are such beings as those whom we call angels, in the common acceptation of the term, is evidently taught in the Bible. It might, therefore, seem impossible for any one to deny their existence who believed the Scriptures to be worthy of credit; and yet, as St. Luke informs us, the Sadducees asserted that there was "neither angel nor spirit." There have been some in modern times also who have coincided with the Sadducees in denying the existence of angels, affirming that when they are spoken of as real beings the term is to be understood in a figurative sense. Thus we are told that good angels signify good thoughts, and evil angels sinful thoughts. But with such as make thus free with the Scriptures, and subvert their plainest teachings, it would be useless to reason; for if the Bible history of the existence and doings of angels is to be understood in a figurative sense, we may as well discard the whole volume of revelation as an idle dream.

But relying upon what God has revealed concerning this class of his moral creatures, and understanding this revelation in its plain and obvious sense, we will proceed to offer such remarks as will elicit all the leading features of their history.

From the Bible we learn that angels are divided, in reference to their moral condition, into *holy* and *unholy*, or into *good* and *evil.* Let us, then, inquire briefly concerning each of these classes.

I. OF HOLY ANGELS.

These are so denominated because they have continued in that state of holiness or moral purity in which they were originally created; and also, to distinguish them from the apostate "angels which kept not their first estate." In our remarks respecting them we will notice,

1. *The time of their Creation.*—To the question, When were the angels created? we can return only a general answer. Of this event Moses has given us no information, unless, with some, we suppose angels to be included in the *host of heaven;* but this phrase seems rather to signify the celestial luminaries, the sun, moon, and stars. We have no reason to think, however, that the creation of angels preceded the time to which Moses refers in the first chapter of Genesis. A prior date has been assigned by many; but it is a mere conjecture, and seems

to be at variance with the general language of Scripture. The sacred historian does most certainly teach that the *heavens* were created at the same time with the earth; and though he takes no notice of the *inhabitants* of the heavenly world, yet there is ground to believe that they also were created at the same time. On what day they were created is a question of mere curiosity; but it is supposed by many that God spoke of the angels when he said to Job, " Where wast thou when I laid the foundations of the earth? when the morning stars sang together, and all the sons of God shouted for joy?" Job xxxviii, 4, 7. If by the *morning stars*, and the *sons of God*, the angelic host is meant, which seems to be probable, it will follow that the angels were present when the mighty fabric of the universe was completed, and that they celebrated, on that occasion, the praises of the Divine Architect.

2. *Their Natural Attributes.*—Of angels it may be affirmed that they are spiritual beings, that they are immortal, that they are highly intelligent, and that they possess astonishing power and activity.

(1.) *They are* SPIRITUAL *beings.*—As such they are represented in the fourth verse of the hundred and fourth Psalm, which is quoted in Heb. i, 7: "Who maketh his angels *spirits*, and his ministers a flame of fire." Angels, then, are spirits; and no better definition of a spirit can be given than the one presented by our Lord, though it is of the negative kind, when he said to his terrified disciples, " Handle me, and see; for a spirit hath not flesh and bones, as ye see me have." Luke xxiv, 39. It would be in vain for us to inquire into the *essence* of a spirit, because it is perfectly beyond our grasp; but it is not more so than is the essence of matter, of which we know only the properties.

(2.) *They are* IMMORTAL.—The immortality of angels may be inferred from the language of our Lord respecting the future condition of the righteous. " Neither can they die any more; for they are equal unto the angels." Luke xx, 36. It may be supposed that their immortality is the natural consequence of their immateriality; but the proper ground is the will of God. He willed that the angels should never die, even though they should sin; but in this respect they have no pre-eminence above the souls of men, which are not injured by the stroke of death, but merely separated from those portions of matter which they had animated for a time, and are destined to animate again.

(3.) *They are highly* INTELLIGENT.—The superior intelligence of angels may be argued: 1. From their spirituality. Their spiritual nature is not weighed down by the frailties of weak and perishing bodies. 2. From their superior order. They are confessedly creatures of a higher order than men; and it is, therefore, reasonable to believe that the degree of intelligence which they possess is in proportion to the superiority of their rank. 3. From the place of their abode. Their proper home is the heaven of heavens, where they ever behold the face of God, and dwell amid the effulgence of heavenly light. The angel who appeared to Zachariah in the temple said, "I am Gabriel, that stand in the presence of God." 4. From their long observation and experience. A capacity to increase in knowledge enters into the very nature of rational creatures, and this is surely as true of angels as it is of men. For multiplied ages they have been gazing upon the unfolding attributes of God, and winging their unwearied flight to various and distant parts of heaven's dominions, to execute the Divine will, and to witness the wonders of the Divine administration. To what lofty heights, then, must they be elevated in regard to knowledge and wisdom! That the Jews believed in the superior knowledge of angels, is evident from the words of the woman of Tekoah to David: "My lord is wise, according to the wisdom of an angel of God, to know all things that are in the earth." 2 Sam. xiv, 20.

(4.) *They possess astonishing* POWER *and* ACTIVITY.—In Psalm ciii, 20, David exclaims, "Bless the Lord, ye his angels, that *excel in strength;*" and St. Paul tells us that "the Lord Jesus shall be revealed from heaven with his *mighty angels.*" 2 Thess. i, 7. *Strong angel* and *mighty angel* are phrases in the Apocalypse which are expressive of the same character.

Proofs of the power with which these exalted beings are endowed are in several instances recorded in the Scriptures. It is highly probable that when "the Lord slew all the first born in the land of Egypt" in a single hour it was done by the ministry of an angel, who is, therefore, called "the destroyer." Exod. xii, 23. An angel destroyed seventy thousand persons in three days in consequence of the sin of David in numbering the people. And an angel put to death in one night of the army of Sennacherib a hundred and eighty-five thousand. These instances show that angels possess a power which to us is utterly incomprehensible.

But their *activity* is equally wonderful. Their nature, in this respect, is briefly described in Psalm civ, 4: "Who maketh his angels spirits, and his ministers a flaming fire." The word here rendered *spirits* most commonly signifies *winds.* But in either sense the phraseology forcibly declares the eminent activity of angels, who are thus represented as moving with the swiftness of winds, or of that which is peculiar to spirits, and as operating with the astonishing energy of flaming fire. Moreover, they are represented as flying on wings; and as they are purely spiritual in their nature, we may suppose that they can travel from world to world with the velocity of thought. Of this we have a striking instance recorded in the ninth chapter of Daniel. From this remarkable passage we learn that Daniel set himself to seek the Lord in fasting and prayer; that after his prayer was begun the Angel Gabriel was commanded to visit him with a message of Divine instruction; and that ere his supplication was closed the angel touched him "about the time of the evening oblation." Hence, during the time in which Daniel was employed in uttering his prayer, Gabriel came to him from the heavenly world. This is a rapidity of motion which exceeds all comprehension of the most active imagination; surpassing, beyond any comparison, the amazing swiftness of light.

3. THEIR MORAL CONDITION.—In regard to the moral condition of angels we may remark,

(1.) *That they are* HOLY *beings.*—Such they must have been when they came from the hand of the Creator; and such they have continued to be, though others have fallen into sin. Hence they are expressly denominated by our Lord "*the holy angels.*" Matt. xxv, 31. They are also called the "ministers of" God, "that do his pleasure," (Psa. ciii, 21;) and they are placed before us, in the prayer which Christ taught his disciples, as patterns of holy obedience. "Thy will be done in earth *as it is in* heaven." Matt. vi, 10.

The holiness of angels may be inferred from their place of residence. Heaven is a holy place, and no unholy being can ever dwell in that holy habitation. This has been the home of the holy angels for almost six thousand years, and in no instance have they done anything displeasing to God. They were no doubt tempted; but they indignantly resisted the solicitation of counsel and example. They have witnessed many a foul display of human and angelic depravity, but they have not received the slightest moral taint.

(2.) *Angels are* BENEVOLENT *beings.*—It is in general true that the more men are advanced in holiness the more pleasure they take in the welfare of others, and in the diffusion of morality and piety. But if this is the case with men it must be eminently so with the holy angels. We see here why the plan of human redemption engages their attention, and fills them with delight and wonder. It is a subject which "the angels desire to look into." 1 Pet. i, 12. The chorus in which "the heavenly host" united, when celebrating the nativity of our Lord, is beautifully expressive of angelic piety and benevolence. "Glory to God in the highest, and on earth peace, good-will toward men." Luke ii, 14. Our Lord tells us that "there is joy in the presence of the angels of God over one sinner that repenteth." Luke xv, 10.

(3.) *They are* HAPPY *beings.*—This may be inferred from the holiness of their nature. With them the recollection of the past creates no remorse, and the prospect of the future awakens no fear or anxiety. They have always served God with fidelity, and they will always enjoy his love. They drink immortal joys from the pure fountain of bliss, and feast continually on the enrapturing visions of the Divine glory.* Nor is their happiness impaired by their visits to earth. The offensive scenes which they here behold must excite their strong disapprobation, but they cannot produce the least disquieting emotion. They have acts of vengeance to perform; but as they detest sin, and glow with zeal

* See Matt. xviii, 10.

for the honor of God, they perform with pleasure any service which he requires.

4. THEIR GREAT NUMBER.—The numerousness of angels is most clearly taught in the Scriptures, which everywhere represent God as being surrounded by a great multitude of heavenly servants, or, as they are called by Jacob, "God's host."* "The chariots of God," says the psalmist, "are twenty thousand, even thousands of angels: the Lord is among them, as in Sinai, in the holy place." Psa. lxviii, 17. The same truth is set forth in the language of our Lord. "Thinkest thou that I cannot now pray to my Father, and he shall presently give me more than twelve legions of angels?" Matt. xxvi, 53. St. John tells us that he "beheld, and heard the voices of many angels round about the throne, and the beasts and the elders;" and that "the number of them was ten thousand times ten thousand, and thousands of thousands." Rev. v, 11.

5. THEIR EMPLOYMENT.—It is the employment of the holy angels,

(1.) *To glorify God, and to celebrate his praise.*—When God laid the foundations of the earth these morning stars rejoiced together and shouted for joy. When on Mount Sinai, amid thunderings and lightnings, and a flame of devouring fire, he published his holy law, "the chariots of God, even the thousands of angels," attended him at this awful solemnity. When the Son of God became incarnate an angel proclaimed his birth to the shepherds of Bethlehem, and "a multitude of the heavenly host" praised God on that occasion in the noblest hymn that earth ever heard. And when he ascended on high, having finished the work of redemption, the same exalted beings attended him, singing, as they approached the heaven of heavens, "Lift up your heads, O ye gates! and be ye lifted up, ye everlasting doors! and the King of Glory shall come in." Psa. xxiv, 7. So, also, their constant employment in their heavenly home is to praise and worship God.†

(2.) *Angels are employed in studying God's works and dispensations.*—St. Paul tells us that "God created all things by Jesus Christ; to the intent that now unto the principalities and powers in heavenly places might be known by the Church the manifold wisdom of God." Eph. iii, 9, 10. And as God designed that a knowledge of his dispensations to the Church should be made known to the angelic host, "the principalities and powers in heavenly places," so we learn that the disposition of angels is in perfect accordance with this design. "Which things the angels desire to look into."

(3.) *Angels are employed in executing the judgments of God upon men.*—The first judgment inflicted upon man—his exclusion from Paradise—appears to have been committed to the ministry of angels. In like manner they were the immediate instruments in the infliction of Divine vengeance on the Israelites, on the army of Sennacherib, on

---

* Gen. xxxii, 2.   † See Rev. v, 11, 12; vii, 11, 12.

Nebuchadnezzar, and on Herod. In the same manner, also, they are represented in the Apocalypse as pouring out the vials of Divine wrath upon the nations of our guilty world.

(4.) *Angels are also employed in ministering to the people of God.*— "Are they not all ministering spirits, sent forth to minister for them who shall be heirs of salvation?" Heb. i, 14. Here we are plainly taught that to minister to the saints is a standing employment of angels. Accordingly they are exhibited in Jacob's vision of the ladder (Gen. xxviii, 12) as ascending from earth to heaven, and descending from heaven to earth, in the discharge of this great duty; and the Scriptures furnish numerous examples of their actual ministry to the children of God.

First, in revealing to them the Divine will. An angel instructed Abraham, Joshua, David, Elijah, Daniel, Zechariah the prophet, Zachariah the father of John the Baptist, the Virgin Mary, and others. It was an angel that conducted Joseph and Mary to Egypt, Philip to the eunuch, and Cornelius to Peter. So also it was by the ministry of an angel that God revealed his will to John in the isle of Patmos.

Secondly, in protecting and delivering them from evil. " There shall no evil befall thee, neither shall any plague come nigh thy dwelling; for he shall give his angels charge over thee, to keep thee in all thy ways." Psa. xci, 10, 11. The angel of the Lord encampeth round about them that fear him, and delivereth them." Psa. xxxiv, 7. Thus angels delivered Lot from Sodom, Jacob from Esau, Daniel from the lions, his three companions from the fiery furnace, and Peter from Herod and the Jewish Sanhedrim. We are not to conclude, however, that ministering angels are to preserve the saints from every calamity of life; for it is the will of God that they should sometimes suffer affliction for their own good. But we have reason to believe that these guardian spirits are continually about our path, encircling us with an invisible wall of protection.

Thirdly, in affording them comfort. Thus they comforted Jacob at the approach of Esau; Daniel in his peculiar sorrows and dangers; Joseph and Mary in their perplexities; CHRIST in his agony in the garden; the apostles and their companions after our Lord's resurrection; and St. Paul immediately before his shipwreck.

Fourthly, in conveying the souls of the saints to the mansions of bliss. Having attended them through the journey of life, they will not forsake them in their dying hour; and when their spirits leave the earthly tenement they will bear them in triumph to the upper sanctuary. When Lazarus died he " was carried by the angels into Abraham's bosom." Luke xvi, 22. We look upon death as a scene of sorrow and distress. But if the spiritual world were not hidden from us, we should behold, in the presence of the dying Christian, ministering angels; and we should hear them commingling their sweetest songs with the groans of the sufferer, and the lamentations of weeping friends, and softly whispering, "Sister spirit, come away."

Lastly, the angels will minister for the saints at the second coming of Christ. At the great harvest of the world, as our Lord has taught us, the angels will be the reapers; and as they will then pluck up the tares and cast them into the fire, so they will gather the wheat into the garner. Christ "shall send his angels with a great sound of a trumpet; and they shall gather together his elect from the four winds, from one end of heaven to the other." Matt. xxiv, 31.

Thus we have given a faint outline of the creation, the nature, the moral condition, and the employment of the holy angels as revealed in the Scriptures. How noble and exalted a portion are these celestial beings of the wonderful works of the great Creator! How large and extended must be their views of the infinite wisdom and goodness of God! How profound must be their adoration! How glorious is their employment! Day and night they are fulfilling their Maker's will, not as a dull task, but as a most delightful service. Lord, help us to do thy will on earth as angels do it in heaven!

II. Of Unholy or Evil Angels.

That this class of created spirits were originally both holy and happy, may be clearly inferred from the Divine character. He who is perfectly holy and good could not have produced unholy and miserable beings. It follows, therefore, that they were once holy angels, and in every respect similar to those who now stand in the presence of God; that they are distinguished from the latter, not in their origin nor in their natural attributes, but in their moral character and condition; and that their present character and condition can only be accounted for on the principle that they are fallen creatures. Let us then direct our attention to their fall, their moral condition, their employment, and their destiny.

1. *Their Fall.*—That these unholy angels were once holy and happy, and fell from that exalted state, is clearly taught in the following passages: "Ye are of your father the devil, and the lusts of your father ye will do. He was a murderer from the beginning, and abode not in the truth." John viii, 44. "God spared not the angels that sinned, but cast them down to hell." 2 Pet. ii, 4. "The angels which kept not their first estate, but left their own habitation, he hath reserved in everlasting chains." Jude 6. Thus we learn that the devil "abode not in the truth," which implies that he was once in it; and that the sinning angels "kept not their first estate, but left their own habitation."

Of this wonderful event—a revolt in the heavenly world, and among the highest order of created intelligences—we have no regular history in the Scriptures. Still we are abundantly assured by them that this event did actually take place. By various declarations and allusions which they contain we are taught that Satan, an angel of pre-eminent distinction in heaven, rebelled against his Maker; and that in this deplorable enterprise a multitude of the heavenly host united with him, and, with the same disposition, violated the law of God, and revolted from his government.

There is a diversity of opinion with respect to the first sin of the fallen angels. Some suppose that it consisted in tempting our first parents; but this opinion is refuted by the consideration that they must have been sinful themselves before they could be inclined to lead others into sin. Some have thought that their sin was *envy*—envy either of those angels who were superior to them in rank and dignity, or of man whom God had created in his own image, and invested with dominion over this lower world. But the most probable opinion is that it consisted in *pride* and *ambition*. St. Paul, in speaking of a bishop, says that he must not be "a novice, (νεοφυτος, *a new convert*,) lest being lifted up with *pride* he fall into the *condemnation of the devil.*" 1 Tim. iii, 6. Here it is clearly implied that the devil was condemned for *pride;* and it is fairly presumable that the same sin was the source of condemnation to his companions.

How it was that these angels sinned without being tempted, or, if self-tempted, how they could have originated the temptation within their own nature, which was at first pure, we cannot fully comprehend; but the facts are revealed, and we are compelled to believe them. That they were under a law is clear from the fact that they sinned. But if they were under a law which it was possible for them to violate, they must have been in a state of trial, and of accountability to God; and, to such a state, the possibility of sinning is essential. To say that holy creatures could not have sinned without a tempter, is the same as to assert the eternity of moral evil, which is absurd; or, that God is its author, which is blasphemous.

2. *Their Moral Condition.*—The fall of angels destroyed none of their natural attributes. With respect to their essence they are still spiritual beings. They are also immortal, highly intelligent, and possessed of great power and activity. But their *moral* qualities have undergone a total change. Of their original holiness not a vestige remains. Sin is now so natural to them that it seems almost to be their essence. It is the element in which they live and move.

The depravity of men is, in some degree, checked and concealed by certain natural feelings and affections, which, though not virtuous, have the effects of virtue in restraining them from acts of malice and cruelty, and in leading them to perform deeds of justice and beneficence. But we have no ground to believe that there is anything analogous to these affections and feelings in apostate angels. Sin rages in them unrestrained. It is the subject of their thoughts, and gives character to all their actions.

We may judge how sin produced immediately its full effect upon fallen angels from the conduct of the tempter. After being expelled from heaven, what was his first work? He visited our earth with the most nefarious and vindictive design to mar its beauty, and to poison and destroy human nature in its source; and he accomplished it by a train of deliberate falsehood and systematic cruelty. There was no relenting at the thought of plunging our whole race into eternal misery. His dark mind rejoiced in the expectation that myriads of human beings should forever endure the same agonies with himself. "He was a murderer from the beginning, and abode not in the truth, because there is no truth in him. When he speaketh a lie, he speaketh of his own, for he is a liar, and the father of it." John viii, 44. This passage illustrates, in a very striking manner, the depravity of fallen angels, for what is true of one is true of them all.

Various names are given to these fallen spirits in the Scriptures, which are descriptive of the depravity of their nature. They are called *evil* spirits, *unclean* spirits, *lying* spirits, the *rulers of the darkness* of this world, and spiritual wickedness. Their leader is denominated *Satan*, or the destroyer; the *devil*, or the accuser; *Apollyon*, or the destroyer; the old serpent; and "the prince of the power of the air."

But the fallen angels are as *unhappy* as they are unholy. This may be inferred from the place of their habitation. Peter says, that "God spared not the angels that sinned, but cast them down to *hell*," or *Tartarus;* for the apostle uses the verb ταρταρωσας, thrusting them down to Tartarus. Neither the verb, nor the noun ταρταρος, from which it is formed, occurs in any other place in the New Testament; but they are both frequently employed by Greek writers, from whom we must learn their meaning. By Tartarus, they understood the lowest of the infernal regions, where the souls of the wicked were supposed to be imprisoned and tormented. The word, as adopted by the apostle, conveys the same general idea. It answers to the Jewish word גיא הנם, and to the Greek γεέννα, and is, therefore, properly rendered *hell*, the place of punishment "prepared for the devil and his angels."

But these unhappy beings are also in a state of *penal suffering*, for God "delivered them into chains of darkness." Having incurred the wrath of their Creator, they can experience only evil, and are bound, as with a chain of iron, to the darkness and misery of their gloomy abode. Their positive misery is very forcibly expressed by our Lord when he represents them as "seeking rest, and finding none;" but still more so when he speaks of their proper abode as a place of "everlasting fire." We are not to conclude, however, that they are constantly confined to that place. It appears from their history that they are prisoners at large; and that they are permitted frequently to visit the home of man, which seems to be the principal theater of their nefarious operations.

3. *Their employment.*—It will appear that the employment of fallen

angels corresponds with the depravity of their nature and the malevolence of their dispositions. It is their constant aim to dishonor God and to injure men, and in prosecuting their wicked designs they submit to no restraint but Almighty power. We learn from the Scriptures,

(1.) *That they are permitted to exercise power over the bodies of men and other material objects.*—In proof of this we may appeal to the history of Job, which fully sustains and illustrates the proposition. But we may appeal to the writings of the Evangelists, also, as furnishing numerous instances of demoniacal possessions, and of the power of evil spirits over the bodies of men.

By some it has been alleged that these were not cases of real possession; that the patients labored under common diseases, such as palsy, epilepsy, and madness; and that they were said to be "possessed of devils," either in a figurative sense, or in accommodation to the opinions of the Jews. But when we consider that the number of demons in particular possessions is given, that their actions are expressly distinguished from those of the persons possessed, that their language in regard to their expulsion is recorded, and that accounts are given of the manner in which they were actually disposed of, it is impossible to deny their reality without admitting that the sacred historians were either deceived themselves or intended to deceive others.

(2.) *That they have power to exercise an evil influence over the human mind.*—This alarming truth is proved, in the first place, by the history of the fall; and in the second place, by many facts and declarations and admonitions in the Scriptures.

It was Satan who tempted Judas to betray his Master,[*] and who put it into the heart of Ananias and Sapphira "to lie to the Holy Ghost."[†] Our Lord told his disciples that Satan had desired to have them, that he might sift them as wheat.[‡] He is called "the spirit that now worketh in the children of disobedience." Eph. ii, 2. St. Peter says, "Your adversary the devil, as a roaring lion, walketh about seeking whom he may devour." 1 Peter v, 8. And St. Paul says, in the name of all his brethren, "We are not ignorant of his devices." 2 Cor. ii, 11.

These and many other passages fully prove that evil spirits are employed in tempting men to sin. Of the mode of their agency we can have no certain knowledge, and to indulge in conjectures would serve no valuable purpose. One thing is certain, that they cannot compel men to sin, for such a power would be destructive of man's moral agency, and would, therefore, defeat their own design, which is to involve us in guilt.

4. *Their* DESTINY.—The degradation and punishment of the fallen angels are not yet completed. They are delivered "into chains of darkness, *to be reserved unto judgment.*" They will then be tried and con-

[*] John xiii, 2.　　　　　[†] Acts v, 3.　　　　　[‡] Luke xxii, 31.

demned for all the evils which they will have wrought during the history of time. These evils, however gratifying to them in the perpetration, will, after the judgment of the great day, return upon their own heads, and will cover them with eternal shame, and overwhelm them with endless ruin. The chains which they now wear will confine them unto the judgment, so that they cannot escape; and will confine them forever in the sufferance of that misery to which they have destined themselves by a voluntary devotion. For them, therefore, there is no redemption, no mercy, no hope.

The question has been proposed, Why might not provision have been made for the recovery of fallen angels as well as for that of man? but to this no decisive answer can be returned. It is enough for us to know that God, who always does right, and is too good to be unkind, has passed them by. Still, there are some circumstances connected with their history, as also with the history of our race, which may reflect some light upon this mysterious subject, and which are therefore worthy of our attention. 1. They were doubtless superior to man in intellectual endowments, and, therefore, less liable to be deceived. 2. As man was partly material, and subject to the influences of the senses, his attention might have been diverted and his judgment biased by allurements addressed to them. But angels were purely *spiritual* beings, and therefore could not have been liable to any such temptations. 3. The progenitor of the human race sustained a federal relation to all his posterity. In him they stood; in him they fell. But among the angels no such relation existed. Each one stood or fell for himself alone. 4. Man sinned, in the earthly paradise, through the subtilty of a tempter; but angels sinned, in the heavenly paradise, without a tempter. For, though we do not possess a history of their apostasy, yet we know that they were not solicited, as man was, by some being of superior artifice, because they were the sole inhabitants of heaven.

Whether these considerations are sufficient to account for the fact that angels were not redeemed we will not pretend to say; but one thing appears to be evident, that their apostasy, under all the circumstances of the case, was more unprovoked and atrocious than that of man. We conclude, then, that the eternal destruction of fallen angels is no more incompatible with the character of God than will be the eternal punishment of wicked men. They had their day of trial; but they chose the evil, and must eat the fruit of their doings.

CHAPTER X.

OF DIVINE PROVIDENCE.

DIVINE *Providence* is that care and superintendence which God exercises over his creatures. As he is the *Creator* of all things, he possesses the power and the right to use them according to his own pleasure; and to cause them, and all which is done by them, to promote his own designs. In the discussion of this subject three things demand our attention: 1. The proofs of a Divine Providence; 2. Its nature; and, 3. Its objects.

I. PROOFS OF DIVINE PROVIDENCE.

The doctrine of Providence may be established by a variety of arguments, which may be drawn both from reason and from revelation. We begin with the former.

1. *Proofs from Reason.*—This class of proofs depends upon the truth of the proposition that God created the world. Presuming that this position may now be considered as fully established, we derive proofs of the Providence of God,

(1.) *From his Nature and Attributes.*—That God is both able and willing to take care of his creatures is demonstrable from the idea of an absolutely perfect being. That he is *able* to do this appears from his *omniscience*, by which he knows the circumstances and wants of all his creatures; from his *wisdom*, by which he understands in what manner and by what means the world may be sustained and governed; and from his *omnipotence*, by which he can accomplish all his purposes. That he *will* do this follows alike from his *wisdom* and *goodness*. Can it be supposed that God, after he had created all things, should abandon his own works and be indifferent to the well-being of the countless myriads of creatures that he brought into existence, and formed with desires and a capacity for happiness? It is certainly more reasonable to believe that he will take care of them, and provide for them according to their respective wants. But as God is *just* and *righteous* in all his doings, he must exercise a moral government over his rational creatures, and reward or punish them according to their actions; and, in the course of his providence, so overrule them as to promote the ultimate end of his administration.

(2.) *From the dependent nature of creatures.*—God alone exists by necessity of nature, or, in other words, has the ground of existence in himself. The existence of all other beings is therefore dependent upon the will and power of God; and as they might or might not have been created, so they may cease to be, there being nothing in the nature of things to insure their continuance. Nothing can be more expressive of the dependent nature of all created things than the following words of Scripture: "In him we live, and move, and have our being." Acts xvii, 28. Of the same import is the language of the apostle, when he speaks of the Son of God as "upholding all things by the word of his power." Heb, i, 3. The assertion of divines, that the preservation of existence is a *continual creation*, is not merely a rhetorical figure, importing that the power of God is as truly admirable in preserving all things as in creating them, but is a literal statement of an important fact. For, as all things were created by the power of God, so their preservation depends upon a continued exertion of the same power, as the flowing stream depends upon an uninterrupted supply of water from the fountain.

(3.) *From the order and harmony observable in the course of nature.* —Though the universe is composed of many parts, they are all retained in their proper places, and perform their peculiar functions with such order and harmony as to promote the general good. In this immense and complicated machine no part ever goes wrong. Its motion is never suspended or embarrassed, and its operations are carried on with such regularity that they are made the subject of definite calculation. The heavenly bodies perform their revolutions in their appointed times, without ever interfering with one another. The sun, the source of light and heat, though he has ministered to the system of which he is the center for thousands of years, has lost no portion of his splendor or of his influence. The seasons succeed each other in their regular order. The earth still retains its native fertility, though many generations have been supported by its products. The sea continues within its ancient boundaries, and leaves the dry land to be the abode of terrestrial animals. The various classes of animals and vegetables have continued to propagate themselves, so that the earth is still stocked with inhabitants and with a full supply for their wants. When, therefore, we contemplate this immense system of nature, so wonderful in its contrivances, so constant in its movements, and proceeding from age to age without the slightest confusion, we must necessarily conclude that it is under the *continual government* of an all-controlling Mind.

It may be objected, that the order which prevails throughout the universe may be accounted for by the laws of nature, without an immediate interposition of the Deity; and that it only proves the wisdom of its original constitution. But what is meant by the *laws of nature?* A *law*, in its primary signification, is a rule established and enforced by authority, and obviously implies intelligence and power. But when the term is applied to inanimate things, it signifies nothing more than the *stated and regular order* in which they are found to subsist. Thus, finding that bodies on or near the surface of the earth tend toward its center, and that the planets of our system tend toward the sun, we call this the law of gravitation; and in like manner we speak of other laws by which matter is governed, as the laws of motion and the laws of light. But the truth is that these are only *facts*, and are called laws solely on account of their uniformity.

From observation and experience we know that bodies gravitate toward a center, and that the rays of light are subject to refraction and reflection; but we know not the true cause of these phenomena. Are we to suppose that nature possesses intelligence, or activity, or power of any kind? Let us not forget that matter is inert, and totally incapable of exertion. It can neither put itself in motion, nor stop itself when in motion. Every modification which it undergoes is the effect of some external power. What, then, are the *laws of nature?* They are the *particular modes in which God exerts his power*, which, being uniform, are accounted natural, while any deviation from them is pronounced to be miraculous. It follows, therefore, if this is a just description of what are called the laws of nature, that so far from their accounting for the order which is maintained in the universe, they necessarily imply the actual and constant interposition of the Creator, and as irresistibly suggest the idea of a lawgiver as do the laws of any human society.

(4.) *From those moral sentiments and feelings which are common to men.*—St. Paul tells us, that even the Gentiles who " have not the law, are a law unto themselves;" and that they " show the work of the law written in their hearts." Rom. ii, 14, 15. There is a principle in every man who has received any degree of cultivation which distinguishes between right and wrong, and which lies at the foundation of all our moral feelings. This principle, which we call *conscience*, never fails to remind us that we are subjects of moral government, and accountable to God for our actions; and to pronounce a sentence of approbation or disapprobation upon our conduct, according as we believe it to be good or bad. If there were no Providence, conscience would be an illusive faculty; its decisions would have no better foundation than the hopes and terrors of superstition; but if it is an original principle of our nature, as we may infer from its universality, it is God's own testimony within us to his moral administration and superintending Providence. But we may argue the truth of this doctrine,

(5.) *From its necessity to piety and virtue, and to the happiness of human life.*—Were it not that God exercises a constant and watchful care over his works all piety would immediately cease. A God who did not concern himself in the affairs of the world, and especially in the actions of men, would be to us the same as no God at all. In that case the pious and virtuous could not hope for his approbation, and the guilty would have no punishment to fear. The persecuted could think of him only as the idle spectator of their wrongs, and the suffering and sorrowful could find no consolation. But if, on the other hand, we have a right to believe that God, as a Father, cares for us, that he guides and protects us, and supplies all our wants, and that "in him we live, and move, and have our being," we may then be composed and unshaken even in times of the greatest adversity, "casting all our care upon him" who cares for us.

There are several other arguments which might be advanced in proof of a Divine Providence, such as the experience of every individual, the judgments which are occasionally executed upon notorious transgressors, the great historic events which have taken place in the world, the proportion which exists between the two sexes, and the variety in the human countenance, which answers so many valuable purposes.

2. *Proofs from Scripture.*—The Bible establishes the doctrine of Divine Providence,

(1.) *By express declarations.*—"O, Lord, thou preservest man and beast." Psa. xxxvi, 6. "The eyes of all wait upon thee; and thou givest them their meat in due season. Thou openest thine hand, and satisfiest the desire of every living thing." Psa. cxlv, 15, 16. "The eyes of the Lord are in every place, beholding the evil and the good." Prov. xv, 3. In the New Testament we may consult Matt. vi, 25–32; x, 29–31; and Acts xvii, 24–28. These, and many other passages, clearly prove the Providence of God.

(2.) *By Prophecies.*—This argument is of great weight, and might be very extensively applied, but our limits will only permit its mere adduction. The rise of mighty kingdoms from small beginnings to extensive dominion, and their subsequent fall into decay and dissolution, may be accounted for, to some extent, by the operation of second causes; but they are often accompanied by circumstances which manifestly point to the hand of Divine Providence. This is particularly the case in the revolutions of the great monarchies of ancient times, when viewed in connection with the prophecies concerning them; for who can doubt that they were accomplished by Him who foretold them ages before they took place? Who can read the predictions of Scripture respecting the captivity and restoration of the Jews, the coming of the Messiah, and the spread of the Gospel, and compare them with their actual fulfillment, without being convinced that in all these events God exercised a special Providence?

(3.) *By Miracles.**—As miracles can be performed only by Divine power, to admit the truth of the Scripture history respecting them is, in effect, to admit that God exercises a particular providence over the affairs of men. Even the magicians of Egypt, though employed to oppose the servants of the Lord, were forced to exclaim, on witnessing one of the miracles of Moses and Aaron, "This is the finger of God!"

* See Book I, chap. 1, Miracles; also chap. 6.

The same is true in regard to every miracle which the sacred Scriptures record.

(4.) *By extraordinary events in the life of individuals.*—This argument, if it were followed out to its full length, would involve the entire subject of sacred biography; a subject which fully exhibits the Providence of God in its most interesting light. How clearly is this seen in the history of Noah, of Abraham, of Lot, of Joseph, of Elijah, of Daniel, and a host of others! Time would fail us "to tell of Gideon, and of Barak, and of Samson, and of Jephtha; of David also, and Samuel, and of the prophets."

II. Nature of Divine Providence.

The *nature* of Divine Providence respects the *manner* in which it is concerned in the affairs of the universe. Divines are generally united in the opinion that Providence includes two acts, that is, *preservation* and *government*.

1. *Of Preservation.*—By *preservation* we mean, that efficient agency of God by which all creatures, with their respective essences, powers, and faculties, are kept in being. No idea can be more false than to suppose that the creation of beings renders them independent of the Creator, for what is derived must always be dependent. Created things, it is true, are perfectly distinct from their Creator, as any other work is from the workman; but they are as dependent on him for the continuance of their being, as vitality in the branch is dependent upon the juice which flows from the trunk, or as the growth and life of the human body is dependent upon the blood which is propelled from the heart. Hence the Scriptures declare, not only that God created all things, but that " by him all things consist;" and that he upholds " all things by the word of his power." This absolute dependence upon God for preservation is as true of man as it is of the lower orders of creation; "for in him *we* live, and move, and have our being."

It has been objected, that the absolute dependence of all things upon God implies a reflection upon his wisdom; as if he had executed a work so imperfect as to require his constant interference to prevent it from perishing. Men, it is said, construct works which, when finished, have no further need of their care. A house will stand though the builder should never see it again; and a watch or a clock will point to the hour after it has passed out of the hands of the maker. But it should be considered, that in such cases men merely give a particular form or arrangement to certain pre-existent materials. They neither make them nor uphold them in being, and consequently the durability of their works plainly depends upon some other cause than their own power. With respect to the operations of any piece of machinery, as a watch or clock, let it be further considered that the process does not depend upon the mechanic in any other sense than that he made a proper disposition of all the parts. The real cause of motion is not in the machine itself, but in some weight, or spring, or other power, which is continually acting upon it, and from which all its motions are derived. So likewise the motivity in the immense machine of the universe does not belong to itself, but is to be ascribed to God. Hence the objection leads us to the very conclusion which it is brought to overthrow.

2. *Of Government.*—The *government* of God is that exercise of his agency by which he so overrules all creatures and all events, that nothing can come to pass but what he either wills or permits.*

The actions of God himself, and those of his creatures, embrace all the phenomena which occur in the universe. Every motion or action of any inanimate creature which is not produced by the voluntary effort of a moral agent is to be ascribed to God; but if the motion or action is caused by some moral agent, it is to be attributed directly to the agent who exerts this influence. If my house is consumed by lightning, it is a direct visitation from God; but if I am prostrated upon the ground by the club of a highwayman, God indeed permits it, but it is the robber, a moral agent, who is the *efficient* cause of the crime.

God is perfectly acquainted with all the *efficient causes* which exist, both those which are free in their agency and those which are otherwise. He knows every *act* of these causes, and all the *effects* which they produce, and he guides and controls them all so as to make them subservient to his own designs, and promotive of the highest good of the whole. But though he governs all his creatures, he does not govern them all after the same manner. With respect to such as are irrational he only applies his power; but he governs his rational creatures partly by his power and partly by moral laws—we say partly by his power, because as to life and faculties they are as dependent upon God as other creatures are. But, to be a little more particular, we may observe,

(1.) That God governs the physical universe according to those general and established laws which are usually called the laws of nature, but which are more properly styled *mode of Divine agency.* He keeps the sun in his place as the center, and wheels the planets round him in their respective orbits. He fixes the mountains on their bases, and confines the ocean within its ancient boundaries. Hence, in figurative language, he is said to command the sun to rise, the stars to shine, and other natural events to take place. And, as the laws by which he governs the material universe are only the regular modes of his agency

---

* When we say that God *permits* any event, we are not to understand the term to indicate that he allows it, or consents to it; but rather, that *he does not exert his power to prevent it.* God permits sin, but he does not approve of it; for, as he is infinitely holy, sin must always be the object of his abhorrence. Accordingly, he testifies against the very sins into which he permits men to fall, denouncing his threatenings against them, and actually punishing them for their crimes.

in the production of effects, it is evident that he governs it by an immediate exertion of his power.

(2.) God governs the lower animals by periodical appetites, by instincts, and by some traces of intellect, not amounting, however, to responsibility. Impelled by these principles of animated nature, they propagate their species, seek the food that is provided for them, and perform the various functions for which they are qualified. Thus the ant "provideth her meat in the summer, and gathereth her food in the harvest." "The stork in the heaven knoweth her appointed times; and the turtle, and the crane, and the swallow observe the time of their coming." God sometimes employs irrational animals as instruments to accomplish his will. Thus, frogs, lice, and flies were his instruments in punishing the Egyptians; and ravens were his ministers to carry food to the prophet Elijah. These and other similar facts, recorded in the Scriptures, show that all animated creatures are under the government of that Being who gave them existence. But,

(3.) *God governs the voluntary actions of men by moral laws.*—Of the physical, the intellectual, and the moral constitution of men God is the efficient cause; but with respect to their moral actions the case is quite different. Of these he could not become the efficient cause without destroying their very nature; for no action can be *moral* unless it is *free.* If men were not free to choose and to act they could not be accountable for their actions, for in that case their actions would not be within their own power. If, then, we would not overturn the first principles of morality, if we would not degrade ourselves below the standard of moral beings, and if we would not falsify the dictates of that moral feeling which God himself has so deeply implanted in our hearts, we must firmly maintain the doctrine that man is *morally free.* We are not to expect, therefore, that the government of God over moral beings will be shown by his *compelling* them to perform either good or bad actions.

But while, on the one hand, the freedom of the human will is unimpaired by the government of God, on the other the government of God is unobstructed and undisturbed by the free actions of men. For, though men are free in what they do, their actions are nevertheless under his most perfect control. This will appear evident if we consider, 1. That the moral actions of men depend upon their *moral powers,* of which God alone is both the author and the preserver, and of which he can deprive them at any moment; 2. That the external circumstances connected with those actions are all under the Divine control; and, 3. That God will reward the obedient and punish the disobedient, in exact accordance with their moral character, in the retributions of the eternal world. If to these considerations we add that God foresees the free actions of his moral creatures, and all the consequences of them, as well as those which result from necessary causes, and that the plans and purposes of his providence were formed in full view of all these events, we shall find no great difficulty in reconciling the unobstructed operation of the Divine government with the free-agency of man.

We must not, then, lose sight of the fact that the government of God over the voluntary actions of men is purely of a moral character. He defines their duty by moral laws. He enforces these laws by moral motives, such as the authority of the lawgiver, the equity of the laws themselves, the advantages of obedience, and the evil consequences of sin. He, moreover, lays upon men such external restraints, and affords them such internal assistances of grace as are sufficient, if properly improved, to withhold them from evil and to lead them to what is right. But still it is within their power to yield obedience to the laws of God or to transgress them; and in either case they are the authors of their own free actions.

III. The Objects of Divine Providence.

The objects of Divine Providence, so far as we know, consist of three classes—inanimate things, creatures endowed with life and activity, but possessing no rational or moral powers, and moral beings. Providence, in relation to its objects, is divided into *general*, *special*, and *particular*. The *general* providence of God extends to all creatures; his *special* providence has respect to men and human affairs; and his *particular* providence is restricted to men of virtue and piety.

1. *The General Providence of God.*—This extends to all created things in the universe—to the small and most insignificant, as well as to the great and most important. "Though the Lord be high, yet hath he respect unto the lowly." Psa. cxxxviii, 6. "O Lord, thou preservest man and beast." Psa. xxxvi, 6. "Are not two sparrows sold for a farthing? and one of them shall not fall to the ground without your Father. But the very hairs of your head are all numbered." Matt. x, 29, 30.

Some talk of a general providence, by which they mean that God upholds the general system of nature without attending to matters of minor importance. Hence they tell us that he takes care of the species, but not of the individuals; not perceiving that it is hardly possible, in so many words, to express a greater absurdity. A species is a general name by which the common and distinguishing properties of a number of individuals are denoted. The species is nothing but the individuals under a particular classification. How, then, can the species be taken care of if the individuals are neglected? If all things, even the smallest, were not subject to the providence of God, scarcely anything could be said to be governed by him; for such is the order, connection, and dependence of causes and effects that in many cases the least causes produce the greatest results. The providence of God, therefore, either extends to *all* things, even to those which we denominate small, or there is no providence; but as the latter is most absurd and impious, the former must be admitted.

Men are accustomed to regard many things as small, insignificant, useless, and even injurious, because they are unable to see their use and importance in the connection of things. This, however, is only a proof of the weakness of the human understanding, and of the great imperfection of human knowledge. But as God *created* all these things, and continually prolongs their existence, he must regard them as useful and necessary, and as adapted to promote his designs in their connection with the whole. How, then, can it be inconsistent with the majesty of God to watch over the most minute things in creation and to preserve them? If it was not dishonorable for him to give them existence, it cannot be dishonorable for him to preserve to them the existence which he has given them. And, indeed, his wisdom, power, and goodness are as evident in his least as in his greatest works.

2. *The Special Providence of God.*—This, we have said, has respect to men and human affairs. Men are the only creatures upon the earth who possess a moral nature, or who have reason and freedom of will; and as possessing these, they are capable of a far higher degree of perfection and happiness than the lower orders of creation. Hence the care of God for them is more apparent, and seems to be more active and efficient than for his other creatures. Of this special providence, or watchful care of God over man, we have abundant proof in the history of our race.

(1.) *It extends to human Life.*—This is true in regard both to its *origin* and to its *termination.*

First, it extends to the *origin* of human life; for though our parents, as the instruments of God, are the means by which we come into the world, yet God is truly our Creator, and the author of our existence. This doctrine is most clearly taught in the sacred Scriptures. Job says, in addressing God, "Thine hands have made me, and fashioned me together round about. Thou hast clothed me with skin and flesh, and hast fenced me with bones and sinews. Thou hast granted me life and favor, and thy visitation hath preserved my spirit." Job x, 8, 11, 12. "My substance," says David, "was not hid from thee, when I was made in secret, and curiously wrought in the lowest parts of the earth. Thine eyes did see my substance, yet being unperfect; and in thy book all my members were written, which in continuance were fashioned, when as yet there was none of them." Psa. cxxxix, 15, 16.

Secondly, Providence is concerned in the *termination* of human life. The causes of death are various, as accident, old age, and disease, either slow or rapid in its progress; but all these causes are under the control of Divine Providence. And as nothing is more precious than human life, it cannot be by chance that men are deprived of it, that their day of trial is terminated, and that their spirits are called into the presence of God to give an account of the deeds done in the body. If a sparrow cannot fall to the ground without the notice of our heavenly Father, it would be most unreasonable to suppose that his providence should not be concerned in the dissolution of every human being. But on this point the Scriptures are clear: "Seeing his days are determined, the number of his months are with thee, thou hast appointed his bounds that he cannot pass." Job xiv, 5. "Thou turnest man to destruction; and sayest, Return, ye children of men." Psa. xc, 3.

It has long been a question of considerable controversy, whether the *time* of every man's death is so fixed and determined that his life can neither be prolonged nor contracted. Some divines think that the affirmative of this question is established by Job xiv, 5, and by some other passages; but others entertain a very different opinion. This much, however, we may safely affirm: 1. That God knows, with absolute certainty, the time of every man's death; 2. That with respect to some the term of life was immutably fixed, as in the case of Moses and of Hezekiah; and, 3. That in regard to all men the term of life is limited, and confined within certain bounds. "The days of our years are threescore years and ten; and if by reason of strength they be fourscore years, yet is their strength labor and sorrow; for it is soon cut off, and we fly away." Psa. xc, 10.

But that God has determined the time of every man's death by an immutable decree is not so evident. Against this opinion various passages of Scripture may be objected. Take, for instance, the promise which is annexed to the fifth commandment, "that thy days may be long upon the land which the Lord thy God giveth thee." Exod. xx, 12. Likewise Psa. lv, 23: "Bloody and deceitful men shall not live out half their days." Another passage is 2 Samuel xxiv, 12–15, where the option which was granted to David seems to imply that God had *not* predetermined the time and manner of the death of those seventy thousand persons who were cut off by pestilence, for if he had there could have been no choice in the case.

It may be objected, also, that this theory leads to the fearful consequence of making God the author of sin. For, where the end is absolutely intended, there the means must also be absolutely intended. Consequently, if God has predetermined the time of every one's death, and if in some cases it is effected by intemperance and murder, these means must likewise have been predetermined.

Moreover, where this doctrine is thoroughly believed, and consistently carried out into action, it must lead to the neglect of the necessary precautions against danger, and of the proper means of recovery from sickness. For, one who is of this opinion may say, If the fixed time of my death has now arrived, these precautions and remedies can be of no service to me; and if it has not yet come, they are wholly unnecessary. If any one should reply that the means of preserving and of losing life are likewise determined, then nothing more remains but that we should wait until God effects within us, and without us, whatever he has decreed.

(2.) *It is concerned in the events of human life.*—It has been said that man is the artificer of his own fortune, and this saying is founded upon the influence which his conduct is frequently observed to have upon his temporal condition. But the remark is more worthy of a heathen or an atheist than of a believer in the Bible. We find, indeed, that certain actions are commonly followed by certain consequences, and it is important that it should be so, because we should otherwise have no motive to act in one way rather than in another. This regularity, however, like the order maintained in the material system, is so far from invalidating the argument for the Divine interference in human affairs that it confirms it. But in the history of men this order does not everywhere prevail. There are frequent deviations from it, which compel us to acknowledge the controlling power of God. "The race is not" always "to the swift, nor the battle to the strong." In many cases industry is frustrated of its reward, and the plans of wisdom prove abortive. Worldly wealth is not apportioned according to any fixed law. It often falls to the lot of the weak and the worthless, while men of superior talents contend for it in vain. The same remarks may be applied to earthly honors, and hence, in the language of worldly men, temporal blessings are called the gifts of fortune, to intimate that they are distributed blindly and without regard to merit. But the true doctrine is, that all these things are controlled by the sovereign will of God. "Promotion cometh neither from the east, nor from the west, nor from the south. But God is the judge: he putteth down one, and setteth up another." Psa. lxxv, 6, 7.

(3.) *It extends to human actions.*—The moral actions of men are regarded as being either good or bad; but whatever their character may be, they are all, in one way or other, under the control of Divine Providence.

First, that God is concerned with the *good* actions of men will not be denied. Their goodness may seem to justify his interference, and the assistance which he gives will be deemed worthy of the purity and benevolence of his character. It will be readily acknowledged that God excites men to good actions, that he presents to them proper objects and proper motives, that he imparts to them spiritual strength and spiritual comfort, that he encourages them to persevere in well-doing, and that he enables them, in many instances at least, to accomplish what they intend. "It is God which worketh in you," says the apostle, "both to will and to do of his good pleasure," and on this fact he grounds the exhortation, "Work out your own salvation with fear and trembling." Phil. ii, 12, 13. But,

Secondly, the providence of God is to be considered in its relation to *moral evil.* The discussion of this question will be attended with some more difficulty; for as, on the one hand, we must be under the strictest guard lest God should be represented as the author of sin, so, on the other, we should be cautious, lest it should be totally removed from under the control of his providence. In the first place, then, this ought to be laid down as a principle of indubitable truth, and as the foundation of all religion, that God is not, in any sense whatever, the author of sin. He neither wills sin nor commits it, otherwise he would be neither holy, just, nor good. "Thou art not a God that hath pleasure in wickedness; neither shall evil dwell with thee." Psa. v, 4. "Let no man say when he is tempted, I am tempted of God: for God cannot be tempted with evil, neither tempteth he any man." James i, 13.

But though God is not the author of sin, yet it is still subject to his control and superintending providence. He permits sin; he limits it; and he overrules it for good.

First, God *permits* sin. This is not a *moral* permission, as if he approved of sin, but physical, by which he suffers it to be committed. The meaning is that he does not interfere in the exercise of his power, as he doubtless might do, to prevent sinful actions. If God should thus prevent his moral creatures from sinning he would force their will and destroy their agency and accountability. Therefore, for wise and holy ends he permits sin. "My people would not hearken to my voice; and Israel would none of me. So I gave them up to their hearts' lust; and they walked in their own counsels." Psa. lxxxi, 11, 12. "Who in times past suffered all nations to walk in their own ways." Acts xiv, 16.

Secondly, God *limits*, or sets bounds to sinful actions. We are not to suppose that when he permits men to sin he exempts them entirely from his control. Such a supposition would be inconsistent with the dependent condition of creatures, and with the character of God as the governor of the world. Wicked men, therefore, are at all times under the superintendence of Divine Providence, and subject to such restraints as God in his wisdom may see proper to impose. He can say to them, as he says to the raging waves of the sea, "Hitherto shall ye come, but no further." Means are always at the command of Providence to circumscribe the wicked actions of sinners. "Surely the wrath of man shall praise thee," said the psalmist; "the remainder of wrath shalt thou restrain." Psa. lxxvi, 10.

Thirdly, God *overrules* sinful actions so as to bring good out of evil. The introduction of sin into the world, though followed by most dreadful consequences, has nevertheless given rise to the brightest manifestation of the glory of God; as also to the highest exercise of his benevolence in the mediation of Christ and the salvation of the guilty through his blood. The sons of Jacob, in selling their brother Joseph into Egypt, committed a great sin; but God overruled it for good both to

Joseph himself and to all his father's family. "As for you," said he to his brethren, "ye thought evil against me; but God meant it unto good, to bring to pass, as it is this day, to save much people alive." Gen. 1, 20. But though God can bring good out of evil, it by no means follows that men may commit sin that good may come. The natural tendency of sin is only to evil; and under the management of creatures, nothing but evil can result from it. The process by which good is deduced from it can be carried on *only* by infinite wisdom and almighty power.

We are not yet done, however, with this important and mysterious subject. The most difficult part remains—the physical agency of God in sinful actions. To understand this matter clearly it will be necessary to distinguish between the moral *powers* with which God has endowed man, and the *exercise* of these powers in voluntary actions. The powers of action come from God, but the use and exercise of these powers he has left to men. This is involved in the very idea that man is a moral being; for, if he were subject to the control of necessity, and not suffered to choose and to do what he sees best, according to the laws of freedom, he would cease to be a moral agent. God is not, therefore, the efficient cause of the free actions of men. He gives them the powers of action, and preserves these powers every moment; but the actions themselves are their own. Thus, for instance, when a man opens his mouth to lie or to blaspheme, God grants him the power at that very moment to open his mouth and to speak; but the *use* of the power is left to the man himself, and he might open his mouth to speak the truth and to glorify God. The action, therefore, whatever it may be, is his own, and for it he alone is accountable; which could not be the case if it proceeded from another.

3. *The Particular Providence of God.*—This has respect to the virtuous and pious, or, in other words, to the people of God, and is therefore sometimes called his *peculiar* or *gracious* providence. No careful reader of the Bible can avoid the conclusion that, though God takes care of all his creatures, and especially of men, yet he exercises a more particular providence toward those who are employed in his service. We do not claim that it is miraculous. It does not suspend the laws of nature in favor of its objects, though it occasionally did so in former times; nor does it consist in visible interpositions. The righteous, so far as we can see, are placed in the same external circumstances with other men. They are rich or poor; they are sick or in health; they meet with successes and disappointments; they have their sorrows and their comforts; but in all God's providential dispensations toward them there is this peculiarity, that in his wisdom and goodness they are rendered subservient to their most important interests. "We know that all things work together for good to them that love God."

The providence of God toward his people is a uniform dispensation of love. He protects them from a thousand evils into which others are permitted to fall. "Whoso hearkeneth unto me shall dwell safely, and shall be quiet from fear of evil." Prov. i, 33. "He shall deliver thee in six troubles; yea, in seven there shall no evil touch thee." Job v, 19. He supports them in times of trial. "When thou passeth through the waters, I will be with thee; and through the rivers, they shall not over-flow thee. When thou walkest through the fire, thou shalt not be burnt; neither shall the flame kindle upon thee." Isa. xliii, 2. He bestows upon them his richest spiritual blessings. "For the Lord God is a sun and shield; the Lord will give grace and glory: no good thing will he withhold from them that walk uprightly." Psa. lxxxiv, 11. And finally, if he chastises them, it is the correction of a Father. "For whom the Lord loveth he chasteneth, and scourgeth every son whom he receiveth." Heb. xii, 6. In a word, the ultimate end of providence is the glory of God in the salvation of his people. To this end the evils of life, as well as its good things, are mysteriously made to contribute. This might be illustrated by an appeal to the Scriptures, which are a history of Divine Providence in relation to the world at large, but particularly of its procedure toward the Church and its genuine members.

BOOK III.

DOCTRINES RESPECTING MAN.

THE scriptural character of God having been adduced from the inspired writings, we now proceed, in pursuance of our plan, to consider their testimony respecting MAN, both in the estate in which he was created, and in that lapsed condition into which the first act of disobedience plunged the primitive pair and their whole posterity.

CHAPTER I.

MAN'S PRIMITIVE STATE.

IN turning our attention to the primitive character and condition of *man*, we will consider him, not so much in a physical, as in a moral light.   In order to this we will inquire, in the first place, into the nature of that law under which man was originally placed; and secondly, his moral condition and capabilities, as they are exhibited in the history of his creation.

I. THE NATURE OF THE LAW UNDER WHICH MAN WAS ORIGINALLY PLACED.

Here we may remark,

1. That besides the natural government which God exercises over all the various parts of the great visible creation, there is evidence of an administration of another kind.   This we call *moral* government, because it has respect to the actions of rational creatures, considered as good and evil, which qualities are necessarily determined by the law of God.

2. All the moral and accountable creatures with which the Scriptures make us acquainted are ANGELS, DEVILS, and MEN, and there is reason to believe that the LAW under which all are placed is substantially the same, and that it is included in this epitome: "Thou shalt love the Lord thy God with all thy heart, and with all thy soul, and with all

thy mind; and thy neighbor as thyself." Matt. xxii, 37, 39. For, though this is addressed to men, yet as it is founded, in both its parts, upon the natural relation of every intelligent creature to God and to all other intelligent creatures, it may be presumed to be universal. Every rational creature owes obedience to God, and a benevolent Creator could only seek, in the first instance, the obedience of love.

From the revealed character of the Creator we must conclude that every rational creature was made, not only to show forth his glory, but that itself might enjoy happiness. The love of God is that affection which unites a created intelligent nature to the Creator, the source of all true happiness, and prevents, in all cases, obedience from being felt as a burden, or regarded under the cold conviction of mere duty. If, therefore, a cheerful obedience from the creature be required, as that which would constantly promote the felicity of the agent, this law of love is to be considered as the law of all moral beings, whether angels or men. Its comprehensiveness is another presumption of its universality; for, unquestionably, it is a maxim of universal import, that "love is the fulfilling of the law," since he who loves must choose to obey every command issued by the sovereign, or the father beloved, and when this love is supreme and uniform the obedience must be absolute and unceasing.

The second commandment is like the first in these respects; it is founded on the natural relations which exist among the creatures of God, and it comprehends every possible relative duty. Thus by these two great first principles of the Divine law, the rational creatures of God would be united to him as their common Lord and Father, and to each other as fellow-subjects and brethren. Indeed, if rational creatures are under a law at all, it cannot be conceived that less than this could be required by their Creator. They are bound to render all love, honor, and obedience to him by a natural and absolute obligation; and, as it has been demonstrated in the experience of man, anything less would be not only contrary to the Creator's glory, but fatal to the creature's happiness.

3. From these views it follows, that all particular precepts, whether they relate to the duties which we owe to God or to other rational creatures, arise out of one or other of these two great commandments, and that every particular law supposes the general one. Our Lord has told us that "on these two commandments *hang* all the law and the prophets;" and St. Paul teaches the doctrine, that all relative duties are briefly comprehended in this saying, "Thou shalt love thy neighbor as thyself."

It was not, therefore, when the law of Moses was engraven on tables of stone by the finger of God, that LAW was first introduced into the world. Men were accounted righteous or wicked between the giving of the law and the flood and before the flood, and were dealt with accordingly. Noah was "a righteous man," Abel was "righteous," and Cain was "wicked." Now as the moral quality of actions is determined by law, and that law the revealed will of God; and as every punitive act on his part, and every bestowment of rewards on account of righteousness, supposes a regal administration, men were under law up to the time of the fall, which law, in all its particular precepts, presupposed the two great commandments.

That our first parents were under law is evident; nor are we to conclude that the command which was given them in the form of a prohibition was the sole measure of their obedience. It was a particular command, which, like those of the Decalogue, and in the writings of the prophets, presupposed a general law of which this was but one manifestation.

Thus are we conducted to a more ancient date of the Divine law than the solemnities of Sinai, or even the creation of man. It is a law coeval in its declaration with the existence of rational creatures, and in its principles with God himself. Under this condition of rational existence must Adam and every other moral creature have come into being, a condition, of course, to which he could not be a party, and to which he had no right to be a party had that been possible. He was *made* under law, as all his descendants are born under law.

But that we may more exactly understand man's primitive state, condition, and capabilities, considered morally, and the nature, extent, and consequences of his fall, it is necessary to consider,

II. The History of his Creation.

The manner in which this event is narrated indicates something peculiar and eminent in the being to be formed, and gives us an intimation of a trinity of persons in the Godhead, all *Divine* because all equally possessed of *creative power*, and to each of whom man was to sustain sacred and intimate relations. "And God said, Let us make man in our image, after our likeness." In what, then, did this "*image*" and "*likeness*" consist?

Human nature has two essential constituent parts: the BODY, formed from the earth, and a LIVING SOUL, breathed into the body by an *inspiration* from God. Did, then, the image or likeness of God in which man was created relate to his body? Certainly not, for "God is a Spirit," without bodily shape or parts, and, therefore, the body of man could not, as such, be in the Divine image.

Nor did this image consist, as some have supposed, in his having *dominion* over the other creatures. Limited dominion may, it is true, be an image of absolute dominion; but it is not said that man was in the image of God's dominion, but in the image and likeness of God himself—of something which constituted *his nature*. Still further, man was evidently made in the image of God *in order to* his having dominion, as the Hebrew imports. His dominion, then, was subsequent to his being made in the Divine image, and could not be that image itself.

It is in vain to say that this image consisted in some *one essential* quality of human nature which *could not be lost;* for we shall find that it comprehended more qualities than *one*, and that while revelation places it, in part, in what was essential to human nature, it included also what was not essential, and what might be both lost and regained. It consisted in what divines have called the *natural* and the *moral* image of God.

1. *His* NATURAL *image.*—The natural image of God in which man was created was essential and ineffaceable, and comprised his *spirituality*, his *immortality*, and his *intellectual powers*. It consisted,

(1.) *In spirituality.*—When God is called "the Father of spirits," a likeness is intimated between man and God in the spirituality of their nature. This is also implied in the argument of St. Paul, Acts xvii, 29: "Forasmuch, then, as we are the offspring of God, we ought not to think that the Godhead is like unto gold, or silver, or stone, graven by art and man's device." Here the apostle argues the spirituality of God, and, consequently, his immateriality, from the spirituality of man; for if man possesses a spiritual nature, that nature must be also immaterial. The argument of the apostle is this: as man is a spiritual and immaterial being, if he is the offspring of God, then God must be a spiritual and immaterial being; consequently, the Godhead cannot be "like unto gold, or silver, or stone."

Nor is it a valid objection to say that immateriality belongs to the lower animals as well as to man; for though we allow them to be actuated by an immaterial principle, it is obviously of an inferior *kind*. The spirit which is incapable of rational induction, and of moral knowledge, must be of an order greatly inferior to the spirits which possess these capabilities; and this is the kind of spirituality which is peculiar to man. But this image consisted,

(2.) *In immortality.*—This applied originally to man's entire compound nature; for even his body would not have died had not sin entered into the world. This is the irresistible conclusion from the reasoning of St. Paul, where he shows that "by one man sin entered into the world, and *death by sin*." Rom. v, 12. The same fact is implied in the original penalty of the law: "In the day thou eatest thereof, thou shalt surely die." In this there was most certainly a promise implied that if man would continue in obedience he should live.

Again, we may clearly infer that immortality was included in the image of God in which man was created from Gen. ix, 6: "Whoso sheddeth man's blood, by man shall his blood be shed; for in the image of God made he man." The criminality of homicide seems here to be measured by the value of life to an immortal being, whose probationary state is to end in eternal happiness or misery, and whose life, on this very account, is not to lie at the sport of human passions.

Though we allow, as the Scriptures seem clearly to teach, that the immortality of man related originally to his entire being, yet, without running into the absurdity of what is called the "natural immortality" of the human soul, that essence must have been constituted immortal in a high and peculiar sense. Hence it has ever retained its immortality amid the universal death, not only of inferior animals, but of the bodies of all human beings. Men may "kill the body, but are not able to kill the soul." Matt. x, 28.

(3.) *Man's intellectual powers were also included in this image.*—This we prove from Col. iii, 10: "And have put on the new man, which is renewed in *knowledge* after the image of him that created him." Here is a plain allusion to the image of God in which man was originally created. He was made capable of knowledge in regard both to natural and moral subjects, and endowed also with *liberty* of *will*.

As to the *degree* of knowledge which man originally possessed commentators have widely differed. Some have represented him as having been, in this respect, almost in a state of infancy; while others have exalted him to almost, if not altogether, angelic perfection. The truth lies between these two extremes. That his knowledge was exceedingly great, may be inferred from the purity and perfection of his nature, and from his capability of holding converse with his Maker. But that he was in this respect inferior to angels, is clearly implied in that declaration of the psalmist: "Thou hast made him a little *lower* than the angels." Psa. viii, 5.

2. *His* MORAL *image.*—The natural image of God in which man was created was the foundation of that MORAL IMAGE by which also he was distinguished. Unless he had been a spiritual being, possessing knowledge and the power of volition, he would have been wholly incapable of *moral* qualities. That he had such qualities eminently, and that in them consisted the image of God, as well as in the natural attributes just stated, may be argued,

(1.) *From the express testimony of Scripture.*—"Lo, this only have I found," said Solomon, "that God made man UPRIGHT." Eccl. vii, 29. There is also an express allusion to the *moral image* of God in which man was at first created in Eph. iv, 24: "Put on the new man, which after God is created in righteousness and true holiness." In this passage the apostle represents the change produced in true Christians, by the Gospel, as a *renewal* of the image of God in man; as a new or second creation of that image; and he explicitly declares that this image consists in "righteousness" and in "true holiness." It follows, therefore, that man was created in the *moral* image of his Maker. But this may be argued,

(2.) *From that satisfaction with which the Creator viewed the works of his hands.*—"And God saw *everything* that he had made, and behold, it was very good." Gen. i, 31. But, as to man, this goodness must have implied moral qualities as well as physical. Without them he would have been imperfect as *man;* and had they existed in him perverted and sinful he could not have been pronounced "very good."

As to the *degree* of moral perfection in the first man, there are two extreme opinions. Some have placed it at an elevation which renders it exceedingly difficult to conceive how he should have fallen into sin at all, and especially how he should have fallen so soon as seems to be represented in the narrative of Moses. On the other hand those who either deny, or hold very slightly, the doctrine of our hereditary depravity, delight to represent Adam as little, if at all, superior in moral perfection and capability to his descendants.

We may not be able to ascertain the exact degree of his moral perfection; but it is evident, from the Scriptures above quoted, that there is a certain standard below which it cannot be placed. Generally, he was made in the *image of God;* which, as we have proved, is to be understood *morally* as well as *naturally.* We must conclude, therefore, that man, in his original state, was SINLESS, both in *act* and in *principle.* "God made man UPRIGHT."

The Hebrew word ישׁר, which is here translated *upright*, signifies just, upright, perfect, righteous, and is, therefore, indicative of moral rectitude. It expresses the *exactness* of truth, justice, and obedience; and comprehends both the state of the heart and the habit of the life. Such, then, was the state of primitive man. There was no obliquity in his moral principles—his mind and affections; none in his conduct. He was perfectly sincere and exactly just, rendering from the heart all that was due both to God and to the creatures. All this is fully implied in the language of the apostle, when he places the image of God in which the new man is created in "*righteousness* and *true holiness.*"

It may be proper to observe here, that the "*knowledge*" in which the apostle places the image of God in the renewed man does not merely imply the faculty of the understanding, which is a part of the natural image of God, but that which might be lost, because it is that in which the new man is "*renewed.*" It is, therefore, to be understood as designating more particularly the knowledge of *God;* that knowledge of God which is the result of holy communion and fellowship with him, that knowledge of God which may be fitly denominated *experimental.*

We see, then, that in the primeval condition and character of man the "kindness and love of God" eminently appeared. He was made a rational and immortal spirit, with no limits to the constant enlargement of his powers. He was made holy and happy, and was admitted to intercourse with God. He was not left alone, but had the pleasures of society. He was placed in a world of grandeur, harmony, beauty, and utility, which was canopied with other distant worlds, to exhibit to his very senses a manifestation of the extent of space and the vastness of the universe, and to call into vigorous and salutary exercise his reason, his fancy, and his devotion. He was placed in a paradise where probably all that was sublime and gentle in the scenery of the whole earth was exhibited in *pattern*, and all that could delight the innocent sense, and excite the curious inquiries of the mind, was spread before him. He had labor to employ his attention without producing weariness, and time for his highest pursuits in the knowledge of God, his will and his works. Such was our world and its rational inhabitants, the first pair; and thus did its creation manifest, not only the power and wisdom of the Creator, but also his benevolence.

CHAPTER II.

THE FALL OF MAN.

THE Mosaic account of this sorrowful event is given in the third chapter of Genesis, and is substantially this: that man was placed in the garden of Eden to dress and to keep it; that in this garden two trees were especially distinguished, one as "the tree of life," the other as "the tree of the knowledge of good and evil;" that of the fruit of the latter Adam was commanded not to eat, and the command was enforced by the announcement of the penalty, "In the day thou eatest thereof thou shalt surely die;" that through the temptation of the serpent the woman was induced to eat of the forbidden fruit, and through her the husband also; and that for this act of disobedience they were expelled from the garden, made subject to death, and laid under other maledictions.

Interpreters of this account may be divided into three classes: those who deny the literal sense of the relation entirely; those who take it to be in part literal and in part allegorical; and those who, while they contend for the literal interpretation of every part, consider some of the terms used and some of the persons introduced as conveying a meaning more extensive than the letter, and as constituting several symbols of spiritual things and of spiritual beings.

In directing our attention to the scriptural account of the fall we will first prove that it is to be understood in its *literal sense;* and in the second place we will consider some objections which have been urged against the Divine administration, as connected with the circumstances of the fall of man.

I. The Mosaic account of the Fall is to be understood in its Literal Sense.

That this account is to be taken as a matter of real history, and according to its literal import, may be established by the following considerations:

1. *That it is a part of a continuous history.*—To select from a regularly conducted narrative a particular portion, as allegorical, when all the other parts in the connection are admitted to be plain history, is contrary to all rules of interpretation. If we may make thus free with the third chapter of Genesis why not the first, and thus deny the reality of the creation? Why not make a similar disposition of the Mosaic history from Abel to Noah, or from Noah to Abraham? One of these consequences must therefore follow: either that the account of the fall must be taken as a history of facts, or that the historical character of the five books of Moses must be given up. But the literal sense of this history is established by the consideration,

2. *That as a simple relation of events it is referred to in various parts of the Scriptures.*—The prophets frequently speak of "the garden of Eden," and of "the garden of God." We have "the tree of life" mentioned several times in the book of Proverbs and in the Revelations. The enemies of Christ and of his Church are spoken of under the name of "the serpent," and the habit of the serpent to "lick the dust" is also referred to by Micah.

If the history of the fall as recorded by Moses were an allegory, or anything but a literal history, several of the above allusions would have no meaning; but the matter is put beyond all possible doubt in the New Testament, unless the same culpable liberties be taken with the words of our Lord and St. Paul as with those of the Jewish lawgiver. Our Lord says, Matt. xix, 4, 5: "Have ye not read, that he which made them at the beginning, made them male and female, and said, For this cause shall a man leave father and mother, and shall cleave to his wife: and they twain shall be one flesh?" Here, although he does not quote immediately from the history of the fall, yet he quotes a portion of the same continuous narrative; consequently he must have regarded it as a real history.

St. Paul says, "By one man sin entered into the world;" "In Adam all die;" and again, "I fear, lest by any means, as the serpent beguiled Eve through his subtilty, so your minds should be corrupted from the simplicity that is in Christ." 2 Cor. xi, 3. In this passage the instrument of the temptation is said to be a *serpent*, [ὄφις,] which is a sufficient answer to those who would make it any other animal; and Eve is represented as being first seduced, according to the Mosaic account. This the apostle repeats in 1 Tim. ii, 13, 14: "Adam was first formed, then Eve. And Adam was not deceived, but the woman being deceived was in the transgression."

When we consider that these passages are made the basis of grave reasonings in regard to some of the most important doctrines of Christianity, and of important social duties and points of Christian order and decorum, it would be to charge the sacred writers with the grossest absurdity, nay, with even culpable and unworthy trifling, to suppose that they would argue from the history of the fall as a narrative, when they knew it to be a mere allegory. We must allow, therefore, that our Lord and his apostles regarded it as a real history. This view of the subject will be strengthened if we consider,

3. *The absurdity of supposing the account of the fall to be partly allegorical.*—No writer of true history would mix allegory with plain matter of fact in one continued narrative without any intimation of a transition from one to the other. If, therefore, any part of this narrative is matter of fact, no part is allegorical. On the other hand, if any part is allegorical, no part is naked matter of fact ; and the consequence of this will be, that everything in every part of the whole narrative must be allegorical. Thus the whole history of the creation would be an allegory, of which the real subject is not disclosed, and in this absurdity the scheme of allegorizing would end.

4. Though the literal sense of the history is thus established, yet *that it has in several parts, but in perfect accordance with the literal interpretation, a* MYSTICAL *sense,* is equally to be proved from the Scriptures.

It is a matter of established history that our first parents were prohibited from the tree of knowledge, and after their fall were excluded from the tree of life; that they were tempted by a serpent, and that various maledictions were passed upon them and upon the instrument of their seduction. But, rightly to understand this history, it is necessary to recollect that man was in a state of trial ; that the prohibition of a certain fruit was but one part of the law under which he was placed ; that the serpent was but the instrument of the real tempter, and that the curse on this instrument was symbolical of the punishment reserved for the real agent.

(1.) That man was in a state of trial appears on the very face of the history; but to a state of trial the power of moral freedom is essential. That our first parents possessed this power is as evident as that they were placed under rule and restraint. They are contemplated throughout the whole transaction, not as mere instruments, but as voluntary agents, and as such, capable of reward and punishment. Commands were issued to them which supposes a power to obey; but a power to obey necessarily implies a power to refuse and rebel. The power to obey and disobey being then mutually involved, that which determines a moral agent to the one or to the other is the *will.* For, if it were some power *ab extra,* operating necessarily, he would be no longer an *actor* but a mere passive instrument, and, therefore, in order to man's account-ability we must allow his free-agency.

In that state of excellence in which man was created his *will* must have exerted an absolute sovereignty over his thoughts, desires, words, and conduct. This, however, did not exclude solicitation or strong influence from without, provided we allow that it was resistible, either by man's own strength, or by means of assistance from a higher source. But though freedom of will is essential to a rational creature in a state of trial, yet the circumstances of the trial may be varied, and made more easy or more difficult, according to the will of the Divine Governor.

Our first parents, in their primitive state of trial, were evidently sub-ject to temptation from *intellectual pride*, from *sense*, and from *passion*. The first two operated on Eve, and, probably, on Adam also; to which was added, in his case, a passionate subjection to the wishes of his wife. If, then, these were the facts of their temptation, the circumstances of their trial are apparent. Their passions and appetites, so far from being in themselves sinful, were doubtless intended, under the control of rea-son, to be the instruments of great good; but it was at the same time possible that they should yield to those appetites and passions contrary to the dictates of reason, and thus suffer them to become the occasions of much mischief. To this cause the commission of the first transgression is evidently ascribed. "The woman saw that the tree was good for food, and that it was pleasant to the eyes, and a tree to be desired to make one wise." This view of its qualities, together with the sugges-tions of the tempter, induced her to act contrary to the express com-mand of God.

It is therefore manifest, that the state of trial in which our first parents were placed required of them, in order to the preservation of their virtue, vigilance, prayer, and the active exercise of the dominion of the *will* over solicitation. No creature can be absolutely perfect, because every creature is finite; and it would appear, from the example of the first pair, that an innocent rational being, though perfect in its *kind*, is kept from falling only by *taking hold on God*. As this is an act, there must be a determination of the will to it; and so, when the least carelessness, the least tampering with the desire of forbidden grat-ifications is induced, there is always an enemy at hand. Thus, "when lust hath conceived, it bringeth forth sin; and sin, when it is finished, bringeth forth death." James i, 15.

This is the only rational account of the origin of moral evil, and it resolves itself into three principles: 1. The necessary imperfection, in *degree*, of finite creatures. 2. The liberty of choice, which is essential to rational, accountable beings. 3. The influence of temptation on the *will*. That Adam might have resisted the temptation is a sufficient proof of the *justice* of God throughout this transaction; and that the circumstances of his trial were made precisely what they were, is to be resolved into a *wisdom*, the full manifestation of which is not to be expected in this life.

(2.) The prohibition of a certain fruit was but one part of the law under which man was placed. We have already seen that all rational creatures are under a law which requires supreme love to God and entire obedience to his commands; and that, consequently, our first parents were placed under this equitable obligation. We have also seen that all specific laws emanate from this general law, and are manifestations of it. The Decalogue was such a manifestation of it to the Jews, and the prohibition of the *tree of knowledge* is to be considered in the same light. This restraint presupposed a right in God to command, and an obligation in his creatures to obey.

But it would be absurd to suppose that this prohibition was the only rule under which our first parents were placed; for then it would follow that had they become sensual in the use of any other food than that which was forbidden, or had they refused to worship their Creator, it would not have been sin. This precept was, however, made prominent by special injunction; and it is enough to say that it was, as the event shows, a sufficient test of their obedience.

(3.) The visible agent in man's seduction was the serpent, but the real tempter was that evil spirit called the Devil and Satan. It is evident, from the attributes and properties ascribed to the serpent, that some superior intelligence was identified with it in the transaction. Surely the use of speech, reasoning powers, a knowledge of the divine law, and seductive artifice, are not the faculties of an irrational animal. The solemn manner, too, in which God addressed the serpent in pronouncing the curse, proves that an intelligent and free agent was arraigned before him; and it would indeed be ridiculous to suppose the contrary.

This shows that the ridicule of some, as to the serpent, is quite misplaced, and that one of the most serious doctrines is involved in the whole account—the liability of man to diabolical influence. Though we have but general intimations of the existence of an order of apostate spirits, and know nothing of the date of their creation, or of the circumstances of their probation and fall, yet this is clear, that they are permitted to have influence on earth; to war against the virtue and the peace of man, though under constant control and government; and that this was one circumstance in the trial of our first parents, as it is also in ours. Here, then, without giving up the literal sense of the history, we must look beyond the letter, and regard the serpent as only the *instrument* of a superhuman tempter.

(4.) In like manner the sentence pronounced upon the serpent, while it is to be understood literally as to that animal, must be considered as teaching more than is expressed by the letter, and the terms of it are therefore to be regarded as symbolical. The cursing of the serpent was a symbol of the malediction which fell upon the devil—the real agent in the temptation; while the prediction respecting the bruising of the serpent's head by the *seed of the woman* was indicative of man's redemption from the malice and power of Satan by our Lord Jesus Christ. This symbolical interpretation of the passage is confirmed by two considerations:

First, if the serpent was only a mere instrument employed by Satan, as was obviously the case, justice required that the curse should fall with its greatest weight upon the real seducer. But to interpret the history in a *merely* literal sense would confine the punishment entirely to the serpent, and leave the prime mover of the offense without any share of the malediction.

Secondly, it would be ridiculous to suppose, under the circumstances, that the prediction respecting the bruising of the serpent's head was intended to be understood in no other than a literal sense. We see the offenders before God in the utmost distress; and we hear him pronouncing upon them pains, and sorrows, and misery, and death. But are we to imagine that we hear him foretelling with great solemnity, in the midst of all this scene of calamity and woe, that at some future period a serpent should wound the heel of one of Adam's posterity, and that he should revenge himself by bruising its head? What had this trivial circumstance to do with man's fallen condition? What comfort could the condemned offenders have derived from such a prediction? Adam surely could not have understood the prophecy in this light, though some of his sons have so understood it.

II. We will consider some objections which have been urged against the Divine administration as connected with the circumstances of the Fall of Man.

1. It is asked by way of objection, *Could not God, who certainly foresaw man's apostasy, have prevented so great an evil?* And if so, *how can we reconcile the fall of man with Divine goodness?* That God foresaw the fall we firmly believe, for he declares " the end from the beginning ;" and that he could have prevented it we freely admit, for he can do whatever does not imply a contradiction and is consistent with his own perfections.

We do not suppose that God was necessarily compelled to create man. The fact that he did not perform this work till a few thousand years ago is sufficient evidence that he might, had he seen proper, have suspended it even till now. If, then, he was not compelled to create man at first, but acted with perfect freedom, it would follow that he might still continue to exercise the same freedom and unmake what he had made, or so change it as to constitute it something entirely different. So far, then, as the simple question of *power* is concerned, God could have prevented the fall. He could have prevented it by omitting to create man. He could have prevented it by making man anything else than a moral agent. But that he could have prevented it consistent with his own attributes without destroying the moral agency of man is what cannot be proved.

But if the only way by which God could have rendered the apostasy of man impossible was, to withhold from him the power of moral agency, the question then amounts to this : Was it best, upon the whole, that moral agents should be brought into existence? Before the Divine administration in this case can be justly impugned, it must be shown either that it was improper to create moral agents, or that the possibility of transgressing is not essential to the character of a moral agent. That it was improper to create moral agents is contradicted by the fact that God did create such beings. We are, therefore, compelled to allow, that in the judgment of God more good than evil would result from their creation, and that it was best, upon the whole, that such beings should be created.

That the possibility of apostasy is essential to the character of a moral agent is easily proved. 1. A moral agent is one who is capable of performing moral actions. 2. Moral actions imply a law by which they are determined to be right or wrong. 3. A law for the government of moral actions must necessarily be such as may be either obeyed or disobeyed by the subject, otherwise there could be neither virtue nor vice ; there could be no praise attached to obedience, no blame to disobedience. Thus it is clear that moral agency necessarily implies the power to obey or disobey; consequently, God could not have prevented the possibility of man's apostasy without destroying his moral agency.

2. *The prohibition under which our first parents were placed has often been made the subject of ridicule.*—" What harm could there be in eating an apple," it is asked, " that they should be placed under a restraint so strict and unreasonable ?"

Here it may be observed that the objection does not lie against the fact of man's being placed under law ; for the propriety of this is generally acknowledged. The ground of complaint is in the peculiar character of the law itself; and particularly in its being a *positive* precept, and not a *moral* one. The difference between positive and moral precepts is, that " moral precepts are those the reasons of which we see ; positive precepts those the reasons of which we do not see. Moral duties arise out of the nature of the case itself prior to external command ; positive duties do not arise out of the nature of the case, but from external command. Nor would they be duties at all, were it not for such command received from Him whose creatures and subjects we are."*

But as the obligation of all duties, whether moral or positive, rests

* Butler's Analogy.

upon their being made *law* by the authority of God, no valid objection can lie against the making of a positive precept the special test of man's obedience. To see or not to see the reasons of the Divine enactments, whether moral or positive, is a circumstance which does not affect the question of duty. But that God has sufficient reasons for all that he requires of us, though we may not see them, is a conclusion as rational as it is pious; and to slight *positive* precepts, therefore, is to refuse obedience to the Lawgiver only on the proud and presumptuous ground that he has not made us acquainted with his own reasons for enacting them.

Nor was this positive injunction without some obvious moral reason, which is probably the case with all positive precepts of Divine authority. That all moral creatures should acknowledge subjection to the Creator is equally required by the Divine glory, and by the benefit of the creatures themselves. Man was required to do this by a free and voluntary obedience, in abstaining from the fruit of a single tree, thus acknowledging the common Creator to be his Supreme Lord, and himself to be dependent upon his bounty and favor. The prohibition was simple and explicit, it was not difficult to observe, it accorded with the circumstances of those on whom it was enjoined, and as a test of obedience no injunction could have been more suitable. This view of the transaction in Paradise gives it an aspect so noble and dignified that we may well shudder at the impiety of that poor wit by whom it has been sometimes ignorantly assailed.

3. It has also been objected, that *if the serpent was but the mere instrument of the real seducer, the sentence pronounced upon it was unjust.*—To this the reply is, that it could not be a matter of just complaint to the serpent that its form should be changed, and its species lowered in the scale of being. To its former superior rank it had no original right, but held it at the pleasure of the Creator. If special pain and suffering had been inflicted upon the serpent there would be a semblance of plausibility in the objection; but it suffered no more in consequence of the fall than other irrational animals.

Its degradation was evidently intended as a memento to man; and the real punishment, as we shall show, fell upon the real transgressor, who used the serpent as his instrument. But the enmity of the whole race of serpents to the human race, their cunning, and their poisonous qualities, appear to have been wisely and graciously intended as standing warnings to us to beware of that spiritual enemy who ever lies in wait to wound and destroy.

4. *The penalty annexed to the Adamic law has been made a ground of complaint, as being excessively rigorous and entirely disproportionate to the offense.*—To understand this subject it will be necessary for us to take into the account,

(1.) *Man's primitive condition as a responsible being.*—In order that he might be a proper subject of moral government he was made a rational being, capable of understanding his duty and the reasons of it. He was made capable of perceiving and feeling the influence of motives, and was endowed with every attribute of a free moral agent. His duty was plainly prescribed; while light, like the unobstructed rays of the sun, flowed into his soul by a direct communication from God. No necessity impelled him to transgress the Divine law, for he was in possession of every necessary faculty to enable him to obey. Such was his primitive condition, and such were the circumstances by which he was rendered accountable for his actions.

(2.) *The nature of that authority by which he was bound, and to which he was held responsible.*—It was the supreme authority of the infinite God, enforced by the strong obligations of truth, justice, holiness, and gratitude. Such obligations, as high as heaven and as sacred as God himself, could not be relinquished or disregarded. The honor of the eternal throne forbade it.

(3.) *The character of man's offense.*—Surely, it could not have been so trivial a thing as those seem to suppose who speak so flippantly of the mere circumstance of tasting an apple. The eating of the forbidden fruit was the external act of the transgression; but the seat of the crime lay deep in the soul. There, where all had been holiness and love, pride and lust and unbelief were allowed to reign in triumph. The word of God was contradicted, his authority was thrown off, man's allegiance to heaven was relinquished, and the claims of gratitude were entirely disregarded. How exceedingly defective, then, must be the views of those who represent the first sin as a venial impropriety, of scarcely sufficient magnitude to merit the notice of God!

In view of all these circumstances we have no room to complain that the penalty of death was annexed to the Divine law. The whole history of the case, when properly understood, proves that the penalty, so far from being an evidence of cruelty on the part of the Lawgiver, was a benevolent enactment. In all good governments the object of penal sanctions is not primarily the punishment of the subjects, but the prevention of crime. So, likewise, that Adam might be deterred from transgression, and thereby be preserved in his primitive state of holiness and happiness, the penalty was annexed to the Divine precept, "In the day thou eatest thereof thou shalt surely *die.*" If the prime object of the penalty was the prevention of crime, then the *severity* of the penalty, if such it may be called, is an evidence of Divine *goodness*, which made the inducements to obedience as strong as possible without destroying man's accountability.

CHAPTER III.

THE EFFECTS OF THE FALL

HAVING investigated, in the preceding chapter, the circumstances of the *fall*, we turn to the consideration of its EFFECTS. On this subject three leading opinions are entertained :

First, the view of Pelagius and of the modern Socinians is, that though Adam, by his transgression, exposed himself to the displeasure of his Maker, yet neither he nor his posterity sustained any *moral* injury by his disobedience; that the only evil he suffered was expulsion from Paradise, and subjection to severe labor; that he was created mortal, and would have died had he not sinned; that his posterity, like himself, are placed in a state of trial; and that we may maintain our innocence amid surrounding temptations, and may also daily improve in moral excellence by the proper use of reason and other natural powers.

The *second* opinion is the psuedo-Arminian or semi-Pelagian theory of Dr. Whitby and several other divines of the English Church. It is this: that though Adam was naturally mortal, yet his life would have been forever preserved by the bounty of his Creator had he continued obedient; and that he was a kind of natural representative of his posterity, so that all the effects of his fall, to some extent, are visited upon them; not, however, as penal, but as natural consequences, and as children are often compelled to suffer by the negligence or fault of their parents.

The *third* opinion, and, as we believe, the only rational and scriptural view of this subject, is that Adam, by his transgression, incurred the Divine displeasure, lost the moral image of God in which he was created, and became subject to temporal death, and exposed to death eternal; that as he was the federal head and legal representative of his posterity they fell in him as really as he fell in himself, and thus became liable to all the penal consequences of his transgression; that man, in his fallen condition, "is very far gone from original righteousness, and is of his own nature inclined to evil, and that continually ;" and that he has no power, without divine grace, to do anything that is really good or acceptable to God.

This is the view which was entertained by Arminius, and which is held by that large body of Christians who follow the theological opinions of Mr. Wesley. Nor is there any material discrepancy between this statement of man's fallen condition and the doctrine of the Augsburg Confession, the Church of England, the French Churches, the Calvinistic Church of Scotland, and, so far as this doctrine alone is concerned, of Calvin himself. True Arminianism, therefore, as fully as Calvinism, admits the total depravity of human nature in consequence of the fall of our first parents ; and to represent this doctrine as being exclusively Calvinistic, which has often been done, it an entire delusion.

But in order to a further investigation of this subject is will be necessary to consider, 1. The nature of that DEATH which was made the penalty of sin ; 2. The legal relation which Adam sustained to his posterity ; and, 3. The moral condition in which men are actually born into the world.

§ 1. *The Nature of that Death which was made the penalty of Sin.*

That this penalty includes the very "fullness of death," as divines have justly termed it, death *bodily, spiritual,* and *eternal,* is a doctrine which cannot be puffed away by mere sarcasm, but which stands upon the firm basis of inspired truth. A few remarks will show the justness of this conclusion.

1. The Pelagian and Socinian notion that Adam would have died had he not sinned, requires no other refutation than the words of St. Paul: "By one man sin entered into the world, and *death by sin.*" Rom. v, 12. It evidently follows, therefore, that if sin had not "entered into the world," so far at least as man is concerned, there would have been no death.

2. In addition to that death which stands opposed to animal life, and which consists in the separation of the rational soul from the body, the Scriptures speak of death in a *moral* sense. This consists in a separation of the soul from communion with God, and is manifested by the dominion of earthly and corrupt dispositions and habits, and an entire indifference or aversion to spiritual and heavenly things. All who have not been made alive by the power of divine grace are regarded as being in this state of spiritual death. "And you hath he quickened, who were DEAD in trespasses and sins." Eph. ii, 1.

In accordance with this view, that moral change which unites the soul to God is represented as a resurrection from the dead, and a passage "from death unto life." To interpret, then, the death pronounced upon Adam as including moral death, is in perfect agreement with the language of Scripture. For, if a state of sin in the unregenerate is a state of spiritual death, then a state of sin in him was a state of spiritual death ; the same cause producing the same effect. And, as God withdraws himself from all communion with the guilty, they are thereby separated from the only source of spiritual life, and thus suffer a *deprivation* from which a *depravation* consequently and necessarily follows.

3. But the highest sense of the term death, in the Scriptures, is the punishment of the soul in a future state by a loss of happiness, a separation from God, and a positive infliction of Divine wrath. It was in this sense that our Lord used the term when he said, "If a man keep my sayings, he shall never see death." John viii, 51. This state of hope-

less misery is also called "the second death," and is evidently included in the penalty of the Divine law; for it is to be regarded as an axiom in the jurisprudence of heaven, that "the wages of sin is DEATH." Nor do the Scriptures give us the least intimation that any sin whatever is exempt from this penalty; or that some sins are punished in this life only, and others in the life to come. The degree of punishment will doubtless be proportionate to the offense; but death is the penalty attached to all sin, unless it is averted by pardon. What was there, then, in the case of Adam to take him out of this rule? His act was a *transgression* of the law, and therefore *sin;* and, as such, its wages was *death,* which means, in its highest sense, future and eternal punishment.

§ 2. *The Legal Relation which Adam sustained to his Posterity.*

The question now to be considered is, whether Adam is to be regarded as a mere individual, the consequences of whose conduct terminated in himself, or no otherwise affected his posterity than incidentally, as the misconduct of an ordinary parent may affect his children; or whether he was the legal *head* and *representative* of the human race, who in consequence of his fall have fallen with him. The latter opinion seems best to accord with the teachings of the holy Scriptures, as we will immediately proceed to show.

1. The testimony of the Scriptures in support of this position is so explicit that all attempts to evade it have been in vain. St. Paul, in the fifth chapter of his epistle to the Romans, evidently contrasts the public or federal character of Adam with that of Christ. He shows that the evils which mankind suffer are the consequences of Adam's transgression, and that the benefits which are graciously bestowed upon them are the effects of Christ's obedience. It is with allusion to this representative character that Adam is called "the figure ($\tau\acute{v}\pi\sigma\varsigma$, *type* or *model*) of him that was to come."

The apostle also adopts the phrases "the first Adam" and "the second Adam," which mode of speaking can only be explained on the ground that as sin and death descended from one, so righteousness and life flow from the other; and that what Christ is to all his spiritual seed Adam was to all his natural descendants. On this, indeed, the parallel is founded, 1 Cor. xv, 22: "For as in Adam all die, even so in Christ shall all be made alive;" words which on any other hypothesis can have no natural signification.

2. The condition in which this federal connection between Adam and his posterity placed the latter is next to be considered. This involves what theologians call "the imputation of Adam's sin to his posterity," in regard to which three leading views have been taken.

(1.) Some hold the doctrine of MEDIATE *imputation,* which is, that in virtue of our derivation from Adam, our bodies are mortal and our moral nature is corrupt. This opinion, however, though embracing truth, does not go to the length of Scripture, which must not be warped by the reasonings of erring man.

(2.) Another view is, that Adam's sin is accounted *ours* in the sight of God by virtue of our federal relation. This is called IMMEDIATE *imputation*, and is supported by the assumption that Adam and his posterity constitute *one moral person*, and that the whole human race was in him, its head consenting to his act. But this opinion is inconsistent with that individual agency which enters into the very notion of an accountable being, while it destroys the distinction between original and actual sin. It asserts the imputation of the actual commission of Adam's sin to his descendants, which is false in fact; it makes us chargeable with the full latitude of his transgression and all its attendant circumstances, and it constitutes us separate from all actual voluntary offense, equally guilty with him, all which are equally repugnant to our consciousness and to the equity of the case.

(3.) The other view of this subject, and that which we believe to be in accordance with the Scriptures, is, that the *imputation* of Adam's sin to his posterity is confined to its LEGAL RESULTS. If a man has committed treason, and has thereby lost his estate, his crime is so imputed to his children that they, with him, are made to suffer the penalty of his offense. We do not mean, however, that the *personal act* of the father is charged upon the children, but that his guilt or liability to punishment is so transferred to them that they suffer the legal consequences of his crime.

Thus the sin of Achan was so imputed to his children that they were stoned to death on account of it.* In like manner the covetousness of Gehazi was imputed to his posterity, when God declared, by the mouth of his prophet, that the leprosy should cleave unto him and his seed for ever.† So also the Jews: "His blood be on us and on our children;" that is, let us and our children be punished for it.

In this sense, then, we may safely contend for the imputation of Adam's sin to his posterity; and this agrees precisely with the apostle Paul, who speaks of the imputation of sin to those "who had not sinned after the similitude of Adam's transgression;" that is, to all who lived between Adam and Moses, and consequently to infants, who personally had not offended. He also declares, that "by one man's disobedience many were made," constituted, accounted, and dealt with as "sinners," and treated as though they themselves had actually sinned. For that this is his sense is clear from what follows: "So by the obedience of one shall many be made righteous;" constituted, accounted, and dealt with as such, though not actually righteous, but in fact pardoned criminals. The legal consequences, then, of this imputation are as previously shown, death *temporal*, *spiritual*, and *eternal*.

* See Josh. vii, 25.　　　　　　　　　　† See 2 Kings v. 27.

An objection has been raised against this view of the imputation of Adam's sin to his posterity on the ground of its supposed *injustice*. Before we give a direct reply to the objection it may be proper to remark, that if this imputation is unjust in any of its parts it must be unjust in every part. If it is unjust to make the descendants of Adam liable to eternal death because of his offense, the infliction of temporal death is unjust also; the *duration* of the punishment making no difference in the simple question of justice. If punishment, whether of *loss* or of *pain*, is unjust, its measure and duration may be greater or less injustice, but it is unjust in every degree. If, then, we confine the legal result of Adam's transgression to bodily death, we are in precisely the same difficulty, as to the equity of the proceeding, as when it is extended further. The only way out of this dilemma is to consider death not as a punishment but as a blessing, which involves the absurdity of supposing that God pronounced a blessing upon Adam as the consequence of sin.

But in meeting this objection it is only necessary to show that it rests upon a false foundation. It supposes, contrary to truth, that the legal consequences of Adam's transgression are to be considered apart from that evangelical provision of mercy which includes the whole human race. The redemption of man by Christ was certainly not an after thought, brought in upon man's apostasy. It was a *provision*, and when man fell he found justice hand in hand with mercy. If we look at the subject in this light every difficulty will be removed.

As to the case of Adam and his *adult* descendants, it will be seen that all became liable to bodily death. Here was *justice*. But by means of the atonement, which effectually declares the justice of God, this sentence is reversed by a glorious resurrection. Again, when God, the fountain of spiritual life, withdrew himself from Adam, he died a spiritual death and became morally corrupt; and, as " that which is born of the flesh is flesh," all his posterity are in the same condition. Here is *justice*. But spiritual life visits man from another quarter and through other means. The second Adam " is a quickening Spirit." Through the atonement which he has made the Holy Spirit is given to man, that he may again infuse into his corrupt nature the heavenly life and regenerate and sanctify it. Here is the *mercy*. And as to a future state, eternal life is promised to all who perseveringly believe in Christ, which reverses the sentence of eternal death. Here, again, is the manifestation of *mercy*.

In all this it is impossible to impeach the equity of the Divine administration, since no man suffers any loss or injury ultimately by the sin of Adam but by his own willful obstinacy. The " abounding grace" by Christ has placed before all men upon their believing, not merely compensation for the loss and injury sustained by Adam, but infinitely higher blessings, both in kind and degree, than were forfeited in him.

As to *adults*, then, the objection taken from Divine justice is unsupported.

We come now to the case of *infants*. The great consideration which leads to a solution of this case is found in Romans v, 18: "Therefore, as by the offense of one judgment came upon all men to condemnation, even so by the righteousness of one the free gift came upon all men unto justification of life." In these words the sin of Adam and the merits of Christ are pronounced to be co-extensive, the words applied to both being precisely the same. " *Judgment* came upon ALL MEN,"— " the *free gift* came upon ALL MEN." If the whole human race is meant in the former clause, the whole human race is meant in the latter also; and then it follows, that as all are benefited by the obedience of Christ, so all children dying in infancy must be partakers of this benefit.

The "free gift" which "came upon all men" is said to be "unto justification of life," a full reversal of the penalty of death, and a title to life eternal. But the benefit did not so come "upon all men" as to relieve them immediately from the penalty of the law; for they are by nature still both morally dead, and liable to the death of the body. This is true, not only of adults, but of children also, whether they die in infancy or not; for we have no reason to conclude that children dying in infancy were born with a purer nature than those who live to maturity. The fact of their being born liable to temporal death, a part of the penalty, is sufficient to show that they are born under the whole malediction.

It is, therefore, incorrect to suppose, as some have done, that children are born in a justified and regenerate state; but they are all born under " the free gift," the effects of which extend to "all men," εις, *in order to* "justification of life." It follows, then, that, in the case of infants, this gift may be connected with the end for which it was given, as well as in the case of adults, or it would be given in vain. All the mystery of the subject arises from this, that in adults we see the "free gift" connected with the *end*, actual justification, by a voluntary acceptance of its benefits; but as to infants, the same end is reached without their voluntary consent, and by a process which is entirely hidden from us. If, however, an infant is not capable of a voluntary acceptance of the benefits of the "free gift," neither, on the other hand, is it capable of a voluntary rejection of them, and it is by rejecting them that adults perish.

We must not overlook the fact that the benefits of this "free gift" are bestowed largely even upon adults, independent of anything they do. This is seen in the longsuffering of God, the instructions of his word, the corrective dispensations of his providence, and, above all, in *preventing grace* and the *influences of the Holy Spirit*, exciting in men various degrees of religious feeling, and enabling them to repent and believe the Gospel. In a word, "justification of life" is offered to them; nay, more, it is pressed upon them, and they fail of it only by rejecting it.

If, then, the very power and inclination to seek "justification of life" is thus prevenient, and in the highest sense *free*, it follows, by the same rule of Divine conduct, that the Holy Spirit may be given to children; that a divine and effectual influence may be exerted on them, which, meeting with no voluntary resistance, shall cure the spiritual death and corrupt tendency of their nature; and that the principle of administration, in their case, does not greatly differ from that in the case of adults.

When, therefore, the doctrine of imputation is considered in this its *whole* and *scriptural* view, the objection which is urged against it, on the ground of its supposed injustice, entirely vanishes; and, at the same time, the evil of sin is manifested, and also the justice of the Lawgiver.

§ 3. *The Moral Condition in which Men are actually born into the World.*

Having established the import of the *death* threatened as the penalty of Adam's transgression, and having shown that the sentence included the whole of his posterity, our next step is to ascertain that moral condition in which men are actually born into the world notwithstanding the gracious provision of redemption. This subject involves the entire question of HUMAN DEPRAVITY, the full discussion of which our limits will not allow; but we will state the doctrine as we believe it to be taught in the Scriptures, and adduce the leading proofs by which man's native depravity is established.

Pelagians, Socinians, and others of kindred sentiments, deny the doctrine of man's native depravity altogether. They hold that the human soul, at its entrance upon the stage of life, is as pure as Adam was when he came from the hand of his Creator.

There are others who teach that all men have suffered to some extent in their moral powers by Adam's transgression; but they define this result to be, not the total depravity of their moral nature, but merely a greater liability to go astray, and to lose that degree of moral purity which they by nature possess.

But as neither of these opinions has any foundation in the sacred Scriptures, nor can be established by any rational argument, we will direct our attention,

I. *To a statement of what we believe to be the true scriptural doctrine respecting the moral condition of man.*

This doctrine is thus expressed in our seventh article of religion: "Original sin standeth not in the following of Adam, (as the Pelagians do vainly talk,) but it is the corruption of the nature of every man, that naturally is engendered of the offspring of Adam, whereby man is very far gone from original righteousness, and of his own nature inclined to evil, and that continually."

Here we have a clear recognition of *human depravity* under the denomination of ORIGINAL SIN—a subject which we will now examine, both as to its *nature* and its *degree*.

1. *Its* NATURE.—As to the *nature* of original sin, some divines have supposed that it consists in a *positive evil*, infused into man's nature by a judicial act of God, which has been transmitted to all Adam's posterity. Others, and those the greater number, both Calvinistic and Arminian, have resolved it into *privation*. Arminius himself calls it "a privation of the image of God," and asserts that the "absence alone of original righteousness is original sin." But he so explains this privation as to include in it both the forfeiture "of the gift of the Holy Spirit" by Adam, for himself and his descendants, and the loss of original righteousness as the consequence. He tells us, therefore, that this state of destitution renders "all men obnoxious to death temporal and eternal;" and that it is "sufficient for the commission and production of every actual sin whatever."

This is by some divines called, with great aptness, "a depravation arising from a deprivation," and is certainly much more consonant with the Scriptures than the opinion that God infused evil qualities into the nature of man.   The resulting of moral evil from a mere privation may be fitly illustrated by the consequences of temporal death.   For, as the mere privation of animal life causes the extinction of heat, and sense, and motion, and surrenders the body to the operation of chemical decomposition; so from the loss of *spiritual* life followed moral inability, the dominion of irregular appetites and passions, aversion to restraint, and estrangement from God, and even enmity against him.

To perceive this subject in its scriptural light it may be proper to remark,

(1.) *That the life which the Holy Spirit supplies is the only source of righteousness in Man.*—This may be inferred from the *new creation*, which is the renewal of man "in righteousness and true holiness," and which is the work of the Holy Spirit; for, before man is thus quickened by the Spirit he is "dead in trespasses and sins." But even after this change, this being "born again," he is not able to preserve himself in the renewed condition into which he is brought but by the continuance of the same quickening and aiding influence.

(2.) *That the loss of spiritual life included in it the retraction of God's Spirit from offending man.*—For, if "Christ hath redeemed us from the curse of the law, that we might receive the promise of the Spirit," as the apostle declares, then it follows that the loss of God's Spirit was included in the curse which fell on apostate Adam.

(3.) *That the necessary consequence of this privation was the total corruption of Man's moral nature.*—If our spiritual life is supplied alone by the spirit of God, it is reasonable to conclude that the withdrawing of that Spirit from Adam when he willfully sinned, and, consequently, from all his posterity, was the cause of the death and depravation which followed.

2. *The* DEGREE *of human depravity.*—In regard to this we may safely affirm, as being the doctrine of the Bible, that man is by nature *totally depraved.* Some, it is true, who are generally reputed as orthodox, have hesitated to adopt the phrase *total depravity* merely because the *term* is not in the Scriptures. But if it expresses, when properly defined, the Scripture doctrine upon this subject, to reject it merely on this account is perfectly puerile.

Others have rejected this phrase because they have attached to it an improper meaning. They have represented it as implying depravity in the greatest possible degree and in every possible sense. They have, therefore, argued that if all men are totally depraved, no one even in practice can be worse than another, and no one can ever become worse than he is. To these conclusions they have opposed the obvious fact that some are more wicked and depraved than others, as likewise the testimony of Scripture, that "evil men and seducers wax worse and worse;" and they have supposed these arguments to be a triumphant refutation of the doctrine of total depravity.

It is worthy of remark, however, that those who have taken this view of the subject have represented the doctrine of depravity in a very distorted light, and hence their arguments have been directed against a mere fiction of their own imagination, leaving the doctrine in its true sense undisturbed. No sensible advocate for total depravity ever contended that all men are wicked in the same degree, or that wicked men may not still become worse; nor can any such inference be fairly drawn from the doctrine when correctly understood.

Human depravity may be justly denominated *total,* because,

(1.) *It extends to all the powers and faculties of the soul.*—The judgment, the memory, the will, the imagination, the affections, and all the moral powers of our nature, are depraved and polluted by sin. "The whole head is sick, and the whole heart faint." Isa. i, 5.

(2.) *It implies the absence of all positive good.*—"For I know," says St. Paul, "that in me (that is, in my flesh) dwelleth no good thing." Rom. vii, 18. In this sense the doctrine of total depravity is very clearly taught in our eighth article of religion: "The condition of man after the fall of Adam is such that he cannot turn and prepare himself by his own natural strength and works to faith, and calling upon God, wherefore we have no power to do good works, pleasant and acceptable to God, without the grace of God by Christ preventing us, that we may have a good-will, and working with us when we have that good-will." This implies a total loss by the fall of all spiritual good; a complete and total erasure of that moral image of God in which man was created.

(3.) *The entire capacity and powers of the soul abstract from grace are filled and continually employed with evil.*—That this is one sense in which the doctrine of total depravity is to be understood may be seen by a reference to our seventh article of religion, already quoted: "Man is very far gone from original righteousness, and of his own nature inclined to evil, and that continually." This is in exact accordance with the testimony of Divine truth. "God saw that the wickedness of man was great in the earth, and that every imagination of the thoughts of his heart was only evil continually." Gen. vi, 5.

Having stated the doctrine of man's native depravity as held by the great body of orthodox Christians, and having inquired to some extent into its nature and degree, we will proceed,

II. *To adduce the leading proofs* by which *it is established.*

The native and total depravity of all mankind may be argued,

1. *From the penalty of the Adamic law, and the relation which Adam sustained to his descendants.*—That the penalty of the law included death *temporal, spiritual,* and *eternal,* and that Adam was the *federal head* and *representative* of his posterity, have been fully established. But if this relationship existed between Adam and his posterity, it will necessarily follow that all the penal consequences of his transgression must legally fall upon all mankind. In him we were seminally created, and as all mankind were represented in him, our common nature was identified with him in the offense. Had he been annihilated the moment he transgressed, the millions of his posterity would have perished with him, and never could have realized a state of conscious existence. As Adam was the *natural* head of all our race, it is not unreasonable, nay, it appears almost necessarily to follow, in view of the law under which he was placed, that he should have been constituted our *federal* head also. As such, by his one offense he "brought death into the world and all our woe;" and, therefore, whatever the penalty of the law may have been, he incurred it not only for himself, but for all his posterity.

It may here be inquired whether the posterity of Adam stand chargeable with his actual transgression. To this our reply is, that as God looks upon things as they really are, and as the transgression of Adam was not personally committed by his posterity, therefore it cannot be imputed to them as their *personal act.* But as Dr. Watts has remarked, "Sin is taken either for an *act of disobedience* to a law, or for the *legal result* of such an act; that is, the *guilt* or *liableness to punishment.*" Hence it is clear that the full penalty of Adam's sin may be justly charged upon his posterity without making his transgression their personal act. A nation or a community may be justly chargeable with all the consequences of the act of their legal representative, as fully as though they had done the same thing personally; even so, if Adam was the legal head and representative of his posterity, they are justly chargeable with all the legal consequences of his offense. The act was theirs, not personally, but through their representative, and they, therefore, incurred the guilt and the penalty which legally and necessarily resulted from his act of disobedience.

This we believe to be the scriptural view of the subject, and one which necessarily results from the federal relation that Adam sustained to all his descendants. If he had not been their federal head, his guilt could not have been imputed to them without violating the principles of justice; and if his guilt had not been imputed to them, it would be impossible to justify the Divine administration in executing upon them the dreadful penalty. But if we admit, as we must, that Adam was our federal head and representative, then our guilt and subjection to the penalty of death will necessarily follow as legal consequences.

2. *This doctrine is confirmed by experience and observation.*—In entering upon this feature of the subject it may be proper to state that there are several facts of history and experience which must be accounted for in any theory that we may adopt respecting man's moral condition.

(1.) That in all ages great, and even general wickedness has prevailed among those large masses of men called *nations*.

As to the immediate descendants of Adam, a murderer sprung up in the first family, and the world became increasingly corrupt, until " God saw that the wickedness of man was great in the earth, and that every imagination of the thoughts of his heart was only evil continually;" that " all flesh had corrupted his way upon the earth;" and that it " was filled with violence." Gen. vi, 5, 12, 13. Only Noah was found righteous before God; and because of the universal wickedness—a wickedness which spurned all warning and resisted all correction—the flood was brought upon the *world of the ungodly*.

The same course of increasing wickedness was pursued after the flood; and from Abraham to Moses idolatry, injustice, oppression, and gross sensuality characterized the people of Canaan, Egypt, and every other country mentioned in the Mosaic narrative.

The obstinate inclination of the Israelites to idolatry through all their generations until the Babylonish captivity, their abounding wickedness after their return from Babylon, and their general corruption in the time of our Lord, are prominently set forth in the sacred writings, and in those of Josephus, their own historian.

In all heathen nations religious error, idolatry, superstition, fraud, oppression, and vice of almost every description show the general state of society to be exceedingly and even destructively corrupt. And, though Mohammedan nations escape the charge of idolatry, yet pride, avarice, oppression, injustice, cruelty, sensuality, and gross superstition are all prevalent among them.

The case of Christian nations, though in them immorality is more powerfully checked than in any other, and many bright and influential examples of the highest virtue are found among their inhabitants, sufficiently proves that the majority are corrupt and vicious in their habits. It is, therefore, evident that men in all ages and in all places have been generally wicked.

(2.) Another fact to be accounted for is the *strength* of this tendency to general wickedness. This can only be measured by the consideration of two circumstances. The *first* is, the greatness of the crimes to which men have abandoned themselves. If the corrupting principle had only led to trifling errors and practical infirmities, a softer view of man's moral condition might be taken; but in every age, and among all nations, men have been guilty of the most atrocious crimes, both against God and their fellow-men.

The *second* circumstance to be considered is the *number* and *character* of the checks and restraints against which this tide of wickedness has urged on its almost resistless course. It has opposed itself against the law of God, which is in some degree found among all men; against the voice of conscience; against the restraints and penalties of human laws; against the known and acknowledged fact that vice is a never-failing source of misery; against the terrible judgments of God upon wicked nations and individuals; and against the counteracting and reforming influences of God's various dispensations of grace and mercy to our fallen world. We cannot consider the number and power of these checks without acknowledging that the principle in human nature which triumphs over them, and gives rise to so much moral evil, is one of great strength and fearful tendency.

(3.) The third fact to be accounted for is, that the seeds of the vices which exist in society are discoverable in children in their earliest years. We see in them selfishness, pride, envy, deceit, resentment, falsehood, and often cruelty; and to restrain and correct these evils is the principal object of moral education.

(4.) The fourth fact is, that every man is conscious of a natural tendency to many evils. Some are inclined to pride, ambition, and excessive love of honor; some to anger, revenge, and implacableness; some to cowardice, meanness, and fear; some to avarice, care, and distrust; and others to sensuality and prodigality. Where is the man who has not his peculiar constitutional tendency to some evil in one or other of these classes? But there are also evil tendencies which are common to all men. These are, to forget God; to be indifferent to our obligations to him; to love created objects more than the Creator; to desire the praise of men more than the Divine approbation; and to be more influenced by visible things which surround us than by those which are invisible and eternal.

(5.) The last fact which we shall name in this connection is, that even after men have seriously resolved to live "soberly, righteously, and godly," they meet with strong and constant resistance at every step from evil passions, appetites, and inclinations. This is so clearly a matter of universal experience that, in the moral writings of every age and country, and in the very phrases and turns of all languages, virtue is associated with difficulty, and represented under the notion of a warfare.

As these five facts of universal history and experience cannot be denied, and as it would be most absurd to discuss the moral condition of human nature without any reference to them, they must be accounted for. The advocates of man's natural innocence have no way of accounting for these moral phenomena but by referring them to bad example and a vicious education.

Let us take the *first*. To account for general wickedness they refer it to bad example. But we remark,

First, That this does not account for the *introduction* of moral evil. It was not till after the repentance of our first parents, and their restoration to the Divine favor, that their children were born. From what example, then, did Cain learn malice, hatred, and murder? Nor will example account for the fact that the children of virtuous parents often become immoral. If they were naturally good, the good example always present ought to be more influential than bad examples at a distance and only occasionally seen.

Secondly, Example will not account for the general prevalence of vice. If man's natural disposition is more in favor of good than evil, then there ought to have been more good than evil in the world, which is contradicted by fact. But if it is indifferent to good and evil, then the quantum of virtue and vice in society ought to have been pretty equally divided, which is also contrary to fact; and on neither supposition can the existence of general wickedness be accounted for.

Thirdly, This very method of explaining the viciousness of society admits the superior power of bad example, which is almost giving up the matter in dispute; for, why should it be more influential than good example, unless there is a proneness in man to be corrupted by it?

Fourthly, Example does not account for that strong bias to evil in men which in all ages has borne down the most powerful restraints; nor for the early manifestation of wrong principles, tempers, and affections in children, since they appear at an age when example can have no influence; nor for the conflict which always attends a virtuous life.

Let us, then, see whether a bad education, the other cause usually alleged to account for these facts, will be more successful. In regard to this we may observe,

First, That this cause will no more account for the introduction into the family of Adam of passions so hateful as those of Cain than will example. As there was no example of these evils in the primeval family, so certainly there was no education that could incite and encourage them. We are also left still without a reason why, in well-ordered and religious families, where both education and example are good, so many instances of their inefficacy should occur. If bad education corrupts a naturally well-disposed mind, then a good education ought still more powerfully to affect it and give it a right tendency.

Secondly, No reason can be assigned why education as well as example should become generally bad if men are not predisposed to evil. Of education men are usually more careful than of example. The lips are often right when the life is wrong; and many practice evil who will not go so far as to teach it. If human nature is born pure, or at worst, equally disposed to good and evil, then the existence of a generally corrupting system of education in all countries and among all people cannot be accounted for.

Thirdly, It is not the fact that education is directly and universally corrupting in its influence. In many cases it is, indeed, defective; but it has only in a few instances been employed to encourage those vices into which men have commonly fallen. It is in those very vices, against which all education, even the most defective, is designed to guard us, that the world has most obviously displayed its depravity.

Fourthly, If we come to the other facts which must be accounted for, education is placed upon the same ground in the argument as example. The evil dispositions of children appear before education commences, and that opposition to good and proneness to evil of which every man is conscious are in direct opposition to those very principles with which education has furnished his judgment.

It is only, then, by the scriptural account of the natural and hereditary corruption of the human race, commonly called *original sin*, that these facts are fully accounted for, and as the facts themselves cannot be denied, they are strongly confirmatory of the doctrine of man's total depravity.

3. *This doctrine is fully established by the direct testimony of Scripture.*—It has already been shown that the full penalty of Adam's offense passed upon his posterity, and consequently that part of it which consists in spiritual death. A full provision has been made, as we have seen, to meet this case; but that does not affect the state in which men are born. It is a cure for an actually existing disease, and not a preventive.

If, then, we are all born in a state of spiritual death, that is, without that Divine influence upon our faculties which is necessary to give them a holy tendency and to maintain them in it, and if that influence is restored to man only by a dispensation of grace and favor, it follows that by nature he is born with sinful propensities, and is incapable in his own strength of anything that is good.

When it is said (Gen. v, 3) that "Adam begat a son in his own likeness," there seems to be an implied opposition between the likeness of God in which Adam was made, and Adam's "own likeness," in which his son was begotten. It is not said that he begat a son in the likeness of God; which would have been an appropriate declaration, and one apparently called for, if human nature had suffered no injury by the fall.

It is asserted (Gen. viii, 21) that "the imagination of man's heart is evil from his youth." Here it is to be observed, 1. That these words were spoken when there were no human beings upon the earth but righteous Noah and his family. 2. That they were spoken of *man* AS MAN; that is, of human nature, and, consequently, of Noah himself and those saved with him in the ark. 3. That it is affirmed of MAN, that is, of mankind, that the imagination of his heart "is evil from his youth." This passage, therefore, affirms the natural and hereditary tendency of man to evil.

The book of Job, which embodies the patriarchal theology, gives ample testimony to this, as the faith of those ancient times. Thus, Job xi, 12: "Vain man would be wise, though man be born like a wild ass's colt." He is "*born*," literally, "*the colt of a wild ass*." Again, "Who can bring a clean thing out of an unclean?" Job xiv, 4. The word *thing* is supplied by our translators, but *person* is evidently understood. In Scripture language, cleanness signifies holiness, and uncleanness, sin; and, therefore, the text clearly asserts the natural impossibility of any man's being born sinless, because he is the offspring of guilty and defiled parents. The same doctrine is taught, only more fully, in Job xv, 14: "What is man, that he should be clean; and he which is born of a woman, that he should be righteous?"

Psalm li, 5: "Behold, I was shapen in iniquity; and in sin did my mother conceive me." What possible sense can be given to this passage on the hypothesis of man's natural innocence? Again, Psalm lvii, 3: "The wicked are estranged from the womb; they go astray as soon as they be born, speaking lies."

Prov. xxii, 15, and xxix, 15: "Foolishness is bound up in the heart of a child; but the rod of correction shall drive it far from him." "The rod and reproof give wisdom, but a child left to himself bringeth his mother to shame." These passages put together are a plain testimony of the inbred corruption of young children. "Foolishness" in the former is not barely appetite, or a want of knowledge attainable by instruction, as some have said; for neither of these deserves the correction which is recommended. But it is an indisposedness to what is good, and a strong propensity to evil.

Jeremiah xvii, 5: "Cursed be the man that trusteth in MAN." But why this if he were not, by nature, unworthy of trust? On the scheme of man's natural innocence it would surely have been more appropriate to say, Cursed be the man that trusteth indiscriminately in men, some of whom may have become corrupt. But here human nature itself, *man* in the abstract, is held up to suspicion and caution. "The heart," proceeds the same prophet, verse 9, "is deceitful above all things, and desperately wicked: who can know it?" which is the reason adduced for the preceding caution against trusting in man.

Mark vii, 21–23: "Out of the heart of men proceed evil thoughts, adulteries, fornications, murders, thefts, covetousness, wickedness, deceit, lasciviousness, an evil eye, blasphemy, pride, foolishness; all these evil things come from within, and defile the man." But this representation would not be true on the scheme of natural innocence; for it assumes that "all these evil things" come from *without*, and not "from *within*," as their original source.

John iii, 5, 6: "Except a man be born of water and of the Spirit, he cannot enter into the kingdom of God. That which is born of the flesh is flesh; and that which is born of the Spirit is spirit." Our Lord here declares the necessity of a spiritual birth, in contradistinction to our natural birth, in order to our entrance into the kingdom of God; and he places the necessity of this moral change in the fact that "that which is born of the flesh is *flesh*." The term *flesh* is often used in the Scriptures to denote man's depraved nature. Thus, "In my *flesh* dwelleth no good thing." "They that are in the *flesh* cannot please God." "If ye live after the *flesh* ye shall die." "The *flesh* lusteth against the Spirit." These passages serve to fix the meaning of the term *flesh* as it is used by our Lord in his conversation with Nicodemus, and to confirm the opinion of those who understand him to teach that man is by *nature* corrupt and sinful, and, consequently, unfit for the kingdom of heaven unless he is "*born again;*" and that all amendment of his case must result, not from himself, but from the regenerating influence of the Holy Spirit.

The universal corruption of mankind is strongly set forth in the third chapter of Paul's Epistle to the Romans. His language, as quoted from the fourteenth Psalm, is, "They are all gone out of the way, they are together become unprofitable; there is none that doeth good, no, not one." He shows that "both Jews and Gentiles are all under sin," and that all men are "guilty before God." He then proposes the means of salvation by faith in Christ, on the express ground that "*all* have sinned and come short of the glory of God." Whoever reads the apostle's argument, and considers the universality of the terms employed—ALL, EVERY, ALL THE WORLD, BOTH JEWS AND GENTILES—must conclude, in all fairness of interpretation, that the whole human race, of every age, is intended.

We have now seen that the doctrine of man's total depravity rests upon a solid foundation—that it is clearly implied in the penalty of the Adamic law, and the relation which Adam sustained to his posterity; that it is confirmed by experience and observation; and that it is explicitly taught in the sacred Scriptures. It would, therefore, be the greatest absurdity to call in question the truth of this doctrine, since it is so fully established by evidence which cannot be rejected.

We will close this chapter by considering two objections which have been urged against the doctrine of man's native and total depravity. It has been objected,

1. That "as we have our souls immediately from God, if we are born sinful he must either create sinful souls, which cannot be supposed without impiety, or send sinless souls into sinful bodies, to be defiled by the unhappy union, which is as inconsistent with his goodness as his justice. Add to this, that nothing can be more unphilosophical than to suppose that a body, a mere lump of organized matter, is able to communicate to a pure spirit that moral pollution of which itself is as incapable as the murderer's sword is incapable of cruelty."

To this objection we reply, that however weighty it may have been regarded by some, it rests entirely upon an assumption which cannot be proved; that is, that we have our souls immediately from God by *creation*. This objection will fall to the ground if we can prove that our souls, as well as our bodies, have descended from Adam by *traduction*. And that this is the fact we are led to believe from the following considerations:

(1.) It is said that God "rested on the seventh day from *all* his work" of creation. It is, therefore, unscriptural as well as unreasonable to suppose that he is still engaged in *creating souls*, as the bodies of mankind multiply upon the earth.

(2.) Eve was originally created *in* Adam. God breathed no breath of life into her, to make her "a living soul," as he did into her husband. Therefore, when Adam saw her he said, "She shall be called Woman, because she (her whole self, not her body only) was taken out of man." If, then, the soul of the first woman sprung from the soul of Adam, as her body did from his, what reason is there to believe that the souls of their posterity are produced by immediate creation?

(3.) It is admitted by all that, under God, we receive *life* from our parents. But if so we must derive from them our *soul*, which is the *principle of life ;* for "the body without the *spirit* is dead."

(4.) Other animals have power to propagate animated beings like themselves. Why, then, should man be but half a father? When did God restrict him to the propagation of the mere *shell* of his person—the body without the soul? It surely was not when "he blessed him and said, "Be fruitful and multiply." When he spoke thus he must have addressed the soul as well as the body; for the body alone is incapable of either understanding or executing a command. It is, therefore, highly reasonable to conclude that the *whole* man, by virtue of the Divine appointment and blessing, can "be fruitful and multiply," and that our souls as well as our bodies come into existence by *traduction*.

(5.) Hence Moses informs us that "Adam begat a son in his own likeness, after his image." But had he generated a body without a soul he would not have begotten "a son in his own likeness," since he was not a mere mortal body, but a fallen *embodied spirit.*

The usual objection to the doctrine of traduction is, that it tends to materialism. But this arises from a mistaken view of that in which the procreation of a human being lies. It does not consist in the production out of nothing of either of the parts in man's compound nature, but only in the uniting of them substantially with one another. As the matter of the body is not then first made, so neither is the soul by that act first produced. The creation of both belongs to a higher power; and then the question is, whether all souls were created in Adam, and are transmitted by a law which is peculiar to themselves. Since, therefore, the *traduction* of the human soul is more rational and scriptural than its *immediate creation,* the objection which we have been considering is shown to be groundless. But,

2. It is objected to the doctrine of man's total depravity, that we often discover *virtuous traits of character in unregenerate men.*

To this our reply is, that all the moral excellence which can be justly claimed for unregenerate men may be easily accounted for without giving up the doctrine of man's total depravity. In doing this we remark,

(1.) That there is often the appearance of virtue where none really exists. It is well known that various vices may, from their very nature, to some extent counteract one another, and thus produce a kind of negative virtue. The passion of avarice may lead men to the practice of industry, and the love of fame may incline them to perform acts of ostentatious benevolence; but in neither case can there be any real virtue, because the principle of action is not spiritually good.

(2.) That selfish motives may sometimes lead men to a course of conduct which may seem to be morally good. A mere love of self-interest induces many to endeavor to establish a good moral character on account of the standing and influence which it will give them in society. All this, however, is perfectly consistent with the view which we have taken of man's moral corruption.

(3.) That the character of men often appears much better than it really is, merely because surrounding circumstances have not called into action the latent principles of the soul. They may have in them the seeds of a thousand evils, but these may lie measurably dormant for the want of exciting causes to call them forth.

(4.) That it does not follow, from the doctrine of man's moral corruption, that there should be nothing virtuous and praiseworthy among men until they are truly regenerated. It is to be remembered that we are not left to ourselves, and to the unrestrained influence of our corrupt nature. In consequence of the atonement made by Christ, a day of grace is given to all men, during which the Holy Spirit operates upon their hearts in various ways, repressing the risings of their native depravity, and moving them to that which is good. In some cases the issue is life, in others an aggravated death. But in nearly all this Divine influence cannot fail to correct and prevent much evil, and to bring into existence some good, though it may be as the morning cloud and the early dew, and to produce civil and social virtues. None of these effects, however, are to be placed to the account of *nature*, or used to soften our views of its entire alienation from God; but they are to be ascribed to the working of Divine *grace*, which is ever employed in seeking and saving the lost, and which alone is the cause of all that is really and spiritually good among men.

CHAPTER IV.

MAN'S MORAL AGENCY.

THE *moral agency of man* is a subject of great interest and importance. Indeed, if men were not free moral agents their actions could not be either virtuous or vicious; they could neither deserve praise nor be justly liable to blame.

Philosophers of every age since the earliest date of metaphysical science have examined this subject with a greater or less degree of particularity, but it must be acknowledged that much of their labor has tended more to darken counsel than to place truth before the mind in a clear and intelligible light. Their metaphysical speculations and finespun theories have so bewildered the public mind that it is exceedingly difficult to exhibit the subject in a clear, concise, and satisfactory manner. Difficult, however, as the task may be, we will try to present such views of man's moral agency as will be found to accord with the word of God and with the principles of sound philosophy. Let us then consider, *first*, its nature; and *secondly*, the proofs by which it is established.

I. THE NATURE OF MAN'S MORAL AGENCY.

A *moral agent* is one who is capable of performing such voluntary actions as are determined by some rule or law to be good or evil. "Moral good and evil," says Locke, "is the conformity or disagreement of our voluntary actions to some law whereby good or evil is drawn upon us from the will or power of the law-maker."

In regard to the simple question of man's *agency* we presume there will be no controversy. We do not contend that he is an *independent* agent. In this sense agency belongs to God alone, for he only possesses the power of action in an underived and independent sense. All created agents derived this power from the Creator, and are dependent on him for its continuance; yet in the exercise of this derived power they are capable of acting. Thus they are distinguished from inanimate matter, which moves only as it is moved by some external force.

That man is a *moral* agent will not be denied by any who believe the holy Scriptures. By these inspired records his actions are determined to be either right or wrong. He is everywhere regarded as being capable of virtue or vice, and susceptible of praise or blame. But in regard to that liberty or freedom which man possesses in the performance of moral actions, very different views have been entertained. Though these views are both numerous and variant, yet upon close examination it will be found that they all harmonize with one or the other of two general or leading theories—that of *necessity*, on the one hand, or that of *free moral agency* on the other. We will notice,

1. *The doctrine of necessity.*—Those who advocate this theory teach that the actions of men are in some way so overruled and directed that they cannot be different from what they are. There is, to be sure, a wide difference in the manner in which this class of writers express themselves upon this subject. Some do it in the most unequivocal terms, openly denying that man has any control whatever over his moral conduct. Others, from the language which they employ, seem to espouse the doctrine of moral liberty in its highest sense; but when their definitions and teachings are scrutinized they are found to result in the doctrine of necessity, or, at least, to be reconciled to it.

Under the general term of *necessity* there are three different schemes of doctrine included, which we should carefully distinguish. The first scheme is called *materialistic fatalism;* the second, *Stoical fatalism;* and the third is that which is now commonly distinguished from the two former as the theory of *moral necessity.*

Materialistic fatalism is based upon the fundamental doctrine that there is nothing in the universe besides matter and motion. This scheme, of course, denies the spirituality of God and of the human soul, and discards all moral distinctions. It is surely not necessary to attempt a refutation of so baseless a theory. A mere statement of its doctrines is enough to convince every sober mind of its extreme absurdity.

Stoical fatalism rises above the former in regard to dignity and purity of character. Its fundamental doctrine is that all things, both in heaven and earth, are bound together by an "implex series and concatenation of causes." The advocates of this theory believe in the existence of God, but they regard him merely as the greatest and brightest link in the adamantine chain of universal necessity. According to this scheme, though it includes the notion of moral distinctions, the idea of moral liberty is inconceivable and impossible.

The theory of *moral necessity,* while it harmonizes with the two former schemes in denying moral freedom to *man*, differs from them in maintaining the absolute freedom of GOD. Its fundamental doctrine is that God is the central and all-controlling power of the universe; that from all eternity he decreed whatever should come to pass, including even the deliberations and volitions of men; and that by his own power he now executes his decrees. "We do not, with the Stoics," says Calvin, "imagine a necessity arising from a perpetual concatenation and intrinsic series of causes contained in nature; but we make God the arbiter and governor of all things, who, in his own wisdom, has, from all eternity, decreed what he would do, and now by his own power executes what he decreed."*

The great reformers, Calvin and Luther, while they maintained the absolute freedom of God, denied the freedom of the human will. They allowed, indeed, that man, in his original state, possessed freedom. "I admit," says Luther, "that man's will is free in a certain sense; not because it is now in the same state it was in Paradise, but because it was made free originally, and may, through God's grace, become so again."† Man "was endowed with free-will," says Calvin, "by which, if he had chosen, he might have obtained eternal life."‡ But it is well known that Luther wrote a work on the "Bondage of the Human Will," and that Calvin, in his Institutes, has written a chapter to show that "man, in his present state, is despoiled of freedom of will, and subjected to a miserable slavery." Thus, according to both Luther and Calvin, man was by the fall despoiled of freedom of will.

They admit that man is free from compulsion or restraint, but they repudiate the idea of calling this a freedom of the will. "Lombard at length pronounces," says Calvin, "that we are not therefore possessed of free-will because we have an equal power to do or think either good or evil, but *only because we are free from constraint*. And this liberty is not diminished, although we are corrupt, and slaves of sin, *and capable of doing nothing but sin*. Then man," Calvin proceeds, "will be said to possess free-will in this sense, not that he has an equal free election of good and evil, but because he does evil voluntarily, *and not by constraint*. That, indeed, is true; but what end could it answer to deck out a thing so diminutive with a title so superb?"§ And truly, if Lombard meant nothing more by that liberty for which he contended than mere freedom from external restraint, Calvin might well contemptuously exclaim, "Egregious liberty."

It has come to pass, however, since the days of the great reformers, that philosophers and theologians have decked out this very kind of liberty, this diminutive thing, with the superb title of *the freedom of the will*, and have passed it off for the highest and most glorious liberty of which the human mind can form any conception. In this category we

* Institutes.   † Scott's Luther and Ref., vol. 1, pp. 70, 71.
‡ Institutes, book 1, chap. 15. § Id., book 2, chap. 2.

may place Sir John Locke and President Edwards. The definition of liberty which is given by Locke, in his "Essays on the Human Understanding," is this: "Liberty is a power to act or not to act, according as the mind directs." President Edwards defines liberty to be the "power, opportunity, or advantage that one has to do as he pleases."* That these two definitions are in perfect harmony will be admitted by every one who weighs the terms in which they are stated. They both teach the doctrine that human liberty consists in a power to act according to the dictates of the mind.

We admit that this theory of liberty rests upon high and distinguished authority; but believing it to be at war with the true doctrine of man's moral agency, we will not shrink from the task of pointing out some of its most obvious errors and defects. And here we may remark,

(1.) That the definition of liberty in which these philosophers agree is no definition of *moral* liberty—it touches not the real question at issue. It evidently confounds moral liberty with the freedom of bodily actions. These philosophers seem to take for granted that if a man has power to conform his actions to the dictates or directions of his mind he possesses moral liberty in its highest sense. But who does not see that if liberty consists in the power to act as the mind directs, or in the power to do as we please, that it can relate to bodily actions alone, as distinguished from those of the mind? In other words, it is made to consist in the unrestrained opportunity of following the directions or volitions of the mind, but not in the power of the mind itself to originate its own volitions.

This may be a correct view of *civil* liberty but not of *moral*. Civil liberty consists in the power or opportunity of doing what we please and of going where we please, so as not to infringe upon the rights of others. Here the external actions of the agents are mainly considered without any reference to the manner in which their volitions originate. In this sense the body might be free to follow the determinations of the mind, though the mind itself should be fast bound in the chains of absolute necessity. This kind of liberty, therefore, has nothing to do with the *freedom of human volitions*, but is confined entirely to the *power or opportunity of acting in accordance with them.*

That this is the only kind of freedom contended for by President Edwards may be seen from his own language. In explaining what he means by the term *liberty*, he says that it is the "power and opportunity for one to do and conduct as he will, or according to his choice; without taking into the meaning of the word anything of the cause of that choice, or at all considering how the person came to have such a volition." In whatever manner a man may come by his choice, "yet, if he is able, and there is nothing in the way to hinder his pursuing and executing his will, the man is perfectly free according to the primary and common notion

* Inquiry, part 1, sec. 5.

of freedom."* This, we repeat it, may be natural or civil liberty, but it cannot be moral liberty. It is that kind of liberty which may be associated with the most absolute fatalism in regard to the volitions of the human mind.

(2.) Another difficulty in this definition of freedom is, that it claims for man what no man ever possessed: a "power to do as he pleases, or as his mind directs." If this is freedom, then it is to be found nowhere but in God; for no one but an independent and omnipotent being can "do as he pleases." Suppose my child falls into the water, where he is in danger of being drowned. The feelings of my nature strongly impel me to save him. Accordingly, I exert myself with all my might to accomplish the desired object, but without being successful. Have I here the power to do as I please? Doubtless I have not, and consequently, according to the definition of President Edwards, I am not at liberty to save my child. I know it may be said that my immediate will is not to save my child, but only to exert myself in order to save him. Such, however, is evidently not the case. My first and governing intention is to save him. This lies at the foundation of all my exertions; for if I did not will to save my child I could not voluntarily exert myself to that end. It follows, then, that no man has the power to "do as he pleases;" and consequently that, in this respect, the definition which we are considering implies too much. But,

(3.) A man may have the power, in certain cases, to "do as he pleases," while at the same time he has no liberty to do otherwise. Suppose a man to be conducted into a room where he meets a friend whom he had long desired to see. Without his knowledge he is locked in; but he is so delighted with his company that he continues in the room most willingly, without any desire to leave it. Will any one pretend to say that his staying with his friend is not voluntary? We think not, and yet he has no liberty to do otherwise. We see, therefore, that a man may do as he pleases in some cases when he has no liberty to act in any other way. Consequently in such cases he cannot be free, unless we confound all language, and say that liberty and necessity are the same thing.

From what we have seen, it is very evident that there is no real difference between the views of President Edwards in regard to human liberty and those of Luther and Calvin. They all agree that in order to man's accountability he must be free from compulsion. Thus, suppose a man wills to perform an external action, but is prevented by some outward restraint; or suppose he is constrained to do an action against his will, he is said to be under compulsion, co-action, or natural necessity, and cannot, therefore, in either case be held accountable. The reformers held this freedom from co-action or compulsion to be consistent with *necessity*, so far as our volitions are concerned, and accord-

* Inquiry, part 1, sec. 5.

ingly they denied the freedom of the human will. President Edwards takes up this same doctrine of freedom from co-action, and expands it into his far-famed theory of the free-agency and accountability of man, a theory which is perfectly consistent with the most absolute necessity in regard to the will itself.

That we do not misrepresent his views in this matter his own language will show. He tells us that "the plain and obvious meaning of the words *freedom* and *liberty*, in common speech, is *power, opportunity, or advantage, that any one has to do as he pleases.* Or, in other words, his being free from hinderance or impediment in the way of doing or conducting in any respect as he wills. And the contrary to liberty, whatever name we call that by, is a person's being hindered or unable to conduct as he will, or being necessitated to do otherwise." Again, "there are two things that are contrary to this which is called liberty in common speech. One is *constraint;* the same is otherwise called force, compulsion, and co-action, which is a person's being necessitated to do a thing contrary to his will. The other is *restraint;* which is his being hindered, and not having power to do according to his will."*

These quotations show that the liberty for which Edwards contends is merely a freedom from co-action and not from necessity. It has no relation to the question as to how a man comes by his volitions; whether they are put forth by the mind itself without being necessitated, or whether they are necessarily produced by some other cause. "Let the person come by his volition or choice HOW HE WILL," says Edwards; let it happen without a cause, let it be determined by an antecedent volition, let it be produced by a direct exertion of Almighty power; "yet if he is able, and there is nothing in the way to hinder his pursuing and executing his will, the man is fully and perfectly free, according to the primary and common notion of freedom."† We see, therefore, that this scheme of moral agency claims for man only that freedom from compulsion or restraint which allows him to act according to his own volitions; and that, so far as these volitions themselves are concerned, it is perfectly reconcilable with the most absolute scheme of necessity or fatalism that the world has ever seen.

Accordingly, it is assumed by Edwards that our volitions are the passive and necessary effects of motives. He tells us that "every act of the will whatever is excited by some motive;" that "if every act of the will is excited by a motive, then that motive is the cause of the act of the will;" and that "volition is *necessary*, and is not from any self-determining power in the will."‡ Thus the human mind is reduced to the condition of a mere machine, capable only of acting as it is acted upon by some external force; and if this is the real state of the case, as the advocates of philosophical necessity must allow, then we have no more to do with our volitions than with the circulation of our blood.

---

* Inquiry, part 1, sec. 5.   † Ibid.   ‡ Id., part 2, sec. 10.

But as this theory is too absurd to be adopted by any one who believes in moral distinctions, we will direct our attention,

2. *To what we conceive to be the true doctrine of free moral agency.*— A *free agent* is one who is capable of acting without being necessitated to do so by some cause extrinsic to himself.

That such an agent may exist cannot be denied without denying to God the original power to produce creation. It is admitted that he only existed from eternity. And, as creation was produced by the act of God when nothing had previously existed but himself, it necessarily follows that he could not have been impelled to the work of creation by any extrinsic cause. To suppose that God cannot put forth an act without being impelled thereto by a power back of his own, is to suppose a power greater than his, on which the exercise of his omnipotence depends. By a parity of reason we should be compelled to suppose another power still back of that, and so on, *ad infinitum*, which would be both absurd and impious. Hence we are forced to the conclusion that God is a free agent in the fullest sense of our definition, being self-active, and wholly independent of all extrinsic influences whatever.

Now, it is not difficult to conceive that God should create moral agents, bearing his image in this, namely, the possession of a *self-active power*—agents who are capable of acting without being necessitated to act, by some efficient cause beyond themselves. Nor is it more difficult to conceive that man possesses self-active power than it is to conceive that such a power belongs to God; for though, in the former case, this power is limited and dependent, and in the latter infinite and independent, yet in both, so far as the simple question of free-agency is concerned, it is the same. We must admit the possibility that man should be endowed with self-active power, for to deny this is to deny the omnipotence of God. It follows, therefore, that the great question in regard to free-agency is, whether man, in the exercise of that power with which God has endowed him, is capable of acting, without being efficiently caused to do so by anything extrinsic to himself. If he possesses this self-active power he is a free agent, and is properly the author of his own actions; but if not, he is no more the real author of what he does than a passive machine.

When we claim for man a self-active power in the exercise of volition, we do not mean that the will is altogether uninfluenced by motives and external circumstances. The mind is the efficient agent that wills; but the act itself is performed according to the laws which properly belong to a self-moving and accountable being. Though motives and external circumstances can exercise no efficient agency in reference to the will, yet, speaking figuratively, they may be properly said to influence the mind, and to be conditions or occasions of the mind's action in willing. In this sense they may be said to influence the *will;* but they cannot exercise over it an absolute and irresistible controlling influence. In no case can they efficiently cause an act of volition without destroying its freedom.

Necessitarians seem to have taken for granted, in their arguments upon this subject, that there is no medium between absolute necessity and perfect independency; but the true doctrine of man's free moral agency is at an equal distance from both these extremes. We deny, on the one hand, that the volitions of men are so determined by things external to themselves as to be fast bound in the chain of absolute necessity; and on the other, that they are so perfectly disconnected with surrounding circumstances and things external as to be entirely uninfluenced by them. The point in controversy, therefore, between the advocates of necessity and the defenders of free agency is, not whether man is influenced, in the exercise of volition, by motives and external circumstances, for this is admitted by all; but whether his will is thus necessarily and absolutely controlled, so that his volitions could not be different from what they are.

It is a fact of great importance in the investigation of this subject that there are three leading attributes or faculties of the human mind which are clearly distinguishable from each other, namely, the *intelligence*, the *sensibility*, and the *will*. In other words, the human mind is capable of *thought*, of *feeling*, and of *volition*. Now it will be found, on examination, that the phenomena which pertain to these .several departments of capability possess different characteristics, according to the attribute or faculty to which they belong. Of these differences we must form clear conceptions, if we would avoid that obscurity and confusion in which the philosophy of the will is mostly involved.

Let us suppose, for the sake of illustration, that I fix my attention upon an apple. I conclude, in my own mind, that it is round and red. This decision or judgment of the mind is a state of the *intelligence*—a state which does not depend on any effort of my own; for I could not possibly come to any other conclusion respecting the form and color of the apple if I would. Hence this decision, this judgment, this state of the intelligence, is necessitated; and so also is every other perception or state of the intelligence. But while I continue to look upon the apple, I experience a strong desire to eat it. This desire or appetite is a state of the *sensibility*; and in this case, as well as in all our feelings, the mind is as clearly passive as in the former. It follows, therefore, that every state of the intelligence and of the sensibility is a necessary result of its proximate cause, and for this reason it cannot be free.

Again, though I have experienced the judgment that the apple is round and red, and have felt the desire to eat it, yet, hitherto, I have put forth no voluntary effort, except in fixing my attention upon it. But now I determine to eat the apple, and accordingly this determination is carried into effect. Here, then, is an entirely new phenomenon.

It is an *effort*, an *act*, a *volition* of the mind; and my consciousness assures me that in this I am free.

If these remarks are just, it will at once be seen how important it is that we should distinguish the *will* from both the intelligence and the sensibility, in order that we may perceive its true nature, and wherein its liberty consists. Necessitarians have generally confounded these distinct faculties of the human mind; and as their theory is based upon this false psychology, it is not strange that they should deny the proper freedom of the will. "By whatever name we call the act of the will," says Edwards, "choosing, refusing, approving, disapproving, liking, disliking, embracing, rejecting, determining, directing, commanding, forbidding, inclining or being averse, being pleased or displeased with—all may be reduced to this of choosing."* Thus it is manifest, according to the psychology of this author, that the phenomena of the intelligence, the sensibility, and the will are identified, as are also these faculties themselves. With him approving, liking, being pleased or displeased with, and willing, are all the same. His psychology admits of no distinction between the impression which is made on a man's intelligence or sensibility by the presence of an apple, and that act of the will by which he puts forth his hand to eat it. "I humbly conceive," says Edwards, "that the affections of the soul are not properly distinguished from the will, as though there were two faculties."† And again, "all acts of the will are truly acts of the affections."‡ Thus this great metaphysician, by confounding things which are perfectly distinct in their nature, has been led to the adoption of views respecting the human will which are contrary to truth, involved in obscurity, and self-contradictory.

We readily admit that in the perception of truth the intelligence is perfectly passive. The mind can no more avoid the conclusion that two and two are equal to four, than it can determine that white is black, or that light is darkness. We admit also that every state of the sensibility is a passive impression—a necessitated phenomenon of the human mind. No matter what fact or truth may be presented to the mind either by its own voluntary attention or by any other agency, the impression which it makes upon the sensibility is beyond the control of the will, except by refusing to give it the attention of the mind. But in the act of willing the case is very different. Here the mind is perfectly free, because it possesses a power of acting over which there is no controlling power either within or without itself. This is what we understand by the free moral agency of man. Let us consider,

II. The Proofs by which Man's Free Moral Agency is established.

In defending the proposition that man is a free moral agent, we may reply,

1. *Upon our own consciousness.*—By this we mean that knowledge

* Edwards's Works, vol. 2, p. 16.   † Ibid., vol. 4, p. 82.   ‡ Ibid.

which we have of what passes in our own minds. Thus, when we are joyful or sad, when we love or hate, when we hope or fear, we are immediately conscious of the fact. This kind of knowledge is not derived from an investigation of testimony, nor does it result from a course of reasoning, but rises spontaneously in the mind. In regard to things of which we are conscious arguments are superfluous. They can neither strengthen our convictions, nor cause us to doubt. We cannot persuade a man whose heart is elated with joy that he is at the same time oppressed with grief; nor can we convince any one who is writhing under the influence of a painful disease that he is in the enjoyment of perfect health. The reason is that consciousness carries with it its own demonstration, and from it there is no appeal.

What, then, is the testimony of consciousness in regard to the freedom of the human will? It is evidently this, at least, that the mind is not controlled in its volitions by any extrinsic cause. Who can convince me that I have not the power to write, or to refrain from writing; to sit still, or to rise up and walk? And this consciousness of a self-determining power of the mind is universal. A false philosophy may occasionally confuse the understanding in regard to this subject, but still the conviction comes home to every man with resistless force, that he has within himself the power of volition, and that he exercises this power freely.

That we are free to choose either good or evil, and not impelled in our moral actions by any law of absolute necessity, is a position which accords with every man's consciousness, a position which we can no more rationally doubt than we can doubt our own existence. Hence it is that all men have a sense of blame when they do wrong, and of approbation when they do right. If you convince a man who is charged with the commission of a crime that the act was unavoidable, he can no more blame himself for having committed it than he can blame the tree which fell upon his neighbor and killed him. Remorse for past offenses depends, for its very existence, upon a conviction that we are morally free. We conclude, therefore, that our consciousness demonstrates the freedom of the human will. To set aside its testimony would be as unphilosophical as to conclude that it is midnight when we behold the full blaze of the meridian sun. But we argue this doctrine,

2. *From the general history of the world.*—If we turn our attention to any period of the world's history, we will find among all nations, in their language and common modes of speech, terms and phrases which clearly indicate their general belief in the freedom of the human will. Terms expressive of blame and of praise are everywhere employed, clearly recognizing the principle that men have power to control their own actions, and that when they do wrong they are blamed because they *might* and should do otherwise. No one is ever seriously blamed for doing an act which is believed to be unavoidable. The very

idea of blame, therefore, implies the principle for which we are contending.

Again, the laws of all civilized nations punish criminals upon the supposition that they have power to control their own moral conduct. Suppose a man to be accused of homicide. If it could be made appear that in the act in question he was not a voluntary agent, but was constrained by an external force which he had not the power to resist, there is not a government upon the earth that would find him guilty, and for this simple reason, that in the event he was merely a passive instrument.

We know that rewards and punishments are connected with the statutory provisions of all civilized governments, and that they are constantly held out before the community. But why should these sanctions of law be thus exhibited if men are not free moral agents? Can these motives induce men voluntarily to conform their actions to law, if they really possess no such voluntary power? But perhaps it may be said that these motives are designed to determine the will itself, independent of any active agency in the man. This, however, cannot be granted; for if motives are to determine the will, why is the man required to attend to the motives, to weigh them carefully, and to make a correct decision in reference to their real weight? We see, therefore, that all men in all ages of the world, and in all places, have regarded themselves as free moral agents.

If man has not the power to control his own actions, why is he censured for any crime that he may commit? " Why, we might ask, are jails and penitentiaries and various modes of punishment, more or less severe, everywhere prevalent in civilized lands? If the advocates of necessity really believe in the truth of their system let them be consistent, and go throughout the civilized world and plead for the destruction of all terms of language expressive of blame or praise; let them decry the unjustifiable prejudice of nations, by which benevolence and virtue have been applauded, and selfishness and vice contemned. Let them proclaim it abroad that the robber and the murderer are as innocent as the infant or the saint, since all men only act as they are necessarily acted upon; and let them teach all nations to abolish at once and forever every description of punishment for crime or misdemeanor. Such would be the consistent course for sincere necessitarians."* Again, we argue the free moral agency of man,

3. *From the Divine administration toward him, as exhibited in the Holy Scriptures.*—Here we shall see that revelation beautifully harmonizes with nature; and that the evidences of our free-agency which are derived from experience and observation are abundantly confirmed by the book of God. In presenting the argument, which is drawn from the Divine administration, we may remark,

* Ralston's Elements, p. 248.

(1.) That God has placed man under moral government. Immediately after his creation a moral law was given him to keep, and a severe penalty was annexed to its transgression. If man had not been created a free agent, to have given him a moral law for the government of his actions would have been inconsistent with the Divine wisdom; for a moral law commanding what is right and prohibiting what is wrong, can only be adapted to beings capable of doing both right and wrong. Hence we argue, that as God placed man under a moral law he must have been a free moral agent, capable alike of obedience and of disobedience.

To this conclusion we are also conducted by the history of the fall. To suppose that all the volitions and actions of men are absolutely determined by causes over which they have no control, is to suppose that the sin of Adam was absolutely necessary. But to suppose that the penalty of the law was inflicted upon the first transgressor for an act which he could not possibly avoid, is to suppose the Divine administration to be unjust and cruel. Can any rational man believe that God would place Adam in such circumstances as would render his act of disobedience absolutely necessary, and then say to him, "In the day thou eatest thereof thou shalt surely die?" Most certainly not. The whole history of the fall, if viewed in the light of reason, of common-sense, and of what we know of the character and government of God, proclaims, in language clear and forcible, that man is a free moral agent.

Though man is now in a fallen condition, and robbed of his primitive glory, yet he is still under moral government. God has given him a law for the rule of his life. He enforces this law by promises and threatenings, thus proving most clearly that man is in a state of probation. But this implies that he is a free moral agent—that he is capable of conforming his actions to the rule of life under which God has placed him. For, if the volitions and actions of men are necessitated by some power over which they have no control, to suppose them to be in a state of probation is most absurd. We might as well ascribe a probationary state to the beasts of the field, or the fowls of the air. If, then, we are in a state of trial we are free moral agents.

(2.) The freedom of the human will is everywhere acknowledged in the Scriptures. "I call heaven and earth to record this day against you, that I have set before you life and death, blessing and cursing: therefore *choose* life, that both thou and thy seed may live." Deut. xxx, 19. "*Choose* you this day whom you will serve." Josh. xxiv, 15. To *choose* is to *determine* or to *will;* and men are here exhorted to choose for themselves. But if the will is not free—if every volition of the human mind is necessarily determined by a necessary cause, such exhortations are nothing better than solemn mockery.

Our Lord said to the Jews, "How often would I have gathered thy children together, even as a hen gathereth her chickens under her wings, and ye *would not!*" Matt. xviii, 37. And again, "Ye *will not* come to me, that ye might have life." John v, 40. These, and numerous other passages of a similar import, refer expressly to the will of men as being under their own control. And on no other principle could the Saviour of the world upbraid men in terms of the deepest solemnity, and denounce against them the severest punishment for the obstinacy of their will. According to the notion of President Edwards and other necessitarians all our volitions are necessarily fixed by antecedent causes; but if so, they are no more under our control than the motions of the heavenly bodies. It does not require the eye of a philosopher, however, to see the antagonism between this theory and the teachings of the Holy Scriptures, and it cannot be difficult to determine which we should adopt. But we may remark,

(3.) That God holds men to an account for their moral conduct. It is the doctrine of the Bible that "every one of us shall give account of himself to God;" that "we must all appear before the judgment-seat of Christ; that every one may receive the things done in his body, according to that he hath done, whether it be good or bad." These and many other Scriptures clearly set forth the doctrine of a general judgment and of future rewards and punishments. But if man were not *free* in his volitions and moral actions, how could we reconcile the retributions of the great day with the attributes of God? As well might we suppose that an all-wise and merciful Being would reward men for breathing the surrounding atmosphere, or punish them for permitting the blood to circulate in their veins. As well might we suppose that he would punish or reward the fish for swimming in the ocean, or the birds for flying in the air!

President Edwards and others have attempted to reconcile the doctrine of necessity with the proper freedom and accountability of man. They have contended that though the will is necessarily determined, yet man is properly a free moral agent merely because he has a will, acts voluntarily, and is free from constraint. But to say that he enjoys freedom merely because he is at liberty to obey his will, is as absurd as to contend that the man who is subject to the edicts of a cruel tyrant enjoys freedom in a civil sense merely because he is at liberty to obey the laws under which he is placed. Will any man contend that civil liberty consists in the privilege of obeying law? Surely not; for this would be to assume that a man may enjoy civil liberty and at the same time be a slave. No one will deny that even slaves have liberty to obey the law under which they are placed: but can they be persuaded that for this reason they are properly free? We know they cannot. And yet this is the very kind of freedom that President Edwards ascribes to man in a moral sense. The will, according to his theory, is unalterably fixed; but as man has the liberty to do as he wills, he is therefore a free moral agent, and accountable to God for his moral actions.

We deny, however, that this kind of liberty can render its possessor an accountable moral agent. "Indeed, there is no difference between the liberty attributed to man by the learned President of Princeton College, and that possessed by a block of marble as it falls to the earth when let loose from the top of a tower. We may call the man *free*, because he may act according to his will or inclination while that will is determined by necessity; but has not the marble precisely the same freedom? It has perfect liberty to fall; it is not constrained by natural force to move in any other direction. If it falls necessarily, even so, on the principle of Edwards, man acts necessarily. If it be said that the marble cannot avoid falling as it does, even so man cannot avoid acting according to his will, just as he does. If it be said that he has no disposition, and makes no effort to act contrary to his will, even so the marble has no inclination to fall in any other direction than it does. The marble moves *freely*, because it has no inclination to move otherwise; but it moves necessarily, because irresistibly compelled by the law of gravitation. Just so man acts freely, because he acts according to his will; but he acts necessarily, because he can no more change his will than he can make a world. And thus it is plain, that, although necessitarians may say they believe in free-agency and man's accountability, it is a freedom just such as pertains to lifeless matter.

"If, according to Edwards, man is free, and justly accountable for his actions, merely because he acts according to his own will when he has no control over that will, upon the same principle the maniac would be a free, accountable agent. If, in a paroxysm of madness, he murders his father, he acts according to his will. It is a voluntary act, and necessitarians cannot excuse him because his will was not under his control; for, in the view of their system, it was as much so as the will of any man in any case possibly can be. The truth is, it is an abuse of language to call that freedom which binds fast in the chains of necessity. Acting voluntarily amounts to no liberty at all, if I cannot possibly act otherwise than I do. The question is, not whether I have a will, or whether I may act according to my will, but what determines the will? This is the point to be settled in the question of free-agency. It is admitted that the will controls the actions; but who controls the will? As the will controls the actions, it necessarily follows that whatever controls the will must be accountable for the actions. Whoever controls the will must be the proper author of all that necessarily results from it, and consequently should be held accountable for the same."[*]

From the whole of this reasoning we feel ourselves safe in the conclusion that the theory of moral necessity cannot be reconciled with man's accountability and the retributions of the judgment day. Men may talk as they please about moral agency and the freedom of the human will;

[*] Ralston's Elements, pp. 252, 253.

but unless man possesses a self-controlling power over his own moral actions, he can no more be justly rewardable or punishable than the beasts that roam in the forest. This controlling power can only be exerted in acts of volition, and hence we contend that the *will of man is free.*

CHAPTER V.

MAN'S MORAL AGENCY: OBJECTIONS.

AGAINST the doctrine of the free moral agency of man, as presented and defended in the preceding chapter, several objections have been urged. We are told that this doctrine is absurd in itself, that it is conflictive with the established doctrine of motives, and that it is irreconcilable with the foreknowledge of God. To each of these grave objections we propose to give our candid attention and to return a suitable reply.

I. IT IS ALLEGED THAT OUR DOCTRINE OF FREE-AGENCY IS ABSURD IN ITSELF.

President Edwards has argued at great length to prove the absurdity of the doctrine, that the human mind in the exercise of volition is self-active. He alleges that it involves the absurdity either of an infinite series of volitions, or of an effect without a cause. Let us then for a moment examine this supposed dilemma. And,

1. It is here assumed that, according to our theory of the freedom of the human will, every act of volition implies a preceding volition by which it is determined. If this were really our doctrine of free-agency; if it implied, as Edwards supposes it does, that " each active volition is necessarily preceded by another," it would, indeed, involve the notion of an infinite series of volitions, the absurdity of which is so obvious that arguments to prove it are altogether unnecessary. But though this has often been asserted of the Arminian system of moral agency, it has never yet been proved and never can be. Our doctrine is, not that one volition determines another, but that the mind itself, as a living, active, and intelligent agent, puts forth its own volitions. When we speak of *free-will* we do not mean that the will is a distinct *agent* of which freedom is an attribute, but that it is an act of the mind, and that the mind, in the act of willing, is free from the control of any efficient cause extrinsic to itself. In other words, the mind is the active intelligent agent, to whom both freedom and volition belong.

Is it then true that, according to the Arminian doctrine of the self-determining power of the mind, every act of volition must be preceded and determined by another act of volition? We think not. We cannot see why there may not be an act of willing performed by the mind itself without any previous act of volition to determine it. To say that there can be no such free act of the mind; that man, in the possession of those powers with which God has endowed him, and independent of any predetermining cause operating upon him, cannot exercise free volition, is the same as to say that he is a slave to the most absolute fatalism.

But this is not all. To say that the doctrine of a self-active power in the exercise of willing is *absurd in itself*, is as much as to say that there is not a free agent in the universe, for this would lead to the fearful conclusion that even God himself has not the power of free volition, but is moved alone by the impulse of fatality. As it is absurd to suppose that every volition of the human mind is determined by a previous volition, so such a supposition must be equally absurd when applied to God. It must, therefore, be admitted, either that the will of God is efficiently determined by external causes, or that in the exercise of volition he possesses a self-determining power. To suppose that his volitions are efficiently determined by external causes, is in effect to suppose that he cannot be the Creator of all things. For, before he exerted creative power he must have willed to do so; but as nothing then existed external to himself, that volition could not have been produced by any external cause. It follows, therefore, that it must have originated in his own self-active nature.

If, then, the Divine mind can will freely without being impelled to do so, either by a previous act of volition or by any extrinsic cause, to suppose that the human mind possesses a similar power cannot be absurd in itself. And if God possesses in himself the power of free volition, the only question is, whether he can confer this exalted ability on created beings. To deny that he possesses this power himself is to deny his independence and free-agency; and to deny that he can confer it on creatures is to deny his omnipotence. But we may proceed to observe,

2. If we avoid the absurdity of an infinite series of volitions by denying that one act of volition is preceded and determined by another, then we are told that, according to our theory of the self-determining power of the mind, volition is an effect without a cause. In replying to this feature of the objection, if we would not dispute about mere words, we should know precisely what is meant by the terms *cause* and *effect*.

President Edwards tells us that he sometimes uses the term *cause* "to signify any antecedent, either natural or moral, positive or negative, on which an event so depends that it is the ground and reason, either in whole or in part, why it is rather than not, or why it is as it is rather than otherwise."[*] So also he tells us that, in accordance with this definition of a cause, he "sometimes uses the word *effect* for the consequence of another thing which is perhaps rather an occasion than a cause, most properly speaking."[†] But when he employs the term *cause*

* Inquiry, part 2, sec. 3.   † Ibid.

in what he regards to be its proper sense, he uses it "to signify only that which has a positive efficiency or influence to produce a thing or bring it to pass."* In other words, he uses the term to indicate what is properly called an *efficient* cause. This is the sense in which he is to be understood when he speaks of motives as being the cause of volition. Consequently, when he calls volition an *effect*, his meaning must be that it is the correlative of an efficient cause.

But now let us ask, Is it indeed true that volition is an *effect?* If we mean by the term whatever comes to pass, of course volition is an effect, for no one can deny that volitions come to pass. Or, if we include in the definition of the term everything which has a sufficient reason and ground of its existence, it will certainly embrace the idea of volition; for, under certain circumstances, the human mind furnishes a sufficient reason and ground for the existence of volition. But if we take the term in its proper sense, as the correlative of an efficient cause, the sense in which it is evidently employed in the objection, we may unhesitatingly deny that volition is an *effect*.

There are no two things in nature which are more perfectly distinct than action and passion. When an effect is produced in anything by the action or influence of something else, the object in which the effect is produced is wholly passive in regard to it. An effect cannot be the act of that in which it is produced, because it results wholly from that which produces it. To say, then, that a thing acts, is the same as to say that its act is not produced by the action or influence of anything else. To suppose that an act is produced by an efficient cause, is to suppose it to be a passive effect, and therefore no act at all.

If these remarks are correct, it will necessarily follow that an act of the mind cannot be the effect of an efficient cause. The ideas of action and passion, of cause and effect, are opposite, and contrary the one to the other. Hence it is absurd to assert that the mind may be caused to act, or that a volition can be produced by anything acting upon the mind as an efficient cause. It is in this restricted sense that we use the term in question when we deny that volition is an *effect*.

It is perhaps impossible to gain a clear conception of the nature of volition, while we continue to view it in the light of that relation which an effect sustains to its efficient cause. The reason is, that volition involves no such relation, and to view it as an effect is to look at it in the light of a false psychology. We know it has been said, and very generally believed, that "all things fall under the one or the other of the two following relations : the relation between subject and attribute, or the relation between cause and effect." It is in this last category that volitions are supposed to be included; but truth requires that they should be placed under a very different relation, namely, the relation of *agent* and *action*. Unless this relation be admitted, and clearly distin-

* Inquiry, part 2, sec. 3.

guished from that of cause and effect, it will be impossible that we should rightly understand the phenomena of the will. Indeed, it may be safely affirmed that the true philosophy of volition is not to be determined by abstract considerations, or alone by the power of words, because it is not so much a question of logic as of psychology. If, therefore, we would really understand the phenomena of the will, we must not undertake to accomplish the end by a mere process of reasoning. We must fix the mind upon its own inward workings, and subject our volitions to a rigid investigation in the light of consciousness.

What, then, is the testimony of consciousness in regard to the nature of volition? Does it appear to be the passive result of a previous act of the mind, or of motive, or of anything else? In other words, is it properly an *effect?* President Edwards has more than once told us that "the mind can be the cause of no *effect*, except by a preceding act of the mind;" that "an effect results from the action or influence of its cause," and that "nothing is any further an effect than as it proceeds from that action or influence." Does our idea of volition correspond with this notion of an *effect?* Does it appear to us that volition, like the motion of body, is the passive result of something else? Most assuredly not. Volition is action itself, and not the result of action. It is an act of the mind, and not a passive state. It is a determination, and not that which is determined. It is itself an original producing cause, and not a produced effect. He, therefore, who reflects upon this subject in the light of experience can hardly fail to see that there is a clear and manifest distinction between an ACT and an EFFECT.

Now if volition is *not an effect*, then it will follow that our theory of the self-active power of the mind *does not* involve the absurdity of an effect without a cause; for it does not at all acknowledge the relation of cause and effect in the exercise of volition, but only that of *agent* and *action.* We readily allow that there is in the powers and capabilities of the human mind a sufficient ground or reason for the exercise of volition, but we deny that it is efficiently caused either by a previous volition or by anything else. Thus we think that the doctrine of man's free moral agency is successfully vindicated from the charge of absurdity and self-contradiction.

II. IT IS OBJECTED THAT THE LIBERTARIAN VIEW OF THIS SUBJECT IS CONFLICTIVE WITH THE DOCTRINE OF MOTIVES.

Necessitarians of every class have uniformly regarded motives as being the efficient cause of volition. Dr. Hartley contends that the thoughts and feelings of the soul result from the various vibrations of the brain, and that these vibrations are produced by the influence of motives or surrounding circumstances. He frankly admits that his theory implies "the necessity of human actions," and says, "I am sorry for it, but I cannot help it." Lord Kames represents the universe as "one vast machine composed of innumerable wheels, all closely linked together, and moving as they are moved." He considers man as "one wheel fixed in the middle of a vast automaton, moving just as necessarily as the sun, moon, or earth." President Edwards represents "motives and surrounding objects as reaching through the senses to a finely wrought nervous system, and by the impressions made there necessarily producing thought, volition, and action, according to the fixed laws of cause and effect."

Thus it is assumed, by the advocates of philosophical necessity, that volition is the passive and unavoidable result of motives and surrounding circumstances, or in other words, that it is necessarily determined by the strongest motive. If this is what we are to understand by the doctrine of motives, we are ready to admit the truth of the objection and to declare our opposition to any such doctrine.

But here it may be proper to inquire, What do necessitarians mean by the strongest motive? Is it the motive which has the most weight and importance in itself? Surely not. To say, in this proper sense of the phrase, that the will is always determined by the strongest motive, is the same as to say that it is always determined by the best reason; for motive, being but a reason of action considered in the mind, the best reason, being in the nature of things the strongest, must always predominate. But this is evidently contrary to fact and experience. If it were not, all men would act reasonably and none foolishly; or, at least, there would be no faults among them but those of the understanding, none of the heart and affections. The weakest reason, however, too generally succeeds when appetite and corrupt affections are present; that is to say, the weakest motive. For if this be not allowed, we must say that under the influence of appetite the weakest reason also appears to be the strongest, which is also false in fact, for then there would be no sins committed against *judgment* and *conviction*. But we cannot deny that many of our sins are of this description.

When necessitarians say that the strongest motive always prevails, do they mean, by the strongest motive, that which has the greatest influence on the mind at the time and under all the circumstances of the case? This is doubtless what they mean. But if so, they only utter this simple truism, that the prevailing motive always prevails—a proposition which no one in his senses will deny. What, then, it may be inquired, is the precise question in controversy between us? It is not whether the mind wills and acts under the influence of motives; for this is freely admitted by every libertarian. But it is simply this: Do motives exert an efficient, absolute, and irresistible influence over the will, so as in all cases to make it necessarily what it is? This is the only point in the doctrine of motives on which the controversy turns. Necessitarians affirm, and libertarians deny; and in support of this denial we offer the following remarks:

1. The doctrine of philosophical necessity is based upon the false foundation that volition is the passive result of motive. Its advocates

assume that there is no difference between mind and matter in regard to the attribute of *passivity*. The notion inculcated is, that motives influence the will just as a weight thrown into an even scale poises it, and inclines the beam. This is the grand metaphysical blunder of necessitarians of every school and of every age. The ancient Manichees, the Stoics, the Atheistic and Deistic philosophers, Spinoza, Hobbes, Voltaire, Hume, and others, adopted this principle; and they have been followed in this confounding of mind and matter by many learned and excellent men, such as President Edwards of Princeton, and President Day of Yale College. Indeed, the whole treatise of Edwards on the "Freedom of the Will" is based on this error. He assumes that the mind, like matter, can act only as it is acted upon; and from assumption he infers that the mind, like matter, is governed by necessity, and that the will is therefore necessarily determined by motives.

It must be admitted either that God has created beings capable of acting without being necessarily caused to act by something else, or that he has not. If he has not created such beings, then it will follow that he himself is the only agent in existence, and that angels and men are no more self-active than a clod of lifeless matter. This conclusion is not only subversive of the distinction between matter and mind, but directly repugnant to the whole tenor of Scripture and to the plainest dictates of common-sense. And yet this is the only view of the subject which accords with the scheme of necessity.

But now let us suppose, according to Scripture and common-sense, that God has endowed his intelligent creatures with a self-moving energy; and that, in the exercise of their derived powers, and independent of the absolute control of anything extrinsic to themselves, they are capable of voluntary action, and it will be easy to see that there is an essential distinction in nature between these intelligent beings and mere lifeless matter. And if this distinction be admitted, then it will follow that the laws by which intelligent creatures are regulated must be as different from those which govern mere matter as mind and matter are different in their essential qualities.

2. Another fundamental error involved in the scheme of necessity is, that motives possess an independent and active influence. To see the absurdity of this notion let us thoughtfully inquire, What are motives? Are they created beings endowed with self-moving energy? Are they capable not only of moving themselves, but of imparting their force to what is external to themselves, so as to produce action in that which could not act without them? If we answer these questions in the affirmative, we ascribe to motives all that self-controlling and self-determining energy which libertarians claim for the mind itself; and if a power to act without being acted upon must be ascribed either to mind or to motives in order to account for volition, it is certainly more rational to ascribe it to the former than to the latter.

If it be said that motives do not possess an *independent* influence, but that they derive their power from some antecedent cause, then it will follow either that they are connected with an infinite series of causes, which is absurd in itself, or that they depend upon God alone both for their existence and efficiency. But if motives themselves do not act—if God acts upon man, and determines his volitions by the instrumentality of motives, why is the doctrine still maintained that motives determine the will? This is the same as to say that motives do not act and that they do act at the same time, which is a contradiction. It is, in fact, to give up the argument for necessity, which is founded upon the supposed influence of motives. Again, if motives are only the instruments by which God determines the volitions of his rational creatures, then he is the only agent in the universe; while angels and men are mere passive instruments, acting only as they are acted upon by Divine power.

But now, if we answer these questions in the negative, as truth requires us to do, then we must allow that motives, considered in themselves, can no more act on the mind so as necessarily to determine its volitions, than one portion of inert matter can, of its own accord, act upon another. The truth is, that motives themselves do not act at all. Independent of the mind they can have no existence. It is the mind that acts upon them and gives them all the influence which they possess. But if motives depend upon the mind both for their existence and influence, is it not most unreasonable to suppose that they should control the mind in all its acts of volition? We conclude, therefore, that though the mind acts in view of motives, yet the controlling power is not in the motives, but in the mind itself.

This view of the subject is established by the very nature of motives. "What are they? Are they not arguments, reasons, or persuasions? Now, if the mind can exercise no free-agency of its own, in attending to arguments, examining reasons, or yielding to persuasions, why address them to man, and exhort him to give them their due weight? The very fact that they are motives, arguments, reasons, or persuasions, is proof sufficient that they are designed to influence the will, not necessarily and irresistibly, but only through the agency of man." What, then, is it that gives to motives their prevailing influence? It is not any inherent power in them, but it is the act of the mind itself, by which it yields to that influence in the exercise of free volition. If it should be asked why the mind yields to one motive rather than another, our reply would be that the reason is in the mind itself. God has endowed us with this power, without which we could not be moral and accountable agents.

3. The doctrine of necessity proceeds upon the false assumption that the mind can exercise no agency whatever in regard to motives. The theory is that the will is determined by motives; that motives arise from

circumstances; that circumstances are ordered by a power above us and beyond our control; and that, therefore, our volitions necessarily follow an order and chain of events appointed and decreed by Infinite Wisdom. If this is true, it will necessarily follow that we have no power to displace one motive by another, or to control those circumstances from which motives flow.

But who will say that a person may not shun evil company and fly from many temptations? Either this must be allowed, or else it must be a link in the chain of necessary events, fixed by a superior power, that we should not shun evil company or fly from temptations. Hence it would follow that the exhortations, " when sinners entice thee consent thou not," and "go not in the way of sinners," are very impertinent, and only prove that Solomon was no philosopher. But we are all conscious that we have the power to alter, and control, and avoid the force of motives. If we have no such power, why does a man resist the same temptation at one time to which he yields at another without any visible change in the circumstances? Why does he at one time resist a powerful temptation, which is the same as to resist a powerful motive, and yield, at another time, to one that is feeble, knowing that he does so?

But further, the motive or reason for an action may be a bad one and yet be prevalent for the want of the presence of a better reason or motive to lead to a contrary choice and act; but in how many instances is the true cause why a better reason or stronger motive is not present, that we have lived thoughtlessly and in ignorance? And if so, then the thoughtless might have been more thoughtful, and the ignorant might have acquired better knowledge, and thereby have placed them-selves under the influence of stronger and better motives. Thus the theory of necessity does not accord with the facts of our own conscious-ness, but contradicts them. It is also refuted by every part of the moral history of man, and it may be, therefore, concluded that those speculations on the human will, to which the theory of philosophical necessity has driven its advocates, are equally opposed to the Holy Scriptures, to the philosophy of mind, to our observation of what passes in others, and to our own convictions.

4. The doctrine of motives, as it is held by necessitarians, is disproved by the absurdity of its logical consequences. We will not attempt to push this argument to its utmost extent. It is only necessary that we should notice some of the most obvious absurdities which result from the doctrine that volitions are necessarily determined by motives. And,

(1.) If volitions are efficiently caused by motives, then the dominion of absolute necessity is *universal*. The steps by which we reach this fearful conclusion are few and easily traced. Volitions cannot be produced by motives without being preceded by them, as the effect must always be preceded by its cause. Nor can they exert any influence over the motives by which they are produced; for they do not even come into existence till their producing motives have finished their operation. Indeed, no effect can modify its cause unless it can act before it exists, which is absurd. But if volition cannot influence the motive by which it is produced, it certainly cannot influence the antecedent to that motive; and so of every other antecedent in a retrospective series, until we reach the first cause. If, then, volition sustains a necessary relation to its producing motive, as our opponents assume, there can be no room for freedom between the volition and the first cause; for, if volition is *necessary*, all that precedes it up to the first cause must be so too.

But may there not be freedom between volition and its *effect?* By no means. Both the volition and its sequence, by the theory, are *effects;* and as every effect sustains a necessary relation to its cause, both the volition and all its sequences are necessary. It is, therefore, impossible to avoid the conclusion that all human volitions are only so many links in the adamantine chain of universal necessity. But what renders this conclusion a thousand times more startling is, that it applies to God as well as to man. The theory maintains that volition from its *very nature*, without a motive cause, would be an absurdity. But if the *nature* of volition demands a motive cause, that demand must be as applicable to the volitions of God as to those of his creatures; for, whatever differences may exist between created minds and the Infinite mind, the theory allows none in regard to volition. The very ground on which necessity is predicated of human volition requires that it should also be predicated of *Divine volition.* If motives are the only possible cause of volition in some minds they are so in all minds. And if this motive-control makes the volitions of all minds necessary, it must make all events equally so. The will of God, no less than the will of man, must be passive. Eternal necessity must rule the one no less than the other.

(2.) Another consequence of this doctrine of motives is, that it destroys the very foundation of moral distinctions. If all minds, without exception, are under the control of absolute and eternal necessity, then human virtue and human vice are impossible.

It is one of the plainest dictates of common-sense that the criminality of an evil act is grounded on the power of the agent to refrain from it. But who can contend successfully against an eternal necessity? Indeed, it is impossible that any one should even *attempt* to act otherwise than he does. For if every volition is the necessary effect of some motive, how can the mind command a different volition until it is produced by a different motive? And if this different motive lies entirely beyond the control of the agent, the very *attempt* to act otherwise than he does lies as far beyond his control as are the movements of the heavenly bodies.

Hence we are forced to the conclusion, if we argue correctly, that all moral creatures are equally undeserving of either praise or blame. For, though we are told that the character of an act lies in the *will*, yet the cause of the will lies in the *motive*, and over this the agent has no control. The greatest crimes in the universe are as necessary as the most distinguished virtues; and though we may regard the criminal as being unfortunate, yet in view of this necessity, and of the claims of eternal justice, we dare not pronounce him *guilty*. As well might men be accounted guilty for becoming hungry or thirsty; or for any other effect that is necessarily produced by the established laws of their physical constitution.

(3.) This doctrine of the causality of motives is injurious to the character of God. If motives are the only possible cause of volition, and if an effect sustains a necessary relation to its cause, then we must allow either that God puts forth no volitions at all, which would contradict both Scripture and reason, or that his volitions are caused by motives, and therefore necessary; but in either case we would deny his free-agency. To say that his volitions are determined by motives is to place him under the same law of necessity which is supposed to govern his creatures, and thus to deny his absolute independence. Nay, it is virtually to say that eternal necessity, and not God, governs the world.

But if we suppose God to be the free and independent governor of all things, and confine our notions of moral necessity to the actions of his intelligent creatures, still this scheme is derogatory to the Divine character. If virtue alone existed in the moral world, we could trace with pleasure the necessitating hand of God in the volitions and actions of his intelligent creatures. But when we fix our attention upon the ungodly deeds of wicked men, and are told that these were rendered necessary from all eternity by the immutable decree of God, and secured in time by a necessary chain of causes and effects, we instinctively inquire, Is there not some other solution of this awful subject which would exhibit the Supreme Governor of the moral world in a more amiable and engaging light? Is it not a most fearful conclusion, indeed, that falsehood, treachery, murder, and blasphemy are declarations of the Divine will? Yet such they must be if the doctrine of philosophical necessity is true.

III. *The last objection we will notice is, that* FREE MORAL AGENCY IS IRRECONCILABLE WITH THE FOREKNOWLEDGE OF GOD.

This is the most frequently employed argument of necessitarians against the doctrine of free moral agency, and one on which they rely with the greatest degree of confidence. Luther calls the foreknowledge of God "a thunderbolt, to dash free-will to atoms."* And Dr. Dick, a distinguished Calvinistic divine, has said that if our actions are certainly

* Bondage of the Will.

foreknown, "it is as impossible to avoid them, as it is to pluck the sun from the firmament." * Hence necessitarians tell us that we must either deny the foreknowledge of God or give up the doctrine of man's free moral agency. But our reply is, We will do neither the one nor the other.

As to the Divine foreknowledge, we believe that it extends to all things great and small, whether necessary or free, and that it is perfect and certain. We believe, moreover, that what God foreknows will certainly come to pass. In this respect the conclusion is the same, whether it be deduced from foreknowledge or concomitant knowledge. If a thing is known *now* to exist, it follows, by an absolute *certainty*, that it does exist; for otherwise it could not possibly be known to exist. So, likewise, if an event is certainly foreknown, it follows, with equal *certainty*, that it will come to pass. We conclude, therefore, that what God foreknows will most certainly and infallibly take place; but this infallible certainty has nothing to do with the manner in which future events will be brought about. It does not determine whether they will take their existence on the principle of *necessity* or on that of *free moral agency*.

By the *necessity* of any action or event we are to understand the impossibility that it should *not* be, or that it should be *different* from what it is. It is in this sense the term is employed when necessitarians tell us that Divine prescience implies *necessity*. If anything can be free from this kind of necessity, one would expect to find it in human volition; but according to the theory of President Edwards, the *will* is absolutely and efficiently determined by the influence of motives. So also Dr. Dick tells us that "a man chooses what appears to be good, and he chooses it necessarily, in this sense, that he *could not do* otherwise." † This sense of the term is evidently implied in the objection; for, as our doctrine of free moral agency acknowledges the *certainty* of future events, it cannot be irreconcilable with the foreknowledge of God, unless his foreknowledge is supposed to imply their absolute *necessity*.

But does the foreknowledge of God imply the necessity of all future events? This is what we deny, and what, we believe, can never be proved. Those who take the affirmative of this question are bound to admit one of two things—either that the foreknowledge of God makes future events necessary, or that he cannot foreknow them unless they are necessary. Let us, then, look for a moment at the consequences of each.

1. To say that the Divine prescience makes future events necessary, is the same as to say that necessity governs all things in heaven and earth. It is to say that all the volitions and actions of angels and men are as necessary as the movements of the planets—that the rebellion of holy angels, the sin of our first parents, and all the ungodly deeds that wicked men have ever committed, were rendered necessary by the foreknowl-

* Dick's Theology, Lec. 34.   † Ibid.

edge of God, and could not have been avoided. Moreover, if whatever is foreknown is thereby rendered necessary, and cannot be otherwise, then, as God foreknows from eternity every act that he would perform throughout all duration, he is a necessary agent in all that he does, acting only as he is acted upon by stern necessity. Thus we see that the "thunderbolt" of the great Reformer, which was supposed to "dash free-will to atoms," falls with as destructive weight upon the free-agency of man in Paradise, and even upon the freedom of God himself, as it does upon the free-will of man in his present condition.

But is it not most glaringly absurd to suppose that the great Jehovah, in all his acts, is impelled by necessity? This is to suppose the eternal existence of some superior power, separate and distinct from himself; which is at once to deny his independence and supremacy. It cannot, therefore, be true that all the acts of God are brought about by necessity. Yet they are foreknown; and if the foreknowledge of God does not render his own acts necessary or destroy his free-agency, so neither can it render the actions of his moral creatures necessary, nor destroy their free-agency.

To suppose that the Divine foreknowledge makes future events necessary is incompatible with the very nature of knowledge in general. What is knowledge? Is it an active power, possessing a distinct and independent existence? We answer, No. It is nothing more than a clear and certain perception of truth and fact. It is, therefore, passive in its nature, and possesses only a relative and dependent existence. And though it is often said that "knowledge is power," yet nothing more is intended by this expression than that it directs an active agent in the exertion of his power. What influence can mere knowledge exert upon any event, whether past, present, or future? Evidently none at all; and for this reason, that it is knowledge and not power.

2. But now let us turn our attention to the other alternative, namely, that God cannot foreknow future events unless they are necessary. This seems to be the position which is generally assumed by necessitarians, and which appears to be based upon the supposition that the volitions and actions of free moral agents are in their very nature uncertain. "There must be a certainty in things themselves," says President Edwards, "before they are certainly known."* But what is this certainty in things themselves, or in human volitions, without which they are incapable of being foreknown? The answer is obvious; for Edwards everywhere contends that unless our volitions are brought to pass by the influence of moral causes—that unless they are necessarily produced by an "effectual power and efficacy," they are altogether uncertain. Hence he clearly maintains, that unless human volitions are brought to pass by the necessitating influence of motives, they are not certain in themselves, and are therefore incapable of being foreknown.

*Inquiry, Part 2, sec. 12.

That this mode of reasoning may hold good in regard to human knowledge we will not deny; but that it will apply to the foreknowledge of God is what cannot be shown. If there is anything in us approaching to foreknowledge, it must result from a knowledge of something now existing between which and the event foreknown there is a necessary connection. But is it proper to conclude, because this is the case with man, that it must also be the case with Deity? Shall we make our own limited and feeble intellects the measure of all possible modes of knowledge with God?

We freely admit that an event cannot be foreknown unless it will certainly come to pass. But why may not the free volitions and actions of moral creatures be as certain as those events that are necessary? To say they cannot, is a mere assumption which never can be proved. To suppose them to be certain and uncertain at the same time would involve a contradiction; but there is no contradiction in supposing them to be future, certain, and free.

That we can gain as clear and certain knowledge of a past free action as of one that was necessarily produced, no one will deny. May we not then reasonably suppose that God can foreknow the free volitions and actions of his moral creatures, as well as those events that are necessary? That he cannot, is more than any finite being should presume to declare.

But if all future events must be necessary in order to be foreknown, then it will follow, either that this necessity exists in the very nature of things themselves or in God. To say that this necessity arises from the nature of things themselves, is to take one's stand upon the platform of Stoical fatalism. It is to assume that all things in heaven and earth are bound together by an intricate series and concatenation of causes; that fate and not God governs the world; and that all moral creatures in the universe, with the *Infinite One* in the same category, are bound by the fetters of eternal necessity. These are only some of the absurd and shocking consequences which result from this scheme of necessity, but they are sufficient to refute it.

Are we, then, to place the necessity of all things in God? This is our only alternative; and this, we believe, is what necessitarians maintain. "If we allow the attribute of prescience," says Mr. Buck, "the idea of a decree must certainly be allowed also, for how can an action that is really to come to pass be foreseen if it be not determined? God knew everything from the beginning, but this he could not know if he had not so determined it."* Again: "No effect can be viewed as future," says Dr. Dick, "or, in human language, can be the object of certain expectation, but when considered in relation to its efficient cause, and the cause of all things that ever shall exist is the purpose of God."†

* Theological Dictionary.   † Dick's Theology, Lec. 21.

In these two brief quotations we have the fundamental principles of the necessitarian scheme. They are these: 1. That God is the moving and efficient cause of all things; 2. That all things are made necessary by his purpose or determination; and, 3. That he foreknows future events, because he has made them necessary. Neither time nor space will allow us to enter into an extended examination of this theory. We can only glance at some of its consequences. And,

First, If God is the efficient cause of all things, then the horrible consequence must follow, that he is the efficient cause of all the moral evil that ever existed or ever will exist. It is no answer to this difficulty to say that God is only the cause of the *act* that is sinful, but not of its sinfulness. Wherein does the sinfulness of an act lie? Is it not in the will? But according to this theory, God controls the will and makes that as necessary as the act itself.

Secondly, If the purpose or determination of God makes all things necessary, then it will follow that a necessity as absolute as Stoical fatalism governs the moral world; and that falsehood, treachery, blasphemy, and murder are rendered as necessary by the Divine purpose as piety and virtue.

Thirdly, To say that God foreknows future events because he has made them necessary, is to say that an essential *attribute* of Deity is dependent for its existence upon an *act* of the Divine mind, the foreknowledge of God upon his purpose or decree.

The conclusion, then, which we draw from the whole argument is this, that though our doctrine of free moral agency is incompatible with the necessitarian notion of Divine foreknowledge, yet it is in perfect harmony with the true doctrine upon this subject, and so the objection falls to the ground.

TEXTS MORE OR LESS ILLUSTRATED.

GENESIS.

Ch.	Ver.	Page
1	2	231
1	6	248
1	26	182
3	7–9	416
3	15	223
3	22	182
4	3, 4	345
5	3	304
6	5	299
6	5, 12, 13	300
6	9	450
8	20, 21	345
8	21	348
9	4	345
9	6	518
15	9, 10	346
17	1	448
17	6	214
17	10, 11	566
18	25	338
18	33	190
22	15, 16	191
22	18	223, 467
28	12	255
31	11, 12	191
32	2	254
32	26	492
48	15, 16	191
49	33	605
50	20	273

EXODUS.

Ch.	Ver.	Page
3	6	191
3	14	191
4	2	434, 442
5	3	349
10	21, 23	84
12	23	252
12	26	496
12	29, 30	84
14	21–23	84
16	23–30	502
18	21, 22	534
20	1–17	468
20	8–11	505
20	12	270
20	24	200
22	20	209
23	20	193
30	12	350
31	14	506
34	6	172

LEVITICUS.

Ch.	Ver.	Page
5	15, 16	350
14	6	574
15	31	351
19	2	169
19	15	534
19	35, 36	521
20	10	527
26	12	442

NUMBERS.

Ch.	Ver.	Page
6	24–27	183
8	17, 18	65
11	9	575
21	14	59
23	19	163
27	21	64

DEUTERONOMY.

Ch.	Ver.	Page
4	33	191
5	6–21	468
6	4	140, 182
6	7	496
10	15	390
11	18, 19	64
14	1	42
18	15	223
18	18	64
25	4	75
29	10–12	564
30	6	426
30	15, 16	491
32	29	478
33	25	459
33	28	575

JOSHUA.

Ch.	Ver.	Page
3	5	66
3	15	66
4	6	496
4	18	66
10	13	59
7	25	293
10	6, 7, 9	463

1 SAMUEL.

Ch.	Ver.	Page
20	6	496
28	15	463
31	4	463

2 SAMUEL.

Ch.	Ver.	Page
6	20	496
14	20	575
18	33	359
20	9	16
23	3	534
24	12–15	270

1 KINGS.

Ch.	Ver.	Page
8	27	149
8	39	200

2 KINGS.

Ch.	Ver.	Page
3	11	575
5	27	293
20	18	214
25	5–7	117

1 CHRONICLES.

Ch.	Ver.	Page
16	34	172
29	29	59

2 CHRONICLES.

Ch.	Ver.	Page
32	4	579

JOB.

Ch.	Ver.	Page
1	1	450
1	4, 5	348
1	6	442
10	8, 11, 12	269
11	7	178
11	7–9	140
11	12	304
12	13	159
13	15	484
14	4	304
14	5	270
14	10	605
15	14	304
17	9	459
17	11	601
23	13	236
24	7	254
26	6	152
26	7–10	147
26	13	231
26	14	148
28	24–27	159
33	4	231
34	12	166
36	5	159
38	4	246
38	7	442
42	7, 8	349

PSALMS.

Ch.	Ver.	Page
5	4	272
7	11	516
8	5	279
9	5	199
16	11	635
19	1	147
19	7	430
22	4	484
22	22	566
23	1, 6	443
27	4	492
30	11	157
31	5	605
33	4	162
33	5	172
33	6	331
33	9	147
33	11	236
34	7	255
36	6	203, 268
37	24	444
38	4, 7	251
39	10	647
40	12	474
41	9	464
49	11	600
49	12, 14	600
50	3, 4	623
51	3	474
51	5	304
51	10	449
51	10, 11	431
55	23	270
57	3	304
66	18	493
68	17	254
72	18, 19	178
73	3–5	638
75	6, 7	271
76	10	272
78	43	647
81	11, 12	272
82	6	442
83	18	196
84	2	492
84	11	274, 443
86	5	172
86	10	140
89	30–35	457
89	34	163
90	2	145, 198
90	3	270
90	10	270
91	10, 11	255
99	9	169
102	25–27	145, 157
103	5, 6	638
103	21	253
104	4	252
104	24	159, 249
104	30	231
105	4	498
112	7	484
116	15	647
117	2	163
121	5–8	443
127	1	443
138	6	268
139	1, 2, 11, 12	152
139	7–10	149
139	15, 16	269
145	3	178
145	9	172
145	15, 16	264
147	5	152

PROVERBS.

Ch.	Ver.	Page
1	23	589
1	24–26	385
1	28	341
3	5	489
8	13	516
10	15	647
12	22	523
15	3	264

TEXTS MORE OR LESS ILLUSTRATED.

Ch.	Ver.	Page
19	17	526
19	18	647
22	6	530
22	15	304
29	15	304
30	4	214

ECCLESIASTES.

Ch.	Ver.	Page
3	19, 20	600
7	29	279
9	5	601
10	20	536
12	14	623

ISAIAH.

Ch.	Ver.	Page
1	3	478
1	18	448
6	3	169, 183
8	13	168
9	6	200
9	7	567
33	22	204
40	3	195, 197
40	12	147
40	13, 14	236
40	17	147
43	2	274
43	2, 3	444
43	10	200
44	3	589
44	6	200
45	22	140
46	9, 10	201
46	10	236
54	5	182
55	6	498
55	7	474, 601
58	13, 14	516
60	8	516

JEREMIAH.

Ch.	Ver.	Page
17	5	212, 304
17	10	200
23	5, 6	196
23	24	149
31	3	458
31	31, 32	194
52	10, 11	117

LAMENTATIONS.

Ch.	Ver.	Page
3	41	498
5	7	360

EZEKIEL.

Ch.	Ver.	Page
14	6	474
18	24	460
18	26, 27	158
18	32	386
33	7–9	17
33	11	386
36	25	448, 589
36	25, 26	426, 560

DANIEL.

Ch.	Ver.	Page
4	33	575
4	35	159
6	10	496
12	2	612
12	2	640, 649
9	2	203
9	2–8	67
9	6	204
10	1–7	68
10	20	79, 228
10	28	279, 606
10	29, 30	268
10	29–31	264
10	30	153
10	37	531
12	21	485
12	32	233
12	36, 37	627

HOSEA.

Ch.	Ver.	Page
12	3–5	191

JOEL.

Ch.	Ver.	Page
2	28, 29	589
2	32	197

JONAH.

Ch.	Ver.	Page
3	4, 5	481
3	10	237

MICAH.

Ch.	Ver.	Page
5	2	213
6	8	517

HABAKKUK.

Ch.	Ver.	Page
3	6	147

ZECHARIAH.

Ch.	Ver.	Page
12	10	493

MALACHI.

Ch.	Ver.	Page
1	6	182
3	1	194
3	6	157

MATTHEW.

Ch.	Ver.	Page
1	21	448
1	23	198
2	22	359
3	1, 2	476
3	2	472
3	5, 6	577, 584
3	11	558, 561
3	16	577
3	16, 17	215, 229
3	17	193, 212
4	12	583
4	17	475
5	8	145, 446
5	17	507
5	22	516
5	44	524
5	48	448
6	5	493
6	6	495
6	10	253
6	14, 15	494, 517
6	25–32	264
6	30	481
7	7	479, 492
7	8	499
7	12	517
7	21	16
8	10	481, 485
8	11	635
13	3	580
13	42	642
13	43	620
13	50	642
14	15–21	67
14	23	495
14	33	205
15	4–6	531
15	28	481
16	18	566
16	21	358
16	24	474, 483
17	3	606
17	5	193
18	3	428
18	18–20	68
18	20	200
18	37	320
19	4, 5	282
19	5	563
19	16–22	517
19	17	239
19	17–19	469
19	4–6	527
20	1–16	167
21	29	472
22	32	607
22	36–40	471
22	37, 38	505
22	37–39	147, 276
22	39	515
22	42	223
23	37	385
24	14	382
24	29	148
24	31	256, 624
25	31	253
25	31, 32	623
25	32	148, 204
25	34	628
25	41	642, 648
25	46	148, 649
26	26, 27	554
26	27, 28	591
26	53	254
27	3	472
27	42	199
27	50	605
28	19	232, 558
28	20	200

MARK.

Ch.	Ver.	Page
1	2	194
1	4, 5	564, 581
1	15	384, 475
1	24	483
2	27	513
3	5	516
3	29	649, 650
6	12	476
7	3, 4	575
7	21–23	305
8	38	484
9	43	649
9	44	642
9	45	650
10	14	570
10	45	359
11	24	494
11	25	494
14	21	650
16	15, 16	558
16	16	239, 384, 458, 562

LUKE.

Ch.	Ver.	Page
1	6	450
1	68–75	567
2	14	253
3	17	642
4	8	208
6	12	495
6	37	494
7	3	472
7	11–15	67
10	7	75
11	11	359
11	13	232, 431
12	6	153
12	11, 12	79
12	48	526
13	3	239, 476
13	29	631
15	10	253
16	9	636
16	22	255
16	23	643
17	5	481
18	13	474
18	13, 14	494
20	36	251
21	25, 26	624
22	31	259, 634
22	70	217
23	43	608
23	46	605
24	39	251, 613
24	46	358
24	47	382
24	51, 52	206

JOHN.

Ch.	Ver.	Page
1	3	216
1	12	442
1	14	216
1	15	187
1	28	578
1	47	450
1	49	199
2	1	582
2	1–10	67
2	24, 25	201
3	2	89
3	3, 7	426, 427
3	5	558
3	5, 6, 8	230, 426
3	13	177, 200
3	17	216
3	18	419
3	19	627
3	23	579
3	36	384, 419
4	9, 10, 14	216
4	24	143
4	50	480
5	4, 18	230
5	17, 18	217
5	18, 29	216
5	19	201
5	20	199
5	21	204
5	22, 23	624
5	24	458
5	28	148
5	28, 29	204, 612, 616, 640
5	37	215
5	40	220, 385
6	39	616
6	62	189
6	63	231
6	64	201
8	7	187
8	26	580
8	44	256, 434
8	51	291, 636
9	7	480
9	35, 36	480
9	35–38	205
10	18	212
10	27, 28	458
10	28	455
10	31–33	217
10	37, 38	482
10	40	578
11	24	614
11	25	204
11	26	636
12	24	358
12	42, 43	484
13	1	459
13	2	259
13	17	10
13	18	464
13	27	464

Ch.	Ver.	Page
14	2, 3	249, 630
14	6	493
14	16, 26	229
14	26	78
15	1, 2, 6	460
15	18	187
15	19	393
15	22	473
15	26	228
16	8	473
16	13	78
16	15	201
17	3	458
17	5	189
17	9	379
17	11	459
17	17	449
17	20	482
18	36	111
20	4, 8	187
20	5	581
20	28	188
20	30, 31	482

ACTS.

Ch.	Ver.	Page
1	5	561
1	24	205
1	25	464
2	19, 20	624
2	23	235
2	33	230
2	34	603
2	37	480
2	38	462, 475
2	38, 41	559
2	43	580
5	3	259
5	3, 4	230
5	29	536
5	31	475
6	15	620
7	38	566
7	59	605
7	59, 60	206
8	12	559
8	22	601
8	29	229
8	36	559
8	37	483
8	38, 39	577
9	18	587
10	34, 35	392
10	36	197
10	42	624, 641
10	44	590
10	46–48	562
10	47, 48	587
11	15	590
11	18	472
11	33	212
14	16	272
14	17	175
15	18	152, 235
16	24–34	588

Ch.	Ver.	Page
16	31	419
17	24–28	264
17	27, 28	149
17	29	278
17	30	384, 477
17	31	627
19	2	229
20	21	475
23	5	536
23	6	616
24	15	640
26	20	474
26	27	483
28	25, 26	184

ROMANS.

Ch.	Ver.	Page
1	7	207
1	16	482
1	17	481
1	25	208
2	4	478
2	5	338
2	6	166
2	14, 15	263
2	14, 15	626
2	16	624
2	29	426, 569
3	24	363
3	24–26	366
3	25	362
3	28	361, 423
3	31	507
4	3	415, 416
4	11	566
4	11, 12	567
4	20	480
4	20–22	417
5	5	462
5	6–8	359
5	10	364, 647
5	12	278, 291
5	15, 18	380
6	1, 2	422
6	2	582
6	3, 4	580
6	4	569
6	14	427
6	22	446
7	7	507
7	9	478
7	12	169, 338
7	24	647
8	3	219
8	7	518
8	9	228, 561
8	10	515
8	11	231
8	13, 14	232
8	14	230, 444
8	15–16	435
8	17	424, 445
8	26	493
8	28	235, 443
8	29	239

Ch.	Ver.	Page
8	35–39	455
8	38, 39	459
9	30	417
10	4	417
10	10	483
10	13	197
10	14, 17	482
11	7	391
11	17, 18, 21, 22	461
12	1	448
12	17, 19	517
13	1, 2	535
13	3, 4	534
14	1	481
14	10	623
14	12	204

1 CORINTHIANS.

Ch.	Ver.	Page
1	2	206
1	13	560
1	27–29	113
2	6	450
2	9, 10	81
2	10	230
2	12	228
4	11, 13	70
5	21	355
6	9	428
6	19	230
6	19, 20	363, 617
8	6	140
8	11	381
9	27	459
10	1–5	464
10	2	575
10	4	568
10	4, 11	353
10	9	195
10	12	465
10	16	555
11	23–25	591
11	26	555
12	6–11	230
12	13	582
14	15	430
14	37	76
15	16–18	603
15	22	292, 380
15	22, 23, 52	616
15	51, 53	614
15	54, 55	617

2 CORINTHIANS.

Ch.	Ver.	Page
1	1	235
2	11	259
3	17	143, 230
4	6	462
4	7	113
4	14	616
5	1	636
5	6–8	609

Ch.	Ver.	Page
5	10	204, 365
5	17	426
5	18	364
5	19	365
5	21	360
7	1	448, 451
8	7	526
8	12	526
9	7	526
10	4	111, 430
11	3	282
12	7–9	206
13	14	185, 232

GALATIANS.

Ch.	Ver.	Page
1	12	81
2	21	417
3	8	568
3	8, 9	566
3	13	177, 363
3	26	442
4	4	216
4	4–6	436
4	5	434
4	6	228
4	19	427
5	14	523
5	22, 23	439
5	25	232
6	10	526

EPHESIANS.

Ch.	Ver.	Page
1	4–6	397
1	5	235
1	7	363
1	9	234
1	11	158
1	13	485
1	18	462
1	21	203
2	1	291
2	7	177
2	10	426
2	12	434
2	16	364, 365
2	18	493
2	19	434
3	2–5	77
3	3–5	81
3	11	236
3	14–19	449
4	10	631
4	24	279, 426
4	25	523
4	32	517
5	2	355
5	22, 23, 25, 33	528
6	1	531
6	2	470
6	5	531
6	8	532

PHILIPPIANS.

Ch.	Ver.	Page
1	21	610
2	7, 8	177
2	12, 13	271
3	15	450
3	20	619
3	21	612
4	6	494, 498

COLOSSIANS.

Ch.	Ver.	Page
1	14, 15	227
1	16, 17	203
1	20	364
1	22, 23	455
1	27	427
2	10	203
2	10, 12	580
2	17	353
3	10	278, 426
3	20	531
3	21	529
4	1	532
4	2	498
4	16	59

1 THESS.

Ch.	Ver.	Page
4	6	521
4	16	624
4	17	614
5	23	449, 451

2 THESS.

Ch.	Ver.	Page
1	3	481
1	7	252
1	9	649
2	8	498
2	13	393, 482
2	13, 14	396

1 TIMOTHY.

Ch.	Ver.	Page
1	17	159
1	18, 19	461
1	19, 20	465
2	1–3	536
2	3, 4	386
2	5	493, 563
2	8	493
3	6	257
4	10	485
5	8	528

2 TIMOTHY.

Ch.	Ver.	Page
3	15	430
4	1	625, 641
4	14	461

TITUS.

Ch.	Ver.	Page
1	9	16
2	11, 12	16
2	13	199
3	7	428

PHILEMON.

Ch.	Ver.	Page
	10	430

HEBREWS.

Ch.	Ver.	Page
1	1	231
1	2	202, 216
1	3	203, 262
1	5	213
1	6	207
1	7	147, 251
1	8	199, 219
2	1	465
2	3, 4	482
2	9	359
3	12	465
3	14	255, 482
4	1	465
4	15	224
4	16	479
5	7	498
5	9	636
6	1	446
6	4–6	461
6	18	163
8	8–13	194
8	10	434
9	14	230
9	22	362
9	27	623
9	27	641
9	28	360
10	1	353
10	22	561, 589
10	26–29	462
10	29	381
10	35	465
10	38	465
11	1	481
11	3	202, 242
11	4	345, 347
11	6	475
11	9, 10	566
12	6	274
12	21	506
12	22–24	443
12	24	589
13	16	526
13	20, 21	449

JAMES.

Ch.	Ver.	Page
1	13	272, 426
1	15	284
1	17	157
1	18	426
1	22	10
2	19	483
2	23	423
4	11	517

1 PETER.

Ch.	Ver.	Page
1	2	239, 394
1	3	424
1	5	455
1	11	74, 231
1	11	82
1	12	253
1	13	168
1	18, 19	363
1	23	426
1	23	430
2	3	462
2	13, 14	534
2	13, 14	535
2	18	531
2	24	360
3	9	386
3	12	499
3	18	231
5	8	259
5	10	636

2 PETER.

Ch.	Ver.	Page
1	5–7, 10	456
1	11	636
1	16, 17	482
1	21	74, 231

2 JOHN.

Ch.	Ver.	Page
	1	542

Ch.	Ver.	Page
2	1	381
2	4	148
2	4	256, 625
2	4–7	641
3	10	229, 627
3	17	465
5	1	542

1 JOHN.

Ch.	Ver.	Page
1	5	163
1	8, 17	200
1	9	166, 367
1	9	448
2	2	361
2	9	516
3	2	442, 635
3	9	427
3	14	647
3	15	516
3	17	526
3	21	622
4	8	169
4	8	184
4	10	360

JUDE.

Ch.	Ver.	Page
	7	642
	13	641

REVELATION.

Ch.	Ver.	Page
1	5, 6	207
1	8	201
1	10	510
1	15	280
1	20	553
2	7	632
2	23	201
3	14	609
5	9	364
5	11	254
7	15	635
7	16	633
7	17	635
19	10	208
20	12	623
20	12	613
21	3	565
21	4	619
21	8	523
21	8	642

INDEX TO SUBJECTS.

	PAGE
Abel's sacrifice	347
Ability, natural and moral	374
Abraham's sacrifice	346
—— offering up of Isaac	346
Adam, legal relation of, to his posterity	292
Adam's sin imputed to his posterity	293
Administration of God toward man, of a mixed nature	100
Admission into the Church, power of, with ministers	548
Adoption, benefits of	441
—— defined	433
——, evidences of	435
——, evidences of, different theories respecting	436
——, nature of	433
Adultery, criminality of	527
Affection, mutual, demanded by the conjugal relation	528
Affusion the proper mode of Christian baptism	583
Age, Augustan, one of great learning	70
Agency, man's moral	308
Agency, man's moral, proofs of	316
——, man's moral, true doctrine of	314
——, moral, defined	308
Alexander, an example of total apostasy	465
All-sufficiency of God	177
Ancient writers testify to the existence and antiquity of Moses	52
Angel, import of the term	250
"Angel of the Lord," a designation of Christ	199
Angels, creation of	250
——, holy, employment of	254
——, holy, great number of	254
——, holy, moral condition of	252
——, holy, natural attributes of	254
——, unholy, employment of	258
——, unholy, fall of	256
——, unholy, final destiny of	259
——, unholy, moral condition of	257
——, unholy, various titles of	258
——, unholy, why not redeemed	260
Animals, distinction of, into clean and unclean	344

PAGE

Annihilation not the penalty of the law 647
—— not the future punishment of the wicked 647
Annihilationism, theory of 598
—— inconsistent with itself 647
Antiquity of the Holy Scriptures 53
Apollinarians, doctrine of 221
Apostasy, Calvinistic theory respecting 456
——, general agreement respecting... 455
——, total, arguments in support of... 460
——, total, examples of 463
——, total, possibility of 455
——, total, Calvinistic arguments against, considered 456
Apostles, office of 540
Arguments for the existence of God... 130
Arianism 222
Aristocratical government, what...... 533
Arminianism 376
Atmosphere, creation of 248
Atonement 343, 349, 356
——, Arminian view of 376
——, Calvinistic theory of 371
——, doctrine of 101
——, extent of 377
——, sacrificial, for bodily disorders .. 351
——, supposed injustice of 369
——, Universalist notion of 374
Attributes of God 139
——, Divine, ascribed to Christ 199
Authority, Church, ends of 549
——, Divine, of the sacred Scriptures 71
98, 109

Baptism a seal 561
—— a sign 560
—— by affusion, proofs for 583
—— by immersion, arguments for, refuted 573
——, emblematical import of 588
——, infant, arguments in support of.. 565
——, infant, objections to, obviated... 562
—— initiatory 560
—— in the room of circumcision 568
——, John's, circumstances of 583
——, mode of 573
——, nature of 557
—— not regeneration............... 431
—— of Cornelius................... 587
—— of the eunuch 586
—— of Saul of Tarsus.............. 587
—— of the jailer................... 588
—— of the three thousand.......... 584
——, sacramental import of 560
——, subjects of 561
——, universal obligation of 557
Baxter's theory of the extent of the atonement 372
Believers proper subjects of baptism .. 562
Benedictions, origin and nature of..... 207
Benefits of the atonement, general view of 403
Benevolence required by the law of love 523
Bible, supposed demoralizing influence of 118

Bishop, office of 541
Blessedness of the saints in heaven endless........................ 636
Blood, why prohibited 350
Body, human, a proof of the Divine existence........................ 136

Cain and Abel, sacrifice of 345
Calvin denied the freedom of the will.. 310
——, theory of, respecting the Lord's Supper 593
Calvinism, brief view of............. 371
Canon, sacred, how determined....... 62
——, sacred, integrity of 58
——, sacred, term defined........... 62
Catalogues, early, of Christian Scriptures 56
Cause, as defined by Edwards 323
Causes, classification of............. 131
Cautions prove the possibility of apostasy 465
Change of the Sabbath from the seventh to the first day of the week 508
Character of God 337
Children, duties of, to parents........ 530
—— of believers proper subjects of baptism 562
Christ a propitiation 356, 361
—— a reconciler................... 364
—— a redeemer................... 363
—— came down from heaven 188
——, creation ascribed to........... 201
——, death of, necessary to man's salvation........................ 357
——, death of, propitiatory 356
——, death of, vicarious 358
—— died for all men.............. 378
—— died for those who may perish... 380
——, Divine attributes ascribed to.... 199
——, Divine titles ascribed to 195
——, Divine works ascribed to 201
——, Divine worship paid to 205
——, Divinity of................... 187
——, errors respecting the Divine nature of 222
——, errors respecting the human nature of 221
——, eternity ascribed to 200
—— existed before the world........ 189
——, existence and antiquity of...... 52
—— is called God 197
—— is called Jehovah.............. 196
—— is called King of Israel......... 199
—— is called Lord................. 196
——, miracles of................... 85
——, omnipresence ascribed to....... 201
——, omniscience ascribed to 200
—— our final Judge 204, 624
——, person of.................... 221
——, pre-existence of.............. 187
——, preservation ascribed to 203
——, raising the dead ascribed to 204
——, real existence of.............. 52
——, resurrection of................ 86

PAGE

Christ, Semiarian doctrine respecting.. 222
——, sinlessness of................. 224
——, Sonship of................... 210
—— subject to innocent infirmities ... 224
—— the Jehovah of the Old Testament 190
——, the two natures of, constitute one
person........................ 224
—— was before Abraham........... 188
—— was truly man 223
—— worshiped by heavenly beings .. 207
—— worshiped by his disciples...... 205
——, worship of, a proof of his Divinity 208
Christianity, ameliorating influence of. 113
——, institutions of 538
——, instruments employed in the propagation of 112
——, marvelous diffusion of, in the first
three centuries 109
——, morals of................... 467
—— not suited to the carnal mind.... 112
—— strongly opposed in the beginning 111
Christians, relation of, to one another.. 539
Church, constitution of............. 543
——, Christian, a continuation of the
Abrahamic covenant 567
——, Christian, officers of the....... 540
——, Christian, punitive discipline of
the 539
——, Christian, what 538
Circumcision a sign and seal of the
Abrahamic covenant............. 566
Clarke, Samuel, theory of, respecting
Christ........................ 222
Compensation, adequate, meaning of
the phrase..................... 368
Condition, moral, in which men are born
into the world.................. 296
Confession an element of true repent-
ance 474
Conflagration, general............. 629
Conformity to truth required by justice 523
Connection between Divine justice and
the penalty of the law 338
Conscience, liberty of.............. 522
Consciousness a proof of man's moral
agency........................ 316
Consent, common, a proof of the Divine
existence...................... 131
—— of the will essential to saving
faith 483
Consideration a means of repentance.. 477
Consubstantiation, doctrine of........ 593
Contents, table of................. 5
Contrition essential to true repentance 473
Conviction precedes repentance....... 473
Correction, Divine, a privilege of God's
people 444
Covenant, Abrahamic, the covenant of
grace 565
Creation ascribed to Christ 201
—— ascribed to the Holy Ghost..... 231
—— a proof of the Divine goodness .. 172
——, date of.................... 245
——, extent of.................. 248

PAGE

Creation in general................. 242
—— in particular................. 249
—— of angels................... 250
—— of man, history of............ 277
—— of the world not discoverable by
reason 25
Credibility of the sacred writers....... 68

Darkness, plague of................ 84
Days of the creation literal days...... 247
Dead, resurrection of the, ascribed to
the Holy Ghost................. 231
Death, nature of that, which was made
the penalty of the law........... 291
—— not annihilation.............. 598
—— of Christ necessary to man's salvation 357
—— of Christ propitiatory 356
—— of Christ, reality of the 86
—— of Christ rendered the salvation
of all men possible.............. 378
—— of Christ vicarious............ 359
Decalogue binding on all Christians... 507
—— imposed no new duties........ 505
Decrees of God................... 234
——, existence of the 234
——, nature and properties of the.... 235
Deity and personality of the Holy Ghost 227
Depravity, human, degree of......... 298
——, human, nature of............ 297
——, human, proofs of 299
——, human, objections to, obviated.. 306
Design a proof of the Divine existence 134
——, examples of................. 136
Destructionism, how defended 599
—— refuted 604
——, theory of.................. 598
Destruction of the first-born......... 84
Devil, the real agent in man's original
temptation 285
Diffusion of Christianity an evidence
of its Divine authority........... 111
—— in the first three centuries...... 109
Dispensation, the remedial 336
Divinity of Christ................. 187
Doctor S. Clarke's theory respecting
Christ........................ 222
Doctrine of atonement 101
—— of Divine influence 104
—— of the Trinity, importance of 180
Doctrines of Scripture, excellency of... 98
Dueling, criminality of 519
Duties of children to parents 530
—— of masters.................. 532
—— of parents to their children 528
—— of rulers 534
—— of servants 531
—— of the subjects of government ... 535
—— to our neighbor 527

Education of children, duty of........ 599
Effects of Christ's death 380
—— of the fall 290
Elders, office of.................. 541

Election, Calvinistic view of 394
—— defined 389
—— of bodies of men to eminent privileges........................... 390
—— of persons to eternal life........ 393
—— of persons to perform special services............................ 390
Elevation, inspiration of 80
Enemies of Christianity, testimonies of the 57
Enjoyments, heavenly, nature of 632
——, heavenly, will be endless 636
Episcopacy may be a matter of expediency 542
Equivalent, a full, meaning. of the phrase 368
Errors respecting Christ's Divine nature 222
—— respecting Christ's human nature. 221
Eternity ascribed to Christ 200
—— of God, proofs of the.......... 145
—— of God not inconsistent with successive time..................... 145
—— of matter refuted 243
—— of the world in its organized state refuted 244
Evangelists, office of................ 541
Evidence, collateral.............. 50, 109
——, different kinds of 40
——, external.................... 40
——, internal 48, 98
——, internal, nature of 48
——, internal, rank of............. 48
Evidences necessary to authenticate a revelation 40
Existence of God argued from common consent 131
—— of God argued from marks of design 134
—— of things a proof of the Divine existence 133
Expulsion from the Church, power of, with ministers................... 548
Extent of the Atonement........ 371, 377
——, Calvinistic theory of the 371
——, Universalist theory of 374
Eye, human, a proof of the Divine existence 136

Failure to obtain salvation man's own fault........................... 385
Faith defined..................... 417
—— implies previous knowledge..... 480
—— imputed for righteousness 415
—— is based on evidence 480
——, justifying, what.............. 481
—— may exist in different degrees ... 481
——, nature of, in general 479
—— operates according to the fact believed 481
——, saving, properties of 481
—— the only condition of justification. 419
Faithfulness of God, what........... 165
Fall of man...................... 281
——, effects of 290

Fall, history of, to be taken literally... 282
Fatalism, materialistic 309
——, stoical 309
Fathers, Christian, testimony of, to the inspiration of the Scriptures 73
Fear of God, implied in love to him... 489
——, nature of the................. 489
Fellowship with the Church, the duty of all........................... 538
Fidelity, a duty demanded by the conjugal relation................... 527
First-born, destruction of........... 84
Foreknowledge of God............. 153
—— consistent with man's moral agency...................... 331
—— does not imply necessity 332
—— not dependent upon his decrees... 135
——, objects of................... 153
——, theories respecting........... 154
Forgiveness of sins ascribed to Christ. 203
Fraud, what 520
Functions, animal, prove design...... 137

Gambling, injustice of 521
Genuineness of a book, what 51
—— of the Scriptures, how established 51
Geologists, notions of, respecting the date of creation 245
Gilgal, the twelve stones of.......... 66
Gnostics, doctrines of, respecting Christ 221
God, a knowledge of, fundamental to religion 180
——, arguments for the existence of .. 130
——, a title given to Christ.......... 197
——, attributes of 139
——, benevolence of, manifested in our creation 174
——, character of.................. 337
——, decrees of 234
—— defined 125
——, derivation of the term 125
——, doctrines respecting.......... 124
——, existence of................. 124
——, existence of, not discoverable by reason 23
——, general Providence of 268
——, idea of, derived alone from revelation 130
——, idea of, not acquired by rational induction..................... 126
——, idea of, not innate 126
——, immutability of............... 156
—— is all-sufficient............... 177
—— is perfect 177
—— is unsearchable 178
——, prescience of................ 153
——, secret and revealed will of 241
——, special Providence of.......... 269
——, unity of.................... 140
God's moral government, principles of. 337
Goodness of God 170
Government, Church, nature of....... 539
——, Church, necessity of 539
——, Church, to whom committed.... 540

Government, civil, different kinds of .. 533
——, civil, of Divine authority...... 533
——, Divine, included in the idea of
Providence 266
—— of children a parental duty...... 528
Governors, duties of................ 534
Gospel, a means of regeneration...... 430
-——, Christians shall be judged by the 626
—— to be preached to all men 382

Heathen shall be judged by the law of
nature 626
Heaven, a place 630
——, the glory of.................. 632
Heavens, creation of 247
——, what they include 248
Hebrew ceased to be a living language
soon after the captivity 54
History, evangelical, impressed with
marks of credibility 70
—— of the world a proof of man's
moral agency 317
Holiness of God 167
Holy Ghost, Arius's opinion respecting 228
——, Deity of..................... 230
——, designated by Divine titles..... 230
——, Divine works ascribed to 231
——, personality of 228
——, possesses Divine attributes..... 230
——, procession of................ 228
—— the object of supreme worship... 233
—— the source of inspiration........ 231
——, works of 231
Hymeneus an example of total apostasy 465

Image of God in which man was cre-
ated 277
Immersion, arguments for, examined.. 573
Immortality of the soul 597
—— not understood by the heathen .. 27
Immutability of God................ 156
Impossibility of corrupting the sacred
Scriptures 59
Imputation, doctrine of 292
—— of Adam's sin to his posterity... 293
—— of Christ's righteousness 410
—— of faith for righteousness 415
——, the term explained 418
Infants, objections to the baptism of,
obviated...................... 562
——, proofs for the baptism of...... 565
Infidelity, moral effects of 118
Influence of the Holy Spirit 104
Inspiration ascribed to the sacred penmen.......................... 73
—— a work of the Holy Spirit....... 23
—— claimed by the sacred penmen... 74
—— defined 71
——, different opinions respecting.... 77
——, extent of................... 77
——, necessity of................. 72
—— of elevation 80
—— of suggestion 81
—— of superintendence 79

Inspiration, plenary, import of 78
——, possibility of................. 72
——, reasonableness of............. 72
——, testimony of the Fathers respecting 73
Instinct and appetite govern the lower
animals 267
Institutions of Christianity 538
Instruction, Divine, a privilege of God's
people 444
Integrity of the Scriptures 58
Introduction 3
Israelites who fell in the wilderness,
examples of total apostasy 464

Jehovah, a title given to Christ 196
Jews, apostasies of, predicted........ 94
——, final restoration of 96
——, prophecies respecting 94
—— shall be judged by Moses and the
prophets 626
——, threatened punishments of 95
Judas an example of apostasy 464
Judgment, final, ascribed to Christ ... 204
——, general, rule of............... 626
——, general, time of 627
Justice, general 165
——, judicial 166
——, legislative 165
—— of God................. 165, 338
—— of God requires the penalty of sin
to be executed 340
——, particular 165, 338
——, universal 338
——, vindictive or punitive 166
Justification, Antinomian scheme of .. 410
——, Arminian doctrine of 415
——, Calvinistic theory of........... 411
—— distinguished from sanctification. 409
—— does not make men actually righteous 409
——, eternal, absurdity of 408
——, how obtained 409
—— is by faith alone.............. 419
——, is by faith in the blood of Christ. 366
——, method of, peculiar to the Scriptures 409
——, nature of 406
——, preliminary remarks concerning. 403

"King of Israel," a title given to Christ 199
Knowledge of God................. 152

Law, Adamic, nature of 275
——, moral, how made known in the
Scriptures 467
——, moral, of the New Testament, a
fuller revelation than the Old 470
——, moral, of the Old Testament,
received into the New............ 469
——, moral, summarily comprehended
in the Decalogue................ 468
——, moral, what................. 467
—— of Moses, two Hebrew copies of.. 54

INDEX OF SUBJECTS.

Law of the Sabbath 512
——, sacrifices of the.............. 349
Laws of nature, what................ 266
Leslie's four rules for determining the truth of history...:............... 64
—— four rules applied to the books of Moses 64
—— four rules applied to the Gospel history........................... 67
Liberty a natural right of man 521
—— defined by Locke and Edwards.. 311
——, natural, what 521
—— of conscience 522
—— of God 158
—— of person 521
—— of speech and of the press 522
Life a natural right of man 518
Light of nature, what 19
Lord Herbert's primary principles of religion 158
Lord's supper 590
——, general observations respecting.. 595
——, institution of................. 591
——, nature of 592
——, perpetual obligation of 591
——, theories respecting............ 592
——, true sacramental character of... 594
Lotteries a species of gambling....... 521
Love, filial....................... 530
—— of our neighbor 515
——, parental 528
—— to God a fruit of the Spirit...... 487
—— to God essential to obedience ... 487
—— to God, nature of.............. 486
—— to God, obligations of 490

Man, doctrines respecting 275
——, fall of....................... 281
—— held accountable for his moral actions 318
·——, history of the creation of....... 277
·—— in his fallen condition.......... 174
—— made in the image of God 278
——, moral condition of 99
——, primitive state of 275
——, voluntary actions of, governed by moral laws....................... 267
—— was originally in a state of trial.. 283
——, what God has done for the recovery of 177
Manna, miracle of 85
Manner of observing the Sabbath 512
Man's moral agency 308
—— consistent with Divine foreknowledge 331
——, nature of 308
——, objections to 322
——, proofs of..................... 316
——, true doctrine of 314
Man's original transgression, character of 281
—— true moral condition 296
Manuscripts, ancient, of the Old Testament, agreement of............... 60

Masters, duties of.................. 532
Matter not eternal 243
Meditation a means of repentance 478
Mercy-seat, as applied to Christ...... 362
Messiah, prophecies respecting....... 96
Ministers, unworthy, trial of......... 548
Ministry, Christian, nature of 14
——, Christian, responsibilities of 17
Miracle of Christ's resurrection....... 86
Miracles, an external evidence of Divine revelation............. 41, 42, 83
——, circumstances under which they become an authenticating evidence.. 42
——, competency of human testimony to establish the credibility of 43
——, how distinguished 41
——, Hume's objection to, answered.. 44
——, instances of................... 41
——, nature of 41
—— of Christ..................... 85
—— of Moses..................... 84
——, possibility of 42
Morality, Christian, motives of....... 106
——, Christian, superior nature of.... 106
——, Pagan, principles of, mere abstractions............................ 106
——, Pagan, what 28
Morals, a perfect system of, found only in the Bible...................... 106
—— of Christianity 467
—— of the Scriptures, how proposed.. 467
Monophysites, doctrine of, respecting Christ............................ 221
Moses, existence of................. 51
——, miracles of 84

Nations rewarded in this life......... 167
Nature, human, has two essential parts 277
——, laws of, what 266
Necessity defined.................. 332
——, different kinds of 309
——, doctrine of................... 309
—— incompatible with moral freedom. 320
Neighbor, duties to our............. 527
——, the love of our 515
Nestorians, doctrine of, respecting Christ............................ 221
New Testament Scriptures, ancient date of........................... 56
——, early catalogues of............ 56
——, quoted by early Christian authors 56
Noah, sacrifice of on leaving the ark.. 345

Obedience, filial................... 531
—— to civil laws the duty of subjects 535
Objection to the doctrine of imputation answered 294
Objections to the Bible answered..... 114
—— to the Divine administration answered............................ 286
—— to the doctrine of justification answered............................ 420
—— to the Mosaic history of the fall.. 286

	PAGE
Objections to the spirituality of God	144
Objects of Divine foreknowledge classified	152
Obligations to love God	490
Observance of the Sabbath	501
——, manner of	512
Offense is followed by penal consequences	102
Office, sacred, nature and responsibilities of	11
Omnipotence ascribed to Christ	201
—— of God	146
Omnipresence ascribed to Christ	200
—— of God	149
—— of God, manner of the	151
Omniscience ascribed to Christ	200
—— of God	151
—— of God, objects of	152
Ordination, power of, with presbyters	546
Pagan religions, demoralizing influence of	33
Pagans have no conception of pure morality	10
Paine, objection of, to the truth of prophecy	116
Pardon not an act of mere prerogative	102, 408
—— not secured by mere penitence and reformation	102
Parents, duties of, to their children	528
Passover, sacrifice of	351
Pastors, Christian, office of	541
——, Christian, qualifications of	12
Patriotism a duty	535
Penalty of sin, nature of	291
Perfection of God	177
Personality and Deity of the Holy Ghost	227
Person, as applied to God	178
——, liberty of	521
—— of Christ	221
—— of Christ, errors respecting	221
—— of Christ, Scriptural doctrine of	223
Piety necessary to true morality	515
Philosophers, heathen, concessions of	32
Plague of darkness	84
Pleasures, the portion of the saints in heaven	635
Polity of the Jews proves the existence and antiquity of Moses	51
Prayer a means of regeneration	430
—— an aid to repentance	479
——, duty of	492
—— for rulers, the duty of subjects	536
——, nature of	492
——, obligations of	497
——, private	495
——, public	497
——, utility of	499
——, various kinds of	494
Precepts, moral and positive	287
—— of the Old Testament received into the New	469
Predestination	387
——, Calvinistic view of	388
—— defined and stated	388
Prediction respecting the coming "SHILOH"	93
Predictions relate chiefly to the scheme of redemption	90
Pre-existence of Christ	187
Preface	3
Prescience of God	153
Presbyters, office of	542
Preservation an element of Divine Providence	265
—— ascribed to Christ	203
—— ascribed to the Holy Ghost	231
Press, liberty of	522
Probation implies the possibility of apostasy	466
Proofs of the goodness of God	172
Property a natural right	520
Prophecies respecting the Jewish nation	94
—— respecting the Messiah	96
Prophecy a proof of Divine revelation	46
——, an objection to, answered	47
——, double sense of	92
——, ends of	91
——, extent of	90
——, force of the evidence of	46
—— found only in the Scriptures	91
——, nature of	46
—— respecting the coming "SHILOH"	93
—— respecting the seed of the woman	92
——, supposed obscurity of	91
Prophets, office of	540
Propitiation, Christ a	356, 361
Protection, Divine, a privilege of God's people	443
Providence, Divine, nature of	265
——, Divine, proofs of	261
——, Divine, objects of	268
——, Divine, with regard to moral evil	271
——, doctrine of, not discoverable by reason	26
——, general	268
——, particular	273
——, special	269
Provision, Divine, a privilege of God's people	443
Punishment, endless, doctrine of	648
——, endless, not incompatible with the Divine perfections	644
——, endless, of the wicked	637
——, endless, objection to	649
——, future, a state of intense suffering	642
——, future, nature of	641
——, future, not reformatory	643
——, future, will be endless	643
—— of the Jews predicted	95
—— of sinners not always disciplinary	644
Raising the dead ascribed to Christ	204
Reality of Christ's death	86

INDEX TO SUBJECTS.

Reason a source of theology........ 18
—— defined 18
——, extent of the discoveries of..... 18
——, insufficiency of, in religion 23
——, limitations of................. 22
——, use of, in religion............. 20
Reconciliation by Christ............. 364
Redemption by Christ 363
Red Sea, the dividing of the 84
Reformation impossible without grace. 102
—— included in true repentance..... 474
Regeneration a concomitant of justification.......................... 427
—— defined...................... 425
——, general remarks respecting..... 424
——, means of 429
——, nature of 424
——, necessity of.................. 428
Relation, conjugal 527
——, filial...................... 530
——, legal, of Adam to his posterity.. 292
——, parental.................... 528
——, servile 531
Relations, domestic 527
——, political 532
Religion, as distinguished from theology 10
——, Christian, a proof of the existence
and antiquity of Christ 52
——, doctrines of, not presented in the
Bible in a systematic form......... 14
——, natural, articles of 115
—— understood objectively 10
—— understood subjectively 10
Remedial dispensation.............. 336
Repentance alone cannot secure pardon....................... 102, 341
—— and faith required of all men.... 384
—— includes contrition 473
—— includes reformation........... 474
—— is the gift of God............. 472
——, means of 477
——, nature of................... 471
——, necessity of.................. 476
—— not regeneration 428
——, order of, in its connection with
faith and regeneration 475
Reprobation, doctrine of 399
Republican government, what 533
Restoration of the Jews, prophecy respecting 96
Restorationism, theory of 643
——, untenable 643
Resurrection body, properties of 617
——, certainty of.................. 614
——, nature of................... 611
—— of Christ.................... 86
—— of the human body 611
—— of the same body that dies...... 612
——, will be universal.............. 614
Retribution, future, connected with the
general judgment 640
——, future, subsequent to the general
resurrection..................... 640
Revelation as a source of theology.... 22

Revelation defined 22
——, Divine, evidences of.........39, 84
——, Divine, necessary...........23, 31
——, Divine, probable character of ... 35
——, Divine, possible 22
—— is all that could be reasonably ex-
pected 36
Righteousness, explanation of the term 417
—— of Christ, how imputed to us.... 412
Right to liberty................... 521
—— to life secured by the law of God. 518
—— to property, secured by the Di-
vine law 520
Rights, natural, what............... 518
—— of God cannot be given up...... 340
Robbery, what 520

Sabbath, change of, from the seventh to
the first day of the week.......... 508
——, Christian, honored of God...... 512
——, inclusion of, in the Decalogue... 505
——, law of, what it forbids........ 513
——, law of, what it requires........ 514
——, manner of the observance of.... 512
——, observance of the............ 501
——, primitive institution of........ 501
——, recognition of, in the wilderness. 502
——, universal and perpetual obligation of 501
Sabellianism 222
Sacraments, Catholic view of 553
——, institution of, by Christ........ 554
——, nature of 552
——, number of 556
——, Socinian notion of 554
——, true Protestant doctrine respecting 554
Sacrifice of Abraham............... 346
—— of Cain and Abel............. 345
—— of Noah on leaving the ark 345
—— of the Passover 351
——, vicarious, what............... 350
Sacrifices, ante-Mosaic, expiatory..... 346
——, Levitical, typical character of... 349
——, Levitical, types of a better sacrifice 352
—— of the law expiatory 349
——, patriarchal, of Divine appointment........................... 343
Sacrificial terms applied to Christ and
his atoning work................. 354
Saints, eternal blessedness of 630
—— eternal blessedness of the, will
be progressive................... 636
—— will know one another in heaven. 636
Salvation ascribed to Christ's death... 356
——, failure to obtain, man's own fault 385
—— of all, will of God concerning the. 386
—— offered to all men in the Gospel.. 382
Sanctification, entire, attainability of .. 447
——, entire, does not differ from regeneration 446
——, entire, does not exclude temptation............................ 447

PAGE

Sanctification, entire, does not imply indefectibility 446

——, entire, objections to, answered.. 453

——, entire, the manner of.......... 452

——, entire, the nature of.......... 446

——, entire, the time of 450

Satan the real tempter of our first parents........................ 285

Satisfaction made to Divine justice, meaning of the phrase............ 368

Saul an example of total apostasy 463

Scape-goat, sacrifice of.............. 351

Scriptures, authenticity of.......... 64

——, Divine authority of ... 71, 83, 90, 98

——, genuineness of 51

——, integrity of 58

——, moral tendency of 105

——, moral tendency of, exemplified in the person of Christ 106

—— worthy of God................ 107

——, Jewish, a catalogue of, by Josephus 53

——, Jewish, antiquity of 51

——, Jewish, translated into Greek... 53

——, Jewish, the impossibility of corrupting the 59

——, New Testament, antiquity of.... 56

——, New Testament, catalogues of .. 56

——, New Testament, could not be corrupted...................... 61

——, New Testament, testimonies of enemies to..................... 57

Seed of the woman, promise of....... 92

Self-examination a means of repentance 478

Semiarianism..................... 222

Serpent, sentence pronounced upon the 285

Servants, duties of 531

Settlement of children, a parental duty. 530

Shiloh, prediction respecting........ 93

Sin not pardoned on mere prerogative...................... 102, 408

—— not pardoned on mere repentance 102

—— not pardoned on repentance and reformation 102

——, original, nature of 297

Solomon an example of total apostasy. 464

Son of God, in what sense Christ is the 213

Sonship of Christ 210

——, false theories respecting the 210

——, importance of the orthodox view of the....................... 219

——, true doctrine of the, established. 213

Soul, the, can exist separate from the body.......................... 604

——, the, exists after death in a conscious state.................... 606

——, immortality of the............ 597

——, immortality of the, not understood by the heathen........... 27

——, immortality of the, proved by Scripture 604

——, nature and powers of, a proof of the Divine existence............. 138

Soul, received by traduction......... 306

Speech, liberty of 522

Spine, human, a proof of design 137

Spirituality of God 142

——, several objections to, answered.. 144

State, future 597

Stonehenge, in Salisbury Plain....... 66

Stones set up at Gilgal 66

Style and manner of the sacred writers 108

Subjects, duties of................. 535

Submission to God implied in love to him...................... 488

Suicide, criminality of 518

Supplies, pecuniary, for the necessities of government, due from subjects... 536

Support of children, the duty of parents 528

Table of contents 5

Teachers, office of................. 541

Terms, sacrificial, applied to the death of Christ 354

Testament, New, agreement of ancient manuscripts of 61

——, New, agreement of ancient versions of, with quotations made by early Christian writers............ 62

——, New, antiquity of............. 56

——, New, contains the fuller revelation of moral law 470

——, New, early catalogues of the books of the 56

——, New, integrity of 61

——, New, quoted by early Christians. 56

——, Old, antiquity of............. 56

Testimony of ancient writers, a proof of the genuineness of the Scriptures. 52

—— of the disciples to Christ's resurrection highly credible............ 87

Theft, what 520

Theology a science................ 10

—— claims universal attention 17

——, didactic 14

——, divisions of.................. 13

—— embraces many controverted subjects 11

——, general utility of.............. 17

——, importance of 11

——, natural..................... 13

——, natural, not to be rejected...... 13

——, natural, principles of, not discovered by reason 29

——, nature of 9

——, objects of................... 12

——, polemic 15

——, practical.................... 16

——, revealed.................... 13

——, sources of 18

——, term explained 9

—— the Christian minister's profession 47

Theologian, what 10

Time, succession of, ascribed to God .. 145

Titles, Divine, ascribed to Christ 195

Traduction of the soul 306

Translation, Greek, of the Old Testament Scriptures a proof of their antiquity ... 53
Transubstantiation ... 592
Tribute, the payment of, the duty of subjects ... 536
Trinity, doctrine of, as affecting our views of God ... 180
——, doctrine of, essential to the credit of the Scriptures ... 181
——, doctrine of, importance of the ... 180
——, doctrine of, lies at the foundation of revealed theology ... 31
——, doctrine of, intimately connected with morals ... 180
——, doctrine of, Scripture proofs of the ... 182
—— in unity ... 178
——, Sabellian notion of ... 222
Trust in God implied in love to him ... 489
—— in God implied in saving faith ... 484
Truth, conformity to, required by justice 523
—— of God, proofs of ... 162
——, when assailed, should be defended 16
Type, what ... 352

Unity of God, proofs of ... 140
Universalism, brief view of ... 374
Universalists, doctrine of, contrary to matters of fact ... 637
——, doctrine of, contrary to Scripture ... 637
——, doctrine of, respecting the punishment of sin ... 637
——, doctrine of, self-contradictory ... 638
——, doctrine of, subverts the whole scheme of salvation by grace ... 639
Universe, physical, governed by the laws of nature ... 266
Unsearchableness of God ... 178

Volition does not imply an infinite series of volitions ... 322
—— is not an effect ... 323
—— is not the unavoidable result of motives ... 326
Voltaire, objection of, to the truth of prophecy ... 116

Warnings prove apostasy possible ... 465
Week, first day of the, called Lord's day 510
——, first day of the, distinguished by God's gracious dispensations ... 511
——, first day of the, observed by the apostolic Churches ... 510
Will, as distinguished from intelligence and sensibility ... 316
——, freedom of, everywhere acknowledged in the Scriptures ... 319
——, how influenced by motives ... 314
—— of God concerning the salvation of all men ... 386
—— of God the only ground of moral obligation ... 467
—— of God, the secret and revealed ... 241
Wisdom of God ... 159
—— demonstrated by his works ... 159
Witness of our own spirit ... 440
—— of the Spirit to our adoption ... 437
—— of the Spirit, different theories respecting the ... 436
Works, Divine, ascribed to Christ ... 201
—— of God ... 242
—— of God declare his wisdom ... 159
World not eternal ... 243
Worship paid to Christ ... 205
—— paid to Christ an evidence of his Divinity ... 208
——, public, obligations of ... 498
——, supreme and inferior, Arian notion of ... 209
——, supreme, paid to the Holy Ghost 232
Wrath ascribed to God ... 363
Writers, sacred, claimed to be inspired ... 74
——, sacred, credibility of ... 68
——, sacred, highly circumstantial in their accounts ... 70
——, sacred, knew what they related ... 69
——, sacred, style and manner of ... 108
——, sacred, were men of exemplary virtue and piety ... 68
——, sacred, were not influenced by worldly motives ... 69
——, sacred, wonderful agreement of ... 107

Zuinglius, theory of, respecting the Lord's Supper ... 593